TRANSLATION AS HOME

ILAN STAVANS

Translation as Home

A Multilingual Life

Edited by Regina Galasso

UNIVERSITY OF TORONTO PRESS
Toronto Buffalo London

© University of Toronto Press 2024
Toronto Buffalo London
utorontopress.com

ISBN 978-1-4875-4792-9 (cloth)   ISBN 978-1-4875-4807-0 (EPUB)
                                    ISBN 978-1-4875-4809-4 (PDF)

Library and Archives Canada Cataloguing in Publication

Title: Translation as home : a multilingual life / Ilan Stavans ;
   edited by Regina Galasso.
Names: Stavans, Ilan, author. | Galasso, Regina, editor.
Description: Includes bibliographical references and index.
Identifiers: Canadiana (print) 20230622941 | Canadiana (ebook)
   20230622976 | ISBN 9781487547929 (cloth) | ISBN 9781487548070
   (EPUB) | ISBN 9781487548094 (PDF)
Subjects: LCSH: Stavans, Ilan. | LCSH: Translators – United States –
   Biography. | LCSH: Translating and interpreting. | LCSH: Language
   and languages. | LCGFT: Autobiographies. | LCGFT: Essays.
Classification: LCC PS3619.T385 Z46 2024 | DDC 418/.02092 – dc23

Cover design: Rebecca Lown
Cover image: Antoni Gaudí. Casa Milà (La Pedrera), Barcelona.
Photo by Regina Galasso (2022).

We wish to acknowledge the land on which the University of Toronto Press operates. This land is the traditional territory of the Wendat, the Anishnaabeg, the Haudenosaunee, the Métis, and the Mississaugas of the Credit First Nation.

University of Toronto Press acknowledges the financial support of the Government of Canada, the Canada Council for the Arts, and the Ontario Arts Council, an agency of the Government of Ontario, for its publishing activities.

[W]hat objection can be made if a translator says to his reader: Here I bring you the book as the man would have written it had he written it in German; and the reader responds: I am just as obliged to you as if you had brought me the picture of a man the way he would look if his mother had conceived him by a different father?

– Friedrich Schleiermacher,
"On the Different Methods of Translating" (1813),
translated from the German by Susan Bernofsky

Contents

Introduction

Room for Language: Moving into Translation, by Regina Galasso   2

Part I: Language on Fire

We Are the Clarion: A Manifesto on Immigration   23
On Packing Up My Library   26
Retelling *Popol Vuh* – in Chinese   32
English as She Is Spoke: The Fallacy of American Studies
    (with Steven G. Kellman)   35
Olga Takarczuk's Messianic Critique   50
Does Literature Teach Us How to Die?
    (with Priyanka Champaneri)   56
The People's Tongue: Language as Character   64
Claudio Lomnitz's Vertigo   82
Rethinking the Classics (with Jenna Tang)   89
Pierre Menard: Retranslation and Approximation
    (with Youssef Boucetta)   95
Fernando Pessoa's Selves   122
On Borges' Blindness (with Max Ubelaker Andrade)   129
How Yiddish Changed America and How America
    Changed Yiddish (with Josh Lambert)   140
The Anxiety of Translation (with Robert Croll)   148
We Are All Drafts: The Erotics of Translation (with Peter Cole)   155

Part II: Dictionaries as Confidants

Notes on Latino Philology   161
The Miasma of Order; or, Why Dictionaries Ought to Be
    Seen as Literature   178
Is American Spanish Healthy?   188
On Decidophobia (with Haoran Tong)   203
"'Clean, Fix, and Grant Splendor'": The Making of
    Diccionario de autoridades   209
Pablo Neruda's "Ode to the Dictionary"   221
Letter to a Young Translator   225
How Dictionaries Define Us (with Margaret Boyle)   228

Part III: Translation as Home

Sor Juana's Nahuatl   247
On Memes as Semiotic Hand-Grenades
    (with Mª Carmen África Vidal Claramonte)   255
Reading Emilio Salgari   268
On Translating *The Disappearance* into Yiddish
    (with Beruriah Wiegand)   271
Is I *Me*, or Who *Is* I?: Conversation with Jim   284
Petrarch's Sonnet #132   287
A Lover Alone in Prison (with Sara Khalili)   289
Jevel Katz in Yingleñol   300
Matching Socks in the Dark; Or, How to Translate from
    Languages You Don't Know   302
Self-translation como survival mecanismo   307
Simply Gimpl   312
Homestead: "La casa pairal," from *The Manuscript of Reus*
    (with Regina Galasso)   314
Translation as Home (with Regina Galasso)   316
Immigrants in Quarantine
    (with Jhumpa Lahiri and Eduardo Halfon)   323

Coda: The Hermeneutics of Translation

Reading the Talmud in Mexico: A Confession   331

Contributors   339
Index   341

Introduction

Room for Language: Moving into Translation

REGINA GALASSO

I.

Welcome to *Translation as Home: A Multilingual Life*. This volume explores immigration, language, and translation, magnifying Ilan Stavans' roots in Hispanic and Jewish cultures and their interconnections with other cultures. It is an attempt to capture and spread his extraordinary enthusiasm for language, written words, and books. Organized in three parts and a coda, *Translation as Home* presents a dynamic range of texts including essays, conversations with writers and translators, and translations that push the boundaries of English and other languages. Readers are invited to start on the first page and end on the last, or enter on any page and skip around from one part to another; they are also encouraged to go beyond its contents and take in some of the other books by Ilan Stavans or by the writers, poets, translators, and scholars who are part of the constellation of this volume. This is a book that will accompany readers throughout their lives as their own relationships with language transform and expand.

Translation as Home, a companion to Stavans' *On Self-Translation: Meditations on Language* (2018), offers an understanding of how, throughout his career, Stavans has advanced the field of translation. Part I, "Language on Fire" includes fifteen chapters that focus on various aspects of the main themes of translation and immigration, book collecting and publishing, literary classics and influential texts, and specific languages: English, French, Portuguese, Spanish, and Yiddish. In half the chapters, Stavans collaborates with another writer, translator, or scholar. The eight chapters of part II, "Dictionaries as Confidants," present more on words, the tomes that gather them, and how words navigate through people's lives via those tomes. It considers what future generations of translators might like to know, and closes with a three-part conversation with Margaret Boyle on how dictionaries define us. The fifteen chapters of part III, "Translation as Home," zoom in on the work of the translator. Stavans highlights Sor Juana's relationship with Latin, Spanish, and Nahuatl and her translations. He has a long conversation with María Carmen África Vidal Claramonte in a chapter entitled "Memes as Semiotic Hand-Grenades." He speaks with the Yiddish translator of his work and confesses that he does not like to translate his own work. He learns from translators of other language pairs and writes about translation from languages he does not yet know. With Jhumpa Lahiri and Eduardo Halfon, Stavans discusses home, family, language, and how relationships with home have shifted during the COVID-19 pandemic. The coda, about reading the Talmud in Mexico, focuses on translation as a hermeneutical reading of an obscure religious text.

Translation as Home is not only about words and their movement in and out of languages, it is also about language when it moves from the page to the stage, the screen, and other media. Adaptation to other media, another form of translation, allows for expanded interpretations of a given source.

This introduction follows some strands of the history of Stavans' work as a translator, relating them to terminology and concepts associated with translation. It identifies moments in in which translation signifies a shift in Stavans' life and his work.

II.

Ilan Stavans, born and raised in Mexico City, grew up speaking Hebrew, Spanish, and Yiddish. In 1985, he immigrated from Mexico City to New York City. New York – a city that is host to many languages and cultures – is where Stavans found his voice in the English language. Almost a decade later, in 1993, he moved to Amherst, Massachusetts, which offered a different linguistic landscape. Stavans' relationship with English is the focus of *On Borrowed Words: A Memoir of Language*, published in 2001, one year before he translated Miguel de Cervantes' seventeenth-century masterpiece *Don Quijote* into Spanglish, an endeavor which would launch him into another period in his relationship with languages – a restless period of translation, a period during which he explores the meaning of home.

Stavans speaks English, Spanish, Spanglish, Hebrew, and Yiddish, among other languages. He writes and publishes, appears on radio shows, gives public talks, and teaches in English, Spanish, and Spanglish.

He translates into English, Spanish, and Spanglish from a lengthy list of languages including Belarusian, Georgian, German, Hebrew, Ladino, Polish, Portuguese, Russian, many variants of Spanish, and Yiddish. *Selected Translations: Poems 2000–2020* (2021), in the Pitt Poetry Series published by the University of Pittsburgh Press, is an introduction to his translations of poetry. Some of the languages he translates from are still unknown to him. Stavans reads literary texts first born into any language. If there is a language he does not read well, he reaches out to a network of colleagues, experts, and students, and is open to expanding that network. He also reads to find undiscovered literary classics, and rereads to find a new story in a familiar text. Stavans publishes books in English translation, a project that was instigated by a conversation with Tom Ashbrook on the National Public Radio show *On Point*. After the show, Ashbrook asked Stavans if he thought of doing something about the small number of books from other languages published in English translation. Soon after, Restless Books was born. Founded in 2013, Restless Books publishes literature in translation and gives immigrant voices a platform. In addition, Restless Classics revives literary classics in any language and commissions new translations of classics and future classics. Restless is not only committed to expanding the range of books available to English-language readers, but also to supporting writers through the Prize for New Immigrant Writing and through its immigrant writing workshops.

It is not only Stavans' collection of languages and activities that defines his multilingual life. It is his style of living in languages. Effective and successful translators understand that language is to be played with, and that every word matters. With experimentation and knowledge comes the need to question everything. In her early years as a translator, Amelia Pérez de Villar was told by a mentor, Antonio Carrilo, "duda siempre":[1] "Si te parece muy fácil, sospecha y consulta; puede que no, pero seguramente será lo que parece. Si te parece muy raro, sospecha y consulta, puede que sí, pero lo mismo no es lo que parece. Duda siempre, y consulta, porque lo más sencillo puede esconder una trampa."[2] Translators cannot confidently translate a text without fully understanding it. In their search to understand, they question words and their usage in and beyond the text they translate, consulting dictionaries and other sources. Steven G. Kellman says that Stavans "tiene

---

1 Amelia Pérez de Villar, *Los enemigos del traductor: Elogio y vituperio del oficio* (Madrid: Fórcola Ediciones, 2019), 68.
2 Pérez de Villar, *Los enemigos del traductor*, 68.

una obsesión cabalística con el poder de las palabras, y sabe que son polisémicas e indeterminadas. Stavans reconoce y disfruta del hecho de que el lenguaje sea un verbo y no un sustantivo, una energía que fluye inestable."[3] Dictionaries of all sorts, other people, and other texts and sources are translators' friends. In becoming aware of the options, translators see a word for what it is and for what it could be. Furthermore, translators rely on context. The context allows translators to know when and how to use the language, to know what the rules are and how they can break them. Translators do not always break rules, but knowing how to break them – what it would mean to break them, what new things that would reveal, how that would innovate language and advance the audience's perspective – is all part of the fun. This curiosity and vision ignited by language are part and parcel of a multilingual life.

In addition to his experience of growing up in and into a multilingual environment, Stavans' Jewishness is central to his conception of language. In "Reading the Talmud in Mexico," the coda to *Translation as Home*, he reflects on feeling "peripheral" to global Jewish culture when he was growing up in a country with a small Jewish community. Thus, he read sacred and secular texts as if in the wilderness, without the camaraderie of other readers with whom to share his inquisitiveness. This experience is intrinsic to his approach to reading: Stavans reads as if from the outside looking in. His quest to belong embraces Jewish multilingualism at various levels. He reads novels, poetry, plays, and other literature gleaned from different parts of the Jewish world in pursuit of common denominators. He translates Jewish texts into English to center himself. Texts traveling to, from, and through languages are essential to his journey. Stavans, especially Stavans as a Jewish translator, seeks a common ground where a community of readers might find each other in dialogue. Translation provides a space for heterogeneous perspectives to meet.

In that regard, it is essential to emphasize the dialogue Stavans establishes with authors like Friedrich Schleiermacher (1768–1834), Walter Benjamin (1892–1940), Jorge Luis Borges (1899–1986), and Susan Sontag (1933–2004), all of whom were passionate about translation. In formal and informal presentations, classes, conversations, and writing, Stavans repeatedly asserts that translation disrupts a text, renews it, and injects it with new meaning. He asks his audiences to consider if a

---

3 Steven G. Kellman, "Prefacio," in *The Translingual Imagination* (Lincoln: University of Nebraska Press, 2000), ix.

text that does not get translated is an unfulfilled text. Does the potential value of a text get bypassed if left untranslated? Conversely, translating a text makes it not only richer but also foreign, as it now acquires meanings perhaps absent from its previous version. In *On Self-Translation: Meditations on Language*, Stavans writes about the difference between the terms "translation" and "transadaptation," as when a text is not only translated but also adapted into a new context with additional content, or when the translator takes liberties that subvert the original. He distinguishes these two terms from a third: "rewriting." Arguably Stavans' most significant publication in this regard is his award-winning *Popol Vuh: A Retelling* (2020); with illustrations by Gabriela Larios, it is a rewriting of the sacred K'iche' creation story. As he mentions in his translator's note, "Retelling the Tale," as well as in the prologue to the Chinese edition (included here in *Translation as Home*), his rendition expands what a reader might expect from a translation. Inspired by Chaucer's *Canterbury Tales*, his objective is to reconfigure the narrative for contemporary sensitivities, for instance by repositioning important segments and deleting repetitive sections. In this case, the translator's task moves in multiple directions, making a historical text palatable to today's readers without sacrificing its essence.

His Jewish sensibility, coupled with his need to bring back Latin American texts from the past, envisions the translator as not only a bridge builder but also a surveyor of past treasures. The translator is a librarian, an artist, and an activist. Stavans performs all those roles. Stavans' intellectual endeavors are not limited to the printed page. They also have a theatrical dimension. He acts them out in front of audiences. As is clear from his memoir *On Borrowed Words*, he inherited this theatricality from his father, a stage actor known for his television roles in Chespirito's *El Chavo del Ocho* and in countless Mexican telenovelas. Stavans himself describes teaching as acting. He has performed in several one-man shows and collaborated with illustrators in making animated films, at times about translation, as in the case of his award-winning short *The Silence of Professor Tösla* (2020), in Yiddish. He has also given numerous TED Talks, which have been translated into more than 30 languages.

III.

Letters, emails, and voice messages threatened to end the multilingual life of Ilan Stavans in the summer of 2002. I learned about them almost a decade later in September 2011, during my first semester on the University of Massachusetts Amherst campus. Like Stavans, I moved from New York City to western Massachusetts to be part of the faculty at one of the five colleges in the Amherst area. Students told me that Professor Stavans received these death threats for having translated *Don Quijote* into Spanglish. My students were fascinated that someone's life could be at risk for having translated a literary work. They hadn't known that the act of translation could carry so much weight. For instance, they hadn't yet heard about the July 12, 1991, death of Hitoshi Igarashi, who at the age of 44 was stabbed to death and found outside his Tsubuka University office for his translation of Salman Rushdie's *The Satanic Verses* (1988). Nor had they heard about the stabbing of 61-year-old Ettore Capriolo, which took place less than two weeks earlier, on July 3, at his Milan apartment, for his Italian translation of Rushdie's same novel. Capriolo survived. I was interested in the death threats Stavans received for other reasons. I wondered where was he when he opened them? Was he home? Was his family around? What are the other details about the making of this translation?

In October 2002, Stavans and a member of the Real Academia Española (RAE), whose name Stavans does not want to remember, were on a Barcelona radio show. The topic was Spanglish. The RAE member said something to Stavans, something he says "sounded remarkable to my ears and ended up defining my whole life": "If Spanglish is to be taken seriously, it must produce a work of art equal to *Don Quixote*, for only a language capable of such depth, such complexity ought to be taken seriously."[4] Stavans responded that it would not be unlikely that this would happen one day. In the meantime, "it would be entertaining" to translate *Don Quijote* into Spanglish.

While back in his hotel room, after the radio show interview, Stavans received a phone call from Sergio Vila-Sanjuán, an editor for *La Vanguardia*, Catalonia's premier newspaper, asking him to translate chapter 1, part 1, of *Don Quixote* into Spanglish. Soon after, Stavans found himself back at home in Massachusetts translating the first chapter. Within a

---

[4] Ilan Stavans, "In Defense of Spanglish," *The Common Reader: A Journal of the Essay* (2014). https://commonreader.wustl.edu/c/cervantes-spanglish/.

week of his request, Vila-Sanjuán had the Spanglish translation in his hands. Cervantes' novel starts like this:

> En un lugar de la Mancha, de cuyo nombre no quiero acordarme, no ha mucho tiempo que vivía un hidalgo de los de lanza en astillero, adarga antigua, rocín flaco y galgo corredor.[5]

In the first published Catalan translation (1891) of *Don Quijote* by Antoni Bulbena i Tussell (1854–1946):

> A un poblet de la Mancha, que del seu nom no vull recordar-me, vivia, no fa gaire temps, un d'aquells *hidalgos* de llança arreconada, darga antiga, rossí magre i llebrer corredor.[6]

And in the John Ormsby (1829–1895) English translation (1885), one of the 22 available English translations, and the one preferred by Stavans:

> In a village of La Mancha, the name of which I have no desire to call to mind, there lived not long since one of those gentlemen that keep a lance in the lance-rack, an old buckler, a lean hack, and a greyhound for coursing.[7]

On Wednesday, July 3, 2002, readers of *La Vanguardia* were now presented with Stavans' Spanglish rendition:

> In un placete de La Mancha of which nombre no quiero remembrearme, vivía, not so long ago, uno de esos gentlemen who always tienen una lanza in the rack, una buckler antigua, a skinny caballo y un grayhound para el chase.[8]

The "global controversy,"[9] as Stavans refers to it, began. The death threats came in from the United States, Spain, Argentina, Colombia, and Mexico. Stavans passed some on to the Amherst College police. "Once or twice, during lectures abroad in Spain and Venezuela, I needed

---

5 Miguel de Cervantes, *El ingenioso hidalgo Don Quijote de la Mancha*, ed. Luis Andrés Murillo (Madrid: Castalia, 1978), 69.
6 Miguel de Cervantes, *L'enginyós cavaller Don Quixot de la Mancha*, trans. Antini Bulbena i Tussell (Barcelona: Ediciones 62, 2005).
7 Miguel de Cervantes, *Don Quixote of La Mancha*, introduction by Ilan Stavans, illustrations by Eko (Brooklyn: Restless Books, 2015), 25.
8 Ilan Stavans, "'Don Quijote' en Spanglish," *La Vanguardia*, 3 July 2002, 5.
9 Stavans, "In Defense of Spanglish."

security," Stavans told me. But the threats didn't stop Stavans. He went on to translate numerous other sections of the novel. In 2014, more than 10 years after the initial publication of the first chapter of *Don Quijote* into Spanglish, Stavans reflected how this act of translation has forever marked his life: "A sentence from it might even make it to my epitaph, let alone my obituaries."[10] Stavans kept pushing the possibilities of this literary classic in Spanglish. In 2018, he published a Spanglish graphic novel adaptation of *Don Quixote of La Mancha* with illustrations by Roberto Weil.

As a result of the initial translation of *Don Quijote* into Spanglish, scholars and *filólogos* focused on Stavans' Spanglish, what his translation means for Spanglish, Spanish, and English, and what it means that a full professor in a Spanish department of a New England elite liberal arts college created this translation. What interests me most is the context that gave birth to this translation. Translations happen because a certain context needs them, asks for them, or sees an opportunity to shift a relationship. The Spanglish translation of *Don Quijxote* is the perfect result of a unique encounter in Barcelona between a local radio show host, a member of the RAE, an editor from *La Vanguardia*, and Stavans. It is hardly surprising that a local listener followed up on Stavans' proposal to translate *Don Quijote* into Spanglish, a language that would challenge Spanish. Had the event taken place in Madrid, this probably would have never happened. In Barcelona, the "friction and complicity between [the city's] two main languages,"[11] Catalan and Spanish, shape all activity. Translation studies scholar Sherry Simon notes that "the history of long years of suppression and the precariousness of a language forced to converse daily with its stronger twin make for the special character of the Barcelona language scene."[12]

Stavans himself appreciates the context from which this project emerged. He says, "Talking about Spanglish in Barcelona is communicating with people who know what it means to traffic in two languages, one a sign of empathy with the empire, the other a ticket to rebellion."[13] Stavans doesn't emphasize the bilingualism of the city or elaborate on who uses which language, or when and how. His focus is on the meaning of the use of two languages in a given context. Since Barcelona is

---

10 Stavans, "In Defense of Spanglish."
11 Sherry Simon, *Cities in Translation: Intersections of Language and Memory* (London: Routledge), 90.
12 Simon, *Cities in Translation*, 90.
13 Stavans, "In Defense of Spanglish."

a bilingual city, with a multilingual backdrop, the written, visual, or aural presence of only one language does not mean the total absence of the other language. In fact, during a lecture at the Universitat de Barcelona in 2015, in response to a quote from the linguist Joan Solà, Stavans told the audience: "I always feel at home in Barcelona, in Catalonia. Because here people live several realities and know that one language can oppress the other, and that a language can come from downstairs and reform everything. You know it perfectly. And you also mix languages, don't you? For better or for worse."[14]

Barcelona is home to additional languages, introduced by all kinds of newcomers and the many tourists that visit every year. The presence of these languages further adds to the relationship between Catalan and Spanish. Thus, Barcelona knows well how language is used and the power of translation. Translation is a way of thinking. It's not reserved for people who are perfectly fluent in at least two languages. And it's not reserved for people who are professional translators. It's an invitation to experiment with language, and to observe the consequences of its use and lack of use. As a way of thinking, in a multilingual context, translation is not an afterthought that waits for something to settle, but an approach that influences a way of living. There isn't one single formula for participating in this multilingual life. In his 2014 piece "In Defense of Spanglish," Stavans called Spanglish "a way to access reality." Likewise, translation can be a way to access reality. Translation is a lens that Stavans applies to the intellectual and creative activities of his multilingual life; *Translation as Home* presents Stavans on translation as a lens to look at languages, literatures, and cultures.

---

14 Ilan Stavans, "Every language that is taking shape goes through a phase similar to Spanglish," *Entrevistes: Universitat de Barcelona*, June 15, 2015, https://web.ub.edu/en/web/actualitat/w/ilan-stavans-every-language-that-is-taking-shape-goes-through-a-phase-similar-to-spanglish.

IV.

Terms traditionally used to talk about translation and language can restrict understandings of a multilingual life. For example, "native" and "non-native," words widely used in academic and professional settings to categorize a speaker's use of language, offer two options that can be challenging to detect or determine owing to circumstances related to birthplace, family, schooling, and other life experiences. The "non-native" label can limit opportunities regardless of one's strengths in a language. "Native" can be impossible to achieve because of one's accent or the use of a wrong preposition despite a stellar range of vocabulary, deep grammatical knowledge, and expansive cultural awareness. The usefulness of these terms is questionable given the bi- and multilingual circumstances of many individuals. More than half the world's population can speak more than one language fluently. However, in the United States, only one in every five adults is fluent in two languages, according to the US Census Bureau.[15] A monolingual perspective of language magnifies the use of "native" and "non-native."

"Life on the hyphen," "in between," "in transit," and similar expressions bring awareness to experiences and understandings of mobility. They often have connotations of being in an unfavorable position, not fitting in, or belonging to a temporary state with disadvantages and without an exit. In the US context, these categories keep many students, referred to as "bilingual," "heritage speakers," or "non-native speakers," from further exploring the advantages of their multilingual lives. Individuals who can't readily define or refuse to define their language A and their language B rarely have an advantage in professional and academic settings. A bi- or multilingual life sees beyond these terms. When I co-taught a course, "Translating the Classics," with Stavans in 2016, we began the semester not by asking the students about which languages they knew and how they knew them but by asking about their relationship to language and to translation. We learned fascinating things about our students' skills, experiences, and thoughts involving language. Thanks to Stavans' commitment to exploring language, *Translation as Home* continues to celebrate translation as a way of living rather than as an origin or destination.

In English, two words associated with translation, "source" and "target," limit the potential of translation. Source refers to the document

---

[15] Elizabeth Gration, "Bilingualism in 2022: US, UK & Global Statistics," updated February 28, 2023. https://preply.com/en/blog/bilingualism-statistics/

or language being translated while target refers to the translated document or language of the translation. To some ears the words source and target sound mechanical and fail to express the creativity, knowledge, and care that goes into translation. Source gives the impression that the text being translated is the origin of everything. In order to effectively and accurately translate a text, translators often turn to other texts, or conduct research that takes them away from the source text. The source text is a guide but it does not contain all the answers to make a quality translation. "Target" has the danger of communicating that there is a single translation of a text. However, there are many ways to translate a text. These terms are rejected by some translators, including the late Gregory Rabassa, who translated Portuguese and Spanish literature into English. Rabassa said, "I am an old infantryman, and we dogfaces were taught to shoot at a target and, ideally, kill it."[16] Because translators think critically about every word, if they do use these terms, they are aware of the deficiencies of jargon and work to compensate in various ways.

Despite the shortcomings of these terms, none of them should be retired. On the contrary, they should exist alongside others, as they give us the opportunity to have discussions about an individual's relationship to language. Translation teaches us not only to question our languages in diverse ways, but also to love our languages. Stavans' love for his languages is evident throughout his work. Translation is not a target or an end goal. Stavans' work is "mucho más allá de un simple instrumento para la comunicación," says María Carmen África Vidal Claramonte.[17] It is a journey, a way of living that sparks interest in languages and nurtures roots in them. Translation is more than a way to get from one language to another; it is much more than a bridge.

---

16 Gregory Rabassa, *If This Be Treason: Translation and Its Dyscontents, A Memoir* (New York: New Directions), 4.
17 María Carmen África Vidal Claramonte, *Ilan Stavans, traductor*, preface by Steven G. Kellman (Granada: Comares, 2002), 5.

V.

In *El fantasma en el libro: La vida en un mundo de traducciones* (2016), Javier Calvo reminds us that "vivimos, más que en ningún otro momento de la historia de la humanidad, en un mundo de traducciones, literalmente rodeados de ellas. En el trabajo, en el cine, en internet, en la publicidad, por la calle. Hemos aprendido a no verlas, pero nuestra relación con ellas es muy íntima."[18] Yet despite our being surrounded by translations, there is still a widespread tendency to focus on what is lost in translation. The biggest loss in translation exists before a translation is even made. It is the lack of a widespread understanding of what translation is, who translators are, and what they do.

A Google image search for translators delivers photos or graphics of professional interpreters or translate buttons on computer keyboards and other machines. Among the mix of interpreters with headsets and translate buttons, is an image of a fifteenth-century painting of Saint Jerome, the patron saint of translators, who translates alone at his desk. These images have perhaps encouraged ideas of the translator as a social recluse, alone in a room with piles of dictionaries and other books. While most translators need their own space to work and access to physical books, this is only a slice of their life. Translators need to get out. Edith Grossman remarked that she prefers being in close contact with people in the city to being isolated in the countryside. In searching for a word or phrase for a translation, she sometimes finds that it rolls off the tongue of someone beside her moving through the city. The city helps her locate the colloquial expressions some of her characters need to say.[19] In the film *Dreaming Murakami* (2017), by director Nitesh Anjaan, Mette Holm plays pinball as part of her research to translate a Murakami novel into Danish. Translators ask about the use of words in certain contexts. Each project has unique needs and needs new connections. "You can't work alone" is a common piece of advice for young translators.

Collaboration with others is necessary for the survival of translators. Stavans embraces collaborations and conversations. His first *Don Quijote* translation into Spanglish and the establishment of Restless Books

---

18 Javier Calvo, *El fantasma en el libro: La vida en un mundo de traducciones* (Barcelona: Seix Barral, 2016), 9.
19 Regina Galasso and Evelyn Scaramella, "Introduction: Translation and the City," in *Avenues of Translation: The City in Iberian and Latin American Writing*, ed. Regina Galasso and Evelyn Scaramella (Lewisburg: Bucknell University Press, 2019), 5.

14 Introduction

were the results of conversations. Many of the pieces in this volume feature Stavans collaborating with scholars from around the world, working in multiple languages: Youssef Boucetta, Margaret Boyle, Priyanka Champaneri, Robert Croll, Peter Cole, Eduardo Halfon, Steven G. Kellman, Sara Khalili, Jhumpa Lahiri, Josh Lambert, Jenna Tang, Haoran Tong, and María Carmen África Vidal Claramonte. The effort to put his thoughts in dialogue with others not only contributes to his prolific output but also allows him to share, expand, and challenge his ideas. This is the translator's approach. Translators know well that translation changes everything, as the title of Lawrence Venuti's 2013 book says. They also know that translation challenges everything. Translating a text challenges not only knowledge of that text and its language, but also the language and content that the text will go into. The thrill of the challenges keeps translators coming back for more.

Fueled by curiosity, an appreciation for immigrant writing, a quest to find undiscovered classics, a love of language, and restlessness, Stavans' approach of getting to know a subject well is exemplified by his work, decades ago, on Felipe Alfau. Born in Barcelona on August 24, 1902, Alfau arrived at the age of 14 in New York City with his family after having lived in the Basque country, the Philippines, and the Caribbean. He lived in New York City until his death in 1999. Alfau translated as part of his day job at a bank. He also wrote literary prose in English and poetry in Spanish. His writing didn't receive much attention until his novel *Chromos*, written about 50 years earlier but never published, was nominated for the National Book Award in 1990. In May 1991, Stavans visited Alfau at his Queens retirement home. He interviewed Alfau and others who knew him. He wrote about Alfau, translated his poetry into English, which he published in *Sentimental Songs: La poesía cursi* (1992), and contributed to and edited the Alfau section of a special issue of the *Review of Contemporary Fiction* (1993). Stavans found Alfau five years after moving to Manhattan, during a time when he was determined to make his own place as a writer.

Stavans was attracted to the ingenuity of Alfau's language. In his 1997 publication, *New World: Young Latino Writers*, Stavans said that Alfau, with the publication of *Locos: A Comedy of Gestures* in 1936, was the author of "the very first novel by a Latino written in English" and the "very first [Latino] to switch languages successfully."[20] However,

---

20 Ilan Stavans, "Introduction," in *New World: Young Latino Writers*, ed. Ilan Stavans (New York: Delta, 1997), 2.

there are traces of Spanish in his English, an "English [that] is Iberian," according to Alfau.[21] As with Spanglish, knowledge of both English and Spanish offers the reader greater appreciation and understanding of the text and of language in general. Alfau's writing needs to be read in translation. Stavans celebrates Alfau's boldness to write in a language that was his own kind of English, an English that never left Spanish, and to explore translation as a central theme. For example, *Chromos* reveals the state of translation that an individual with a certain sensitivity to language can experience. Alfau's characters, some of whom are writers themselves, contemplate language choice in several situations. Among Stavans' efforts to make Alfau and his work available to a larger audience is his inclusion of Alfau in conversations about Latino literature. Alfau's path, one that Stavans' himself follows, suggests that "considerations of translation in Latino Studies can lead to a more complex understanding of the work of translators in multilingual writing in general."[22]

Alfau and Stavans are translingual authors. *Translingual*, a term coined by Steven G. Kellman in his 2000 book *The Translingual Imagination*, refers to "authors who write in more than one language or at least in a language other than their primary one."[23] Stavans discusses his own ideas about translingualism in a conversation with Haoran Tong in *Translation as Home*. Kellman, who continues to work on translingualism, authored the first book-length study on Stavans, *The Restless Ilan Stavans: Outsider on the Inside* (2019), with a focus on his "unlikely rise to prominence within the context of the spread of multiculturalism as a seminal principle within American culture," as stated in the publisher's description of the book. A little over two years later, a professor from Spain's Universidad de Salamanca, María Carmen África Vidal Claramonte, dove deeper into Stavans' relationship with language, highlighting translation as a way of being in her books *Translating Borrowed Tongues: The Verbal Quest of Ilan Stavans* (2022) and *Ilan Stavans, traductor* (2022). Drawing from a vast bibliography, Vidal Claramonte situates Stavans among other translingual writers, from

---

21 Ilan Stavans, "Anonymity: An Interview with Felipe Alfau," special issue, *Review of Contemporary Fiction* 13, no. 1 (1993): 151.
22 Ilan Stavans, "Introduction," in *Oxford Handbook of Latino Studies*, ed. Ilan Stavans (New York: Oxford University Press, 2020), xviii, Stavans on Galasso's chapter in the same volume.
23 Kellman, *Translingual Imagination*, 9.

16   Introduction

Giannina Braschi (1953–) to Guillermo Gómez-Peña (1955–), and the work of translation studies scholars, including Susan Bassnett, Edwin Gentzler, and Sherry Simon to frame Stavans' relationship with language. Her work endorses a postmonolingual era, going beyond a single language as having structured "la vida moderna, los imperios, las instituciones, y que ha prescrito una jerarquía entre lenguas y entre quienes las hablan."[24] The postmonolingual era welcomes the age of translation.

Vidal Claramonte's books not only provide an exploration of translation as a guide for understanding the many aspects of Stavans' work but also focus on the role of the translator and the doors that translation opens for literary inquiry. In doing so, *Ilan Stavans, traductor* and *Translating Borrowed Tongues: The Verbal Quest of Ilan Stavans* contribute to translator studies, a scholarly effort to humanize translation studies.[25] Klaus Kaindl indicates that this translator-centered approach contributes to making "the potentials, options and meanings of the lives of translators accessible to scholarly investigation"[26] while shining a brighter spotlight on translators' "contribution(s) to the cultural and social spheres of life."[27]

Stavans' arrival in the United States marks the beginning of a period of not only a changed use of a specific language but also new understandings of language in general. In *Translation and Transmigration* (2021), Siri Nergaard sees the entire migrant experience as a "complex process of translation" not only between languages but also between places, "cultures, lifestyles, habits, traditions, and thoughts."[28] For Nergaard, the migrant "is translated and she translates herself. She lives in translation" and "translation is the concept through which the encounter with otherness finds its best expression."[29] Keeping in mind the backdrop of continuous shifts, *Translation as Home* promotes an understanding of what it means to use the word "translation" to make sense of a migrant experience, a love for language, a fascination with the use of words, and a commitment to being open to allowing the shapes, sounds, and sizes of all languages

---

24 Vidal Claramonte, *Ilan Stavans, traductor*, 24.
25 Klaus Kaindl, "(Literary) Translator Studies," in *Literary Translation Studies*, ed. Klaus Kaindl, Waltraub Kolb, and Daniela Schlager, 2.
26 Kaindl, "(Literary) Translator Studies," 3.
27 Kaindl, "(Literary) Translator Studies," 23.
28 Siri Nergaard, *Translation and Transmigration* (London: Routledge, 2021), 1.
29 Nergaard, *Translation and Transmigration*, 1.

and words to challenge and feed one's own self-expression. "Living in translation," according to Nergaard, "is a condition that questions all certain belongings, all defined identities, and disrupts the idea of cultures as natural unities of exclusive belonging."[30] Stavans has been a pioneer in sharing lives, including his own, in translation.

VI.

In "How Dictionaries Define Us," Margaret Boyle joins Stavans to discuss words, dictionaries, translation, the pandemic's impact on language and more. Boyle and Stavans point out that "COVID-19" had been accepted into the *Merriam-Webster Dictionary* faster than any other word to date. It took two weeks from its first utterance until it appeared on the company's website. New terms also quickly emerged to express the needs of life during the pandemic, such as "Zooming," "muting," "anti-vaxxers." At the same time, familiar words took on new meanings. "Home" is one of them. In the United States we began to hear "stay at home" or "stay home." Some people were forced to stay home in a home that was not theirs. Others, with multiple homes, had to choose a home to stay at home in. Some people, those without a physical home, had to find a home or were offered a temporary home during this critical period. Other people, including many university students and recent graduates, were forced to move to their parents' home because they could no longer afford the home of their own that they were trying to make. For others, their ideas about home began to change while staying home. "Home delivery," "work from home," and other phrases that included "home" were used more frequently and took on new meanings.

During the lockdown, to stop the spread of COVID-19, in an apartment in the Eixample neighborhood of Barcelona, three roommates, Guillem Bolto, Klaus Stroink, and Rai Benet, sang "Please stay homa (please stay home), don't want the corona (please stay home), Oh God please stay homa (please stay home). It's ok to be alona." They took their group's name, Stay Homas, from the lyrics to that song. They wrote "Confination Songs" in Catalan, English, and Spanish from their rooftop terrace. They went from a play-at-home group that had only one drumstick, household items, their voices, and their creativity to one that tours internationally. Their music helped them and their listeners stay home during a time in which all kinds of feelings about home were surfacing. The familiar word "home" became a source of creativity and new understandings.

---

30 Nergaard, *Translation and Transmigration*, 5.

18 Introduction

Over 130 years earlier, in the same city, Antoni Gaudí i Cornet (1852–1926) was assigned his first project. In 1883, Manuel Vicens i Montaner commissioned the young architect to design and build a house, one that would become his family's summer home in Gràcia, then a village outside the city. Marrying tradition with a ground-breaking design and structural system, Casa Vicens, a UNESCO World Heritage Site since 2005, is considered Gaudí's first architectural masterpiece and the seeds of the Modernisme movement. This project provided Gaudí with the opportunity to think about what a "casa" should be. His ideas are shared in the text "La casa pairal," found in Gaudí's notebook known as *El manuscrit de Reus*; it escaped destruction during the Spanish Civil War thanks to the architect Domènec Sugrañes i Gras (1878–1938), who removed it from Gaudí's studio inside Barcelona's Sagrada Familia.[31] Another architect, César Martinell i Brunet (1888–1973), then rediscovered the notebook while writing his 1967 book *Gaudí: Su vida, su teoría, su obra*. *Translation as Home* includes an English translation of "La casa pairal" that Stavans and I made together especially for this volume. This is Stavans' first published translation from Catalan. For Stavans, Catalan is the language of the fifteenth-century *Tirant lo Blanc* by Joanot Martorell, a work that influenced Cervantes and the conception of *Don Quijote*. Catalan is the language of resistance against Madrid's centralizing agenda, and Stavans' awareness of that instigated his own translations of *Don Quijote* into Spanglish. While there's no doubt that Stavans would consider the journey of "La casa pairal" a good enough reason to translate the text, its translation is also a creative activity to extend and deepen the experience of what it means to build and to write, to build with words, about "casa."

In the process of translation, familiar words are tested to see how far and where they can go. When is "casa" home? When is "casa" house? When is "casa" casa? Is it anything else? Stavans and I explored translation as home in a conversation included in the February 2021 issue of *Latin American Literature Today*, reprinted in this volume. The *LALT* carried on with "language, translation, and the concept of 'home' [to] weave together [the] two main dossiers," as announced by Denise Kripper in her Facebook post promoting the June 22 issue. The idea of translation as home is an invitation to better understand relationships with language, to better understand a multilingual life. It's an attempt to slow down audiences to focus on what translation is, what it does,

---

31 Ramon Gomis and Kimberly Katte, "Antoni Gaudí (1852-1926): The Manuscript of Reus," *Contributions to Science* 12, no. 2 (2016).

and how we can make language and texts our own through translation. Home is where one entertains, recovers, develops, suffers, shares, learns, transforms, and more on one's own terms. *Translation as Home* shares perspectives on language and translation, challenging the reputation of translation as a lofty endeavor reserved for polyglots or a select group of scholars. Translation is an open house.

BIBLIOGRAPHY

Anjaan, Nitesh, director. *Dreaming Murakami*. 2017. 58 min.
Calvo, Javier. *El fantasma en el libro: La vida en un mundo de traducciones*. Barcelona: Seix Barral, 2016.
Cervantes, Miguel de. *El ingenioso hidalgo Don Quijote de la Mancha*. Ed. Luis Andrés Murillo. Madrid: Castalia, 1978.
– *L'enginyós cavaller Don Quixot de la Mancha*. Trans. Antoni Bulbena i Tussell. Barcelona: Edicions 62, 2005.
– *Don Quixote of La Mancha*. Introduction by Ilan Stavans. Illustrations by Eko. Brooklyn: Restless Books, 2015.
Galasso, Regina. "Always in Translation: Ways of Writing in Spanish and English." In *The Oxford Handbook of Latino Studies*, ed. Ilan Stavans, 330–46. New York: Oxford University Press, 2020.
Galasso, Regina, and Evelyn Scaramella. "Introduction: Translation and the City." In *Avenues of Translation: The City in Iberian and Latin American Writing*, ed. Regina Galasso and Evelyn Scaramella. Lewisburg: Bucknell University Press, 2019.
Gomis, Ramon, and Kimberly Katte. "Antoni Gaudí (1852–1926): The Manuscript of Reus." *Contributions to Science* 12, no. 2 (2016): 145–9.
Gration, Elizabeth. "Bilingualism in 2022: US, UK and Global Statistics." Updated February 28, 2023. https://preply.com/en/blog/bilingualism-statistics/
Kaindl, Klaus. "(Literary) Translator Studies: Shaping the Field." In *Literary Translation Studies*, Benjamins Translation Library, vol. 156, ed. Klaus Kaindl, Waltraub Kolb, and Daniela Schlager, 1–38. Amsterdam: John Benjamins Publishing Company, 2021.
Kellman, Steven G. *The Translingual Imagination*. Lincoln: University of Nebraska Press, 2000.
– *The Restless Ilan Stavans: Outsider on the Inside*. Pittsburgh: University of Pittsburgh Press, 2019.
– "Prefacio." In *Ilan Stavans, traductor*, by María Carmen África Vidal Claramonte, xxx. Granada: Comares, 2022.
Martinell i Brunet, César. *Gaudí: Su vida, su teoría, su obra*. Barcelona: Colegio Arquitectos Cataluña y Baleares, 1967.

Martorell, Joanot. *Tirant lo Blanc*. Trans. David Rosenthal. Baltimore: Johns Hopkins University Press, 1996.

Nergaard, Siri. *Translation and Transmigration*. London: Routledge, 2021.

Pérez de Villar, Amelia. *Los enemigos del traductor: Elogio y vituperio del oficio*. Madrid: Fórcola Ediciones, 2019.

Rabassa, Gregory. *If This Be Treason: Translation and Its Dyscontents: A Memoir*. New York: New Directions, 2005.

Simon, Sherry. *Cities in Translation: Intersections of Language and Memory*. London: Routledge, 2012.

Stavans, Ilan. *Sentimental Songs: La poesía cursi*. Elmwood Park: Dalkey Archive Press, 1992.

– "Anonymity: An Interview with Felipe Alfau." Special issue, *The Review of Contemporary Fiction* 13, no.1 (1993): 146–57.

– Special issue, *The Review of Contemporary Fiction* 13, no. 1 (1993).

– "Introduction." In *New World: Young Latino Writers*. Ed. Ilan Stavans. New York: Delta, 1997.

– *On Borrowed Words: A Memoir of Language*. New York: Penguin, 2001.

– "'Don Quijote' en Spanglish." *La Vanguardia*, July 3, 2002, 5–6.

– "In Defense of Spanglish." *The Common Reader: A Journal of the Essay* (2014). https://commonreader.wustl.edu/c/cervantes-spanglish/.

– "Every language that is taking share goes through a phase similar to Spanglish." *Entrevistes: Universitat de Barcelona*, 15 June 2015. https://web.ub.edu/en/web/actualitat/w/ilan-stavans-every-language-that-is-taking-shape-goes-through-a-phase-similar-to-spanglish

– *Don Quixote of La Mancha* (adaptation). By Miguel de Cervantes. Illustrations by Roberto Weil. University Park: Pennsylvania State University Press, 2018.

– *On Self-Translation: Meditations on Language*. Albany: State University of New York Press, 2018.

– "Introduction." In *Oxford Handbook of Latino Studies*, ed. Ilan Stavans, xi–xxi. New York: Oxford University Press, 2020.

– *Popol Vuh: A Retelling*. Illustrations by Gabriela Larios. Foreword by Homero Aridjis. Brooklyn: Restless Books, 2020.

– *Selected Translations: Poems 2000–2021*. Pittsburgh: University of Pittsburgh Press, 2021.

– "Translation as Home: A Conversation with Ilan Stavans." By Regina Galasso, *Latin American Literature Today*. February 2022. https://latinamericanliteraturetoday.org/2021/02/translation-home-conversation-ilan-stavans/

Venuti, Lawrence. *Translation Changes Everything: Theory and Practice*. London: Routledge, 2013

Vidal Claramonte, María Carmen África. *Ilan Stavans, traductor*. Preface by Steven G. Kellman. Granada: Comares, 2022.

– *Translating Borrowed Tongues: The Verbal Quest of Ilan Stavans*. New York: Routledge, 2022.

PART I

Language on Fire

We Are the Clarion:
A Manifesto on Immigration

There is no America without outsiders. Call us pilgrims, slaves, refugees, exiles, immigrants, even tourists – we all, directly or indirectly, come from somewhere else. As a nation, the glue tying us together is the shared sense of destiny we nurture and the conviction that somehow this place is different, unlike any other, even exceptional, and that here we may finally breathe free.

We trade in reinvention. What we were is not who we are and who we will be. It starts with our language, but it eventually affects everything else, how we dress, what we eat, what we think.

If America is a cradle of creativity, it is thanks to us. We are all the "wretched refuse" Emma Lazarus quotes Lady Liberty as saying in her sonnet "The New Colossus," "the homeless, tempest-test" who were rejected in other lands. In *Democracy in America*, Alexis de Tocqueville says that "the happy and powerful do not go into exile, and there are no surer guarantees of equality among men than poverty and misfortune." When we come, we immigrants are all leveled-off. We made the move out of choice. It was our manifest destiny.

American literature is a cornucopia of viewpoints in which immigrants play a starring role. Starting with the diaries of William Bradford and Puritan religious manuals like the *Bay Psalm Book*, our reflections are indeed always about home, for home is the everlasting theme that defines us. Home is also where we resist, where we become ourselves, the way Native Americans, brushed aside by the European colonizers, maneuvered to survive by speaking their name to the wind from one generation to the next.

They have been shoved around, subdued through internal immigration. Yet the indigenous population is undeterred. They are the torch bearer: they own the place the rest of us lease. That's what Robert Frost meant in his poem "The Gift Outright": this land, such as she was, such as she will become, "was ours before we are the land's."

When Phillis Wheatley writes, "To give an higher appellation still, / Teach me a better strain, a nobler lay," she also talks of immigrants. Likewise, when Emily Dickinson states, "I am Nobody? Who are you?," it is newcomers she is addressing, too. And when in "Song of Myself" Walt Whitman says, "I'm very large, I contain multitudes," he is talking of the rest of us, those here today, yesterday, and tomorrow. Immigrants not only hear these clarions; immigrants are the clarion.

We connect America with every single crevice of the world. The world's heart palpitates in us. English is this nation's dominant language but, thanks to immigrants, all other languages (Chinese, Swahili, Bengali, Arabic, Italian, Gaelic ..., even Latin) are here too, through nostalgia and as an effort to trace our roots. H.L. Mencken put it right once: "A living language is like a person suffering incessantly from small hemorrhages, and what it needs above all else is constant transactions of new blood from other tongues. The day the gates go up, that day it begins to die."

Immigrants are the thermometer that announces the health of a language. The moment we become proficient in English in America we feel we belong. Yet our proficiency isn't stagnant. Willingly or otherwise, we keep a transaction with our original tongues. Look at how American immigrant writers are restless, innovative, pioneering: O.E. Rølvaag, Isaac Bashevis Singer, Vladimir Nabokov, Felipe Alfau, Lucette Lagnado, Jamaica Kincaid, Jhumpa Lahiri, and Edwidge Danticat. They turn English upside down and inside out; they also season it with their original spices into a gorgeous polyglot stew.

Undeterred, we immigrant writers have something to prove; that something is that America is an unfinished project. We know we don't have time to lose: the spotlight won't stay with us for long. So we tell the wrenching stories of self-definition that make us who we are. We trace the paths our families have taken, sometimes in great pain. Ours are often stories of isolation, misunderstandings, even regret. Yet for us the act of writing is, in and of itself, a triumph. "We are here! We have arrived!" every immigrant book proclaims.

Immigrants are like converts to a new religion. We become obsessed with knowing everything about it, sometimes far more than the locals. This makes us proud: we are willing to sacrifice so that those coming after us will reap the same benefits.

Yet, what remains beautiful about America is the way individualism and collectivism are in constant opposition. The self becomes powerful to the point of obfuscation. Yet it is constantly humbled, brought back down to earth, being asked not to forget that this country is not mine but ours, that the success of anyone, including mine, is a social act, and, as such, an engine of progress. That's why immigrants are hyper-sensitive about suddenly losing what they fought so hard to gain: because their victory is everyone else's too. Immigrants love freedom; they know well that without it, nothing is worthwhile.

In short, we immigrants, always on the go, outsiders on the inside, assimilating to our new place while making that new place different, less stringent, more elastic, keep America on its toes. The most stable feature in our nation is change, and to a large extent we immigrants are responsible for it.

– American Writers Museum, October 27, 2019

On Packing Up My Library

I live in an old house. On the third floor, there is a small space, six feet by five, bigger than a closet but smaller than a room. The wooden door is beautiful; seeing it, you wouldn't guess that the inside was left unfinished at the time the house was built in 1905. I don't remember when I started using it as a Genizah.

The Hebrew word "Genizah" – meaning "to hide or put away" – refers to a storage place in a synagogue or a cemetery where old Jewish books go to die. They might contain the name of God in any of its variations. In Judaism, names play a crucial role: they hold the secret to their owner's identity. There is no higher secret than the divine name. Placing sacred books in the Genizah is a way to protect them from falling into the wrong hands. You could say that the Genizah is both a holy place and a dustbin. Whenever these storage places become full, someone in the community takes out the content and buries it. That way sacred books are safe forever.

Obviously, Genizahs have enormous historical value. Items in them – mostly prayer books, volumes of the Talmud, and other Judaic texts – represent the memory of their community. Genizahs might be cleaned out once every 50 years, maybe once a century. Or maybe never, like some basements over whose maintenance their owners always procrastinate. The most famous Genizah, at least in modern times, is in the Ben Ezra Synagogue in Fustat, in Old Cairo, Egypt. A collection of 400,000 manuscript fragments representing about 1,000 years of Jewish history, from 870 CE to the 19th century. More specifically, medieval texts from Eastern and North Africa, mostly in Aramaic and Hebrew, and including fragments from Maimonides. In 1896, samples were taken to England by a couple of Scottish scholars, who showed them to their Cambridge colleague Solomon Schechter, who was a lecturer in Talmudics. This led to an astonishing period of revival in Jewish scholarship.

If you ask my family, they will tell you that I don't like keeping things around. If something isn't of value anymore, I don't see the need to keep it. This is true – with one exception: books and other literary artifacts. I keep correspondence, first drafts of manuscripts, photographs, posters, newspapers, and so on. I don't save everything, just what I consider valuable, and that, of course, is an important question. I'm interested in the written word. I want to preserve items that are a statement of the period in which they came to life. I don't know when I developed this habit; it must have been in my teens. I wasn't a bookish boy. In fact, I unequivocally disliked reading. My 80-year-old mother likes to remind me of this. I preferred the outdoors: hiking, camping, playing soccer. It never crossed my mind while growing up that I would be a writer or a scholar or a translator or a publisher. Books were for awkward people. They were unexciting.

In retrospect, books have been my most trustworthy friends. I spend my days with them: reading them, writing them, opening them up in front of others – students, including incarcerated people, middle and high schoolers, and senior citizens. When I really think about it, there are very few moments of my day when books aren't around. In a personal essay published in *Literarische Welt* in 1931, Walter Benjamin, the German cultural critic, describes his passion for collecting books. He says that the book collector relates to books in a way that is different from a book buyer or a library borrower. A book buyer has a pecuniary relationship: the person buys the book to read it, after which the book is put aside. It might end in a bookshelf; it might be given away; or it might be thrown into the garbage. A library patron borrows a book, reads it, and returns it to the archive.

And then there's the book publisher. I'm one of them. The publisher makes books, not his own (though he might do this as well) but other people's. He views books as products, or let's say merchandise. His objective is to bring them to people, to sell them. To these three types of book-related individuals – the buyer, the borrower, and the publisher – the specific copy of a given book is irrelevant: as long as they are reading, say, Kafka's *The Metamorphosis*, it doesn't matter if it's a first edition, if it has a beautiful cover, or if someone has inserted some marginalia into it. By contrast, a book collector looks for a specific copy; no other one will do. That copy has particular value: it might be a first edition, it might be signed, it might have been owned by someone of distinction. The collector wants that copy to sit on a shelf where it will be accompanied by others of significant, relevant material. Curating this collection is a statement of ownership: this gathering of items, it seems to say, forms a family, one that was previously dispersed throughout the vast universe of books; and it is vital that the family members stay together.

Benjamin was a mid-20th-century Marxist who looked at culture from the perspective of dialectical materialism. In other words, he was interested in a kind of messianism: social progress, leading to the end of history. He could never find an academic job, which is a good thing in my eyes because academia would have destroyed his creativity. I have seen too many geniuses wither away in cold and snobbish hallways. "The acquisition of books is by no means a matter of money or expert knowledge alone," Benjamin says.

One of the finest memories of a collector is the moment when he rescued a book to which he might never have given a thought, much less a wishful look, because he found it lonely and abandoned in the marketplace and bought it to give it its freedom – the way the prince bought a beautiful slave girl in *The Arabian Nights*. To a book collector, you see, the true freedom of all books is somewhere on his shelves.

More than 25 years ago, I started placing items in my Genizah. It began with a couple of office boxes that contained my first attempts to write in English, as well as stuff I had accumulated over the years since I emigrated from Mexico in the mid-1980s. When I arrived in New York City, I had with me a few boxes of books I had found it impossible to part with. I talk about those books in the first chapter of my 2001 memoir, *On Borrowed Words*. Soon, the door of the Genizah was covered with manuscripts – letters from family and friends. It was an indistinct space, without personality – a closet really, where I placed material I didn't want to lie around elsewhere. In time, the question of personality became essential. As I developed as a writer, and especially as I came to focus on my Mexican and Jewish background, it became clear to me that the Genizah was becoming the secluded room where I stored aspects of myself. I wasn't hiding them from anyone; by now, the effort of housing them in that space was a matter of survival. These items were a statement of who I had been.

This past November, I finally cleaned out the Genizah. It was an agonizing project. Not only had it grown in uncontainable ways – items covered every inch of it up to the celling in such a way that only spiders could find their way around, and every time I opened the door some fleeting article tried to escape, so I had to close the door quickly and forcefully – but, as my wife and children often repeated to me, it had become a fire hazard.

But it wasn't the Genizah alone that had grown; the entire third floor, or most of it, had become a library. Its content was rather specific. In my journeys through Latin America, the United States, Europe, Israel, and the Middle East, I had realized that what I was interested in, what I often wrote about – the intersections of Jewishness in the Hispanic world – was off the radar of major Judaica and Latino collections. No one was interested in these items, at least not comprehensively. There were libraries with specific interests – for instance, Yiddish literature in general and Latin American in particular, as at the Yiddish Book Center, in Amherst, Massachusetts, not far from where I live, or at the YIVO branches in New York or Buenos Aires. But gathering, say, Argentine Jewish literature or Peruvian Jewish literature or the literature of the *marranos*, not as separate collections but as part of a whole, wasn't done anywhere. That, I told myself, was my contribution: to build a reservoir of material capable of mapping out the experience of Latino Jews from before 1492, when the Jews were expelled from Spain, up to the present.

I'm not a billionaire. Fortunately, I have enough money not to need more. Whenever I've had extra, I have used it to travel, to buy books and manuscripts. My collection reflects my idiosyncrasies. I love translations of the Bible, of Borges, of García Márquez, of Pablo Neruda, of Isaac Bashevis Singer, and of *Don Quixote*; and I'm enamored with dictionaries and their makers: Covarrubias's *Tesoro de la Lengua Castellana o Española*, Samuel Johnson, Noah Webster, the *OED*, *Webster's Third*. These subcategories are also part of what I've accumulated over the years. They are linked to the manuscripts I have been given as presents by friends from across the globe, correspondence I have exchanged with politicians, activists, rabbis, writers, poets, artists, educators, scholars, and a slew of common folks. The letters alone must number close to 50,000. I'm not known for being short of words. The languages of the collection include Spanish, Yiddish, Hebrew, English, Ladino, French, Polish, Russian, German, and K'iche', among others.

Some of the books and other items in the collection are unique; some are old and others new. When I was in the midst of research for my book *The Seventh Heaven: Travels through Jewish Latin America* (2019), I visited the agricultural colonies in the Pampas funded by Baron Maurice de Hirsch. While there, I acquired all kinds of Yiddish material related to theater, poetry, the novel, and music. I fell for Jevel Katz, a Lithuanian-born theater star who immigrated to Argentina, where he became a popular comedian and performer of tangos in Yiddish – or better, in "Casteidish," the local mix of Yiddish and Spanish. He was known as "the Jewish Carlos Gardel." Yiddish in Argentina was a voracious language that thrived for decades, as it did, although more modestly, in Cuba, Brazil, and elsewhere. I followed the same method in connection with the so-called "rat route" that former Nazis took to Paraguay, Bolivia, Chile, and other South American locations, and also in

Northern Mexico and the American Southwest, as I pursued the roots of crypto-Jewish life. In Israel, I spent time with Argentines, Uruguayans, Brazilians, and others who had made *Aliyah* in the '70s.

When I finally took my family's injunction to clean out my collection seriously, I invited Aaron Lansky to breakfast. The founder of the Yiddish Book Center in Amherst, he is an expert in the art of rescuing books. I described my collection: the Genizah as well as the library, which by then included thousands of books, filling various rooms in which I had added shelves, and eventually spilling over into a climate-controlled bunker at the institution where I work. I joked that, on top of being a fire hazard, the collection was also a health hazard. The staircase to the third floor was significantly narrowed because of the piles of books that had accumulated on each side. I stumbled over a pile one night after consulting a handful of dictionaries and fell down, causing several other piles to collapse over me. That, I told Aaron, was the catalyst: I didn't want to be killed by my own collection.

I asked for his advice. I did the same with a number of other close friends and confidants, including Ken Schoen, the Judaica bookseller, who lives and works in a 1930s WPA-built firehouse in South Deerfield, Massachusetts, and whose motto is "books with a past, looking for a future." Soon I had a number of institutions in Israel and the United States interested in an acquisition. The ordeal was torturous. For starters, it meant inviting them to visit. I am not a shy person, but letting others see this portion of my house, in an order that might be perceived as chaos, made me uncomfortable. I suppressed that discomfort because I realized that the worst that could happen wasn't the collection burning down. I was in my mid-50s, and growingly aware of my own mortality. I didn't want to leave the decision of where to place the collection to my survivors – an unfair burden given its magnitude. And I wanted to know that it would be available to others. I wanted to make sure it would serve its prime function: to foster the study of Latin American Jewish civilization and of Jews in the Hispanic world generally.

After intense negotiations, the collection was acquired by the Herbert D. Katz Center at the University of Pennsylvania. The COVID-19 virus hit in early 2020, just as the contract was being drafted. The pandemic naturally delayed the transfer of the material. Arthur Kiron, Schottenstein-Jesselson Curator of Judaica Collections at the Center, kept monitoring the situation. Finally, in late summer, he received the go ahead. It took me several months to pack my library. Opening up the Genizah in order to empty its contents was traumatic. This sacred place contained everything I ever was and would ever be. The same went for my books. They would no longer sit in the place that had been theirs for a long time. Moreover, I needed to put every single item in clearly cataloged boxes. The process wasn't just physically exhausting. Psychologically, I felt as if I were unraveling, splitting from my own past. It wasn't that I was renouncing the books; I was putting them in a foster home. During those months, I engaged in a dialogue with them: a dialogue about separation. I also donated 1,000 or so books to public libraries and to specialized booksellers. And I gave away some items to students, friends, and acquaintances.

The moving truck arrived on a sunny November morning. Two immigrant workers, one originally from outside Lima, Peru, the other from Santo Domingo in the Dominican Republic, were extraordinarily careful in the treatment they gave to the more than 150 shipping boxes. They took the entire day to load the truck. In the late afternoon, the three of us sat on my porch and drank tea. Although they didn't ask, as per company policy, I told them what the boxes contained. They told me that, up until their arrival in the United States, they had never seen a Jew in their lives in their respective countries of origin. I felt satisfied that the collection, with any luck, would help correct that ignorance. Jews in Latin America are insular people, forming communities that deliberately limit their intercourse with the outside world as a survival mechanism.

The Genizah on the third floor is now empty. So are the shelves in the several rooms of my personal library. Not entirely empty, of course: I kept about 100 volumes, from which I just couldn't separate. I'm not planning on dying in the immediate future, and I'm sure I will continue filling up the shelves. Then – slowly – I will ship these artifacts to Philadelphia to be next to their peers, where they belong.

– Los Angeles Review of Books, May 16, 2021,
and *The Book Collector,* Spring 2024

Retelling *Popol Vuh* – in Chinese

Translation is the way literature travels. It gives a book freedom, allowing it to dress up in fashionably different clothes.

I am attracted to books with questionable origins and whose ultimate form was shaped by translation. The *Popol Vuh* is a prime example. It wasn't "written" at a specific time and place. Its birth was in the form of oral tradition in K'iche', a language that, like all languages, changed every time the story was told. That is, the narrative didn't have a single author but a collectivity, which made its content mutate over centuries. Then, around the Spanish conquest, it was written down, a transcription that entails a form of translation.

That transcription had a tangible beginning, middle, and end. It in turn became translated into other languages. The result builds a structure of concentric circles: each time a new language is added, the *Popol Vuh* gains an audience. Is it the same book that the K'iche' hold in their heart? Yes and no. Translators are interpreters: they allow the book to travel *through their own views*. There is no such a thing as an innocent translation. Of course, some translators are more "loyal" than others. As it is impossible, according to Heraclitus, to read the same book twice (by definition, the reader changes), each translation is biased. All translators are commentators.

The Chinese translation by Chen Yang offers an opportunity to reflect on the connections between the Maya and the Chinese. I have had a front seat in her meticulous process and have engaged in dialogue with her throughout. She has sent me numerous intelligent questions about the text: about birds and felines, about the so-called "wood people," about religious manifestations, and so on. It has been a pleasure to answer them to the best of my ability. One of the topics that has repeatedly come up is mythology. For years, I have studied biblical and Greek mythologies. And I look at popular culture (think of superheroes today, or the British royalty) as another mythology. For a culture to coalesce, it needs myths: the hero's journey, the role of fate, etc.

Are myths universal? Or do they respond to local forces? The answer is both. Myths are stories that every generation is drawn to in order to find its place. They might appear in pure, unadulterated form. Or they might deceitfully present themselves as modern. That is to say, certain archetypes are engraved in our DNA. Others are linked to the particular circumstances that define us.

In our conversations, Chen Yang has described to me the way she fell in love with Mayan culture while translating the *Popol Vuh*. Along with the publisher, she wondered if I could offer a preface tailored for Chinese readers, "to open the gate for them, while I lead them into the fantastic world you created, just like Dante's Virgil." She told me of the degree to which her acquaintances have called attention to a number of curious parallels between the cosmologies of China and Mesoamérica. Take Q'uq'umatz. The Great Feathered Serpent might be seen as "kin" to the Chinese dragon, who also controls weather, storms, and rainfall and who represents an important constellation in traditional Chinese astrology. The appearance in the night sky announces the start of spring. Is this sheer coincidence? Or to put it another way, is mythology defined by coincidence?

Another instance is the fact that in Mayan and Chinese culture, each cardinal direction has a color, and therefore a meaning. In China, the east is the green, the vegetation, the spring, represented by a dragon; the south is the red, the fire, the summer, represented by a rosefinch, a bird on fire; the west is the white, the metal, the killing, the bad augur, the autumn, represented by a white tiger; the north is the black, the water, the winter, represented by a turtle-snake "chimera"; and finally the middle/center is the yellow, the earth, which is without a precise representing creature.

A rabbit always follows the Maya moon god/goddess. Likewise, in China the Moon Goddess, Chang'e, has a cute white little rabbit. In Chinese literature, "jade rabbit" is a metaphor for the moon. At one point, Chen Yang mentioned that when she first learned that Juraqan means "one-legged," she immediately thought about the Creation Gods in China: Nvwa 女娲 & Fuxi 伏羲. They are human-serpent, and their serpent tails are a reminder of Juraqan's one leg. The famous twentieth-century Mexican muralist Diego Rivera drew it like two serpent tails.

These similarities stem from their graphic quality as well as the symbolic nature of the two civilizations. Before their languages became regulated by the letters of the Latin alphabet, the pre-Columbian people of the Americas – not only the K'iche' but the Aztec, the Mayas, the Inca, and so on – used visuals to embody their universe. Their architecture, their art, even their languages were populated with animals, flowers, and other objects whose value is precise and tangible. The arrival from Spain of a lettered culture uprooted that quality, creating an epistemological shift of epic proportions. As a result, there is no doubt a schism in K'iche' history, a before and an after. That many of these symbols continue with us today is evidence of perseverance.

Due to these similarities, there is a feeling among Chinese that the Maya might have started in Asia – maybe somewhere in Northern China – from where they moved to America through the Bering Strait that connects the Pacific and Arctic Oceans, the way modern-day migrants might, in the form of caravans, trek from El Salvador, Guatemala, and Honduras to the US-Mexican border. Growing up in Mexico, I myself heard this conjecture, in part because anthropologists are constantly in need of finding a common ancestor. As I have reflected with Chen Yang, the movement of individuals millions of years ago from one geography to another is nothing but a hunch. In our correspondence, she called it "a charming theory" without evidence. There is no solid grounding for such a legend.

Mythology isn't ruled by science, though. Instead, it offers its own set of truths. My impression is that the *Popol Vuh* is likely to ignite the Chinese imagination, not least because of these and other coincidences. To me, the idea that, thanks to translation, the K'iche' classic is once again being liberated from its environment to intellectually fertilize a distant land is invigorating. Translators make a book global. Just as *The Arabian Nights* has been replenished by a thousand and one translations into a multitude of languages (inserting a handful of apocryphal episodes along the way), and as the Bible, *The Odyssey, Beowulf,* and the *I-Ching* go on being "retold" for young, uninitiated audiences, suddenly carrying messages not foreseen by the original, so does this magical tale about the rise and fall of a resolute, indomitable empire whose story shall endure as long as new readers are drawn to it.

– Popul Vuh: A Retelling (Chinese edition), 2022

English as She Is Spoke: The Fallacy of American Studies (with Steven G. Kellman)

STEVEN G. KELLMAN: Let's start with hope, Ilan. The conlang Esperanto ("one who hopes") was concocted in the 1880s by the Polish ophthalmologist Ludwik Zamenhof out of an aspiration for world peace. In the post-Babel world, we are fragmented among linguistic tribes that literally do not speak the same language. Horrified by pogroms sweeping the multilingual Russian Empire, Zamenhof became convinced that a new, neutral second language that would be easy (at least for Europeans) to learn could bring everyone together and eliminate strife and violence. However, linguistic differences did not kill more than a million Americans during the Civil War, nor were they much of a factor in the "Troubles" of Northern Ireland. The fact that Serbian and Croatian are virtually indistinguishable did not prevent genocide in the Balkan Peninsula. Esperanto became the explicit target of idealists of a different sort, when Adolf Hitler inveighed against it as a tool for Jewish world domination and Josef Stalin vilified it as a symptom of anti-Soviet cosmopolitanism. Esperantists, including Zamenhof's own children, were exterminated in Nazi death camps and confined in Soviet gulags. National loyalty and ideological, if not ethnic, purity was demonstrated through the use of German and Russian, respectively, exclusively. Moreover, what a person speaks continues to be fighting words throughout much of the world, including the United States. Linguistic chauvinism has a long history even – or especially – in a country that sometimes prides itself on being a haven for huddled, babbling masses yearning to breathe free. At the time of the Constitutional Convention, when German was the most widely spoken language in Pennsylvania, only 40 percent of Americans were anglophone, and various native and African tongues were widely heard throughout the former colonies, the question of an official language was debated. Should it really be English, the language of the despised imperial power that Americans had just successfully gained its independence from? French, German, Latin, and Hebrew were considered as alternatives. In the end, though the Constitution was written in English, no language was chosen to be official. And, though 32 states have formally declared English their official language, the nation as a whole remains without one.

ILAN STAVANS: In looking up the word "hope" in Merriam-Webster, I found several definitions, prominently as an intransitive verb, "to cherish a desire with anticipation," and as a noun, "expectation of fulfillment or success." I want to start in the pages of the dictionary because, although, as you say, linguistic chauvinism is an international malaise, one experienced with agony in the United States, it is also important to consider the degree to which two concepts, language and nationalism, go hand in hand and are inextricably intertwined. Max Weinreich, the Yiddish sociolinguist, once said, in the speech "Der YIVO un di problemen fun undzer tsayt," delivered on January 5, 1945, that "a language is a dialect with an army and navy." Languages, like people, strive for power. Those that amass it in large quantities emerge as conquerors; and those that don't are, well, hopeless. English is far from being the only language in the United States. Nor is it the exclusive language of American affairs, including American intellectual pursuits. Yet English was embraced as a language of power by the Constitutional Convention in the formative days of the Republic, just as Spanish was endorsed by the Catholic King and Queen Ferdinand and Isabella in 1492, Hebrew was endorsed by David Ben-Gurion in the shaping of Israel as a Jewish state in 1947, and so on. Indeed, there is no empire that doesn't have its own distinct language, no matter how much discomfort that language causes among its dwellers.

SGK: The Latin phrase "e pluribus unum" remains inscribed on the Great Seal of the United States. But Americans' tolerance for many languages and resistance to the imposition of only one have been tested since the infancy of the Republic. As early as 1780, John Adams proposed the creation of an academy along the lines of the Académie Française in Paris to enforce a standardized American English. Striking a blow for linguistic diversity and acknowledging the fact that language cannot be legislated, the Second Continental Congress rejected Adams' proposal. Yet pressures toward linguistic uniformity have reasserted themselves over the decades – among other places, in Noah Webster's prescriptive *Dictionary of the American Language* and Theodore Roosevelt's insistence, in 1917, that "We have room for but one language here, and that is the English language, for we intend to see that the crucible turns our people out as Americans, not as dwellers in a polyglot boarding house."

IS: You brought up Noah Webster. I take that as a signal to talk a bit about dictionaries. To me, the mere idea of a dictionary is utopian: to trap within book covers, and now in a single website, the entirety of a language. No wonder dictionaries, as we know them, are byproducts of the Enlightenment, even in England, where the Enlightenment as such – unlike say France, Germany, etc. – was seen through a different prism. The most ambitious efforts to corral language in its entirety belong to the second half of the 18th century and to the 19th century. Think of Doctor Johnson or of the Brothers Grimm's *Deutsches Wörterbuch*. One of the leading figures in the history of English lexicography, a renaissance man if there ever was one, is Samuel Johnson, unabatedly one of my lifelong heroes. In a recent session, we compared Johnson's "Plan of an English Dictionary" (1747), in which, after being approached by a group of booksellers to prepare a lexicon, he scanned the landscape – contrary to common belief, he wasn't the first to produce a dictionary of English, but he did produce the best a single person might ever aspire to – and mapped out the route he would take to produce what he thought would be the best lexicon of the English language ever to be published. I quote: "I expect that sometimes the desire of accuracy will urge me to superfluities, and sometimes the fear of prolixity betray me to omissions; that in the extent of such variety, I shall be often bewildered, and, in the mazes of such intricacy, be frequently entangled; that in one part refinement will be subtilized beyond exactness, and evidence dilated in another beyond perspicuity. Yet I do not despair of approbation from those who, knowing the uncertainty of conjecture, the scantiness of knowledge, the fallibility of memory, and the unsteadiness of attention, can compare the causes of errour with the means of avoiding it, and the extent of art with the capacity of man: and whatever be the event of my endeavours, I shall not easily regret an attempt, which has procured me the honour of appearing thus publickly." In other words, Johnson wanted to be judged not by what he hoped for but by what he accomplished. Nine years later (he originally thought he could complete his task in three), he included in the first volume the "Preface to the Dictionary" (1755), an invaluable document in which he explains the extent to which his dreams needed to fit into reality. Johnson states: "When first I engaged in this work, I resolved to leave neither words nor things unexamined, and pleased myself with a prospect of the hours which I should revel away in feasts of literature, the obscure recesses of northern learning, which I should enter and ransack, the treasures with which I expected every search into those neglected mines to reward my labour, and the triumph with which I should display my acquisitions to mankind. When I had thus enquired into the origin of words, I resolved to show likewise my attention to things; to pierce deep into every science, to enquire the nature of every substance of which I inserted the name, to limit every idea by a definition strictly logical, and exhibit every production of art or nature in an accurate description, that my book might be in place of all other dictionaries whether appellative or technical. But these were the dreams of a poet doomed at last to wake a lexicographer. I soon found that it is too late to look for instruments, when the work calls for execution, and that whatever abilities I had brought to my task, with those I must finally perform it. To deliberate whenever I doubted, to enquire whenever I was ignorant, would have protracted the undertaking without end, and, perhaps, without much improvement; for I did not find by my first experiments, that what I had not of my own was easily to be obtained: I saw that one enquiry only gave occasion to another, that book referred to book, that to search was not always to find, and to find was not always to be informed; and that thus to persue perfection, was, like the first inhabitants of Arcadia, to chace the sun, which, when they had reached the hill where he seemed to rest, was still beheld at the same distance from them." A humbling idea: to chase the sun only to find out it is unreachable. As complete as Johnson's *A Dictionary of the English Language* is, it is irremediably limited, for in the end language is larger than any one user: vast, infinite, and, therefore, unascertainable. The English language has some of the best, if not the best, dictionaries ever produced in any language, primarily among them the *Oxford English Dictionary* and *Merriam-Webster*. It is an attribute of the language, and the empires it has fostered, to have produced such a feast. Unlike the *OED*, which was finalized 173 years after Johnson's project saw the light of day, Webster's *American Dictionary of the English Language* (I'm moving across the Atlantic now) was done, in 1828 – and remains – outside the halls of academia, that is, a commercial project, susceptible to the rules of the market. Webster wasn't a man of letters so to speak and he got a lot of things wrong in his dictionary, which is to say, he was no American Doctor Johnson. But one thing he had very clear in his mind: as the "Father of American Scholarship and Education," Webster (who, by the way, was one of the founders of Amherst College) saw English as the conduit for the expression of America's dreams, including its future imperial quests. Just as I find lots to admire in Johnson's dictionary, which he revised several times, Webster, another key figure of course, as an individual, is, in my eyes, less commendable. In May 1962, Joseph W. Reed Jr. of Wesleyan published an article in *American Speech* called "Noah Webster's Debt to Samuel Johnson." Looking at Johnson and Webster through the letter "L" – 2,024 words and 4,505 meanings out of approximately 70,000 words and perhaps 150,000 meanings given in the 1828 *American Dictionary*, comparing their definitions. Reed found that Webster, who lambasts Johnson as error-ridden, plagiarizes him in 333 entries and made very slight alterations in 987 other entries to distinguish his work from his British precursor. In other words, not an auspicious beginning for American lexicography. I offer these numbers because the English language, in and of itself, is a battlefield. George Bernard Shaw famously said that "the United States and Great Britain are two countries separated by a common language." The truth goes further: English being autochthonous in England but adopted in the United States, the wars around it aren't quite the same. America (even the name is a misnomer) is a land of immigrants, which means that English has competed here for space, in distinct ways, from the moment it arrived. And those wars have only intensified as time goes by. Even though they mostly were in command of their projects, neither Johnson's nor Webster's dictionaries would have been conceivable without the army and the navy symbolized by the culture that surrounded them. That culture injected their achievements with a kind of gravitas that is only possible, in my mind, in an imperial language. Less vigorous, more vulnerable languages can't muster such elan; their existence is mostly about survival.

SGK: Samuel Johnson might indeed have produced the best dictionary a single person ever aspired to, but anyone examining the monumental achievement of the *Oxford English Dictionary* might find an even greater aspiration at work there. Though he certainly had help from others, James Murray's maniacal dedication to the task of cataloging every word in the language destroyed his health, but he persevered despite his ailments. When he finally died, at age seventy-eight in 1915, he had managed to get as far as the volume "Trink to Turndown." The final volume was not completed until 1928, but of course, as long as language lives and evolves, the lexicographical project is never complete.

IS: No doubt, Steve. The *OED* is as emblematic of English, an unquestionable achievement, as the King James version of the Bible, each of them an illustrious staple of the time in which they came to life. But the *OED* is a corporate venture. Murray was the director of an immense orchestra. Johnson, in contrast, had a few scribes who don't seem to have contributed anything significant in terms of direction. The *OED* used "cheap" labor to harvest entries from around the world. It was a British venture through and through: mathematical in its architecture and obsessive in its ambition. I own a large collection of dictionaries. Although all of them (some 400 in total) are objects of admiration, some are quirkier than others and also more quixotic. What fascinates me is why certain civilizations produce better dictionaries and why.

sgk: Nevertheless, thousands of languages have their own dictionaries, and, though dictionaries have often been exploited to inspire nationalism or imperialism, I do not see a necessary connection between lexicography and chauvinism. The *Woordenboek der Nederlandsche Taal*, a compilation of every Dutch word used since 1500, was, like the *OED*, created during an extended period, from 1863 to 1998. But its compilers proceeded with a more modest sense of Dutch-speakers' place in the world than the publishers of *Webster's Third New International Dictionary of the English Language, Unabridged* imagined for Anglophones. Collective work on the *Comprehensive Aramaic Lexicon Project*, based at Hebrew Union College, proceeds not out of an ambition that the tiny remnant of Aramaic-speakers scattered throughout the Middle East conquer the world but as an instrument for understanding ancient religious texts. When you compiled your own glossary of Spanglish, it served as an antidote to nationalist power structures.

is: Oh, there certainly is a high dose of chauvinism in lexicography, and in philology for that matter. Sebastián de Covarrubias' *Tesoro de la lengua castellana o española* (1611), published when Cervantes was still working on the second part of *Don Quixote*, has the imprimatur of the Spanish Inquisition, which explains, to a large degree, why Covarrubias goes against Jews, Arabs, and other apostates, heretics, and disbelievers with cruel insistence. His entries might be poetic in style but they are vicious in tone. There are intense feelings of Christian Nationalism in Webster's work, such as his moralizing, sermon-like definition in which he extols Christian beliefs, as in the case of "wife" or "religion," the latter's definition featuring this line: "… includes a belief in the being and perfections of God, in the revelation of his will, in man's obligation to obey his commands, in a state of reward and punishment, and in man's accountableness to God; and also true godliness or piety of life, with the practice of all moral duties." Webster is also constantly quoting the New Testament and the Founding Fathers. On the opposite side of the spectrum is *Webster's Third* (1961), which you referred to. At 14 pounds and 2,700 pages, it remains the most controversial of all English dictionaries in America. When it came out, it created a hoopla, especially about the inclusion of the word "ain't" and the tension between prescriptivism and descriptivism. Its permissiveness, trashed by Dwight Macdonald in the *New Yorker*, resulted in the *New York Times*, the *New Yorker*, and other periodicals swearing never to embrace its dictums. These are just two immediate examples. I don't think lexicographers are part of a plotting cabala intent on indoctrinating us in subliminal ways. Yet, like all of us, they are never free of biases. How could they be? After all, they are a product of their time, although, clearly, some more than others. We all belong to the (in) human race. In his dictionary, Johnson vituperates against the Scots (he defined oats as "a grain, which in England is generally given to horses, but in Scotland supports the people"), which makes his relationship with his friend and biographer James Boswell all the more interesting. You and I know well how that chauvinism strives in the United States, and now, in the Trump era, even more so. One gets the feeling it comes and goes in cycles but it isn't true; it is ubiquitous everywhere one goes, even, of course, among us liberals, who take care of delivering it in a more delicate outfit. The fastest, easiest place to look for it is to consider the status of foreign languages in America. Robert Louis Stevenson, whose Victorian novel *Treasure Island* (1882) is as exotic as they come (well, maybe Melville's *Moby-Dick*, published three decades earlier, not quite Victorian but certainly transcendental, wins the trophy) believed that "there are no foreign countries" and that "only the traveler is foreign." For the United States, it's the opposite: everybody is a foreigner until they "adapt" to the American ways. And those ways are frighteningly close-minded: Native Americans shouldn't be foreign yet they are; all immigrants are a menace. At the level of language, this hatred becomes ideology. Suffice to mention the campaigns against bilingual education and the noisy debates surrounding English Only and English First. Fifty years after the Texas Revolution, you could hear aberrations like "If English was good enough for Jesus Christ, it ought to be good enough for the children of Texas." At times, this paranoia translated into censorship, in spite of the nation's First Amendment.

SGK: Yes. During World War I, the teaching of German was banned in the United States, and, in 1918, the governor of Iowa, William L. Harding, went even further; his "Babel Proclamation" declared that "only English was legal in public or private schools, in public conversations, on trains, over the telephone, at all meetings, and in all religious services." The First Amendment, he insisted, "is not a guaranty of the right to use a language other than the language of this country – the English language." In the spirit of the Texan statement you quoted, the governor even claimed that God responded only to prayers uttered in English. As he explained to the Des Moines Chamber of Commerce: "Those who insist upon praying in some other language ... are wasting their time for the good Lord up above is now listening for the voice of English." So, xenolingua phobia has certainly been a powerful force in American culture, as it has elsewhere in the world. But there are counter-forces, and it is hyperbolic – if not paranoid – to claim that all Americans believe that "all immigrants are a menace." Emma Lazarus did not think so, and neither do the millions of Americans who oppose the construction of a wall across the southern border. And not all lexicographers are rabid nationalists.

IS: Turning the Almighty into a defender of monolingualism is obviously a cheap shot. In the first part of chapter 10 of Genesis, the episode of the Tower of Babel, God appears to recant on his effort to make a polyglot world because humans have hubris and will in the end take over the heavens. In other words, it is a precaution the Almighty takes. But God doesn't speak a human language, at least according to the Talmud, but a divine language. It is humans who have created human languages not only to communicate but to control their habitat. Translations of the Bible into English don't acknowledge, obviously, that the language in which readers are accessing the narrative took shape, depending on how one counts, a millennium after the Crucifixion. For English-language advocates, that's beside the point. English is all about dominance, locally and globally. They believe English isn't only the best, most authentic language ever to exist; it is also the last, as if nothing would ever come after it. This view of history is, well, ahistorical.

SGK: Xenolinguaphobia persists in the United States, most overtly in hostility toward the use of Spanish, despite the fact that the United States, with more than 53 million Hispanophones, trails only Mexico as a Spanish-speaking nation. As recently as 2019, La Cantera, a posh resort in San Antonio, Texas, was forced to pay $2.625 million to settle a lawsuit brought by twenty employees over a policy that punished them for speaking Spanish even among themselves, out of earshot of the guests. The name of the resort, La Cantera (i.e., The Quarry), is itself, of course, Spanish.

IS: Spanish is America's officially unofficial second language. As you say, it is spoken in this land, even in its impure form, by more people than anywhere in the Spanish-speaking world with the exception of Mexico. There are more Latinos in the United States than Spaniards in Spain. Still, it is considered a "kitchen" language, unworthy of its tradition. Latino authors, Spanish-speaking and otherwise, constantly look for strategies to emphasize this distortion or else to circumvent it. We are a diaspora of Latin America in the United States. Our approach to the dominance of English is to subvert it from within because we are also one of this country's minorities – the largest and fastest growing. I'm also interested in what happens to English in the outreaches of the empire. English isn't the world's most popular native language. Chinese, in its many varieties, and Spanish are ahead. But English is the spoken non-native language. Four out of every five speakers is a non-native. I have taken to enjoy a book Mark Twain found amusing: *English as She Is Spoke* (1884), by Pedro Carolino, who at times is called by another name, José da Fonseca. It is a Portuguese-English conversational guide, prepared by an absolutely inefficient, inadvertently creative mind whose knowledge of the language is as abundant as water in the desert. There are lines like "The storm is go over" and "the winter no pleases to me." The guide includes "dialogues," designed to teach non-natives how to use English in specific situations. This is "Dialogue 20," subtitled "For to visit a sick":

- How have you passed the night?
- Very bad. I have nots sleeped; I had the fever during all night. I fell some pain every where body.
- Live me see your tongue. Have you pain to the heart?
- Yes, sir, some times.
- Are you altered?
- Yes, I have thirsty often.
- Let me feel your pulse.
- It is some fever.
- Do you think my illness dangerous?
- Your stat have nothing from trouble some.
- It must to send to the apothecary, I go to write the prescription.
- What is composed the medicine what I have to take?
- Rhubarb, and tartar cream, etc.
- You shall take a spoonful of this potion hour by hour.
- It must to diet one's self a day.
- What I may to eat?
- You can take a broth.
- Can I to get up my self?
- Yes, during a hour or two.
- Let me have another thing to do.
- Take care to hold your warme ly, and in two or three days you shall be cured.

In a commendation often used as a preface, Twain states: "In this world of uncertainties, there is, at any rate, one thing which may be pretty confidently set down as a certainty: and that is, that this celebrated little phrase-book will never die while the English language lasts. Its delicious unconscious ridiculousness, and its enchanting naïveté, are as supreme and unapproachable, in their way, as are Shakespeare's sub-limities." Apparently, Carolino didn't know a word of English. He used a Portuguese-French dictionary and then a French-English lexicon to compile his manual. Now that's resourcefulness! To me *English as She Is Spoke* is about the unequivocal force behind global capitalism and its commanding tool, the English language. Do native English speakers feel pressure all the time from the overwhelming number of non-native speakers? At first sight, Carolino's guide is clumsy. But in its pages there are higher, more urgent truths, particularly in regard to English: mistranslation is a sine qua non of modernity; and America's imposition of cultural patterns gives place to derivatives – let's call them "impostor versions" – that are nothing less than omnipresent. The empire's center prides itself in being authentic while the periphery thrives in second-rate spinoffs.

SGK: I'm not sure about an essential connection between English and capitalism. German was certainly an important tool in the development of modern capitalism, as illustrated by *Das Kapital*. If English and capitalism are connected, it is a matter of contingencies, not necessities. I suspect that any European language might have been harnessed to advance the interests of multinational corporations based in the United States. Perhaps if Hebrew, which lacks a verb meaning "to have" (to declare: "I have a book," a Hebrew-speaker says: "Yesh li sefer" [To me there is a book], an expression devoid of possessiveness), had become the dominant language of this country, our economic and social systems might have been less acquisitive and predatory.

IS: I disagree. The chauvinism we are talking about is, in part, a desire to prove to people in the rest of the world that, no matter how much they try to communicate in English, they will never be part of the "inner club" made by natives. If this sounds Trumpian, it surely is: we are great, the rationale suggests, and everyone else isn't.

SGK: Nevertheless, there is nothing intrinsic to the English language that makes it the appropriate medium for an abusive Trump tweet. Thomas Merton, who renounced worldly appetites in favor of a monastic life, also wrote in English. However, it is a truism in Hollywood that American audiences do not go to the movies in order to read, which is why foreign-language features almost always fare better at the box office when remade, sans subtitles, in English. Coline Serreau's *Trois hommes et un couffin* qualified as a foreign hit in the American market when it grossed $2,052,466 in 1985. However, Leonard Nimoy's 1987 remake, *Three Men and a Baby*, took in $167,780,960 domestically. Other countries that dub rather than subtitle foreign-language films enforce an even greater provincialism. In Naples, where any trace of the English language is expunged from the movie-going experience, audiences for *Stars Wars* are not permitted access even to the voices of Mark Hamill, Harrison Ford, and Carrie Fisher. The (American) Academy of Motion Picture Arts and Sciences presents an annual Oscar to the best foreign-language feature, separate from its award for the best overall picture. In 2020, for the first time, a foreign-language feature, Bong Joon-ho's *Parasite*, shot in Korean and shown in the United States with English subtitles, was honored with the best-picture Oscar, as well as several other Oscars, including the one for foreign-language feature. The president of the United States reacted with xenophobic indignation. "How bad were the Academy Awards this year, did you see?" Donald Trump, who admitted to not having seen *Parasite*, asked the crowd at one of his political rallies. "What the hell was that all about? We've got enough problems with South Korea, with trade, on top of that, they give them the best movie of the year?" Until the ignorance and myopia of Mr. Trump's question become apparent to all, language will continue to be an instrument of America First nationalism.

IS: I also find it intriguing that we teach English as "a second language" to immigrants but not as a foreign language. Anyway, happily the Academy of Motion Picture no longer describes that category as "foreign films," so is it a happy coincidence that *Parasite* won both for "best international picture" and "best picture"? What's the difference when the majority of American movies are financed by transnational corporations whose resources aren't made locally? Will there come a time when these two categories will merge into one? Instead of *Parasite*, Trump wanted *Gone with the Wind* and with it a return to the Old South. In any case, I believe it is important to contemplate how linguistic difference fits into the study of race, gender, and class. One example: the embrace, by American academics, of the term "Latinx." I have written about this in the *New York Times*. As I travel through Latin America, I have yet to hear it on the street, in the classroom, in religious settings and political forums. The term surely comes from a genuine desire to be sensitive to linguistic domination. Yet Spanish, Portuguese, French, Italian, and other Romance languages, derived from Latin, cannot avoid using gendered pronouns. It would be impossible to use these languages entirely. The sun is masculine whereas the moon is feminine. A house is feminine but a home is masculine. That's how the world is built in linguistic terms. In my view, this is an example of English-language speakers spreading the gospel of liberalism through a supposedly ungendered approach. Again, the effort is genuine; but it gets across as nearsighted and manipulative, not to say imperial. In a recent edited volume, *The Oxford Handbook of Latino Studies* (2020), I opted for not asking the three dozen contributors to find a common approach. The result is a symphony of well-wishing discordance. I like it, though. To me, language isn't about homogeneity but about difference.

SGK: When you proclaim that "the sun is masculine whereas the moon is feminine," are you not succumbing to the linguistic absolutism you have been attacking? That gender assignment is true in Spanish and other Romance languages, but it is not true, for example, in German, where *die Sonne* is feminine or in Hebrew, where *shemesh* is also feminine. Multilingualism teaches us that any one language immures us within one particular prison house. Since living languages evolve, is it not possible that the hundreds of teachers in France who signed a proclamation opposing the hoary rule that the masculine noun always prevails over the feminine noun (French speakers are taught to say *"L'homme et les femmes sont américains*, not *L'homme et les femmes sont américaines*) will ultimately prevail? Of course, language is a marker not only of nationality and gender but also of many other factors we use to differentiate among human beings. George Bernard Shaw's Henry Higgins could locate the precise birthplace of a speaker by listening to a few sentences, and one need not be a sociolinguist to differentiate between an Alabama drawl and a Mainer's Yankee dialect. And if men are indeed from Mars, women from Venus, they betray their origins in separate speech patterns. In his famous study of social stratification in language, William Labov discovered that New Yorkers pronounce "fourth floor" differently when he studied them at the posh Saks Fifth Avenue, middle-class Macy's, or working-class S. Klein department stores. The reality of Ebonics is that African American differ from others in vocabulary, phonology, syntax, and other linguistic features.

IS: Labov was on target: when we talk about the dominance of English, we are really describing the apparent cohesiveness of the various Englishes that are available.

SGK: Such differences can be exploited to assert dominance and create injustice.

IS: Of course they can. They often are. But they also bring people together. This discussion makes me think of the role social media has today. Helpful? No doubt since it builds countless layers of connectivity, opening us up to previously unreachable stimulation. Pernicious too? No doubt, since we are lonelier than ever, entrapped in our little bubbles. And, equally worrisome, hatred nowadays arguably travels further and faster than ever before. There's much talk nowadays about restricting social media platforms like Facebook, Twitter, Instagram, and others, de facto injecting them with a modicum of censorship in order to make their assets more palatable. The English language is also a social medium, one that is far more versatile than any of the ones I've listed. While its global, hegemonic reach is a threat to minority cultures and languages, it also brings those cultures and languages – and a zillion other things – to the attention of people. Like the Greek god Janus, it has two faces; and, metaphorically, it is also about beginnings and ends, and about transitions. I'm all in favor of pluralism as well as relativism; however, I also see strong benefits to the hope brought about by universalism, a legacy, let it be remembered of the Enlightenment.

SGK: Speakers of supposedly "mongrel" jargons such as Yiddish and Spanglish have been scorned by those who consider their own languages – which do possess armies and navies – somehow "purer." Under the Russification policy of the Stalinist Soviet Union, the teaching of Chechen, Ingush, Udmurt, and other languages could lead to a stint in a gulag, and American Indian children sent to compulsory government schools were punished if caught using their "inferior" native tongues. An extreme example of language as an instrument of oppression might be the use of shibboleths to identify and eliminate an enemy, as when, on the orders of Dominican dictator Rafael Trujillo, suspected Haitian immigrants were told to pronounce the Spanish word *"perejil."* The Haitian francophones would offer a guttural "r," unlike the trilled "r" of Spanish-speaking Dominicans. In the resulting Parsley Massacre, thousands of "mispronouncing" Haitians were put to death. However, if go back to Esperanto, we find that its lesson is that reducing all linguistic difference does not necessarily lead to equality and harmony. If we all spoke the same language in the same dialect, with the same vocabulary and intonations, human beings would surely still find some reasons and means to oppress one another. The solution is not to eliminate linguistic diversity, but to respect it. Monotony does not create equality but banality.

IS: Rita Dove has a lovely two-part poem called "Parsley," part of her collection *Museum* (1983), on the subject. Yes, Esperanto was a utopian dream: a second language designed to bring peace to Europe. L.L. Zamenhoff's mistake is not to be found in his linguistic effort but in his naïve way of looking at human interaction. Peace will always be just a dream. Humans are about control, and language is a means to achieve it. This is not to say, obviously, that a counter-approach shouldn't be vigorously fought for to ameliorate conflict. That, too, is achieved through the mediation of language.

SGK: Since we have been invited to ponder whether American Studies might be conceived in languages other than English, a start might be to recognize the provinciality of American Studies if isolated from a study of the rest of the world. The rest of the world recognizes the pitfalls of provincialism, as evidenced by the existence of important centers for the study of American culture in Bahrain, Beijing, Berlin, and Brussels – to name only a few institutions beginning with B. Those pursuing American Studies in the United States might benefit from an awareness of the perspectives of those *centers* located in the *peripheries*. In addition, an analysis of the concept of Manifest Destiny would be enriched by recognizing that similar impulses have helped shape Australia, Brazil, South Africa, and other nations. The United States is not the only "nation of immigrants," and the histories of Argentina, Canada, and Israel might aid in an understanding of Ellis Island. American theater must be studied alongside Shakespeare as well as Sophocles, Calderón, Molière, Ibsen,

Chekhov, and Brecht. As glorious as are the achievements of Hawthorne, Melville, Dickinson, Whitman, Wharton, Faulkner, Ellison, and others, the treasury of American literature is not exhausted by texts written in English. Expansion of the canon in recent decades to include neglected minority groups, including Jews, African Americans, Latinos, Asians, and American Indians, has been a salutary and necessary antidote to an oppressively restrictive curriculum. However, it remains noxiously insular if it neglects the wealth of literature written in the United States in languages other than English. An educated American ought to be acquainted with the prolific Hawaiian compositions of Queen Lili'uokalani; the slave narrative written by Omar Ibn Said in Arabic; the novel *Dafydd Morgan* written by R.R. Williams in Michigan in Welsh; as well as some of the rest of the vast library created in this country in Spanish, Yiddish, German, Chinese, Russian, Navajo, and other languages. I salute the work of Harvard's Longfellow Institute, especially its *Multilingual Anthology of American Literature*, edited by Marc Shell and Werner Sollors, as well as the efforts of Arte Publico Press's Recovering the US Hispanic Literary Heritage project and of the Yiddish Book Center at Hampshire College. When their discoveries and insights are incorporated into our understanding of literature of the United States, English will cease to maintain its monopolistic and oppressive control of the culture. It can be honored as a member of the global community of languages.

IS: I'm less optimistic, even though I've actively worked in several of the endeavors you just mentioned. I like your response about provinciality. All provinciality is indeed nefarious. Yet provinciality is, to me, the most pernicious virus around today, in this age of super-viruses. Again looking at *Merriam-Webster*, the first definition, unexpectedly, is "the superior of a province of a Roman Catholic religious order. Only later does the reader come across statements like "limited in outlook" and "a person lacking urban polish or refinement." Epistemologically, this, clearly, is about the distinction between the city and the countryside. Dictionaries are written by urbane people for whom the rural landscape is awkward, atavistic, and, therefore, unwelcome. (I have yet to find a lexicographic project of national importance that sprung, and found life, in the so-called provinces.) Of course, just as the word "America" might be uttered in any tongue, so can anything related to it. By this I mean that one can engage in American Studies in any language one pleases, as is clear from the infinite number of academic papers on the topic published every minute anywhere in the world. Yet whether we want it or not, American Studies as a discipline, in my opinion, is also, at its core, English-language studies produced under the guise of cosmopolitanism, which, by the way, means "dweller of the cosmos." Which cosmos are we talking about? One in which people communicate through a lingua franca, the one you and I are employing right now.

SGK: Is it my American origins that make me, like Emerson, want to revert to hope, if not Esperanto? I am not convinced that lexicography is an insidious conspiracy by city slickers to impose their language and thus *Weltanschauung* on helpless country folk. Willie Sutton explained: "I rob banks because that's where the money is." And if dictionaries tend to be based in cities, it might be because their ambition is to record the language as it is actually spoken, and cities are where, by definition, most speakers cluster. The magnificent *Dictionary of American Regional English*, though, draws on thousands of informants located, by its count, in 1,002 American communities. Surely not all of those are urban behemoths. New Haven, where Noah Webster published his first dictionary was not, nor is Springfield, Massachusetts, where the *Merriam-Webster Dictionary* continues to be based. And the hegemony of magisterial American dictionaries is challenged by the proliferation of dictionaries of variant Englishes – South African, Caribbean, Australian, Canadian. Percy Bysshe Shelley has the ruined statue of a once-omnipotent pharaoh proclaim: "My name is Ozymandias, king of kings: / Look on my works, ye Mighty, and despair!" English was not always the world's dominant language, and it is not likely to remain so forever. In 1872, when French was still the dominant language in diplomacy and German in philosophy and science, Frederick Douglass noted: "Five generations ago, Britain was ashamed to write books in her own tongue. Now her language is spoken in all corners of the globe." *Sic transit gloria mundi*, as they say in a language that, like Greek, Persian, and Sumerian, once monopolized discourse. What can deliver us from cultural hubris and linguistic oppression is a recognition of the relativity of speech systems and our ability to discuss it in a common language, whatever that happens to be.

– *Los Angeles Review of Books*, December 19, 2019

Olga Tokarczuk's Messianic Critique

Messianism is the collectively held belief that an individual with supernatural powers will redeem our world from human misery. It is a religious phenomenon directed toward the future, but it has its origins in the material present, in the economic, social, and cultural crises of a particular historical moment. The conviction that the end of time has arrived – or soon will – comes from the hope that this messiah will help the world reverse course.

Ours is a profoundly troubled time, and one with a few false messiahs as well. When Olga Tokarczuk set out to write her mammoth novel *The Books of Jacob* in 2014, these messiahs were perhaps less rooted in the kinds of nationalist movements we have become accustomed to across the world in the past decade and more in the furies of religious fundamentalism found in an earlier century. But her vision of messianism appears no less potent today, as the countercurrents against liberalism have spread across the globe.

Tokarczuk's inquiry begins in the Poland of the 18th century. Charting the movements of Jewish messianism, in particular the so-called Frankists, she also considers the violence and anti-Semitism in Poland that spawned these countercurrents. At the center of her novel is the real-life Jacob Frank, born in 1726, who began his career as a prominent mainstream Jewish thinker before his increasingly messianic views led to his excommunication from the Jewish community, his eventual rejection by Muslim leaders in the Ottoman Empire, and a heresy trial among Christians, which resulted in his imprisonment in a monastery in Częstochowa, a city in southern Poland.

In a display of narrative elasticity, Tokarczuk tells Frank's story not through his own eyes but through how others perceive him. Frank is seen numerous times as a self-proclaimed fool, dispensing all kinds of cockamamie theological theories that seek to dismantle, or else unify, the Abrahamic faiths. Or he is shown committing or inspiring acts of depravity. But his persona is less important than those of the Talmudists, archbishops, noblemen, freethinkers, bodyguards, and his own cadre of radical followers, whose deeply held convictions he massaged into an appealing common faith with astonishing ease.

The Books of Jacob is divided into seven parts with names like "The Book of Sand," "The Book of the Road," "The Book of the Comet," and "The Book of Metal and Sulphur." Each is made up of countless mini-chapters, the vast majority of them written in the third person, with the exception of letters and diaries by a handful of witnesses of Frank's messianic adventures, or peripheral figures whose accounts help explain the major ideological trends of the period. Defying the traditional choice of the past tense as the default verbal conjugation of the novel, Tokarczuk tells her multitudinous tale in the present tense, as if Frank's exploits are happening before our very eyes.

Readers learn that Frank – the titular Jacob in *The Books of Jacob* – was a follower of Shabtai Tzvi, a false messiah from Smyrna whose impact reverberated deeply in Jewish history and whose odyssey was chronicled in minute detail and with enviable insight in a biography by Gershom Scholem. Tzvi's rise as a messiah came about at a time of intense religious violence and anti-Semitism. The Khmelnytsky massacres, in which Cossacks killed an estimated 40,000 to 100,000 Jews living in the Polish-Lithuanian Commonwealth, took place in the middle of the 17th century. It was therefore not surprising that, among Jews living in the region, a sense of impending Armageddon was in the air. An ossified rabbinical hierarchy, often slow to process or respond to the brutality against Jews, only made this anxiety more acute.

For many, mysticism and a more spiritual and unmediated expression of religion became appealing. The *Sefer ha-Bahir*, the *Zohar*, and other mystical documents in circulation for a while acquired new adherents during this period. Tokarczuk's novel incorporates many of these concepts into its text: We read about the Shekhina, the female aspect of the divine; Ein Sof, the Almighty prior to any self-manifestation; and the Merkhava, the celestial light invoked in Ezekiel's biblical vision. And all this otherworldly philosophizing is set against a tapestry of relentless disaster: comets igniting the formation of popular cults, epidemics erasing entire populations, and wars bringing ruin and desolation. The impression one gets is of a cosmic fight between light and darkness.

Many turned to Hasidism. Fostered by Rabbi Israel ben Eliezer (later known as the Baal Shem Tov), this mystical expression of Judaism was not quite messianic. Instead, it emphasized spiritual awakening and fighting against the rationalist straitjacket of the Talmudic status quo, and thus it focused on the joys of encountering the sacred in daily life, encouraging its followers to congregate around storytelling masters who offered lessons about the magical dimensions of the universe. But Tzvi took a different tack: Enormously charismatic, he was visited by extreme mood swings, and his ecstatic experiences were apparently quite performative. This histrionic aspect allowed him to command a large cadre of fanatical believers. His devotees were willing to follow him anywhere, literally – from Smyrna, where he angered the rabbinate, to Salonika, known as a Kabbalistic center, to Constantinople (today's Istanbul). Everywhere he went, Tzvi commanded attention. In Constantinople, he enlisted a Jewish preacher who avowed him as the messiah; and in Palestine and Cairo, where he went next, he was able to penetrate the court of the Turkish governor. His movement developed roots in major European cities, including Venice and London, as well as in North Africa.

Then, in 1666, after being arrested by the Ottoman authorities, Tzvi left his followers. He was given three options by the sultan's vizier in Adrianople: to be put to a special type of trial (an archer would shoot a series of arrows at him, and if they all missed, it would prove he was the messiah); to be impaled; or to choose apostasy. To almost everyone's surprise, Tzvi chose to convert. Renaming him Mehmed Efendi, the sultan made Tzvi his personal doorkeeper. A few of his followers were livid at Tzvi's decision, but others justified his conversion as a vindication of sin. A portion of his followers, who until then had been mostly devout, became antinomians: They believed that to achieve beatitude, they had to become reprobates, for only a divinity that perceived the universe through opposites could be fully empathetic to the chaotic rhythms of nature.

All of this might sound fanciful to us, as if Judas, through his betrayal of Jesus, was responsible for the advent of Christianity, or as if Satan, in the Book of Job, sets the right course for Job to pursue, not the Almighty. But for a young Jacob Frank, attempting to make sense of the violent world around him, Tzvi had decided to embrace a subversive understanding of evil. For Frank and his growing number of followers, Tzvi's thinking, particularly his conversion to Islam, was an invitation to turn morality upside down. Tzvi's decision to surrender his Judaism, the Frankists suggested, was a secret message: Right was now wrong, and vice versa. This attitude – that the accepted moral law in society is useless because faith alone is necessary for redemption – is intrinsic to cults, whose tenets are based on the subversion of ethical hierarchies. In their view, salvation is likely to come only after extreme deprivation.

Tzvi's and Frank's messianic excesses took place against the backdrop of their near opposite: what is known in Hebrew as Haskala, or the Jewish Enlightenment, in which disparate figures from Baruch Spinoza to Moses Mendelssohn repudiated biblical dogmatism and sought to modernize or even secularize Jewish thought, bringing it into accordance with the larger Enlightenment. A central part of this movement was political as well as theological: Even as Europe's Jews experienced the violent furies of anti-Semitism, Haskala thinkers contended that Jews, religious or otherwise, should be able to live as equals in an increasingly secular and enlightened Europe. This pursuit of Jewish emancipation was more a pipe dream than an achievable reality in a world in which Jews were promised civil or political rights whose fruits could not be savored immediately. The fracturing of Jewish culture in the Pale of Settlement – the region in Eastern Europe where the Russian czar had allowed them to live – resulted in a theological splintering that produced all sorts of alternatives, including extremist ones like Jacob Frank's. Some of these alternatives were peaceful and imagined a hopeful future, while others sabotaged that future through the rejection of morality.

The conflict between the Enlightenment and spiritualism, between sectarianism and assimilation, between visions of coexistence and of extreme isolation, runs through Tokarczuk's novel. In it, we meet rationalists who become epicureans, Talmudists who metamorphose into apostates, and law-abiding secular citizens who turn into fundamentalists. Many of these transformations are told through the story of Frank and the Frankists, who spearheaded a movement that sought to revive Shabtai Tzvi's messianic sectarianism in the 1780s.

Frank's energy and charisma were endless, and his life was full of incident: He was imprisoned, declared himself a baron, demanded specific behavior from his followers that baffled everyone involved, and accrued vast wealth for his sect. His followers were drawn to his ideas, including the conviction that salvation could be achieved only through the embrace of what Frank called "the religion of Edom," which had its own ethical system. He built a court around himself and established a militia to defend him against apostates eager to bring down his movement. Called the "Holy Master," Frank railed against his enemies with vicious fury, be they rabbis who cautioned against his insanities or political figures in Poland who saw him as seditious. He gave speeches and sermons about the end of the world, which were posthumously assembled into a volume called, in English, *The Collection of the Words of the Lord Jacob Frank*. Toward the end of his life, after he'd visited Czar Paul I in 1786, he passed the baton to his daughter Eve. She was herself a fanciful character, depleting the wealth her father had accrued until she was forced into bankruptcy – thereby marking the symbolic end to a movement that was a Hollywood-like epic of messianic reorganization, linking prophecy with politics and cultism with commerce.

One of the beauties in narrating this wild story of a lunatic persuading his followers that his fabrications are actually the word of God is the comfort with which Tokarczuk plays with the babel of tongues spoken by the Frankists. At one point, her characters are speaking Yiddish; at another, the Judeo-Spanish language of Ladino. They also communicate in Polish, Turkish, German, Russian, and a variety of code languages. The Jews of Europe were a multilingual lot, often forced to wander from one diaspora to the next, picking up and adapting languages as they made their new homes and cultures their own. Tokarczuk deals deftly with these dialectical adaptations, at times coloring the Polish syntax with Yiddishisms and terms from Turkish, Russian, German, and regional dialects, all of which Jennifer Croft accommodates beautifully in her English translation. There are also extended sections in the narrative in which the verbal cadence of a particular set of characters takes over.

The novel is rife as well with nonverbal code switching, charting the many transformations of different social types as they adapt to their new surroundings. The effect is much like looking at one of Hieronymus Bosch's apocalyptic paintings. While Frank and his entourage serve as protagonists, there are countless other characters, all with their own narrative arc and evolution. While the storyline progresses chronologically, the novel's 965 pages are numbered regressively, as if we were reading backward – perhaps because Tokarczuk wants to emulate how Hebrew is read, but also to remind us that the story we are encountering is, in some ways, being viewed both retrospectively and through a distorted mirror. Time itself seems to move backward too: In the prologue of the novel, as well as throughout its pages and in the epilogue, the character Yente, who is one of Frank's ancestors, lies on her deathbed but cannot die, no matter how hard she tries.

The last section of *The Books of Jacob*, however, is disappointing. Tokarczuk has looked, in intimate detail, at the way the Frankists infiltrated the upper echelons of Polish society. They changed names, becoming confidants of the king, or powerful priests, or barons, merchants, and other kinds of influencers. They became involved in trade that brought tea from China, coffee from Turkey, and chocolate from America. The last episodes take place in the German city of Offenbach, on the bank of the River Main, where Frank's dissolute, profligate children bring his legacy to an end. Here we don't get a *Bildung* of the important characters, their path to achieving a sobering realization of their own shortcomings, but rather a kind of Wikipedia list of what happened with each, the places they lived in, or the artifacts they touched. One of the protagonists, along with his younger brother, dies on the guillotine next to Danton; a Russian czar becomes fascinated with "the Jewish-Christian colony" the Frankists created; and Frank's skull, described as "the skull of a Jewish patriarch," is removed from his grave and makes its way to Berlin, where it serves as an example of "Jewish inferiority" and then, after the Second World War, vanishes without a trace. This last section feels like a concession to modern sensibilities, as if everything in our universe needs to be delivered in a perfectly packaged message – a clean ending to a story with a disorderly beginning.

Tokarczuk's encyclopedic command of her sources – Jewish, Christian, and Muslim, Ashkenazic and Sephardic, Polish and Turkish – is hard to overstate. (Her basic knowledge of Frank's story seems to come, in part, from the scholarship of Paweł Maciejko, author of *The Mixed Multitude: Jacob Frank and the Frankist Movement, 1755–1816*.) And her capacity to recreate the past is just splendid. Filled with black-and-white reproductions, mostly of engravings but also maps and other visual paraphernalia, *The Books of Jacob* was written for a Polish audience, and it is steadfast in its desire to confront readers with the glaring void in Poland's present: Close to 3.3 million Jews lived there in 1939; in 2016, fewer than 3,200 people described themselves as Jews in the national census. It goes without saying that the Nazis did not import anti-Semitism into Poland with their arrival, nor did it end with their departure. Already in 15th-century Krakow, Jews were expelled from some areas and forced to move into others. To this day, Polish stores sell little toys and Christmas decorations that depict a bearded Jew with a sack of money. When you ask about their meaning, the answer you get is that they are good-luck charms.

In this sense, *The Books of Jacob* is a stunningly courageous work of art: The novel becomes a mirror through which it demands that Poland see itself. But *The Books of Jacob* also goes beyond its political and moral ambitions: In its sheer scope, following the Frankists as they breach borders and transcend national histories, and as they and their Jewish contemporaries are persecuted by those who want to police those borders, the novel reminds readers of both the fictions and the powerful extremism found in the idea that worlds can be gated off from one another. In an era in which a new kind of messianism is spreading across the world – one that seeks to reassert a belligerent nationalism we hoped might be transcended – *The Books of Jacob* also reminds us that extreme ideologies are a fixture of every age. Spread a lie and build a movement around it, or vice versa.

– *The Nation*, October 4, 2022

Does Literature Teach Us How to Die? (with Priyanka Champaneri)

ILAN STAVANS: I'm haunted by the idea of a "good death," which is what gives your breathtaking debut novel, *The City of Good Death*, its traction. The story takes place in and around a hostel in the holy city of Kashi in India, also known as Varanasi, on the banks of the Ganges. People go to Kashi to "detach," to let purifying fire release the body from the cycle of reincarnation. I wonder if in the West we know the meaning of a "good death." In the last chapter of *Don Quixote*, the knight dies two deaths: he "gives up the ghost" – just as Hamlet does when he travels to "the undiscovered country" – but before that he relinquishes his persona of Don Quixote to become once again Alonso Quijano. Neither of these deaths are graphic, yet they are wrenching. And even after Quijano "confesses" to the town priest and delivers a living testament, the reader knows there is no afterlife for him. It seems to me that we are horrified by the end, not knowing how to approach it. Death is the conclusion; there is nothing after it. Through death, we as individuals vanish once and for all. What remains? Perhaps memory remains, but even that is fleeting. What is a "good death" for you?

PRIYANKA CHAMPANERI: This is such a complex question, and I will start with the caveat that the answer I give now is subject to change as I get older. But at this particular moment, a good death for me is inextricable from the life that leads up to that end. I cannot expect to have a good death if my life did not accomplish certain specific things. And these things are not material. The goal that I am always striving toward is to balance the scales as much as possible in the time that is given to me. This means fulfilling all my obligations to the people and things I am duty-bound to. But one thing you mention, about "vanishing once and for all" – I don't think of death in that way. Based on the belief system I've chosen for myself, I don't believe I will be erased entirely. I existed in another life before this one, and I'll return in another life after. Certainly, the person that I am now, in this life and in this reality, will vanish when I die. So, is it that loss of identity, then, that makes death horrifying?

IS: Ironically, Don Quixote, in spite of his two deaths, doesn't really die either. Readers have been keeping him alive since 1615, when Cervantes published Part II of the novel. To me, that is life after life. In any case, my friend Sherwin Nuland, a surgeon and author of *How We Die: Reflections on Life's Final Chapter* (1994), frequently pointed out the way death in the West makes us feel ashamed: we avoid talking about it openly, we hide from it. But death is an essential part of our natural cycle. If we don't know how to die, we can't know how to live.

PC: Absolutely. We are all rushing toward death – and I count all living things in this "we," not just humans – yet we ignore this one thing that is a universal certainty. It's akin to getting in a car, going on a journey, and expecting that you'll be driving forever without end. But, of course, there must be a final destination, and accepting that will likely affect the places you'll end up driving to, right? I really feel that, if you're able to accept that end early on, really understand that, yes, the days you have are finite – if you can get to that point, it can only increase your quality of life. Because if you truly understand that death is the inevitable end, then you'll be more apt to make decisions that take that brevity of time into account. You'll be more mindful about the relationships you hold onto and nurture in your life – and, conversely, you'll know which people you need to walk away from. You'll weigh your decisions differently; you'll pull joy out of places where you might not usually do so.

Accepting death is not a sign of surrender. It's knowledge, a tool we can use to recalibrate or refocus when we feel unmoored in the world. But thinking in this way is not easy, and it's not a switch you can just turn on within yourself. It takes constant practice. I can't say I'm very good at it myself. But I've also encountered enough death in my life – and just as impactful, enough *near* death – to goad me to get better at this way of thinking as the years go by. And because of those experiences, whenever I have a decision before me – particularly regarding relationships – I always have the same two questions drumming in the back of my mind. If I am no longer here tomorrow, what will I wish I had done? And if that other person is no longer here tomorrow, what will I regret not doing?

IS: To me, death is a variety of translation. In translation, we "redress" a text so that others might be able to embrace it. This means that the original dies – metaphorically, of course – in order for the translation to be born; or, if it doesn't die, it at least moves aside. There is a kind of transmigration, maybe even reincarnation, in translation: the self travels from one body to another. When I reimagine a poem by Anna Akhmatova,

Paul Celan, or César Vallejo in English, I'm fully conscious of the clash between life and death, between construction and destruction, that is at stake in the creative process. What prompted you to write *The City of Good Death*?

PC: The initial catalyst was reading a Reuters article that turned out to be about the death hostels of Banaras. I was immediately struck by how practical and utilitarian these places are: they essentially offer only the shelter of concrete walls and nothing more. And I could not stop thinking about how intentional these places are. This is not a place to have a holiday. This is not a spa or a meditation retreat. The entire purpose of a death hostel is right in the name: you're there to die. And not just die – you're there to exit the cycle of rebirth completely. And the part of me that had grown up intimately familiar with Hindu philosophy understood all of that and accepted it – but I had also grown up in the United States. And I could equally understand how incongruous this direct confrontation with death can be within a Western society, where the focus is so much more on everlasting life, on holding off death or ignoring it entirely.

I had spent my life up to that point on a steady diet of mostly Western literature written in English. And it was a diet that has given my life so much richness – but I inevitably had to contort myself as a reader to understand the work on a deeper thematic level, which usually always meant having to don a Judeo-Christian lens. I was just desperate to read something that used *my* default lens, one that I knew many other people carried. And this city, the death hostels, the people who journey from afar with the sole purpose of making that final exit – it all held so much potential for a story that I could write using that default lens, and hopefully share with people who either had the same lens or were open to accessing it.

IS: After living a good life, my 79-year-old mother, who lives in Mexico City, is in the process of precipitously losing her sense of self. She has trouble remembering who those that surround her are. The case, I'm told, is one for the books: in two months, from January to March 2021, she has gone through what Alzheimer's patients experience in five, 10, 20 years. On New Year's Day, I had a normal conversation with my mother over the phone. Eight weeks later, she no longer knows what day of the week it is, is afraid of the dark and sleeps poorly, and her sentences are monosyllabic. Day after day, she is ceding the space she occupies. Her thoughts are jumbled. She is disinterested even in reading. It is painful to watch it all because she herself doesn't understand what is happening and, therefore, is quite upset. Anxiety is her modus vivendi now. Just before she entered this state, my mother said to me that she wanted to die. I asked her if she wanted me to inquire about a merciful end. But she was afraid. Among other things, I wonder if she dreams – if in the theater of her mind she sees, when she is unconscious, scenes from her life. That would be a gift, but my impression is that the thief we call Alzheimer's has stolen even that pleasure.

PC: I deeply empathize with your mother, because her fear is real, and it's a humbling thing. It's like standing on a beach and seeing a colossal wave roaring toward you from a great distance. You can see and hear it; its imminent arrival is no surprise. But that knowledge doesn't mitigate the terror you feel as it gets closer, knowing you are about to be swept away into the unknown. What can you do to lessen that terror? How do you comfort yourself before being engulfed? Some might say that having a strong conviction in a belief system can help. But one question I struggle with is how a person can be so certain of how they might react in a theoretical situation, only to have instinct – the deepest, most primal emotions – ultimately override all of that when the actual moment comes. It's all well and good to think about death in a general abstract way, but how can any of us be sure of how we will react when we meet that moment?

I don't want to assume things about your mother's experience, but in general I hypothesize that the fear comes from the unknown, and the aloneness. We will all face that moment when we must stride off the stage and into something we cannot be sure of, and we all must make that journey alone. That fear can be so powerful that even someone who has lived their life confident in what happens to them after the wave comes isn't always immune to it. And it also comes back around to fear of losing your identity. If you have a great attachment to the person you are in this life, then the prospect of leaving that life at the end is going to be difficult. Platitudes are easy to spout from a distance, but really, Ilan, what do I know? What do any of us know? And what does that knowledge matter, if that ocean of fear that comes alongside death is equally inevitable? Is the fear then something to fight against? Something to run from? Something to accept and sink into? I have no answers. But I have an intense sympathy for your mother, for everyone awash in that fear.

IS: In Mexico, people commune with the dead all the time; and on Día de los Muertos, we celebrate with food, music, and candles at the cemetery. Malcolm Lowry, in *Under the Volcano*, recreates the phantasmagoric atmosphere of Day of the Dead. In Jewish culture, the dead are also with us constantly: in the prayer recited every morning, in the High Holidays, on Passover, etc. The Talmud states that sleep is one-sixtieth of death. I love the image: death is with us every night when we surrender consciousness. I feel this in my bones. The full quote in the Talmud is more emblematic. It states that fire is one-sixtieth of hell, honey is one-sixtieth of manna, the Shabbat is one-sixtieth of the World to Come, and dreams are one-sixtieth of prophecy.

PC: I love this idea of these intensely symbolic and sometimes distant abstractions being portioned out in a way we can attach relevance to in our daily lives, especially regarding sleep. It makes me think of John Updike: "Each day, we wake slightly altered, and the person we were yesterday is dead. So why, one could say, be afraid of death, when death comes all the time?" I'm fascinated with all the different ways people around the world have folded the dead into their lives. While this is not something actively practiced in my family or in my house, I've seen many Hindu households with framed photographs of deceased elders – parents, grandparents, and so forth – occupying a space and treated with the same veneration as the household shrine would be – anointed with rice and flowers during daily puja ceremonies and treated with special attention during holidays. And in the 15-day period preceding the holiday of Navratri, food is prepared and left out for any departed family members who may still be lingering, in the hope that it might bring them peace and send them onward to the next life.

On another end of the spectrum, I read a *New York Times* story about the death rituals of the Toraja people of the Indonesian island of Sulawesi. They've perfected very specific ways of preserving their dead so that a body can be exhumed and cleaned every few years or so. They take photographs alongside their dead loved ones and take great pride in caring for the body, all with the idea that the spirits of the dead remain behind to offer the family protection. But the decayed body itself is not feared or viewed as repugnant – it's venerated within this tradition. And so, the dead remain alive in the memories of those left behind, but more than that, death is normalized. If you can recognize that the journey has been taken by so many before you, perhaps you can mitigate some of that fear. I tried to express a similar culture in my novel. Bodies are openly carried through the same cramped lanes that people pass through, going about their daily lives in the city. Families caring for their loved ones in the death hostel are still mired in the worldly troubles that await them when they return home. Death, rebirth, and all the rest are discussed openly as a matter of course rather than a matter of taboo.

IS: In *The Year of Magical Thinking,* Joan Didion tackles that issue through paradox. She doesn't believe memory will allow her to reconnect to her husband, who has suddenly died; instead, she delves into the state of magical thought that is grief. In this state, we aren't fully ourselves; our mental capacity is transformed. I don't know whether to describe it as diminished. Instead of thinking rationally, we are in a nebula. Memory is fleeting: what we remember arrives to us as if through a veil. As you say, the dead are alive but in limbo – a Dantesque theater.

PC: I have two thoughts about this. One thing I wanted to explore in *The City of Good Death* was the idea that a story can become stronger, infused with life, the more and more it is told. And I think that idea translates to our dead as well – the more we recall them, the more we solidify our memories of them by writing things down or speaking the words aloud. It's no different from an incantation. You are conjuring them into being. And conversely, by not doing those things, by suppressing those memories, or hiding your grief, or overriding your emotions so you can get to a place of "normalcy" … well, it's a second death in a way. You lose the person in life, and you lose them in memory as well. We have real power within ourselves, through memory, through ritual, through storytelling, to bring what was dead back to life. But it's worth mentioning that this power can be used in the opposite direction as well. Because not all the dead are worthy of remembrance through the eyes of the living.

My second thought is that, as useful as memory can be in navigating grief, there is a temptation to become addicted to it, and thereby sentence yourself to a future of living in the past. Whether you are mired in memory, or in that nebula of grief, eventually you will have to pull yourself out, you must move on with living your life. But that presents another of those unanswerable quandaries – when do you accept that you have fallen too deeply? When are you allowed to drop the hand of memory and continue forward, alone, without feeling as if you are leaving that departed one behind?

IS: This is a suitable place to talk about oblivion. Often remembrance and forgetting are seen as antonyms – that is, as antagonists. But there is enormous benefit, not to mention health, in forgetting. We can't remember everything. And we shouldn't either. In order to think lucidly, we need to forget a vast amount of information. This allows us to think in abstractions, not in particularities. But forgetting is also a welcome respite. Most things have value in the present. That's where they live. To transpose them to another time coordinate is to needlessly extend their life. Forgetting, in other words, is a palliative. In any case, I hope for myself a "good death": instantaneous, without suffering – switching from being to non-being without my noticing it. It is a foolish, ambitious wish.

PC: You're right – as vessels, we are simply incapable of remembering everything, and that's to our advantage. We have to let go, we have to jettison the things weighing us down in order to move forward. But we equally cannot *force* ourselves to let go – it's important to process and reflect and resolve first, otherwise we're not forgetting so much as suppressing. During Hindu funeral rites, after the pyre has almost completely burned, the chief mourner must turn his back on the body and walk away. Under no circumstances should he look back, because doing so symbolizes that an attachment remains between him and the departed one. I was so captivated by this part of the rites when I was first reading about them, this very tangible action that has such symbolic weight, that it was inevitable that it would show up in the novel. When the death hostel manager Pramesh performs the rites for his cousin, he fails this test, and that failure incites his journey into these memories that he had assumed he had discarded and detached from years before. But really, he'd been carrying them all the while and actively shunting them aside because he couldn't bear to relive those moments.

As for your vision of a good death, it's ambitious perhaps, but entirely universal. In my belief system, the most exalted death is one where a person is entirely conscious and cognizant at the moment it is happening, and if they've attained a certain spiritual level, they can even choose the exact moment to exit their body. And that is considered an incredible gift, because if you can master your moment, you are also able to master your thoughts – and the things contained in your mind and in your heart when you die are critical to determining where you go in the next life. I've thought about my own death quite a bit. But I'm too superstitious to tell you plainly what I hope for, Ilan. Speaking it aloud or writing it down would be akin to jinxing it.

IS: I frequently ask myself – alone and in front of others: friends, students, the general public – if literature teaches us how to live. After reading your novel, I realized I needed to reformulate the question: might literature teach us how to die? A Shakespeare sonnet ("No longer mourn for me when I am dead / Than you shall hear the surly sullen bell"), poems like Christina Rossetti's "Gone far away into the silent land," Rubén Darío's "*Lo fatal*," and Neruda's "Love is so long, forgetting so short," stories such as Isaac Babel's "Story of My Dovecot," Ambrose Bierce's "An Occurrence at Owl Creek Bridge" and Borges's rewriting of it in "The Secret Miracle," as well as Isaac Bashevis Singer's "The Cabalist of East Broadway," mesmerizing novels like Faulkner's *As I Lay Dying*, Gabriel García Márquez's *One Hundred Years of Solitude*, Leo Tolstoy's *The Death of Ivan Ilyich*, and Toni Morrison's *Beloved* ...

PC: I wonder, Ilan, if those two questions actually approach the same gate. Because the process of living *is* the process of dying. Every day that we live is a step forward in the direction of death. Is it too simplistic to suggest, then, that the answer to both questions is also the same? But that aside, I do believe in the power of art to teach, because art, for me, is always about perspective. No matter the medium, art offers me a chance to don someone else's lens and view the world through their eyes. Whether it's about living, or dying, or just being – I always learn something. I always see something new. Art isn't ever going to answer all my questions. But it can offer some clarity. And equally important, it can offer comfort.

IS: You talked about "the ocean of fear." It is intrinsic to life and, thus, primal and irresoluble. Mapping it is perhaps the best we are able to do.

– Los Angeles Review of Books, July 27, 2021

The People's Tongue: Language as Character

A word is dead
When it is said,
Some say.
I say it just
Begins to live
That day.   – Emily Dickinson

1.

TO CREATE A NEW NATION, you need a language. Two, or three, or four might do, but abundance, in this case, can lead to disintegration. One shared language brings cohesion. It also fosters uniqueness. Of course, new languages don't emerge in a vacuum. They evolve slowly from other languages, acquiring their own character only after a long process of decantation. Other ingredients are also required in forging a nation: a territory, a flag, a government, a currency, a postal service, and so on. Language, however, is the crux. Without it, you have no conversation.

The Founding Fathers understood this very well. English had arrived on these American shores with the Pilgrims in 1607. It was the language they used to communicate with one another in their quest for religious freedom. But, inescapably, it was also the language of the persecuting environment from which they fled. The Pilgrims believed they were destined to build their own Canaan. Their separatist effort was a repudiation of British ways. Could their new nation achieve its independence one day with English as its main form of communication? Nowhere, it seems, not in the *Federalist Papers* (1788), nor in any other historical documents, did the Founding Fathers consider the idea of replacing English.

And with what? Several of the Founding Fathers were polyglots. They knew Greek, Latin, biblical Hebrew, French, and other tongues. They knew too that in any imperial age, the empire's language is carried over to the colonies. The Greek language spread as far as Egypt and Asia Minor thanks in large part to the military campaigns of Alexander the Great. Latin was the evangelical language of the Catholic Church, which used it to "civilize" new lands (and to exclude the natives from official discourse). Spanish and Portuguese became imperial tools across the Atlantic. Dutch, French, and to a lesser extent German were global maritime languages. The British Empire stretched as far as the sun could reach, including America. These new arrivals also considered the indigenous languages they encountered in the American Northeast unworthy of their attention. They were "barbaric," without the "proper" lineage. Thus, English for the Founding Fathers was the only instrument to achieve their goals. It would need to be subverted from within – to give birth to its own new vocabulary – in order to make room for the American revolutionary spirit. But sooner or later, the young republic would thrive in it.

The type of English used by the settlers in Plymouth colony, on Cape Cod Bay, and elsewhere in the region, is available to us in diaries, sermons, and correspondence they left behind. Spelling and punctuation were unstable, so much so that one might be forgiven for thinking it a foreign language, or maybe a part of Middle English, the type used by Geoffrey Chaucer in *The Canterbury Tales*. The variety used in England at the time was equally amorphous. That is to say, English, as we understand it today, had not gone through the rigorous "Americanization" (a local type of modernization) we have witnessed in the past couple of centuries, standardizing spelling, grammar, and syntax. It had also not witnessed the astonishing explosion of printed material that technology has fostered and which, inevitably, has pushed the language into a more systematic, coherent mode.

At any rate, the New England settlers, ambitious in their quest, were convinced that a new nation, which they could almost taste, required its citizens to go through a demanding educational training that focused on the use of the right language for the appropriate circumstance. This meant teaching children how to spell through manuals that mothers kept at home and teachers used at school, such as *The New England Primer*, a very popular booklet first circulated in 1687 that helped kids to memorize riddles, rhymes, and folktales. That way they would acquire the proper diction. Such an effort also served to inculcate the right moral values in the next generation, to encourage them to speak the language elegantly, and to instill in the citizenry the traction it needed to go forward.

How exactly English became American is a story that spans more than four centuries. It is an ongoing process, a language that is in constant flux, responding in audacious ways to the stimulation of its environment. Over the years, it has distinguished itself from British English in numerous ways. But it has also done something more: it has become the planet's lingua franca, to the point that in listening to it in its infinite vicissitudes, it is often impossible to know what is American and what is global in it. This anthology looks at that transformation from up close. Chronological in order, it features contributions by poets, musicians, Supreme Court justices, historians, linguists, activists, actors, scholars, journalists, scientists, writers, presidents, playwrights, teachers, translators, comedians, politicians, grammarians, lexicographers, and all kinds of other folks. In that sense, it is fully and unapologetically a people's history. It even includes "pedagogues" like José da Fonseca and Pedro Carolino, authors of the popular *English as She Is Spoke* (1884), a guide designed to teach people English anywhere in the world. Ironically, neither da Fonseca nor Carolino knew English. How about that? The example is actually quite common. When traveling abroad, one often comes across hilarious tourist signs, inadvertently poetic, that purport to give instructions in English. The lesson is clear: the language belongs to those who use it. And the popularization of the language undoubtedly says a great deal about the power of its speakers. The United States, with its mighty economy and ideology, contributes much to the globalization of English and the Englishization of the globe.

It shouldn't surprise anyone to find that a generous portion of this volume is contributed by immigrants. After all, the idea of America is a magnet that brings newcomers from all over to the nation's shores. That journey turns them from outsiders into insiders – a very American reinvention, which is frequently narrated in American English. Put another way, American English might be acquired through heredity, but in numerous cases it is the result of choice. It is obvious, then, that a series of heated debates will always brew at its core. In what way does change, that source of constancy in American English, keep it alive? What roles do purists, those who want it to be static, play? How about those on the other side of the divide, the so-called "assimilationists"? Is there one American English in the United States or are there many? How do age, class, region, ethnicity, and locale define the particulars of the language? Are they equally legitimate? If American English belongs to those who use it, is its well-being the responsibility of anyone in particular?

Wisely or otherwise, in drafting the Constitution at the Philadelphia Convention in 1787, the Founding Fathers did not include the word "official" in connection to any particular language. There is much debate as to why. They probably assumed that, by virtue of its usage, sooner or later American English would become a social congealer, the glue bringing people together. But not everyone thinks this is the case. And that openness to ambiguity has caused a schism. As successive immigrant groups arrive on these shores, the sense that the language is losing its gravitas has persuaded a number of individual states (Arizona, California, Georgia, Kentucky, Massachusetts, Oklahoma, Tennessee, and many more) to make English the official language. For them, not enforcing this law amounts to allowing the English language to wane.

It is an act of supreme irony that Emma Lazarus's "The New Colossus" (1883), arguably the most famous poem ever written in the country, welcomed immigrants – "the huddled masses yearning to breathe free" – in English, since, it is fair to assume, the vast majority of them, coming through Ellis Island, upon seeing the Statue of Liberty (if they actually ever did), where the sonnet is engraved in a plaque in the pedestal, didn't understand a single English word. Shouldn't the sonnet have greeted them in Gaelic, Italian, Yiddish, and all the other languages native to these newcomers? That would have been too much of a concession to their alienness. After all, they were starting anew. Learning the lay of the land is part of the shock of recognition.

Alexis de Tocqueville, the French aristocrat and passionate traveler who authored *Democracy in America* (1735), which has been described as "the bible of democracy," understood that the dream of freedom is what keeps Americans going. But that freedom is difficult to verbalize until one fully digests its tenets. Democracy is a cacophonous system. To function, Tocqueville argued, it depends on opposing views vigorously challenging each other in a civil deliberation, with a common language tying opposing views together:

> The genius of a democratic people is not only shown by the great number of words they bring into use, but also by the nature of the ideas these new words represent. Amongst such a people the majority lays down the law in language as well as in everything else; its prevailing spirit is as manifest in that as in other respects. But the majority is more engaged in business than in study – in political and commercial interests than in philosophical speculation or literary pursuits. Most of the words coined or adopted for its use will therefore bear the mark of these habits; they will mainly serve

to express the wants of business, the passions of party, or the details of the public administration. In these departments the language will constantly spread, whilst on the other hand it will gradually lose ground in metaphysics and theology.

2.

A democracy, no matter how representative it is, depends on a set of visionary individuals to govern it. That group, Thomas Jefferson argued, must be fluent in the language of its constituents in order to lead them through easy and hard times. Jefferson, who lived in Paris for five years, was obsessed with grammar. He wrote treatises on (and in) English in comparison with Greek, Latin, and French. And he wrote to friends about the well-being of the language, often stating that he was no friend "to what is called *Purism*, but a zealous one to the *Neology* which has introduced these two words without the authority of any dictionary." He believed purists oppose what is most beautiful in a language: its innovative drive. For Jefferson, that drive was what gave English its nerve, its beauty, and its copiousness. Still, authority in a language is often represented by a legislative institution empowered to safekeep its health. Fascinatingly, to this day there is still no such governing body in English, not in the United States or anywhere else where English is used. Other languages have academies, like the Académie française for French, the Real Academia Española for Spanish, and the Accademia della Crusca for Italian. Why don't we? Maybe because English loves to escape its confines, to enter alien territories, to lend and borrow words without restraint. Maybe because, while an elite is in command of government, the fluidity of the language has no keepers.

John Adams, our second president (he was in office until 1801, when Jefferson, his longtime friend with whom he served in the Continental Congress, succeeded him), was more conservative. He worried about the language's proper use as well: its consistency, its dignity. "As eloquence is cultivated with more care in free republics than in other governments," he wrote in "Proposal for an American Language Academy" while on a diplomatic mission to Europe during the Revolutionary War, "it has been found by constant experience that such republics have produced the greatest purity, copiousness, and perfection of language." Perfection was what Adams sought: the capacity of a tongue to be always in control. But those not in power, whose indigenous languages were brushed aside – actually, annihilated – in order for English to reign supreme, understood the power dynamic: behind every code of communication seeking to coalesce a nation there are others subjugated in the process.

Such a stance as Adams's has frequently been a target of ire. A century later, Simon Pokagon, a member of the Pokagon Band of Potawatomi Indians and the author of *The Red Man's Rebuke* (1893), rejected this premise, suggesting that when the colonizers rejoice in admiration "over the beauty and grandeur of this young republic and you say, 'behold the wonders wrought by our children in this foreign land,'" they ought not to forget that their success has come through "the sacrifice of our homes and a once happy race," as well as of indigenous languages. Pokagon was among the first indigenous writers in America to fully articulate an argument against the sovereignty of American English. He inaugurated a tradition that remains forceful today via figures like Louise Erdrich and Natalie Diaz. It rightfully condemns the settlers and their successors for ignoring the conditions they encountered. There were approximately three hundred native tongues, from Iroquois to Cherokee, used among the population. The ignominious internal migration its speakers were subjected to – the "Trail of Tears" – pushed them into silence.

Adams remains one of the most distinct voices identified with the defense of American English. He believed in linguistic authority, which meant setting up the proper mechanisms so that the language would remain healthy. Of course, one person's health is another person's malaise. Another way, aside from an academy, for that authority to be implemented is through efficient, up-to-date dictionaries continuously safekeeping – "cleaning up," purists would put it – what is exquisite from what is unpleasant. The first to propose a dictionary genuinely reflecting "the parlance of the people" was Noah Webster, occasionally described as the "forgotten" Founding Father. Webster's idol was Samuel Johnson, the Renaissance man who in 1755 published what is still, in my opinion, the best single-author lexicon of the English language. Webster endeavored to produce a new one applicable to the American reality. The result was *An American Dictionary of the English Language* (1828), in which he incorporated all sorts of terms – "skunk" and "squash," for instance – Americans used. He also reformed spelling, switching "centre" for "center," and "colour" for "color." As stated in his preface, Webster's intention was to look at language as the expression of ideas, "and if the people of one country cannot preserve an identity of ideas, they cannot retain an identity of language." Interestingly, and controversially for future generations, he defined the word "American" (or, in his spelling "AMER'ICAN") as "a native of America; originally applied to the aboriginals, or copper-colored races, found here by the Europeans; but now applied to the descendants of

Europeans born in America." The tension of who gets to be "American" present in Webster's original definition would grow ever more complex in the ensuing decades. Webster's adventure in lexicography remains extraordinarily vibrant. When Webster, a "difficult" person who was probably on the Asperger's spectrum, died in 1843 at the age of eighty-five, his dictionary was acquired by a pair of entrepreneurial siblings in Springfield, Massachusetts: George and Charles Merriam. In time, the Merriams made it stunningly successful, both commercially and in terms of critical reception. The Merriam-Webster dictionary, its sales still in the millions of copies every year, has something its British counterpart, the *Oxford English Dictionary*, which depends on a slow-moving cabal of dons at what Matthew Arnold called "the city of dreaming spires," doesn't: it is a business, that is, it looks to make a profit – a very American endeavor.

   I have included in this anthology a number of entries that evidence the relevance that dictionaries play in America and also showcase the controversies around them. One of them is a piece in the *New Yorker*, published in 1961, by Dwight McDonald. It is a review of *Webster's Third*, as the third major update of the Merriam-Webster enterprise is known. Edited by Dr. Philip Gove and released about three decades after the last major update (call it *Webster's Second*), it is also the most liberal, featuring words like "ain't" that until then had been excluded from the lexicon. McDonald, an acerbic critic, takes stock of the way dictionaries, in their descriptiveness, push American English in utterly new directions. "Dr. Gove conceives of his dictionary as a recording instrument rather than as an authority," McDonald writes. "In fact, the whole idea of authority or correctness is repulsive to him as a lexical scientist. The question is, however, whether a purely scientific approach to dictionary-making may not result in greater evils than those it seeks to cure." There is also an exuberant essay by David Foster Wallace, author of *Infinite Jest* (1996), this one published in *Harper's* magazine, in which he discusses a number of other dictionaries, including Bryan A. Garner's *A Dictionary of Modern American Usage* (1998). And there's Ambrose Bierce's *The Devil's Dictionary*, published as the First World War was approaching. Designed as a satire, it might be read as a countervoice to Noah Webster's nation-building lexicography in its portrayal of lexicographers as scholars with an obtuse, politically driven agenda, and their dictionaries as indoctrination tools. I have divided the content of the anthology into three chronological parts: Part I, "Landing Mode," begins with early colonial writings that evidence unfettered English syntax of the times and continues roughly through the end of the First World War. Part II, "Fly Me to the Moon," goes from 1919 to the early

1980s and encompasses the precise moment (July 20, 1969, at 20:17 UTC) in which English becomes the language of the moon, when American astronaut Neil Armstrong, upon landing on it, describes its surface as "fine and powdery." And Part III, "The Ruckus of Polyphony," brings us to the present, a time of passionate philological belligerence ("I am my language," says poet and activist Gloria Anzaldua), in which every aspect of English has been put up for debate, including pronouns. As a recognizable quantity, American English is over three centuries old. Like any other language, it might be said to have gone through periods of development that resemble those of any living organism: a birth that came about when a conjunction of circumstances took place, an infancy and childhood, an adolescence, and so on. It would be foolish to ascribe concrete years to each of these periods. What is unquestionable is that, after its gestation, American English has come to recognize its own qualities as independent from its British counterpart. George Bernard Shaw once purportedly said that England and the United States are separated by a common language. That separation is what American English has achieved, not without pain.

I myself am a lover of linguistic pollution. A neophyte (I came to the United States from Mexico – and thus to English – in 1985), I'm regularly in awe of the ingenuity of American English speakers. My first exposure to its multifarious character was in the New York City subway, attuning my then innocent ear to the intermingling tonalities of a typhoon of tongues. Instinctively I felt paralyzed by the abundance. But soon paralysis gave way to awe. The copiousness of sounds hypnotized me. What was the meaning behind it? It took me a while to reach a conclusion, yet once I did there was no turning back: American English doesn't really need protection; it has reached a stage in which it cannibalizes everything in its reach, while also keeping its flexible structure intact. Originally a Germanic language spoken by the Angles, Saxons, Jutes, and Frisians, and recalibrating itself through encounters with the Normans, the Vikings, the Bretons, and the French, it has magisterially expanded its horizons, especially since the 1800s, by going from the British Isles to just about everywhere.

As a student of history, my own sense is that it was during the American Civil War, with the fierce debate it fostered around slavery, that the nation's English came into its own. What and how Americans should speak had already been a constant topic. One finds arguments in Walt Whitman's views on American slang, in Lydia Huntley Sigourney's reflections on "Indian Names," and in Thomas Hopkins Gallaudet's case for an American variety of sign language for those who during his time were called "the deaf and dumb." But it was slavery that brought the debate on the principles of the humanity of America into focus, in that a person becomes human through speaking the language of the community. The best paragraphs from the period were uttered by Abraham Lincoln in 1863 in his "Gettysburg Address" at the Soldiers' National Cemetery in Gettysburg, Pennsylvania, on a field where, at a turning point in the war, between 46,000 and 51,000 soldiers from both the Union and the Confederate armies died. I include it here not because it deals with language – it doesn't – but because it summons up the raw emotions of his time. These 272 words are the consummate example of what the nation's language is capable of: eloquence, concision, and beauty. If language is by definition chaotic, President Lincoln created the most admirable semblance of order.

Next to it is *Adventures of Huckleberry Finn*, released in 1883, arguably the greatest American novel ever written. Ernest Hemingway believed the nation's literature begins, and might end, with it. Plotwise as well as symbolically, it is a veritable fountainhead of linguistic elasticity. Told from the viewpoint of a thirteen-year-old boy and a runaway slave who, having befriended one another, navigate the Mississippi River, it is infused with a variety of dialects. In the front matter, Twain says:

> In this book a number of dialects are used, to wit: the Missouri Negro dialect; the extremist form of the backwoods Southwestern dialect; the ordinary "Pike County" dialect; and four modified varieties of this last. The shadings have not been done in a haphazard fashion, or by guesswork; but painstakingly, and with the trustworthy guidance and support of personal familiarity with these several forms of speech. I make this explanation for the reason that without it many readers would suppose that all these characters were trying to talk alike and not succeeding.

The fact that in American literature *Huckleberry Finn* has become the yardstick is, in part, due to Twain's ambitious effort not only to describe different segments of pre-Civil War society but to give them voices.

3.

It is often said that the twentieth century was "the American century." But centuries aren't the most useful way to describe an epoch. When does the American century begin? Most likely with the Spanish-American War, in 1898, when Spain lost control of Cuba, Puerto Rico, and the Philippines, and the United States became the new kid on the block. The industrial revolution had pushed the nation to new heights, allowing cities across the map to prosper, building roads, telegraphs, railways, and other means of communication. And, along with it, shaping the machinery that would perfect "the American Dream" as a democratic ideal. American English was there to disseminate it all, an ever-expansive language ready to seize its place. Before then, during the period we call Reconstruction, the efforts and refusals to redress the inequities of slavery pushed Blacks in centrifugal directions. Along with that movement came the consolidation of an ethnic parlance that had roots in Negro spirituals and was interconnected with different urban scenes. There were successive waves of immigrant groups from a variety of European places entrenched in poverty, including Ireland, Italy, and Russia. It must have felt as if the tapestry of America was being rewoven. All types of mixed tongues were emerging. Henry James, in his travel book *The American Scene* (1907), described the New York demographic landscape with unavoidable puzzlement. He was witnessing significant segments of the population living in indigence – what the German social photographer Jacob Riis referred to when he talked about "how the other half lives." America, it seemed, was in the midst of an outright demographic remapping.

James was interested in the way the demographic and cultural changes before him would ultimately redefine America as a nation. "Once it has set your observation," he writes,

> to say nothing of your imagination, working, it becomes for you, as you go and come, the wonderment to which everything ministers and that is quickened well-nigh to madness, in some places and on some occasions, by every face and every accent that meet your eyes and ears. The sense of the elements in the cauldron – the cauldron of the "American" character – becomes thus about as vivid a thing as you can at all quietly manage, and the question settles into a form which makes the intelligible answer further and further recede.

James was intrigued by the juxtaposition of what he called "the *small* America," that is, the individual one, the one shaped by people in their own private realms, and the big one, the one summing up all these realms, making a huge mosaic of individualities. "Goodness be thanked for the bigness," he concluded in "a state of flat fatigue," not knowing exactly how that bigness could be articulated.

Myriad hybrid languages were on display before him, languages that reshaped the American soundscape. Claude McKay, in his poetry, made Jamaican Creole come alive in American English. Others like Paul Laurence Dunbar, Zora Neale Hurston, and James Baldwin would add a surfeit of ebullient voices from the Black diaspora. Mary Antin's memoir

The Promised Land (1912) recounts her odyssey as a Russian girl in Boston learning the English language, to the point of writing an ode to George Washington that she tries to publish in one of the city dailies. Anti-Italian acrimony and mockery of Italian speech were evident in the press in the early 1920s surrounding the scapegoating of anarcho-syndicalists Nicola Sacco and Bartolomeo Vanzetti, who were convicted of murder and sentenced to death. Henry Roth, an immigrant from the Austro-Hungarian Empire, in his novel *Call It Sleep* (1934) depicts the adventures of a six-year-old Jewish boy in New York's Lower East Side. Portions of the narrative are in a Yiddishized English. And the lively pidgin spoken by Japanese American soldiers in a division from Hawaii in the Second World War is featured in Martin Minoru Iida's lyrics to the war song "Go for Broke" (1944). And there are slam poetry, rap, hip-hop, R&B, *corridos*, salsa, and ranchera. And the experimentation of poets such as Emily Dickinson, Bret Harte, E.E. Cummings, John Ashbery, Judith Ortiz Cofer, Julia Alvarez, and Yusef Komunyakaa. This anthology is as much about *what* is said in America as it is about *how* it is said.

One of the most accomplished – and feisty – chroniclers of the transformation of American English in the first part of the American century was H.L. Mencken, the cantankerous Baltimore journalist and editor, who spent a generous portion of his long career examining slangs, accents, and localisms in his multivolume *The American Language: An Inquiry into the Development of English in the United States* (1919). Reprinted numerous times, it is an invaluable document, especially since it wasn't done by a scholar. Ever cantankerous, Mencken chronicles the vicissitudes of the language of Irish, Italian, German, Polish, and Slavic speakers, among many others. He thoroughly disliked the idea of a prescriptive grammar. In his view, parlance arises in the kitchen, at the bar, on the street, wherever people express themselves freely. Given American values – individualism being the most exemplary – but also the enormous expanse of land encompassed by the nation, Mencken was convinced that American English was substantially more complex than British English. He believed in global interaction as a lifestream. "A living language," he posited, "is like a man suffering incessantly from small hemorrhages, and what it needs above all else is constant transactions of new blood from other tongues. The day the gates go up, that day it begins to die." In response to John Adams's attitude of protecting English from the "barbarians," Mencken opined that "the notion that anything is gained by fixing a language in a groove is cherished only by pedants."

As it unfolded, the American century seemed boundless. There was Albert Einstein explaining the theory of relativity in American English to colleagues and students at Princeton in the thirties. There was Harry Truman announcing the surrender of Germany in 1945, which ended the Second World War. There was *Abbott and Costello* as well as *I Love Lucy*, with their cathartic verbosity, and, after them, Mel Brooks, Richard Pryor, Eddie Murphy, Robin Williams, Jerry Seinfeld, George Lopez, Sarah Silverman, Aziz Ansari, and a host of others who used comedy to push against the bounds of "acceptable" language. In 1972, George Carlin recorded a bit for his stand-up album *Class Clown* called "The Seven Words You Can Never Say on Television," which was inspired by a comedy routine by Lenny Bruce. The words in Carlin's litany – "ass," "balls," "cocksucker," "cunt," "fuck," "motherfucker," "piss," "shit," and "tits" – were taboo at the time. Half a century later, these terms are now ubiquitous on streaming services like HBO, Netflix, and Hulu. On a similar front, in 1975 Richard Pryor hosted *Saturday Night Live* in its first season and performed a sketch with Chevy Chase called "Word Association" that included a slew of racial slurs rarely uttered on network television. The sketch, written by Pryor's co-writer Paul Mooney and included in this anthology, became infamous and put *SNL* on the map. There was Theodor Seuss Geisel, a.k.a. Dr. Seuss, with his children's books *The Cat in the Hat* (1957), *How the Grinch Stole Christmas!* (1957), *Green Eggs and Ham* (1960), and *The Lorax* (1971), all delivered in his anarchically whimsical rhymes in American English. And there was Spock in *Star Trek*, originally played by Leonard Nimoy, a mixed human-Vulcan and a Federation ambassador on the USS *Enterprise*, and, along with him, a cadre of American science fiction writers, like Isaac Asimov, Philip K. Dick, Russell Hoban, and Ursula K. Le Guin, pushing the language "where no man has gone before." And of course Yoda, the Master Jedi, who uttered sentences like "Hard to see, the dark side is" and "To his family, send him." In *Star Wars*, the default trade language of that "galaxy far, far away," is English, which a whole gamut of aliens, droids, and earthlings speak with non-native accents. Radio, television, and Hollywood movies have been the great conduits – and the great equalizers – of the nation's language. Imagine, for a second, if your TV screen just emitted words in other languages. Would America still be America?

In fact, your TV does broadcast in lots of languages, courtesy of Telemundo and other language channels. This wealth emanates from the pluralistic nature of American society and the fact that immigrants never quite surrender their status. The nation's calendar has days for Juneteenth, St. Patrick's Day, Holocaust Day, and so on. American cities turn ethnic enclaves into museums, such as New York's Chinatown, the Lower East Side, and Little Italy. Still, the pull is to celebrate them ecumenically and in English as fossilized relics of an admirable journey toward assimilation.

Translation is at the core of the American experiment. Even if it has privileged one tongue above all others, the nation has always relied on the transactions among languages. To translate is to create bridges, to find common ground, to push beyond one's own parochialism. It is also, inevitably, about making the United States global. Translators are linguistic refreshers: they alert us to etymologies, expand our vocabularies, and remind us that we aren't alone in trying to decipher the universe. That component of translators' work – as agents of change, as chroniclers of day-to-day life, and as facilitators of progress – is in America's collective DNA. It is therefore ironic that a country made of so heterogeneous a people is so allergic to foreign languages. (Miriam Amanda "Ma" Ferguson, governor of Texas in the twenties and thirties, is reported as saying, "If the King's English was good enough for Jesus Christ, it's good enough for the children of Texas!") Truth is, our existence depends on the constant climbing, up and down, of the Tower of Babel.

The engine of that assimilation has been the classroom. Since the dawn of the republic, from the Founding Fathers to Tocqueville, the emphasis has been on the importance of education. Spelling, grammar, and syntax come to life when a teacher explains their patterns to an audience of students. For that reason, whatever doesn't happen in the classroom becomes an absence in the larger canvas that is society. The relocation of Indigenous children away from their parents in order to be "Americanized" turned schools into factories of misery. The same goes for segregation, which continues to this day despite Supreme Court Justice Earl Warren's landmark 1954 opinion in *Brown v. Board of Education*. In 1982, Canadian-born, Japanese-descended California Senator Samuel Ichiye Hayakawa hoped to foster integration through a language amendment that would make English the country's official language. "The wonderful thing about the United States is that kind of cultural intermixing, that cultural melding, is possible," Senator Hayakawa stated, addressing his comments to the then president Ronald Reagan.

> When you go to other parts of the world, you find to your amazement that China is full of Chinese; that Russia is full of Russians and practically nobody else. Italy is full of Italians and Korea is full of Koreans, and so on around the world. But we are full of people from all parts of the world having learned one language and ultimately having learned to get along with each other to create institutions of a multiracial, multicultural

democratic society. Mr. President, that is what I want to preserve when I say I want an amendment that says the English language shall be the official language of the United States.

Not that Hayakawa's bill, which died in action in the House, would have solved the country's racial, economic, or linguistic fractures. Among the most acerbic debates in the history of America have been those around bilingual education. Although bilingual education as a movement began in 1961, in Florida, versions of it have been around since the birth of the republic. With the consolidation of public school as mandated by law, the question became about what is taught in the classroom and how effectively. At what point in the odyssey of immigration does a person fully "assimilate"? One might say that acculturation is a metamorphosis: defined by benchmarks, simultaneously shaped as a journey of arrival in physical terms and as a haphazard interior exploration. At one point, perhaps without noticing it, immigrants achieve their objective: they are now part of "the people."

Richard Rodriguez – whose autobiography, *Hunger of Memory* (1982), sharply divided the Mexican American community – appreciated that while he would have liked to be fluent in Spanish, the language of his parents, his teachers were "unsentimental about their responsibility." Rodriguez applauds them for understanding

> that I needed to speak public English. So their voices would search me out, asking me questions. Each time I heard them I'd look up in surprise to see a nun's face frowning at me. I'd mumble, not really meaning to answer. The nun would persist. "Richard, stand up. Don't look at the floor. Speak up. Speak to the entire class, not just to me!" But I couldn't believe English could be my language to use. (In part, I did not want to believe it.) I continued to mumble. I resisted the teacher's demands. (Did I somehow suspect that once I learned this public language my family life would be changed?) Silent, waiting for the bell to sound, I remained dazed, diffident, afraid.

Along came movements like "English Only," "English First," "English Plus," and other attempts at recentering English in the culture wars. The history of linguistic xenophobia in America is intense. Propelled by the anti-German sentiment that was a fixture of the First World War, in 1918 Iowa governor William L. Harding forbade people in his state to use any other language – even on the telephone. And Teddy Roosevelt, on his deathbed in 1919, announced that there was only one language for Americans and that was the English language.

While perhaps not as heated as in the past, these efforts continue to divide America. The division intensified during the Trump years. As the nation has become more ethnically diverse, some, especially in rural areas, believe it has betrayed the principles espoused by the Founding Fathers. Furthermore, those principles, in their view, ought to be presented in a straight, unpolluted American English, one not tainted by "foreignness." There are in this volume an assortment of entries reflecting that dispute. At times they come in the form of newspaper opinion pieces, such as the *New York Times* columns of linguist John McWhorter, or children's book writer E.B. White's introduction to William Strunk's omnipresent *The Elements of Style* (1979), which, along with other similar handbooks – for instance, the *Chicago Manual of Style* (1906) or the *Associated Press Stylebook* (1953) – show what is tolerable and what is forbidden in terms of language usage. In private, most Americans, known for their allergy toward authority, might perceive these exercises as ridiculous. But judging by their bestsellerdom, there is little doubt they play a central role in the nation's approach to language: be as rebellious and improvisational as you wish when you speak, but writing needs rules, which you better learn if you want to be American.

4.

Has the American century come to an end? Some point to the terrorist attacks on September 11, 2001, as the concluding moment. Through transnational investment, tourism, and a technological boom that, as if by hocus-pocus, erased borders, the nation had engaged in ever-expanding levels of globalization, so much so that it was difficult to say where America began and where it might end. That drive pushed American English to new frontiers. While not the most popular language spoken in the world (Mandarin Chinese plays that role), it is unquestionably the most important for business, education, scientific research, and entertainment. But it might also be said that it is less grounded – less local – than it used to be: a global vernacular, it is everyone's favorite "second" language.

The pressure of such a status is enormous. Aside from the fact that we are moving – rather quickly – into a culture in which visual storytelling will take over our consciousness and the written word will play a smaller role than in the past, there is the reality that for every native speaker of American English in the world, there are approximately a dozen more non-native American English speakers. Keeping the syntactic order in place is challenging. At the same time, social media – Facebook, Twitter, Instagram, Snapchat – pushes American English into a paroxysmal state, one in which users must be "tuned in" 24/7 lest they be seen as antisocial. Brand names like Apple, Cheerios, Coca-Cola, Google, Nike, Q-Tips, and Xerox are an integral part of the language. So are acronyms such as AI, ATM, ICU, and GPS. And texting terms like JK (just kidding), LOL (laughing out loud), IMHO (in my humble opinion), TTYL (talk to you later), NC (Netflix and chill), BFF (best friends forever), and FWB (friend with benefits). With the attention-span needle rapidly moving toward zero, punctuation is erratic, spelling is unstable, and, more dangerous, ideas are truncated to a bit over a hundred characters. What does all this mean? Has the language gone to the dogs, as John Adams suggested? Obviously, it is in a period of intense pressure. Donald Trump, a politician known for his willingness to exacerbate ideological conflict, was a relentless communicator. The *New York Times* published a complete list of his Twitter insults, from the moment he announced his candidacy for president in 2015 until 2021, that is, when Twitter suspended his account. Aside from being infuriating, the English language, while suffocating in its compression, is extraordinarily versatile.

Fortunately, dictionaries retain the banner of authority. How fast should they incorporate new words? And should they feature lewd, demeaning language? The question of profanity is important in its symbolism. A language is about not only propriety but versatility. An example: for a long time, the word "fuck" was deemed unacceptable in Merriam-Webster, and, thus, left out until 1974. Yet it is one of the most adaptable, resourceful words in the language, used as a noun, a verb, an adjective, an adverb, as well as a sheer expression of dismay, excitement, or doubt. Depending on the intonation: fuck? = doubt; fuck! = excitement; fuck?! = dismay + doubt + excitement and a slew of other mixed emotions unconveyable more effectively through other, "cleaner," words. Exiling it from the dictionary was a statement of elitism that finally caved in. But the debate around it brings about all sorts of ramifications: should destructive language be in print? Does that give it legitimacy? As Jesse Sheidlower, once on staff at the *Oxford English Dictionary* and the author of *The F-Word* (1995), writes, "terms that are insulting toward a particular group of people should be handled with sensitivity. But that doesn't mean obscuring the issue ... Discussing a word is not the same as wantonly using a word, just as reporting on racism does not make you a racist." Some publications, like the *New Yorker*, have retrenched in their no-no policy, but others haven't. If expressions can be reduced in texting to a combination of capital letters, is America still so prudish as to not be able to digest "fuck" in the pages of the *New York Times*?

America, willy-nilly, has grown up to discover its cosmopolitanism as a source of pain. Susan Sontag, in her lecture "The World as India" (2002), posited, "We live in a world that is, in several important respects, both mired in the most banal nationalisms and radically postnational ... But there is one intractable feature of our lives that roots us in the old boundaries that advanced capitalism, advanced science and technology, and advanced imperial dominance ... That is the fact that we speak so many different languages. Hence, the necessity of an international language. And what more plausible candidate than English?" Yet Americans are conflicted about that internationalism, fearing they might lose control of its most precious property.

We are witnesses today to ongoing changes to grammar. Efforts at simplifying the language are constantly invoked. Foreign terms, starting with food, are *de rigueur*. The remarkable achievements of the LGBTQ movement have manifested themselves in gender pronouns being contested, such as in the case of Merriam-Webster's declaration of "they" as the word of the year in 2021. The term "Latinx" also seeks to alleviate gender divisions that come about from the Latin roots of Romance languages. And automatic translation machines, such as Google, deconstruct codes in ways that make English seem frenzied. Were Thomas Jefferson, John Adams, and Noah Webster to walk among us again, they would most likely be at a loss as to how Americans go around communicating with one another. They might not feel this is the nation and the language they helped create. Still, if there is a lesson to be learned from history, it is that American English thrives through contradictions. The twenty-first century seems to be pushing the nation's polarization and fragmentation to extremes. Will it be able to re-coalesce into a single unifying whole?

Or will it break apart? Will a second American Civil War soon unfold? It sometimes feels as if the sole element that keeps Americans with divergent viewpoints together is their language. We speak and understand the same words. It's what allows democratic deliberation to take place, the glue holding the nation together. From the start, this nation's language has existed in a state of constant innovation. Innovation means originality, which often requires a defiant stance. Frank Zappa once said that "all the good music has already been written by people with wigs and stuff," which means it is time to turn ugly music into new good music. Change happens astonishingly fast. "The zipper displaces the button," Ray Bradbury wrote in *Fahrenheit 451* (1953), "and a man lacks just that much time to think while dressing at dawn, a philosophical hour, and thus a melancholy hour." In language the good isn't the opposite of the bad but simply its companion. American English is of the people, by the people, and for the people. It answers only to them. This anthology shows the extent to which the nation's tongue is restless.

– Introduction, *The People's Tongue: Americans and the English Language* (2023)

Claudio Lomnitz's Vertigo

Most writers are content to write a book once; others, after publishing a first version, go back and rewrite it over and over again. Sometimes they do so out of aesthetic dissatisfaction. But there is another type of writer (let's call them "translinguals") who returns to a book time and again in order to rewrite it in a different language. In a way, translingual writers might be seen as their own translators, although the term doesn't quite fit because these writers don't simply render their original work into another language; they rewrite it in a peculiar way, creating another original. Like Dr. Jekyll and Mr. Hyde, they inhabit – or, better, are inhabited by – different iterations of who they are; each version of their book represents a different self.

Claudio Lomnitz, who teaches history and anthropology at Columbia and is interested in the family in Latin America as an economic and political unit as well as a fantasy, is such a writer. Born in Chile, he descends from a rich tapestry of Jewish communists, intellectuals, scientists, educators, and political activists (many of them translingual, like Lomnitz himself), who are the subject of his memoir, *Nuestra América*.

Published in Mexico in 2018, the Spanish edition was 332 pages and juxtaposed disquisitions on Jewish life in the Pale of Settlement, anti-Semitism in Europe, and the plight of Ashkenazi Jews in Latin America throughout the 20th century with the history of Latin America itself – in particular, the histories of Chile, Peru, Colombia, and Mexico. Since the topic of Jewish culture remains the domain of a small audience in Spanish, the Spanish edition expanded those horizons, often at the expense of Latin American themes. Most readers would have recognized, for example, how *Nuestra América*'s title was an homage to José Martí's famous 1891 essay, in which the Cuban thinker and revolutionary martyr sought to unite the Americas under a single, anti-colonialist banner.

They likely could also identify many of the Latin American thinkers and radicals Lomnitz's ancestors rubbed elbows with, such as the influential Indigenous philosopher José Carlos Mariátegui, the author of *Seven Interpretative Essays on Peruvian Reality* and a philo-Semite who established Peru's Socialist Party and founded the journal *Amauta* in the 1920s to discuss socialism and culture.

Though much of the Jewish content remains in the English version of *Nuestra América*, published by Other Press, the book in many ways dances to a different beat. At 464 pages, it caters to American readers, offering more intricate histories of Latin American politics and culture as well as a far more intimate portrait of Lomnitz's family. The author's English-language style also stands in stark contrast to his Spanish one: It has a melodious rhythm, and the sentences are shorter and more focused. This might be because of the US tradition of in-house editing, but it appears that the rewriting also honed and sharpened Lomnitz's prose.

Other intriguing differences emerge between the two versions, almost like two divergent Rembrandt self-portraits. The cover of the Spanish edition features a stunning black-and-white photo of Lomnitz's maternal grandfather, Misha Adler, who witnessed firsthand the upheaval of East European Jews, with an Indigenous person who likely witnessed firsthand the upheaval of his own communities at the same time. The message is clear: The book's theme, as the author himself puts it, is "the relationship between the exaltation of 'the Indian' and the destruction of Europe." The cover of the English version is more intimate: It shows a home photo of Lomnitz with his older brother Jorge, who died in 1993. The US edition, while filling in the potential gaps in the reader's knowledge of Latin America, also offers a more domestic narrative. That, after all, is what Americans like in memoirs: a fast track to the domestic realm.

Another way to compare the two versions is through their subtitles. The Spanish one is *Utopía y Persistencia en Una Familia Judía* and emphasizes how Lomnitz's family, like many other Jewish families in the post-Haskalah stage (the period immediately after the Jewish Enlightenment), embraced radical politics and cosmopolitanism. The English subtitle, *My Family in the Vertigo of Translation*, foreshadows a different story: One less about a utopianism that supplanted religiosity than how Lomnitz's family found itself caught between languages. In the introductory section, Lomnitz talks of the way his polyglot family (he brings up the concept of "panglossia") collectively spoke about a dozen tongues, some more actively than others, including German, Spanish, Yiddish, Hebrew, English, Russian, Romanian, and French. But he also discusses what he calls "alingualism," the condition of being left out of a language that others around you speak. His father, the geologist Cinna Lomnitz, a yeque (or German Jew) known for his 1974 book *Global Tectonics and Earthquake Risk* as well as the so-called Lomnitz law, which is used to understand the viscosity of rocks, didn't teach his son German. Meanwhile his mother, Larissa Adler, a famous anthropologist in Mexico who was raised in an Ashkenazi family (she was the oldest daughter of Misha and Noemí Adler), never taught her son Yiddish or Hebrew, perhaps because Jewish history made her feel alien, disconnected. For most of his life, Lomnitz writes, he has remained sandwiched between Spanish and English, feeling comfortable to a certain point in each of these languages, but also insecure in both. "Spanish is my Yiddish, and English is my Esperanto," he explains, "but I have always lacked the perfect language: the one that names things without distorting them. For there is not, nor can there be, a language of paradise such as those possessed by the truly great writers, who make their home in their language. My mother tongue is a linguistic shipwreck; and it is from there that I write the story of my grandparents."

"Vertigo" is an exquisitely poetic way to represent language as both an anchor and a trampoline. In Lomnitz's narrative there are Yiddishists, Hebraists, Esperantists, Hispanicists, Anglicists, and other obsessives. Switching tongues allows them to reinvent themselves in different milieus, but it also confuses them to the point of unsteadiness.

Lomnitz begins his story with his grandparents – and in particular with Misha Adler, the one who appears on the cover of the Spanish edition. Born in 1904 in Bessarabia, which is today part of Moldova and Ukraine, Adler spent his life on a globe-trotting odyssey in search of a satisfying radical politics. Misha's wife, Noemí Milstein, born in 1911 in Mogilev, a district of Podolia, Ukraine, was a politically committed companion on this odyssey. Another passionate intellectual, she belonged to the left-leaning Zionist youth organization Hashomer Hatzair and was part of the circle of socialists and radicals gathered around José Carlos Mariátegui, who was then forming Peru's Socialist Party. Lomnitz follows them, separately and together, from Novo Sulitza, near Czernowitz, to cities like Vienna, Paris, Santiago, Cali, Bogotá, Medellín, Caracas, and Haifa.

In Peru during the reign of the dictator Augusto B. Leguía, the couple edited a short-lived magazine under Mariátegui's mentorship called *Repertorio Hebreo*, and in Colombia they were connected with another, *Nuevo Mundo*, which also published a handful of issues. The pair were lofty in their aspirations: Lomnitz talks about Misha's correspondence with Sigmund Freud and Waldo Frank and Latin American intellectuals like Gabriela Mistral, Manuel Ugarte, and especially Samuel Glusberg, a prominent Argentine Jewish editor who converted to Catholicism (his adopted name was Enrique Espinoza, after Heine and Spinoza) and with whom Misha maintained an incisive dialogue on Jewish–Latin American identity. Being itinerant was for Misha and Noemí a proof of their cosmopolitanism and a way to escape the narrowness of identity, but that did not mean they were reluctant to embrace either their Jewishness or their Latin Americanness. In a 1965 notebook, Misha wrote that "Americanism and Judaica ... have ended up harmonizing and fusing into one another in my intimate thoughts and feelings, to such a degree that they have been reduced to one." The couple's itinerancy was far from being exclusively political; in fact, it was a matter of necessity. In 1930, four months after Mariátegui's death, a coup in Peru brought down the country's liberal president, Augusto Leguía. The new junta was anti-communist and xenophobic. Soon after, Misha's and Noemí's applications for citizenship were denied. They were expelled and forced to move once again from one country to the next.

Lomnitz parades a cast of dozens of other relatives, all the way back to great-grandparents like Shloma "Sina" Aronsfrau, who was born in Bukovina in the Austro-Hungarian Empire in 1859 and murdered in Mannheim, in southwestern Germany, in 1922 by anti-Semitic nationalist terrorists with close connections to the Nazi Party. Lomnitz also looks at Gerardo Reichel-Dolmanoff, an Austrian aristocrat, member of the SS, and a founding figure in Colombian anthropology who was also interested in the "Indian Question in South America." Reichel-Dolmanoff's writing on Indigenous tribes in the Amazon (his books include *Yurupari: Studies of an Amazonian Foundation Myth* and *Indians of Colombia: Experience and Cognition*) was not all that different from Lomnitz's own communist relatives' interest in pre-Columbian cosmogonies. Without actually articulating it, Lomnitz's book poses a probing question to its readers: Were Reichel-Dolmanoff's fascist views on indigeneity and Lomnitz's relatives' utopian ones linked at the core in the way they tried to understand Indigenous culture from the viewpoint of European psychology, religion, and politics?

In a couple of places, Lomnitz states that he wrote his memoir for his two children, Enrique and Elisa. This "domestic" angle gives both the Spanish and English versions a schmaltzy quality, tangible in the assortment of family photographs featured throughout the book. Yet these images also feel organic. After all, Lomnitz is first and foremost a historian who studies the many ways in which people react to their circumstances and how family is often at the center of these reactions. There's a family tree, a map, and copious bibliographical notes in the book's back matter. (An index would also have been useful.) That is to say, Lomnitz's own family – the real and the imagined – has been turned into a subject of scientific research.

Autobiography is a difficult genre to balance. It conceals as much as it reveals. It doesn't have to be confessional in nature. It must give the impression that the author is in control, although the best memoirs are those in which the reader realizes how precarious and foolish this objective is. Lomnitz is humble in this regard: He constantly recognizes how much he doesn't know about his family. The best sections of this book, in fact, are those that dramatize Lomnitz's incapacity to fill in the gaps or that engage with how all autobiography is, in one way or another, a work of fiction. Indeed, if *Nuestra América* has a failing, it is the way it overwhelms its readers with detail. Lomnitz is punctilious to such an extent that the details about Misha and Noemí's journey feel numbing. Does every cameo need a full Wikipedia-like detour? The accumulation can be almost encyclopedic at times: Lomnitz reaches out to everyone he can think of for information about minutiae. Even though what he finds is masterfully arranged, the plot (if the volume can be said to have one) keeps on twisting and turning.

There are hardly any droll sections, any quiet transitions. Instead, there is an abundance of tangential figures making an appearance, sometimes only as a reference, at other times in more vigorous ways. Lomnitz speaks of living in Berlin on the same street as Walter Benjamin. His grandmother sings in a concert conducted by Bruno Walter. He discusses the anti-Semitic legacy of Mircea Eliade, quotes Pablo Neruda, and debates Hannah Arendt's writing. He places his family in celebrated kibbutzim in Israel or connects them to important members of the Knesset, such as Hannah Lamdan and Yitzhak Ben-Aharon. It is all very dizzying. The assassination of Boris Milstein, Lomnitz's other paternal great-grandfather – a death surrounded in mystery – serves up a dollop of suspense. But the tension in these sections is finally dissipated by the onslaught of data. On Jewish history, *Nuestra América* can sometimes feel misguided. Perhaps because of his obsession with the crossroads where politics and daily life meet (the book opens with an epigraph from Marx's *Theses on Feuerbach* about discovering "the secret of the Holy Family," which "must then itself be destroyed in theory and in practice"), and because Lomnitz isn't, as he puts it, a specialist in Jewish history, he does not often engage in a meaningful way with questions of Jewish religion. He portrays Jews as creatures "confined, identified, and punished" in the Christian lands they inhabit, "but also protected so that they could carry out the theological role of the condemned witness: always present but never invited to the banquet.

Someone is always required to envy whatever is deemed to be normal, because normality can scarcely justify itself on its own." And he neglects the fact that European and Latin American Jews have a rich religious tradition. At least in part, this is doubtless because Lomnitz's family didn't introduce him to any theological realms – which is too bad, since in Peru, Chile, Colombia, and Mexico, Jewish religious as well as secular life has flourished, and its exploration would only have deepened his book.

Nuestra América overcomes its limitations, however, by doing something that historians seldom know how to accomplish: turn the scientific eye onto themselves. Lomnitz is serene, steady, and unemotional in his delivery. He makes the reader feel that each of our lives is a galaxy with countless entities. While individuals are obviously important in families, their actions are part of a whole. And it is the whole that matters to Lomnitz: not a self-portrait but a group one. This crucial message comes across especially in his affectionate, indebted depiction of his mother, Larissa Lomnitz. When I was growing up in Copilco, in the southern part of Mexico City, near UNAM, the national university, I knew that the Lomnitz family lived a few blocks away, although I don't remember spending time with them. Larissa, a French-born Chilean, was admired by my mother as a trailblazing ethnographer. She had earned her bachelor's degree at Berkeley and her doctorate at Universidad Iberoamericana (where my mother and I taught) and was on the faculty at UNAM. Her interests moved along the lines of Oscar Lewis's in *The Children of Sanchez*, a book about the ways a poor Mexican family responded to its environment and the death of its patriarch that I was mesmerized by in my youth. (Claudio Lomnitz wrote an introduction in Spanish to its 50th-anniversary edition.)

Larissa was attracted to similar themes but was far more academic in her tone. I remember reading about her fieldwork in Cerrada del Cóndor, a shantytown of about 200 houses in Mexico City, not too far from Copilco. Lomnitz, whose *Death and the Idea of Mexico* follows closely in his mother's footsteps, has more global aspirations – first, because he performs his career bilingually, connecting with two distinct, at times heterogeneous readerships, something I don't believe Larissa succeeded at by comparison. And second, because Lomnitz has devoted his energy to bridging the gap between the academic milieu and the public sphere. He is captivated by the intersection of history, politics, and day-to-day affairs, and he reflects on that intersection not only in scholarly volumes but in the regular columns he writes for the left-leaning newspaper *La Jornada*. Composed "in exile" in New York, Lomnitz's autobiography is an invitation to look at the past and present of Latin American Jewish life with depth and complexity. Talking about columns of a different sort, at one point he refers to what he calls "the column syndrome." As he looks at his family subspecie *aeternitatis*, a particular member "props up, buffers, protects, and endures," allowing others to coalesce as a group. This, he says, is a trait especially visible among Jews, given their propensity to catastrophe. "The role of the column," Lomnitz adds, "comes with a communicative function – to be a source of practical wisdom, to be sure, but also to temper or soften news so that fear doesn't spin into vertigo and paralysis, so that depression doesn't become overwhelming, and blows don't prove fatal." By detailing the intricacies of his own labyrinthine family, *Nuestra América*, in its two complementary versions, turns Lomnitz himself into an exemplary column, thanks to whom it is possible to discern patterns in the never-ending, multilingual, transnational trek that is modern Jewish diasporic existence – the ultimate sense of which, it goes without saying, will always be beyond us.

– *The Nation*, March 7–14, 2022

Rethinking the Classics
(with Jenna Tang)

JENNA TANG: For starters, could you define what a literary classic means for you?

ILAN STAVANS: A literary classic is a book that knows how to be patient, a book with all the time on its hands, capable of waiting for the right readers to come by. It is also a book that "survives" translation. The classics are always in the process of being retranslated, in part because they are in the public domain but also because language ages, which prompts us to refashion them under a fresh new look. Dostoyevsky's *Crime and Punishment*, for example, has been rendered into English thirteen times; Kafka's *The Metamorphosis*, eighteen times; and Cervantes' *Don Quixote of La Mancha*, twenty-two times. Needless to say, when looked at comparatively, the quality of all those translations is, well, unequal. But regardless how atrocious a translation might be, the original survives.

Translators are always pitching new versions as a way to supersede the inefficacies of their predecessors, only to produce, of course, equally inefficacious versions. And new publishers are investing again in the classics because their appeal is perennial. As much as I hate looking at literature as a market commodity, it is ruled by supply and demand. I like what Giancarlo DiTrapano, the late publisher of Tyrant Books, told the magazine *Entropy* in 2015: "Tyrant stuff isn't for everyone, but nothing should be for everyone. Or at least nothing that's worth anything. You know what's for everyone? Water. Water is for everyone. And if you're publishing something for everyone, well, you're publishing water."

JT: Can you recall what was the very first classic title you read?

IS: A fascinating question. I don't know at what precise moment I became aware of the concept of a literary classic. The first time I read *The Little Prince*? At the age of eight, it came with a strong endorsement from my mother. But I don't remember being interested in it. I wasn't into reading; I preferred outdoor activities. The illustrations seemed childish to me. To be honest, the narrative still feels infantile. Clearly, I didn't get the allegorical nature of classics. The little prince wasn't Everyman, a mythological hero in the middle of a journey. I needed to grow up to realize that the book was, well, more than just a book: it was a canvas on which readers could project themselves. That's what classics are: more than just an accumulation of pages, they are the stuff our personal dreams are made of. I've now translated Antoine de Saint-Exupéry's volume into Spanglish, which to me is a way to say thank you. But, frankly, it is peripheral to me in comparison with the Hebrew Bible. That's *the* ur-text. I feel Noah's ark, the Tower of Babel, the story of Abraham's calling, Isaac's *Akedah*, and Jacob's ordeal and Moses' liberation odyssey are imprinted in my DNA. I come from a Jewish-Mexican family in which culture was a form of religion. If pressed, I confess not to remember a specific moment during which I read Genesis. But that's what the classics are: we get them not through reading but by osmosis.

JT: It's important to think of the classics that have influenced us throughout our upbringings. What brought you to start the Restless Classics imprint? You switched from being an author to becoming a publisher. Was that switch challenging? What prompted it? Is there something specific you look for in world classics?

IS: Independent, nonprofit publishers are devoted to bringing out cutting-edge books. Restless Books is devoted to extraordinary literature in translation. It also focuses on giving immigrant voices a platform. I was about to reach fifty – that is, ripe for a midlife crisis, or as Dante would put it in the *Divine Comedy*, "Nel mezzo del cammin di nostra vita / mi ritrovai per una selva oscura / ché la diritta via era smarrita" – when, during an interview about translation on NPR, I spoke about the dire number of books that come from other languages and are published in English. It was a comment frequently made in public. After the show, the host asked me if I got tired of my message and if I ever thought of doing something concrete about it. That might have been the seed for the project. I decided I would either commit myself to a publishing venture or find a new message. In the next few months I talked to several potential funders. I found in one of them an extraordinary partner. She challenged me to educate myself by becoming a student again, taking a business course on start-ups. After taking one, a financial plan was devised. That happened in 2012. Restless Books was launched the following year, first as a for-profit. Honestly, I didn't think the endeavor would go beyond a year, maximum two. One of my models was James Laughlin, who launched New Directions while a student at Harvard in 1936 with money from his father, out of a cottage at his aunt's home in Norfolk, Connecticut, and stored copies in his college room. We live in different times, though. For one thing, the market is now astonishingly crowded. Maybe it's my teacher's self, but I believe it is incumbent upon publishers not just to release books but to help open them in front of audiences in need. If these are perennials, let their durability, in affordable prices, reach segments of our culture frequently left behind. Isn't that the dream of democracy, to allow its dwellers to have a voice? The only way to achieve that is to allow them to appreciate the voices of the past. Penguin Classics and Oxford Classics, obviously, have set the path. As a scholar, I am part of their backlist. But the classics shouldn't be their exclusive purview alone. This essential field of literature needs a jolt. Independent publishers must push in further, more adventurous directions. Reading *Frankenstein* in prison is a unique experience. After all, we see those behind bars as monsters. What do "monsters" think of monstrosity? Or give immigrants *Don Quixote*. Is there a better book about dreaming oneself into a new life? What I look for in the classics is a message that is reinvented every time a new reader opens it. Along with the author, it is the role of the introducer and artist to make a case for that fresh take.

JT: Can you talk about your experiences collaborating with translators to bring more classics to English-speaking audiences?

IS: At Restless Classics we take two approaches. One is to revive a translation that has circulated but still commands attention. Reading a classic, I believe, ought to entail an element of foreignness. If you delve into *Les Misérables* in French, you cannot fail to first recognize, and then, hopefully, to thrive in, the somewhat stilted nature of Victor Hugo's language. Classics are windows into an epoch, not only in content but in form. That's where their allure is found. I don't think translations should turn them into modern artifacts; the feeling of alienation felt in the original should be accessible in the translation as well. But we also commission new translations of classics that either have failed to "arrive" in English, or the available translations of them aren't in the public domain.

JT: Having published so many works in translation across cultures, what are the most urgent questions you think publishers should be asking themselves? What change do you see in the world of publishing translated literature?

IS: It is crucial that, as culture seeks to represent nonwhite voices, our conception of perennial literature undergoes an expansion. We need to make classics from Asia, Africa, and Latin America available to underrepresented readerships. That means recalibrating our definition of a literary classic and explicitly reaching out to translators for new, undiscovered classics. It also means that nonprofit, independent publishers, which are often strapped for money, need to build partnerships in order to subsidize these new translations. For instance, Restless Classics is about to bring out the first English translation ever of a nineteenth-century slave-narrative novella, *The Maroons* by Louis Timagène Houat, from Mauritius, translated by Aqiil Gopee. By the way, I have noticed a distressing phenomenon. Copyright functions as a kind of censoring mechanism. Books that were published recently but failed to gain traction suffer in limbo, out of print but still under copyright, whereas books out of copyright are available to anyone. This means that titles released between, say, 1930 and 2010 are impossible to get other than in libraries.

JT: The Restless Books Prize for Immigrant Writing was established in 2016 to honor debut fiction and nonfiction works by first-generation immigrants. Can you talk about starting this literary prize?

IS: The prize is awarded alternatively to a fiction and nonfiction winner. Restless Books has published Deepak Unnikrishnan's *Temporary People*, Grace Talusan's *The Body Papers*, and Priyanka Champaneri's *The City of Good Death*. They all launched their careers with these books. We also publish the series The Face, in which diverse writers (Ruth Ozeki, Tash Aw, Chris Abani, et al.) use their face as a springboard to reflect on their identity. These are the classics of tomorrow, I hope. Du Bois, in *The Souls of Black Folk*, argued that the theme of the twentieth century was the color line. In my view, the theme of the twenty-first century is immigration. Everything rotates around it: climate change, COVID-19, populism from Trump to other "aspirational" dictators, global finance, etc. It is essential that our conversation opens up to alternative perspectives.

JT: You also run the Immigrant Writing Workshops. What are some of the most important questions and discussions you've had?

IS: These workshops not only inform Restless Books' mission but define it. Immigrants understand what it feels like to live in the margins, peripherally. My impression is that the syncopated dance between the center and the periphery is no longer what it used to be. The center today exists in a state of never-ending doubt, complicit in ancestral crimes that range from colonialism to appropriation. It is minorities who now set the tone of cultural change. They function as translators. The immigrant workshops are regularly offered through various branches of the New York Public Library, starting with the Midtown one, and, similarly, the Los Angeles Public Library.

JT: Translation is not just about languages; it is about the "coming across" among cultures. How does one navigate the marriage of sensibilities between authors and translators? How do you consider gender, ethnicity, and other identities to foster a more balanced and diverse relationship among all the people who are bringing cross-cultural works to the world?

IS: Translators have always been agents of change. The Muslim translators of the Toledo School in the twelfth century, for example, and later on under Alfonso El Sabio, brought Aristotle, Ptolemy, and Hippocrates into Europe. Or Lucretius's *De rerum natura*. Without these translators, there would not be a connection with the classical past. Borges has an inspiring story, "Averroes' Search," about ibn-Rushd tendering in Arabic a couple of terms from Aristotle's lost treatise on comedy.

    Translators open the window to the past to welcome fresh air. They are surveyors of what is significant somewhere else and want to bring that significance home. As we make room for new voices from the world, we must diversify the database of translators. If and when they come from a diverse background, what they propose is likely to be more heterogeneous. A theater teacher of mine used to say to me that what's important is not to give the audience what the audience wants but to teach the audience to want something else. A diverse army of translators will be able to achieve such an objective. The same goes for editors and, of course, publishers: we need otherness to be less alien.

JT: Do the literary classics change over time? If so, what are the changes?

IS: They do, indeed. In two ways. First, one generation's literary classics aren't the same as those of previous or subsequent generations. As I mentioned before, we are currently in the midst of reimagining the classics, making the canon more expansive, less white and Eurocentric. Some titles fall off the shelf as others arrive. Harriet Beecher Stowe's *Uncle Tom's Cabin*, for instance, is, it appears to me, less current than it was a few decades ago. I taught it a couple of years ago, and students found plenty to fault and that is difficult to justify these days. At the same time, the work of immigrant writers – I love the novels by Viet Thanh Nguyen, for instance – is opening new vistas. This is as it should be. Literature, at first sight, might feel static, but it is just the opposite: an organic expression of a particular time and place. The second change has to do with each and every one of its readers. The relationship we develop with a classic is like a lifelong friendship: it goes through ups and downs. Whenever we reopen the book, we are different, and, as a result, what we read is too. This, I think, is another definition of a literary classic: like a mirror, it reflects what is in front of it.

JT: What is the future of the classics in translation?

IS: The future is plentiful. As long as there are readers, literary classics will be in circulation in refashioned versions. The originals are sacred. Taking out a single word of the Hebrew Bible amounts to anathema since we're talking about a narrative supposedly written by the divine. But no translator is godlike; on the contrary, all are miserably human, meaning imperfect in their quest. Therefore, the practice of translation exists, as it should, in a state of constant renewal. Without the classics, we are a *tabula rasa*: we have no memory. We not only open the classics to recreate the past; we also use them to calibrate the present. Look at Shakespeare. I dream of doing a Restless Shakespeare; in fact, the name of this series is already a mission statement. There is arguably no more reprinted author in the English language. Do we need another *Hamlet*, *Romeo and Juliet*, *King Lear,* and *The Tempest*? No doubt we do. He is a kaleidoscope that fluctuates depending on who is looking through it. There is the Elizabethan Shakespeare, the Victorian, the modern, the postmodern, the postcolonial, and so on. And there is also a restless Shakespeare, capable of conveying the perspective of a world always in transit and reorganized at all times – and at all costs – by outsiders. That's the Shakespeare I'm after, one that lives in English but becomes an emblem of a world without a center.

– *World Literature Today*, May 12, 2021

Pierre Menard: Retranslation and Approximation (with Youssef Boucetta)

YOUSSEF BOUCETTA: Why translate "Pierre Menard, autor del *Quijote*" again?

ILAN STAVANS: Simply put, because to me it's far less important what a literary classic says than what it means. As books, classics are survivors. They have successfully overcome the passage of time. Classics are also patient books: they know how to wait for their readers, in contrast with new books, whose existence depends on the urgency with which readers embrace them. Finally, classics are books that overcome translation, so to speak. There are more than a few atrocious versions of *Madame Bovary* in English, yet Flaubert's book is still a classic. The same might be said of *Don Quixote*. Tobias Smollett, who supposedly rendered it in English in 1755, apparently didn't know even the basics of Cervantes's tongue. Yet even his translation doesn't fully deter readers from finding joy in the knight's adventures. The echoes of Pierre Menard's oeuvre are infinite. *Menardian*, as a noun, is the attempt to render the impossible in translation. Borges has taught us, readers, to approach a text according to our own perspectives. The *Talmud* stated it earlier: "we don't understand the world as it is but as we are."

YB: In my understanding of "Pierre Menard," the rewriting serves as a personified allegory of translation. The protagonist is an embodiment of the French language. In this allegorical reading, Borges wants French to re-write Spanish and what better work than *Don Quixote* to represent Spanish.

IS: The choice of Cervantes's canonical novel, as Borges himself states it, isn't accidental. There isn't a more central classic in Hispanic civilization. This is a story about originality. In my opinion, Borges is shifting the coordinates of what passes as original, arguing that Latin America – Argentina, in particular – might be seen as an offspring from Spain yet that perspective allows it to be even more original, especially when it recycles material coming from the so-called Old World.

YB: Borges's vindicating his right as an Argentinian writer to read the *Quixote* and create his own interpretation. This assertion implies his profound desire to revive this monument of the Spanish language from a Latin American perspective, almost in the same way that Raphael's fresco the *School of Athens* wants to reinvent the elegance of classical Greece. He is certainly also making a statement about literary modernity, proposing a renaissance of the reader.

IS: Borges's story is in the form of an essay. Or, maybe, a eulogy. Or a review. In other words, fiction might take different shapes. I've looked at all other English translations of the story, at least those I'm able to access. In translating a classic, the pleasures but also the perils involve having antecedents. One might choose to ignore those who came before or one might want to establish a dialogue with them. I prefer the latter approach.

YB: I decided not to look at any other translations before doing mine to try and see how much my reading would differ from the others'. I eventually ended up reading Paul Verdevoye's 1951 translation but only after I finished my first draft.

IS: For me, it was important to look at the available translations into English of *Don Quixote* – they are all in my personal library – and chose the one most appropriate for the task. I went for John Ormsby's, my favorite, published in 1885, because it is modern yet feels somewhat detached from us in the 21st century. I have introduced it a couple of times in English-language editions. It should be said that the portion that Borges quotes (Part I, Chapter IX) is emblematic of the entire book. It's the episode in which the narrator comes across the original story of *Don Quixote* in Toledo, written by the Arab historian Cide Hamete Benengueli. Cervantes's novel is built as a palimpsest and Benengueli is described as a liar, "just like all Arabs." To thus reflect on truth and history having an impostor as center of gravity is ironic.

YB: Once I was done, as I compared my translation with Paul Verdevoye's, I noticed one main tendency. Verdevoye's sentence structures and syntactic choices often changed Borges' initial formulations. Verdevoye saw Borges as a universal writer, caring less for the aesthetic of the style than for the meaning of the text. The difference between both of our translations is that mine finds a different compromise between style and content. For me, with the impact of globalization and the multiplication of cultural exchanges, the French language is changing much faster and becoming much more accepting of literal formulations in other languages such as Spanish. Therefore, translating Borges from Spanish into French today is probably easier as the cultural proximity of both languages and their interlocutors is much greater. Have you felt any of this with English as well? The importance of Latino culture in the US has obviously made it a much common practice to translate Spanish to English and vice versa. What type of variations did this create between your translation and Ormsby's?

IS: In Spanish, Borges's style is stunningly archaic, even awkward, He writes: "la señoril reserva que la distingue," and "resolvió adelantarse a la vanidad que aguarda todas las fatigas del hombre." Nobody spoke like that in Buenos Aires in 1939; and nobody speaks like that today. Of course, Borges's signature prose isn't about how language is spoken, unless he is mimicking the parlance of *compadritos* and other social types. Youssef, I tell you all this because my attempt was to translate the original as punctiliously as possible, particularly after so many translations into English have been done. In other words, reading "Pierre Menard, autor del *Quijote*" in Spanish entails accepting Borges's self-conscious, obstinate mannerisms. The translation in no way should make the reader's effort less uncomfortable. In the list of works by Menard, at the outset of the story, he gives a date as "October of 1909," rather than the common "October 1909"; I have mimicked that in my rendition. By the way, my choices for those lines are "the dandy-like reserve that characterizes her" and "he resolved to be ahead of the vanity that awaits all human fatigues."

YB: I too have noticed that Borges is using a particularly rare language register. We can see that in the second phrase which is incredibly long. That contributes to the construction of a certain enunciating persona separate from him. What I mean by this is that there seems to be a variation in the literary style of Borges when he narrates a personal story like "El Otro" (El Libro de Arena) and when he composes this type of fiction although both are written in the first person. If we assume that an author's voice is textualized in their literary style, Borges is adopting another voice in "Pierre Menard." This reminds me of Barthes's "The Death of the Author": "Its source, its voice is not to be located; and yet it is perfectly read; this is because the true locus of writing is reading" (talking about a sentence in Balzac's *Sarrasine*). This is obviously the most evident reading we can make of the whole short story, but there is a deeper level to it where we understand the voice in the aforementioned metaphorical sense. I see it as an added layer of discourse that is connoted in the style and serves to extend an invitation to integrate the voice of the reader.

IS: Another thing: Borges, always aloof, injects foreign terms into his paragraphs; he also uses titles in German, French, and English. Rather than translate these into English, I've kept them in their original. Again, my argument is simple: the polyphony of the original needs to be maintained in the translation. It is our duty to approximate Borges's bookish style as much as possible.

YB: To my convenience, most of Borges's foreign-language incursions in this story are in French so it just left me with less to translate. However, there is always a doubt of what to do with something that comes directly in the target language. There is often an additional connotation when a text has foreign terms and in my situation this connotation is lost. Maybe the text was meant to be closer to a Francophone reader than a Hispanophone one. We know that the protagonist is French so he is surely more open to the identification of a Francophone reader. I wanted to accentuate this relationship of the text with the French reader by simply leaving words that were in French as they were. I've seen a translation of *The Death of Ivan Illyich* that chose to put little starry symbols before and after a word that was originally written in French by Tolstoy. This editorial decision is meant to highlight the fact that Tolstoï was initially writing in Russian and that French words are to be taken in relation to Russian 19th-century societal norms as a symbol of cultural capital. I've decided not to make the decision of signaling French words and instead chose to play along with Borges by bringing the short story about Menard back to Menard's language seamlessly. Not having put in place these markers that would constantly remind the reader of the precedence of Spanish, I want to fully move the text and let it find new roots in Menard's language.

IS: Menard makes it clear that, like all things human, every translation is a product of its time. Mine and yours are too, of course. Others shall critique it, as they should, as they attempt their own version. Perhaps the true feast would be to do a translation of "Pierre Menard, autor del *Quijote*" in 2019 that doesn't include any expressions whatsoever that were incorporated into English after 1939. Or, maybe, after the beginning of the 20th century. In that sense, the translator would be bringing the rendition back to its sources. But that isn't an approximation; that's an anachronism. Language exists in constant change. What we do as translators is transpose the era in which a piece was composed into the era in which we live in. That's what humanity is all about – time travel.

YB: That's very interesting. When a text is written in a certain language and is met with long-lasting glory like *Don Quixote,* it remains fixated in the state of the language of the time it was written. However, continued translations constitute a renewal of such texts, adapting them to other languages in the time where the translation was written. In other words, translations are markers in time that update the comprehension of a text with the linguistic sensibilities of an instant in an ever-evolving history.

IS: No retranslation ever fixes a text in the adopted language, since translation is nothing but interpretation, and interpretation, by definition, is relative. *Menardism*, therefore, is relativism.

YB: Were you intimidated by the previous translators of Borges's story?

IS: Not in the least. On the contrary, I felt the need to retranslate "Pierre Menard, autor del *Quijote*" because I wanted to leave behind my own reaction as a reader who has descended, like those before and after me, on Borges's pages. Every night, before I go to bed, I read a section of the Talmud, a non-sequential narrative written between 200 BCE and 500 CE. A page of it is something to behold: parallel columns offer diverse, at times divergent interpretations. I love these parallel universes of reading. To me translation does the same: it opens new vistas by redressing a text, giving it a different look.

YB: Are you more interested in retranslation than in translation?

IS: I am, indeed. In part, this is because, about to turn sixty, I prefer to spend time with the classics. They are lifelong companions whose secrets reveal themselves to us depending on where we are in life. My own interpretations of the Menard story have changed over the years. When I was young in Mexico, I didn't think of it as an invitation to think of Latin America as a landscape where, as a result of the barbarous history of colonialism, originality is always compromised. I also used to think Borges was aloof, stuffy, stoic. Now I don't care. I love his style, his devotion to ideas, his prescriptive relativism.

YB: In *Maghreb Pluriel,* Moroccan author Abdelkébir Khatibi proposes the hypothetical extraordinary event of writing with "several hands," in several languages, in a text that is but a perpetual translation. I find that "Pierre Menard, autor del *Quijote*" bears this extraordinary nature. Borges imbues this story with a sense of profound universalism. He suggests that by merely sharing the condition of being human with Cervantes, Menard can literally rewrite *Don Quixote*. The word "translation" comes from the Latin *translatio*, which means carry across. Borges carries *Don Quixote* from Cervantes's subjectivity to Menard's.

As we read it ourselves, it mixes in with our subjectivity. As we translate the text, we permanently impress this subjectivity over Borges's, Cervantes's, and Menard's in a palimpsestic fashion. When a reader comes upon our translation, they get mixed into the equation. Therefore, as the text births this space of intersubjectivity from the fundamental depth of Menard's universalist philosophy and travels across languages and cultures, it begins to embody Khatibi's proposition of a text residing in a perpetual translation.

– *Translation Review*, volume 17, issue 1 (2020)

Pierre Menard, Autor del *Quijote*

JORGE LUIS BORGES

A Silvina Ocampo

La obra visible que ha dejado este novelista es de fácil y breve enumeración. Son, por lo tanto, imperdonables las omisiones y adiciones perpetradas por madame Henri Bachelier en un catálogo falaz que cierto diario cuya tendencia *protestante* no es un secreto ha tenido la desconsideración de inferir a sus deplorables lectores – si bien estos son pocos y calvinistas, cuando no masones y circuncisos. Los amigos auténticos de Menard han visto con alarma ese catálogo y aun con cierta tristeza. Diríase que ayer nos reunimos ante el mármol final y entre los cipreses infaustos y ya el Error trata de empañar su Memoria ... Decididamente, una breve rectificación es inevitable.

Me consta que es muy fácil recusar mi pobre autoridad. Espero, sin embargo, que no me prohibirán mencionar dos altos testimonios. La baronesa de Bacourt (en cuyos *vendredis* inolvidables tuve el honor de conocer al llorado poeta) ha tenido a bien aprobar las líneas que siguen. La condesa de Bagnoregio, uno de los espíritus más finos del principado de Mónaco (y ahora de Pittsburgh, Pennsylvania, después de su reciente boda con el filántropo internacional Simón Kautzsch, tan calumniado, ¡ay!, por las víctimas de sus desinteresadas maniobras) ha sacrificado "a la veracidad y a la muerte" (tales son sus palabras) la señoril reserva que la distingue y en una carta abierta publicada en la revista *Luxe* me concede asimismo su beneplácito. Esas ejecutorias, creo, no son insuficientes.

He dicho que la obra *visible* de Menard es fácilmente enumerable. Examinado con esmero su archivo particular, he verificado que consta de las piezas que siguen:

a) Un soneto simbolista que apareció dos veces (con variaciones) en la revista *La Conque* (números de marzo y octubre de 1899).

b) Una monografía sobre la posibilidad de construir un vocabulario poético de conceptos que no fueran sinónimos o perífrasis de los que informan el lenguaje común, "sino objetos ideales creados por una convención y esencialmente destinados a las necesidades poéticas" (Nîmes, 1901).

c) Una monografía sobre "ciertas conexiones o afinidades" del pensamiento de Descartes, de Leibniz y de John Wilkins (Nîmes, 1903).
d) Una monografía sobre la *Characteristica universalis* de Leibniz (Nîmes, 1904).
e) Un artículo técnico sobre la posibilidad de enriquecer el ajedrez eliminando uno de los peones de torre. Menard propone, recomienda, discute y acaba por rechazar esa innovación.
f) Una monografía sobre el *Ars Magna Generalis* de Ramón Llull (Nîmes, 1906).
g) Una traducción con prólogo y notas del *Libro de la invención liberal y arte del juego del axedrez* de Ruy López de Segura (París, 1907).
h) Los borradores de una monografía sobre la lógica simbólica de George Boole.
i) Un examen de las leyes métricas esenciales de la prosa francesa, ilustrado con ejemplos de Saint Simon (*Revue des Langues Romanes*, Montpellier, octubre de 1909).
j) Una réplica a Luc Durtain (que había negado la existencia de tales leyes) ilustrada con ejemplos de Luc Durtain (*Revue des Langues Romanes*, Montpellier, diciembre de 1909).
k) Una traducción manuscrita de la *Aguja de navegar cultos* de Quevedo, intitulada *La boussole des précieux*.
l) Un prefacio al catálogo de la exposición de litografías de Carolus Hourcade (Nîmes, 1914).
m) La obra *Les problèmes d'un problème* (París, 1917) que discute en orden cronológico las soluciones del ilustre problema de Aquiles y la tortuga. Dos ediciones de este libro han aparecido hasta ahora; la segunda trae como epígrafe el consejo de Leibniz *Ne craignez point, monsieur, la tortue,* y renueva los capítulos dedicados a Russell y a Descartes.
n) Un obstinado análisis de las "costumbres sintácticas" de Toulet (N.R.F., marzo de 1921). Menard recuerdo declaraba que censurar y alabar son operaciones sentimentales que nada tienen que ver con la crítica.
o) Una transposición en alejandrinos del *Cimetière marin*, de Paul Valéry (N.R.F., enero de 1928).
p) Una invectiva contra Paul Valéry, en las *Hojas para la supresión de la realidad* de Jacques Reboul. (Esa invectiva, dicho sea entre paréntesis, es el reverso exacto de su verdadera opinión sobre Valéry. Éste así lo entendió y la amistad antigua de los dos no corrió peligro.)

q) Una "definición" de la condesa de Bagnoregio, en el "victorioso volumen" la locución es de otro colaborador, Gabriele d'Annunzio que anualmente publica esta dama para rectificar los inevitables falseos del periodismo y presentar "al mundo y a Italia" una auténtica efigie de su persona, tan expuesta (en razón misma de su belleza y de su actuación) a interpretaciones erróneas o apresuradas.

r) Un ciclo de admirables sonetos para la baronesa de Bacourt (1934).

s) Una lista manuscrita de versos que deben su eficacia a la puntuación.[1]

Hasta aquí (sin otra omisión que unos vagos sonetos circunstanciales para el hospitalario, o ávido, álbum de madame Henri Bachelier) la obra *visible* de Menard, en su orden cronológico. Paso ahora a la otra: la subterránea, la interminablemente heroica, la impar. También, ¡ay de las posibilidades del hombre!, la inconclusa. Esa obra, tal vez la más significativa de nuestro tiempo, consta de los capítulos noveno y trigésimo octavo de la primera parte del *Don Quijote* y de un fragmento del capítulo veintidós. Yo sé que tal afirmación parece un dislate; justificar ese "dislate" es el objeto primordial de esta nota.[2]

Dos textos de valor desigual inspiraron la empresa. Uno es aquel fragmento filológico de Novalis – el que lleva el número 2005 en la edición de Dresden – que esboza el tema de la *total identificación* con un autor determinado. Otro es uno de esos libros parasitarios que sitúan a Cristo en un bulevar, a Hamlet en la Cannebiére o a don Quijote en Wall Street. Como todo hombre de buen gusto, Menard abominaba de esos carnavales inútiles, sólo aptos decía para ocasionar el plebeyo placer del anacronismo o (lo que es peor) para embelesarnos con la idea primaria de que todas las épocas son iguales o de que son distintas. Más interesante, aunque de ejecución contradictoria y superficial, le parecía el famoso propósito de Daudet: conjugar en una figura, que es Tartarín, al Ingenioso Hidalgo y a su escudero … Quienes han insinuado que Menard dedicó su vida a escribir un Quijote contemporáneo, calumnian su clara memoria.

---

1 Madame Henri Bachelier enumera asimismo una versión literal de la versión literal que hizo Quevedo de la *Introduction à la vie dévote* de san Francisco de Sales. En la biblioteca de Pierre Menard no hay rastros de tal obra. Debe tratarse de una broma de nuestro amigo, mal escuchada.

2 Tuve también el propósito secundario de bosquejar la imagen de Pierre Menard. Pero ¿cómo atreverme a competir con las páginas áureas que me dicen prepara la baronesa de Bacourt o con el lápiz delicado y puntual de Carolus Hourcade?

No quería componer otro Quijote – lo cual es fácil – sino *el Quijote*. Inútil agregar que no encaró nunca una transcripción mecánica del original; no se proponía copiarlo. Su admirable ambición era producir unas páginas que coincidieran palabra por palabra y línea por línea con las de Miguel de Cervantes.

"Mi propósito es meramente asombroso", me escribió el 30 de septiembre de 1934 desde Bayonne. "El término final de una demostración teológica o metafísica – el mundo externo, Dios, la causalidad, las formas universales – no es menos anterior y común que mi divulgada novela. La sola diferencia es que los filósofos publican en agradables volúmenes las etapas intermediarias de su labor y que yo he resuelto perderlas." En efecto, no queda un solo borrador que atestigüe ese trabajo de años.

El método inicial que imaginó era relativamente sencillo. Conocer bien el español, recuperar la fe católica, guerrear contra los moros o contra el turco, olvidar la historia de Europa entre los años de 1602 y de 1918, *ser* Miguel de Cervantes. Pierre Menard estudió ese procedimiento (sé que logró un manejo bastante fiel del español del siglo diecisiete) pero lo descartó por fácil. ¡Más bien por imposible! dirá el lector. De acuerdo, pero la empresa era de antemano imposible y de todos los medios imposibles para llevarla a término, éste era el menos interesante. Ser en el siglo veinte un novelista popular del siglo diecisiete le pareció una disminución. Ser, de alguna manera, Cervantes y llegar al Quijote le pareció menos arduo por – consiguiente, menos interesante – que seguir siendo Pierre Menard y llegar al Quijote, a través de las experiencias de Pierre Menard. (Esa convicción, dicho sea de paso, le hizo excluir el prólogo autobiográfico de la segunda parte del Don Quijote. Incluir ese prólogo hubiera sido crear otro personaje – Cervantes – pero también hubiera significado presentar el Quijote en función de ese personaje y no de Menard. Éste, naturalmente, se negó a esa facilidad.) "Mi empresa no es difícil, esencialmente" leo en otro lugar de la carta. "Me bastaría ser inmortal para llevarla a cabo." ¿Confesaré que suelo imaginar que la terminó y que leo el Quijote – todo el Quijote – como si lo hubiera pensado Menard? Noches pasadas, al hojear el capítulo XXVI – no ensayado nunca por él – reconocí el estilo de nuestro amigo y como su voz en esta frase excepcional: *las ninfas de los ríos, la dolorosa y húmida Eco*. Esa conjunción eficaz de un adjetivo moral y otro físico me trajo a la memoria un verso de Shakespeare, que discutimos una tarde:

Where a malignant and a turbaned Turk ...

¿Por qué precisamente el Quijote? dirá nuestro lector. Esa preferencia, en un español, no hubiera sido inexplicable; pero sin duda lo es en un simbolista de Nîmes, devoto esencialmente de Poe, que engendró a Baudelaire, que engendró a Mallarmé, que engendró a Valéry, que engendró a Edmond Teste. La carta precitada ilumina el punto. "El Quijote", aclara Menard, "me interesa profundamente, pero no me parece ¿cómo lo diré? inevitable. No puedo imaginar el universo sin la interjección de Edgar Allan Poe:

Ah, bear in mind this garden was enchanted!

o sin el *Bateau ivre* o el *Ancient Mariner*, pero me sé capaz de imaginarlo sin el Quijote. (Hablo, naturalmente, de mi capacidad personal, no de la resonancia histórica de las obras.) El Quijote es un libro contingente, el Quijote es innecesario. Puedo premeditar su escritura, puedo escribirlo, sin incurrir en una tautología. A los doce o trece años lo leí, tal vez íntegramente. Después, he releído con atención algunos capítulos, aquellos que no intentaré por ahora. He cursado asimismo los entremeses, las comedias, la *Galatea*, las *Novelas ejemplares*, los trabajos sin duda laboriosos de *Persiles y Segismunda* y el *Viaje del Parnaso* … Mi recuerdo general del Quijote, simplificado por el olvido y la indiferencia, puede muy bien equivaler a la imprecisa imagen anterior de un libro no escrito. Postulada esa imagen (que nadie en buena ley me puede negar) es indiscutible que mi problema es harto más difícil que el de Cervantes. Mi complaciente precursor no rehusó la colaboración del azar: iba componiendo la obra inmortal un poco *à la diable*, llevado por inercias del lenguaje y de la invención. Yo he contraído el misterioso deber de reconstruir literalmente su obra espontánea. Mi solitario juego está gobernado por dos leyes polares. La primera me permite ensayar variantes de tipo formal o psicológico; la segunda me obliga a sacrificarlas al texto 'original' y a razonar de un modo irrefutable esa aniquilación … A esas trabas artificiales hay que sumar otra, congénita. Componer el Quijote a principios del siglo diecisiete era una empresa razonable, necesaria, acaso fatal; a principios del veinte, es casi imposible. No en vano han transcurrido trescientos años, cargados de complejísimos hechos. Entre ellos, para mencionar uno solo: el mismo Quijote."

A pesar de esos tres obstáculos, el fragmentario Quijote de Menard es más sutil que el de Cervantes. Éste, de un modo burdo, opone a las ficciones caballerescas la pobre realidad provinciana de su país; Menard elige como "realidad" la tierra de Carmen durante el siglo de Lepanto y de Lope. ¡Qué españoladas no habría aconsejado esa elección a Maurice Barrès o al doctor Rodríguez Larreta! Menard, con toda naturalidad, las elude. En su obra no hay gitanerías ni conquistadores ni místicos ni Felipe II ni autos de fe. Desatiende o proscribe el color local. Ese desdén indica un sentido nuevo de la novela histórica. Ese desdén condena a *Salammbô*, inapelablemente.

No menos asombroso es considerar capítulos aislados. Por ejemplo, examinemos el xxxviii de la primera parte, "que trata del curioso discurso que hizo don Quixote de las armas y las letras". Es sabido que don Quijote (como Quevedo en el pasaje análogo, y posterior, de *La hora de todos*) falla el pleito contra las letras y en favor de las armas. Cervantes era un viejo militar: su fallo se explica. ¡Pero que el don Quijote de Pierre Menard – hombre contemporáneo de *La trahison des clercs* y de Bertrand Russell – reincida en esas nebulosas sofisterías! Madame Bachelier ha visto en ellas una admirable y típica subordinación del autor a la psicología del héroe; otros (nada perspicazmente) una *transcripción* del Quijote; la baronesa de Bacourt, la influencia de Nietzsche. A esa tercera interpretación (que juzgo irrefutable) no sé si me atreveré a añadir una cuarta, que condice muy bien con la casi divina modestia de Pierre Menard: su hábito resignado o irónico de propagar ideas que eran el estricto reverso de las preferidas por él. (Rememoremos otra vez su diatriba contra Paul Valéry en la efímera hoja superrealista de Jacques Reboul.) El texto de Cervantes y el de Menard son verbalmente idénticos, pero el segundo es casi infinitamente más rico. (Más ambiguo, dirán sus detractores; pero la ambigüedad es una riqueza.)

Es una revelación cotejar el *Don Quijote* de Menard con el de Cervantes. Éste, por ejemplo, escribió (Don Quijote, primera parte, noveno capítulo):

... la verdad, cuya madre es la historia, émula del tiempo, depósito de las acciones, testigo de lo pasado, ejemplo y aviso de lo presente, advertencia de lo por venir.

Redactada en el siglo diecisiete, redactada por el "ingenio lego" Cervantes, esa enumeración es un mero elogio retórico de la historia. Menard, en cambio, escribe:

... la verdad, cuya madre es la historia, émula del tiempo, depósito de las acciones, testigo de lo pasado, ejemplo y aviso de lo presente, advertencia de lo por venir.

La historia, *madre* de la verdad; la idea es asombrosa. Menard, contemporáneo de William James, no define la historia como una indagación de la realidad sino como su origen. La verdad histórica, para él, no es lo que sucedió; es lo que juzgamos que sucedió. Las cláusulas finales – *ejemplo y aviso de lo presente, advertencia de lo por venir* – son descaradamente pragmáticas. También es vívido el contraste de los estilos.

El estilo arcaizante de Menard – extranjero al fin – adolece de alguna afectación. No así el del precursor, que maneja con desenfado el español corriente de su época.

No hay ejercicio intelectual que no sea finalmente inútil. Una doctrina es al principio una descripción verosímil del universo; giran los años y es un mero capítulo – cuando no un párrafo o un nombre – de la historia de la filosofía. En la literatura, esa caducidad es aún más notoria. El Quijote – me dijo Menard – fue ante todo un libro agradable; ahora es una ocasión de brindis patriótico, de soberbia gramatical, de obscenas ediciones de lujo. La gloria es una incomprensión y quizá la peor.

Nada tienen de nuevo esas comprobaciones nihilistas; lo singular es la decisión que de ellas derivó Pierre Menard. Resolvió adelantarse a la vanidad que aguarda todas las fatigas del hombre; acometió una empresa complejísima y de antemano fútil. Dedicó sus escrúpulos y vigilias a repetir en un idioma ajeno un libro preexistente. Multiplicó los borradores; corrigió tenazmente y desgarró miles de páginas manuscritas.[3] No permitió que fueran examinadas por nadie y cuidó que no le sobrevivieran. En vano he procurado reconstruirlas.

He reflexionado que es lícito ver en el Quijote "final" una especie de palimpsesto, en el que deben traslucirse los rastros – Tenues pero no indescifrables – de la "previa" escritura de nuestro amigo. Desgraciadamente, sólo un segundo Pierre Menard, invirtiendo el trabajo del anterior, podría exhumar y resucitar esas Troyas …

"Pensar, analizar, inventar (me escribió también) no son actos anómalos, son la normal respiración de la inteligencia. Glorificar el ocasional cumplimiento de esa función, atesorar antiguos y ajenos pensamientos, recordar con incrédulo estupor que el *doctor universalis* pensó, es confesar nuestra languidez o nuestra barbarie. Todo hombre debe ser capaz de todas las ideas y entiendo que en el porvenir lo será."

Menard (acaso sin quererlo) ha enriquecido mediante una técnica nueva el arte detenido y rudimentario de la lectura: la técnica del anacronismo deliberado y de las atribuciones erróneas. Esa técnica de aplicación infinita nos insta a recorrer la *Odisea* como si fuera posterior a la *Eneida* y el libro *Le jardin du Centaure* de madame Henri Bachelier como si fuera de madame Henri Bachelier. Esa técnica puebla de aventura los libros más calmosos. Atribuir a Louis Ferdinand Céline o a James Joyce la *Imitación de Cristo* ¿no es una suficiente renovación de esos tenues avisos espirituales?

Nîmes, 1939

---

3 Recuerdo sus cuadernos cuadriculados, sus negras tachaduras, sus peculiares símbolos tipográficos y su letra de insecto. En los atardeceres le gustaba salir a caminar por los arrabales de Nîmes; solía llevar consigo un cuaderno y hacer una alegre fogata.

Pierre Menard, Author of the *Quixote*

JORGE LUIS BORGES

Translated from the Spanish by Ilan Stavans

A Silvina Ocampo

The visible oeuvre this novelist has left behind can be enumerated easily and briefly. Therefore, the unforgivable omissions and additions perpetrated by Madame Henri Bachelier in a fake catalog published in a certain newspaper with a *Protestant* tendency that isn't a secret has had the unpleasant impact on its deplorable readers, although these are few and Calvinist, if not masons and circumcised. Menard's authentic friends have seen this catalog with alarm and even certain sadness. Let us say we gathered yesterday around the final ivory and among the ill-fated cypresses and error is already trying to fog memory. Decidedly, a brief rectification is inevitable.

I'm aware that it's easy to recuse my poor authority. I hope, however, I won't be forgiven from mentioning two high testimonies. The Bacourt Baroness (in whose unforgettable *vendredis* I had the fortune to know the lamented poet) has graciously approved the following lines. The Bagnoregio Countess, one of the most refined spirits of the Monaco principality (and now of Pittsburgh, Pennsylvania, after her recent wedding with the international philanthropist Simon Kautzsch, so frequently libeled, ah!, by the victims of his disinterested efforts), has sacrificed, "to veracity and to death" (these are her words), the dandy-like reserve that characterizes her and, in an open letter published in the magazine *Luxe*, she likewise conceded me the consent. Those judgements, I believe, aren't insufficient.

I have said that Menard's visible oeuvre is of easy enumeration. Having examined with care his particular archive, I have verified that it includes the following items:

a) A symbolist sonnet that appeared twice (with variations) in the magazine *La Conque* (issues of March and October of 1899).
b) A monograph about the possibility of building a poetic lexicon of concepts that are not synonymous or periphrasis of those who inform the common language, "without ideal objects created by a convention or essentially destined to poetic necessities" (Nîmes, 1901).

c) A monograph about "certain connections and affinities" of Descartes', Leibniz's, and John Wilkins' thought (Nîmes, 1903).
d) A monograph on the *Characteristica Universalis* by Leibniz (Nîmes, 1904).
e) A technical article on the possibilities of enriching the game of chess, eliminating one of the tower pieces. Menard proposes, recommends, discusses and ends by rejecting that innovation.
f) A monograph on the *Ars Magna Generalis* by Raimund Lull (Nîmes, 1906).
g) A translation with a prologue and notes of the *Libro de la invención liberal y arte del juego del axedrez* by Ruy López de Segura (Paris, 1907).
h) The drafts of a monograph on George Boole's symbolic logic.
i) An exam of the metrical laws of French prose, illustrated with volumes by Saint Simon (*Revue des Langues Romanes*, Montpellier, October of 1909).
j) A reply to Luc Durtain (who had negated the existence of such laws) illustrated with volumes by Luc Duratin (*Revue des Langues Romanes*, Montpellier, December of 1909).
k) A handwritten translation of *Aguja de navegar cultos* by Quevedo, titled *La Boussole des précieux*.
l) A preface to a catalog of the exhibition of lithographs by Carolus Hourcade (Nîmes, 1914).
m) The work *Les Problèmes d'un problème* (Paris, 1917), which discusses, in chronological order, the solutions to the illustrious problem of Aquiles and the turtle. Two editions of this book have appeared so far; the second one includes, as an epigraph, Leibniz's advice *Ne craignez point, monsieur, la tortue,* and renews the chapters devoted to Russell and Descartes.
n) An obstinate analysis of Toulet's "syntactical customs" (N.R.F., March of 1921). I remember Menard declaring that censoring and celebrating are sentimental operations that have nothing to do with criticism.
o) A transposition of alexandrines of Paul Valéry's *Cimetière marin* (N.R.F., January of 1928).
p) An invective on Paul Valéry, in Jacques Reboul's *Hojas para la supresión de la realidad*. (Such invective, it ought to be said parenthetically, is the exact reverse of Valéry's true opinion. He understood it thus and the old friendship between the two of them didn't run any risk.)

q) A "definition" by the Bagnoregio Countess. In the "victorious volume" the locution is by another collaborator, Gabriele D'Annunzio, which this lady publishes annually to rectify the inevitable stumbles of journalism and to present "to the world and to Italy" an authentic effigy of her own persona, so exposed (in due course of her beauty and her histrionics) to quick and erroneous interpretations.
r) A cycle of admirable sonnets by the Bacourt Baroness (1934).
s) A handwritten list of verses whose efficacy is owed to punctuation.[1]

This is the full extent (without any other omission but some vague circumstantial sonnets for hospitable, and avid, album by Madame Henry Bachelier) of Menard's *visible* oeuvre, in chronological order. I now move to the other one: the subterranean, the unendingly heroic, the unparalleled. Likewise, ah, of human possibilities!, the unfinished one. This oeuvre, perhaps the most significant of our time, is made of the ninth and thirty-eighth of the First Part of *Don Quixote*, and of a fragment of chapter twenty-two. I know such affirmation appears like an absurdity; to justify that "absurdity" is the primary objective of this note.[2]

Two texts of unequal value inspired such an enterprise. One is that philological fragment by Novalis – the one that carries the number 2005 in the Dresden edition – which sketches the theme of *total identification* with a given author. Another is one of those parasitic books that place Christ in a boulevard, Hamlet in the Cannebiére, or Don Quixote on Wall Street. Like any man of good taste, Menard abominated such useless carnivals, only aptly he would say to the occasional plebeian pleasure of anachronism or (which is worse) to captivate us with the prime idea that all epochs are the same or that they are different. More interestingly, although of contradictory and superficial execution, he believed Daudet's famous purpose to be to conjure in a figure, meaning Tartarín, the Ingenious Hidalgo and his squire ... Those who insinuate that Menard spent his life writing a contemporary Quixote libel his clear memory.

---

1 Madame Henri Bachelier likewise lists a literal version Quevedo made of *Introduction à la vie dévote* by Saint Francis de Sales. In Pierre Menard's library there are no traces of that work. It must be our friend's joke, poorly conveyed.
2 I also had the secondary purpose of sketching Pierre Menard's image. But how should I dare compete with the aural pages I am told Baroness Bacourt is preparing or with Carolus Hourcade's delicate and punctual pencil?

He didn't want to make another Quixote – which is easy – but the *Quixote*. It is useless to add that he never confronted a mechanical transcription of the original; he didn't intent to copy it. His admirable ambition was to produce a few pages that coincided, word by word and line by line, with those by Miguel de Cervantes.

"My purpose is merely astounding," he wrote to me on September 20, of 1934, from Bayonne. "The final term of a theological or metaphysical demonstration – the external world, God, causality, the universal forms – isn't less untimely and common than the well-divulged novel. The only difference is that philosophers publish agreeable volumes in intermediary stages of their labor and that I have resolved to lose them." Indeed, not a single draft remains that testifies to that work of years.

The initial method he imagined is relatively simple. To know Spanish well, to recover the Catholic faith, to fight the Moors and against the Turk, to forget the history of Europe between 1602 and 1918, *to be* Miguel de Cervantes. Pierre Menard studied that procedure (I know he achieved a fairly loyal handling of the Spanish of the seventeenth century) but ruled it out because it was easy. Or rather, because it was impossible, the reader might say. It's true, but the enterprise was impossible from the start and of all the means to achieve it, this was the least interesting. In his opinion, to be in the twentieth century a popular novelist in the seventeenth was a diminishment. He deemed less arduous – and, consequently, less interesting – to somehow be Cervantes and arrive to the Quixote than to continue to be Menard and arrive to the Quixote through Pierre Menard's experiences. (That conviction, it ought to be said, made him exclude the autobiographical prologue to the Second Part of *Don Quixote*. To include that prologue would have entailed creating another character – Cervantes – but it would have also signified presenting the Quixote in relation to that character and not to Menard. He, naturally, rejected such an easy route.) "Essentially, my enterprise isn't difficult," I read in another place of his letter. "It would be enough to be immortal in order to achieve it." Shall I confess that I often imagine that he finished it and that I read the *Quixote* – the entire *Quixote* – as if Menard had thought it? A few nights ago, browsing chapter XXVI – never rehearsed by him – I recognized our friend's style and something like his voice in this exceptional phrase: *las ninfas de los ríos, la dolorosa y húmida Eco*. This efficacious conjunction of a moral adjective and another physical one brought to my memory Shakespeare's verse, which we discussed one afternoon:

> *Where a malignant and a turbaned Turk ...*

Why precisely the Quixote? Our reader will say. That preference, in Spanish, would not have been inexplicable; yet it doubtlessly is to a symbolist from Nîmes, an essential fan of Poe, who begat Baudelaire, who begat Mallarmé, who begat Valéry. Who begat Edmond Teste. The above-quoted letter illuminates this point. "The Quixote," Menard clarifies, "interested me deeply, but it doesn't appear to me, how shall I say, inevitable. I cannot imagine the universe without Edgar Allan Poe's interjections:

Ah, bear in mind this garden was enchanted!

or without the *Bateau ivre* or the *Ancient Mariner*, but I'm capable of imagining it without the Quixote. (I speak, naturally, of my personal capacity, not of the historical resonance of the works.) The Quixote is a contingent book, the Quixote is unnecessary. I can premeditate its writing, I can write it, without incurring a tautology. I read it when I was twelve or thirteen years old, perhaps completely. Afterward, I have read with attention some chapters, those I will not deal with now. I have also studied the *entremeses*, the *comedias*, the *Galatea*, the *Novelas ejemplares*, the no doubt laborious works of *Persiles y Segismunda* and the *Viaje al Parnaso* ... My general recollection of the Quixote, simplified by forgetfulness and indifference, might well correspond to the imprecise previous image of a book not written. Once this image is postulated (which no one in good measure can deny me) it is indisputable that my problem is far more difficult than Cervantes'. My complacent precursor didn't reject the contribution of chance: he was shaping the immortal work a bit *à la diable*, carried by the inertia of language and invention. I have contracted the mysterious duty of constructing literally his spontaneous oeuvre. My solitary game is governed by two polar laws. The first one allows me to rehearse variants which are of a formal and psychological type; the second forces me to sacrifice the 'original' text and to reason in an irrefutable way that annihilation ... To these artificial obstacles one must add another congenital one. To compose the Quixote at the beginning of the seventeenth century is a reasonable, necessary, and perhaps fatal enterprise; at the beginning of the twentieth, it is almost impossible. Not in vain have three hundred years gone by, endowed with very complex events. Among them, to mention only one: the very same Quixote."

In spite of these three obstacles, Menard's fragmentary Quixote is subtler than Cervantes'. The latter, in a clumsy way, opposes to the chivalry fictions his country's poor provincial reality; Menard choses as "reality: the land of Carmen during the century of Lepanto and Lope. What Spanish tricks Maurice Barrès and Doctor Rodríguez Larretta wouldn't have advised! Menard, with every natural quality, eludes them. There are no gypsy tricks or conquistadors or mystics or Philip II or autos-da-fé in his oeuvre. He either disattends or proscribes the local color. This disdain indicates a new sense of the historical novel. This disdain condemns *Salammbô* without appeal.

Not less stunning is to consider isolated chapters. For example, let us examine XXXVIII of the First Part, "which deals with the curious discourse Don Quixote made on the arms and the letters." It is known that Don Quixote (like Quevedo in the analogous passage, and after, in *La hora de todos*) resolved the dispute against the letters and in favor of the arms. Cervantes was an old soldier: his choice can be explained. But that the Don Quixote of Pierre Menard – contemporaneous of *La trahison des clercs* and of Bertrand Russell – relapses in these nebulous sophistries! Madame Bachelier has seen in them an admirable and typical subordination of the author to the hero's psychology; others (in no way perspicaciously) a *transcription* of the Quixote; the Bacourt Baroness, Nietzsche's influence. To this third interpretation (which I judge irrefutable) I don't know if I will dare to add a fourth one, which leads well to Pierre Menard's almost divine modesty: his resigned or ironic habit to propagate ideas that were the strict reverse of those he preferred. (Let's recall again his diatribe against Paul Valéry in the ephemeral page by Jacques Reboul.) The texts by Cervantes and Menard are verbally identical, but the second is almost infinitely richer. (More ambiguous, his detractors will say; but ambiguity is wealth.)

It's a revelation to compare the *Don Quixote* by Menard with that of Cervantes. The latter, for instance, wrote (*Don Quixote*, First part, ninth chapter):

> ... *truth, whose mother is history, rival to time, storehouse of deeds, witness for the past, example and counsel for the present, and warning for the future.*

Redacted in the seventeenth century, redacted by the "ingenious layman" Cervantes, this enumeration is a mere rhetorical praise of history. Menard, instead, writes:

> ... *truth, whose mother is history, rival to time, storehouse of deeds, witness for the past, example and counsel for the present, and warning for the future.*

History, *mother* of truth; the idea is astonishing. Menard, a contemporary of William James, doesn't define history as an investigation of reality but as its origin. The true history, for him, isn't what happened; it is what we judge that happened. The final clauses – *ejemplo y aviso de lo presente, advertencia de lo por venir* – are shamelessly pragmatic.

Vivid is also the contrast of styles. Menard's archaizing style – a foreigner, after all – suffers from some affectation. It isn't the case of his precursor, who handles with ease the common Spanish of his epoch.

There is no intellectual exercise that isn't in the end useless. A doctrine is at the beginning a plausible description of reality; years go by and it is a mere chapter – if not a paragraph or a name – in the history of philosophy. In literature, that expiration date is even more noticeable. The Quixote – Menard told me – was first and foremost an enjoyable book; now it's the occasion of a patriotic toast, of grammatical pride, of obscene luxury editions. Glory is an incomprehension and perhaps the worst.

There is nothing new in these nihilist proofs; what is singular is the decision Pierre Menard derived from them. He resolved to be ahead of the vanity that awaits all human toil; he embarked on a very complex enterprise which was futile from the start. He dedicated his scruples and wakefulness to repeat in someone else's language a pre-existing book. He multiplied the drafts; he tenaciously corrected and tore up thousands of handwritten pages.[3] He didn't allow anyone to examine them and he made sure they didn't survive him. I have attempted in vain to reconstruct them.

I've reflected that it's licit to see in the "final" Quixote a kind of palimpsest, in which the traces – tenuous but not indecipherable – must show up the "previous" writing of our friend. Unfortunately, only a second Pierre Menard, investing in the work of the previous one, could exhume and resuscitate those Troys …

"To think, to analyze, to invent (he also wrote to me) aren't anomalous acts, they are the normal respiration of intelligence. To glorify the occasional fulfillment of that function, to treasure old and foreign thoughts, to remember with incredulous stupor what the *doctor universalis* thought, is to confess our listlessness or our barbarism. Every human must be capable of all the ideas and I understand that in the future that will be the case."

Menard (perhaps without wanting it) has enriched, through a new technique, the sustained and rudimentary art of reading: the technique of the deliberate anachronism and of the erroneous attributions. That technique of infinite application encourages us to go through the *Odyssey* as if it was composed after the *Aeneid* and the book *Le jardin du Centaure* by Madame Henri Bachelier as if it was by Madame Henri Bachelier. This technique populates the adventure of the calmest books. To attribute to Louis Ferdinand Céline or to James Joyce the *Imitation of Christ*, isn't it sufficient renovation of those tenuous spiritual advices?

Nîmes, 1939

---

3 I remember his notebooks, his black cross-outs, his peculiar typographic symbols, and insect-like letters. He liked going for walks in the afternoon in the neighborhoods of Nîmes; he used to take a notebook with him and make a happy bonfire.

Pierre Menard, auteur du *Quichotte*

JORGE LUIS BORGES

Traduit de l'espagnol par Youssef Boucetta

À Silvina Ocampo

L'œuvre visible qu'a laissé ce romancier est facile et brève à énumérer. Sont alors impardonnables les omissions et additions perpétrées par Madame Henri Bachelier, dans un catalogue fallacieux, qu'un certain journal, dont la tendance protestante n'est pas un secret, a eu la déconsidération de transmettre à ses déplorables lecteurs – bien qu'ils soient peu nombreux et calvinistes quand ils ne sont pas maçons et circoncis. Les amis authentiques de Menard ont été alarmés par la vue de ce catalogue et même atteints par une certaine tristesse. Il semblerait que nous nous soyons réunis hier devant le marbre final et entre les malheureux cyprès et déjà l'Erreur tente de ternir sa Mémoire… Décidemment, une brève rectification est inévitable.

Je comprends qu'il soit très facile de contester ma pauvre autorité. J'espère cependant, que vous ne m'interdirez pas la mention de deux hauts témoignages. La baronne de Bacourt (chez qui j'ai eu l'honneur de connaître le regretté poète grâce aux inoubliables *vendredis*) a bien voulu approuver les lignes qui suivent. La comtesse de Bagnoregio, un des esprits les plus fins de la principauté de Monaco (et maintenant de Pittsburgh, Pennsylvanie, après son récent mariage avec le philanthrope international Simon Kautzsch, tellement calomnié, Ô ! par les victimes de ses manœuvres désintéressées) a sacrifiée « à la véracité et à la mort » (tels sont ses propres mots) la réserve seigneuriale qui la distingue, et, dans une lettre ouverte publiée dans le magazine *Luxe*, m'a ainsi concédé son aval. Ces jugements exécutoires, il me semble, ne sont pas insuffisants.

J'ai dit que l'œuvre *visible* de Menard est facilement énumérable. Ayant examiné avec soin ses archives particulières, j'ai vérifié qu'elles comprennent les pièces suivantes :

a) Un sonnet symboliste qui est paru deux fois (avec certaines variations) dans la revue *La conque* (numéros de Mars et Octobre 1899).
b) Une monographie sur la possibilité de construction d'un vocabulaire poétique de concepts, qui ne sont ni synonymes ni périphrases de ceux qui forment le langage commun, « mais des objets

idéaux crées par convention et essentiellement destinés aux nécessités poétiques » (Nîmes, 1901).
c) Une monographie sur « certaines connexions et/ou affinités » de la pensée de Descartes, Leibniz et John Wilkins (Nîmes, 1903).
d) Une monographie sur la *Characteristica universalis* de Leibniz (Nîmes, 1903)
e) Un article technique sur la possibilité d'enrichir les échecs en éliminant l'un des pions des tours. Menard propose, recommande, conteste et finit par refuser cette innovation.
f) Une monographie sur l'*Ars magna generalis* de Ramon Llull (Nîmes, 1906).
g) Une traduction avec prologue et notes du *Livre sur l'invention libérale et l'art du jeu d'échecs* de Ruy Lopez de Segura (Paris, 1907).
h) Les brouillons d'une monographie sur la logique symbolique de George Boole.
i) Un examen des lois métriques essentielles de la prose française, illustré avec des exemples de Saint-Simon (*Revue des langues romanes*, Montpellier, Décembre 1909).
j) Une réponse à Luc Durtain (qui a nié l'existence de telles lois) illustrée avec des exemples de Luc Durtain (*Revue des langues romanes*, Montpellier, Décembre 1909).
k) Une traduction manuscrite de l'*Aguja para navegar cultos* de Quevedo, intitulée *La boussole des précieux*.
l) Une préface au catalogue de l'exposition de lithographies de Carolus Hourcade (Nîmes, 1914).
m) L'œuvre *Les problèmes d'un problème* (Paris, 1917) qui débat, en ordre chronologique, sur les solutions de l'illustre problème d'Achille et la tortue. Deux éditions de ce livre sont parues jusqu'à aujourd'hui ; la deuxième a pour épigraphe le conseil de Leibniz *ne craignez point, monsieur, la tortue,* et renouvelle les chapitres dédiés à Russell et à Descartes.
n) Une analyse obstinée des « coutumes syntaxiques » de Toulet (N.R.F, mars 1921). Menard – je me souviens – déclarait que la censure et l'éloge sont des opérations sentimentales qui n'ont rien à voir avec la critique.
o) Une transposition en alexandrins du *Cimetière marin* de Paul Valéry (N.R.F, janvier 1928)
p) Une invective contre Paul Valéry, dans les *Feuilles pour la suppression de la réalité* de Jacques Reboul. (Cette invective, soit dit entre parenthèses, est l'inverse exact de sa véritable opinion sur Valéry. Ce dernier l'a comprise ainsi, et leur vieille amitié n'en a pas été menacée).

q) Une définition de la comtesse de Bagnoregio, dans le « victorieux volume » – la locution vient d'un autre collaborateur, Gabriele d'Annunzio- que publie annuellement cette dame pour rectifier les inévitables faussetés du –ournalisme et afin de présenter « au monde entier et à l'Italie » l'effigie authentique de sa personne, tant exposée (en raison même de sa beauté et sa performativité) a des interprétations erronées où précipitées.
r) Un cycle d'admirables sonnets pour la baronne de Bacourt (1934).
s) Une liste manuscrite de vers qui doivent leur efficacité à la ponctuation.[1]

C'est, jusque là (sans autre omission que quelques vagues sonnets circonstanciels pour l'album avide ou hospitalier de Madame Henri Bachelier) l'œuvre *visible* de Menard, dans son ordre chronologique. Je passe maintenant à l'autre, la souterraine, l'interminablement héroïque, l'hors pair. Aussi, l'inachevée. Ô les possibilités de l'homme ! Cette œuvre, peut-être la plus significative de notre temps, compte les chapitres IX et XXXVIII de la première partie de *Don Quichotte*, et un extrait du chapitre XXII. Je sais qu'une telle affirmation paraît absurde ; justifier cette « absurdité » est l'objectif primordial de cette note.[2]

Deux textes de valeur inégale ont inspiré cette entreprise. L'un est l'extrait philologique de Novalis – celui qui porte le numéro 2005 dans l'édition de Dresde – qui esquisse le thème de *l'identification totale* avec un auteur donné. L'autre fait partie de ces livres parasites qui situent le Christ dans un boulevard, Hamlet à la Cannebière, ou Don Quichotte à Wall Street. Comme tout homme de bon goût, Menard avait horreur de ces carnavals inutiles, aptes uniquement – disait-il – à réveiller le plaisir plébéien de l'anachronisme, ou encore (chose pire), pour nous éblouir par l'idée primaire que toutes les époques sont les mêmes, ou qu'elles sont différentes. Plus intéressante que cela, bien qu'exécutée de façon contradictoire et superficielle, lui paraissait la fameuse mission de Daudet, conjuguer en *une* figure qu'est Tartarin, l'hidalgo ingénieux et

---

1 Madame Henri Bachelier énumère également une version littérale de la version littérale de Quevedo de l'Introduction à la vie dévote de saint François de Sales. Dans la bibliothèque de Pierre Ménard il n'y a aucune trace d'un tel ouvrage. Ce doit être une blague de notre ami, mal entendue.
2 J'ai aussi eu comme propos secondaire de faire une ébauche de l'image de Pierre Menard. Mais comment oser rentrer en compétition avec les pages dorées préparées, m'a-t-on dit, par la Baronne de Bacourt ou avec la plume délicate et appliquée de Carolus Hourcade?

son écuyer… Ceux qui ont insinué que Menard a dédié sa vie à écrire un Quichotte contemporain, calomnient sa mémoire claire.

Il ne voulait pas composer un autre Quichotte – chose qui est facile – mais *le Quichotte*. Inutile de rajouter qu'il n'a jamais fait face à une transcription mécanique de l'original ; il ne se donnait pas comme objectif de le copier. Son admirable ambition était de produire des pages qui coïncideraient – mot pour mot et ligne pour ligne – avec celles de Miguel de Cervantes. « Mon but est tout simplement formidable » m'écrivait-t-il le 30 septembre 1934 depuis Bayonne. « Le terme final d'une démonstration théologique ou métaphysique – le monde extérieur, Dieu, le hasard, les formes universelles – n'est pas moins antérieur et commun que mon roman divulgué. La seule différence est que les philosophes publient dans des volumes agréables les étapes intermédiaires de leur labeur, et que, pour ma part, je me suis résolu à les perdre ». En effet, il n'y a plus un seul brouillon qui témoigne de ce travail de plusieurs années.

La méthode initiale qu'il a imaginé était relativement simple. Bien connaître l'espagnol, reprendre la foi catholique, faire la guerre aux maures ou au turc, oublier l'histoire de l'Europe entre l'an 1602 et l'an 1918, *être* Miguel de Cervantes. Pierre Menard a étudié ce processus (je sais qu'il a atteint une maîtrise assez fidèle de l'espagnol du XVIIème) mais il l'a mis de côté car il s'est avéré être trop facile. Plutôt impossible ! dirait le lecteur. D'accord, mais l'entreprise était impossible à la base, et d'entre tous les moyens impossibles pour la mener à bout, celui-ci était le moins intéressant. Être au XXème siècle un romancier populaire du XVIIème lui paraissait être une réduction. Être, d'une certaine façon, Cervantes et arriver au *Quichotte* lui paraissait moins ardu – par conséquent, moins intéressant – que continuer à être Pierre Menard et arriver au *Quichotte*, au travers des expériences de Pierre Menard. (Cette conviction, soit dit en passant, lui à fait exclure le prologue autobiographique de la deuxième partie de *Don Quichotte*. Inclure ce prologue aurait signifié créer un nouveau personnage – Cervantes – mais cela aurait également signifié présenter le *Quichotte* en fonction de ce personnage et pas de Menard. Ce dernier a naturellement renié cette facilité.) « Mon entreprise n'est pas essentiellement difficile », je lis dans un autre emplacement de sa lettre. « Il me suffirait d'être immortel pour la mener à bout. » Devrais-je confesser qu'il m'arrive d'imaginer qu'il l'a finie et que je lis le *Quichotte* – tout le *Quichotte* – comme s'il avait été pensé par Menard ? Il y a quelques nuits, en feuilletant le chapitre XXVI – jamais essayé par lui – j'ai reconnu le style de notre ami et presque sa voix dans cette phrase exceptionnelle : *les nymphes des rivières, l'Écho douloureuse et humide*. Cette conjonction efficace d'un adjectif moral et d'un adjectif physique m'a remémoré un vers de Shakespeare, que nous avions discuté un après midi:

> *Where a malignant and a turbaned Turk …*

Pourquoi précisément le *Quichotte* ? Dirait notre lecteur. Cette préférence, chez un espagnol, n'aurait pas été inexplicable ; mais elle l'est pour un symboliste de Nîmes, adepte de Poe, qui a engendré Baudelaire, qui a engendré Mallarmé, qui a engendré Valéry, qui a engendré Edmond Teste. La lettre précitée illumine ce point. « Le *Quichotte* », précise Menard, « m'intéresse profondément, mais ne me semble pas, comment dirais-je ? inévitable. Je ne peux imaginer l'univers sans l'interjection de Poe :

> *Ah, bear in mind this garden was enchanted!*

Ou sans le *Bateau ivre* ou l'*Ancient Mariner*, mais je peux l'imaginer sans le *Quichotte*. (Je parle, naturellement, de ma capacité personnelle, pas de la résonance historique des œuvres.) Le *Quichotte* est un livre contingent, le *Quichotte* n'est pas nécessaire. Je peux préméditer son écriture, je peux l'écrire, sans me retrouver dans une tautologie. A douze ou treize ans je l'ai lu, peut être intégralement. Après j'ai relu avec attention certains chapitres, ceux que je n'essaierai pas pour le moment. J'ai étudié les entremets, les comédies, la *Galatée*, les *Nouvelles exemplaires*, les travaux sans doute laborieux de *Persille et Sigismond* et le *Voyage au Parnasse*… Mon souvenir général du *Quichotte*, simplifié par l'oubli et l'indifférence, peut très bien équivaloir à l'image imprécise, antérieure à l'écriture d'un livre. Une fois cette image postulée (que personne de bon aloi ne peut me refuser), il est indiscutable que mon problème est infiniment plus difficile que celui de Cervantes. Mon précurseur dans sa complaisance n'a pas refusé la collaboration du hasard : il composait l'œuvre immortelle un peu *à la diable,* poussé par les inerties du langage et de l'invention. Pour ma part, j'ai contracté le mystérieux devoir de reconstruire littéralement son œuvre spontanée. Mon jeu solitaire est gouverné par deux lois polaires. La première me permet d'essayer certaines variantes d'ordre formel ou psychologique; la deuxième m'oblige à les sacrifier au texte 'original' et à raisonner cet anéantissement d'une façon irréfutable. À ces obstacles artificiels, il faut en rajouter un autre, congénital. Composer le *Quichotte* au début du XVIIème siècle était une entreprise raisonnable, nécessaire, peut être fatale; au début du XXème, cela est pratiquement impossible. Trois-cent ans chargés de faits extrêmement complexes ne se sont pas écoulés en vain. Entre eux, pour en mentionner un seul : le *Quichotte* même. »

Malgré ces trois obstacles, le *Quichotte* fragmentaire de Menard est plus subtil que celui de Cervantes. Ce dernier, de façon grossière, oppose les fictions chevaleresques à la pauvre réalité provinciale de son pays; Menard choisit comme « réalité » la terre de Carmen pendant le siècle de Lépante et de Lope. Quelles espagnolades n'aurait conseillé ce choix à Maurice Barrès ou au docteur Rodriguez Larreta ! Menard, tout naturellement, les contourne. Dans son œuvre il n'y a ni gitaneries, ni conquistadors, ni mystiques, ni Philippe II, ni autodafés. Elle ignore ou proscrit les couleurs locales. Ce dédain indique un nouveau sentiment du roman historique. Ce dédain condamne *Salammbô*, inévitablement.

Il n'est pas moins incroyable de considérer des chapitres isolés. Par exemple, examinons le XXVIIIème de la première partie, « qui traite du curieux discours qu'a donné Don Quichotte sur les armes et les lettres ». Il est connu que Don Quichotte (tout comme Quevedo dans le passage analogue et postérieur de *L'heure de tous*) échoue dans le plaidoyer contre les lettres et en faveur des armes. Cervantes était un ancien militaire : sa défaite s'explique. Mais que le Don Quichotte de Pierre Menard – contemporain de *La trahison des clercs* et de Bertrand Russell – récidive dans cette sophistique nébuleuse ! Madame Bachelier y a vu une admirable et typique subordination de l'auteur à la psychologie du héros; d'autres (sans perspicacité) ont vu une *transcription* du Quichotte; la baronne de Bacourt y a vu l'influence de Nietzsche. À cette troisième interprétation (que je juge irréfutable) je ne sais pas si j'oserais rajouter une quatrième, qui coïncide très bien avec la modestie presque divine de Pierre Menard : son habitude résignée ou ironique de propager des idées qui étaient le strict contraire de celles qu'il préférait. (Rappelons-nous une autre fois de sa diatribe contre Paul Valéry dans la feuille éphémère et surréaliste de Jacques Reboul.) Le texte de Cervantes et celui de Menard sont verbalement identiques, mais le second est presque infiniment plus riche. (Plus ambigu diront ses détracteurs, mais l'ambiguïté est une richesse.)

C'est une révélation que de confronter le *Don Quichotte* de Menard à celui de Cervantes. Ce dernier, par exemple, a écrit (*Don Quichotte*, première partie, chapitre IX) :

> … *la vérité, qui a pour mère l'histoire, émule du temps, dépôt des actions, Témoin du passé, exemple et préavis du présent, avertissement de l'avenir.*

Rédigée au XVIIème, par l'ingénieux ignorant qu'était Cervantes, cette énumération n'est que le simple éloge rhétorique de l'histoire. Menard, par contre, écrit:

> ... la vérité, qui a pour mère l'histoire, émule du temps, dépôt des actions, Témoin du passé, exemple et préavis du présent, avertissement de l'avenir.

L'histoire, *mère* de la vérité, l'idée est merveilleuse. Menard, contemporain de William James, ne définit pas l'histoire comme la recherche de la réalité mais comme son origine. La vérité historique, pour lui, n'est pas ce qui s'est passé; mais comment l'on juge que cela s'est passé. Les clauses finales – *exemple et préavis du présent, avertissement de l'avenir* – sont d'un pragmatisme désarmant. On y perçoit aussi le contraste des styles. Le style archaïsant de Menard – en fin de compte étranger – n'est atteint d'aucune affectation. Celui de son précurseur diffère, maniant avec désinvolture l'espagnol courant de son époque.

Il n'y a pas d'exercice intellectuel qui ne soit finalement inutile. Une doctrine philosophique est au début une description plausible de l'univers; les années passent et c'est un simple chapitre – quand ce n'est pas un paragraphe ou un nom – de l'histoire de la philosophie. Dans la littérature, cette caducité finale est d'autant plus notoire. « Le *Quichotte* » m'a dit Menard « était avant tout un livre agréable ; il est maintenant l'occasion de toasts patriotiques, d'orgueil grammatical, d'obscènes éditions de luxe. La gloire est une incompréhension, peut-être la pire. »

Il n'y a rien de nouveau dans ses constats nihilistes; ce qu'il y a de singulier se trouve dans la décision qu'en a tiré Pierre Menard. Il s'est résolu à être en avance sur la vanité qui accompagne les fatigues de l'homme; il s'est adonné à une entreprise extrêmement complexe et d'avance futile. Il a dédié sa méticulosité et des nuits entières à répéter, dans une langue étrangère, un livre déjà existant. Il a multiplié les brouillons; il a tenacement corrigé et arraché des milliers de pages manuscrites.[3] Il n'a pas permis qu'elles soient examinées par qui que ce soit et il a bien fait attention à ce qu'elles ne vivent pas plus que lui. En vain, j'ai tâché de les reconstruire.

J'ai pensé qu'il est licite de voir dans le *Quichotte* « final » une sorte de palimpseste, dans lequel transparaissent les traces – ténues mais pas indéchiffrables – de l'écriture « préalable » de notre ami. Hélas, seul un deuxième Pierre Menard, en inversant le travail de l'antérieur, pourrait exhumer et ressusciter ces Troies.

---

3 Je me rappelle de ses cahiers quadrillés, ses ratures noires, ses symboles typographiques particuliers et son écriture de fourmis. Dans l'après-midi, il aimait sortir se promener dans les faubourgs de Nîmes, il emportait habituellement avec lui un cahier et allumait un joyeux feu de bois.

« Penser, analyser, inventer (m'écrivait-t-il aussi) ne sont pas des actes anormaux, ils sont la respiration ordinaire de l'intelligence. Glorifier l'accomplissement occasionnel de cette fonction, thésauriser des pensées anciennes et étrangères à soi, se rappeler avec une stupeur incrédule ce que le *docteur universalis* pensait, c'est confesser notre langueur ou notre barbarisme. Tout homme doit être capable de toutes les idées et j'admets que dans l'avenir il le sera. »

Menard (peut être sans le vouloir) a enrichi au travers d'une nouvelle technique, l'art arrêté et rudimentaire de la lecture : la technique de l'anachronisme délibéré et des attributions erronées. Cette technique d'application infinie nous pousse à parcourir l'*Odyssée* comme si elle était postérieure à l'*Enéide* et le livre *Le jardin du Centaure* de Madame Henri Bachelier comme s'il était de Madame Henri Bachelier. Cette technique peuple d'aventures les livres les plus calmes. Attribuer à Louis Ferdinand Céline ou à James Joyce l'*Imitation du Christ* n'est-ce pas rénovation suffisante des faibles avis spirituels de cet ouvrage ?

Nîmes, 1939

Fernando Pessoa's Selves

If ever a writer was fated to bear a particular name, it was Fernando Pessoa. In Portuguese the word *pessoa* means "person"; in Latin it means "mask" or "character." Pessoa spent his life adopting personas, masks, and characters from almost the moment he began his writing career. These alternative personalities were still Pessoa, even when he signed his works under a pseudonym. Many of his alter egos were poets like himself, although only a few were Portuguese. One was an anti-Fascist Italian critic, another a psychiatrist, a third studied engineering; the others included monks, an assistant bookkeeper, a 19-year-old hunchbacked girl who suffered from tuberculosis, a translator of Portuguese literature into English, an inventor and solver of riddles, a French satirist, a toga-wearing lunatic obsessed with Greece who lived in an asylum, and even a Voodooist.

As Pessoa explained in 1928, "Pseudonymous works are by the author in his own person, except in the name he signs." His works were what he called "heteronymous"; they were "by the author" but "outside of his own person. They proceed from a full-fledged individual created by him, like the lines spoken by a character in a drama he might write." Pessoa's heteronyms were people with birthdays and deathdays; they had the whole gestalt – passions, fears, dreams, and clearly traced literary paths. As for him, he was a *fingidor*: a feigner, a pretender, an impostor who believed he could do "more in dreams than Napoleon."

Did Pessoa truly control his alter egos? Or did his creations, in fact, control him? The layers of identities and personalities that make up Pessoa's writing career are what draw readers in, and yet they also make it hard at times to have a sense of who he was and what kind of writer he aspired to be. The mystery of Pessoa is at the center of Richard Zenith's magnanimous new biography, which charts the author's life as well as the many lives he "performed" as he indulged in repeated "projections, spin-offs, or metamorphoses." Should we take seriously Pessoa's claim, which Zenith invites us to question, that "he had no personality of his own, that he was just a 'medium' for the many writers who welled up in him and whom he served as 'literary executor'"? Or, Zenith asks, should we see all of these eccentric scribblers as manifestations of Pessoa and the writer he sought to be – a true "they" inhabiting the "he"?

While scores of writers, from William Butler Yeats to Jorge Luis Borges, used pseudonyms or noms de plume, or else made writers their protagonists or created characters that were manifestations of their alternative personalities, very few have done so to such a degree as Pessoa. His most developed heteronyms were Alberto Caeiro, Ricardo Reis, and Álvaro de Campos, followed by dozens of others like Raphael Baldaya, Vicente Guedes, William Jinks, David Merrick, António Mora, Dr. Gaudêncio Nabos, Frederico Reis, Alexander Search, Bernardo Soares, Baron of Teive, António Mora, and Maria José. (Only the last of these was female.) Some wrote in Portuguese, while others delivered their poems, stories, philosophical studies, linguistic theories, self-analysis, automatic writing, or astrological charts in English or French.

It is no secret that Pessoa's work and that of his fictional writing partners are uneven. Some of his poems are superb. As a prose writer, he can write in a style that is luminous and hypnotizing, but not always. Part of the strangeness of Pessoa's career is that very few of his writings were published while he was alive. Only one of his books of Portuguese poetry, *Mensagem*, was published during his lifetime, even if he published much of his English-language poems in chapbooks. His magnum opus, *The Book of Disquiet*, was published posthumously in 1982 and comprises a galaxy of existential vignettes; Pessoa had left the manuscript in a state of disorder, which was likely not an accident. "To say that this is a book for which no definitive edition is possible," observes Zenith, who translated it in 2015, "would be a flagrant understatement were it not a conceptually erroneous statement, since there is no ur-book begging for definition." Instead, what Pessoa had produced was "a quintessential non-book: a large but uncertain quantity of discreet, mostly undated texts left in no sequential order, such that every published edition – inevitably depending on massive editorial intervention – is necessarily untrue to the nonexistent 'original.'" The same could be said of much of Pessoa's work, whether poems, stories, philosophical essays, or works of fiction.

Pessoa's experiments in form and substance were always bold and difficult. They were also not his alone. He was a representative, like Joyce, Proust, Woolf, Kafka, and Musil, of modernism. His unstable personality wasn't a symptom of schizophrenia but a statement of the anxiety at the heart of the modern sensibility: He was obsessed with being at a time when its meaning had become increasingly transient, precarious, dizzying, unmoored from the absolute truths that had once reigned uncontested. Pessoa's biggest, most vigorous response to this panoply of apprehensions isn't, in my view, the writing he channeled but himself – or the selves he articulated – as a creation.

Zenith, himself the owner of a symbolic last name, is a Boswell to Pessoa's Johnson. At 1,055 pages (the index alone runs for 20 pages, each divided into three columns), his biography, at least a decade in the making, is enviably researched and stylistically nuanced without being obnoxious in its information. In fact, it reads better than most, if not all, of Pessoa's oeuvre, as if Pessoa had exited the stage so that Zenith would finally be able to narrate his subject's many personalities and their vicissitudes. There have been, of course, other biographical investigations, among them João Gaspar Simões's in 1950. Yet no one has produced a richer work than Zenith has both as a scholar and as a translator.

When Pessoa died, at the age of 48, he left a huge trunk of manuscripts full of half-baked literary exercises. That, indeed, was his preferred form: He was prone to abandon enterprises midway, to discard projects filled with ambiguities, paradoxes, and inconsistencies, to leave things in a state of incompleteness. It is a tendency that makes him belong, at least tangentially, to the same club as Walter Benjamin, who was also known for his love of fragments, disconnected quotes, and scattered projects. For the biographer, however, this poses a Herculean task: It has taken decades for Zenith to sort through all the manuscripts, in part because only in the last few decades has Pessoa achieved the status of totemic world-class author, which has led not only to his canonization but also to a vast archival enterprise.

Zenith leads the reader commandingly through Pessoa's house of mirrors. Although his book could be said to be not one biography but many, in order to account for the almost infinite unwrapping of Pessoa's fictional personas, it is, necessarily, a map of his obsessions as well, though the writer is always seen in his historical, social, and aesthetic context. In other words, the book is also a narrative of Portugal as a modern nation whose colonial aspirations were coming to an end. We witness the tenuous control of Angola and Mozambique at the end of the 19th century, the democratic First Republic from 1910 to 1926, and, after a coup d'état, the *Ditadura Nacional* and *Estado Novo* that followed, orchestrated by the economist Antonio Oliveira Salazar, who first became a finance minister with sweeping powers in 1928 and then prime minister in 1932.

Salazar established a conservative, nationalist political regime that would last, through various incarnations, until the late 1960s and that became known for its acerbic anticommunism and its doctrine of *Lusotropicalism*, a term coined by Gilberto Freyre to describe imperial rule in the Portuguese colonies. The political upheavals that shaped Pessoa's day-to-day life give breadth to Zenith's story. His superb scholarship follows the emergence and death of each of the heteronyms, which cumulatively gives the impression that we are dealing with a cast of hundreds. It all reads very much like a novel – or several novels tied at the neck.

I first came across Pessoa as a young man in Mexico City, after reading Octavio Paz's 1961 essay on him, "El desconocido de sí mismo," which roughly translates as "The Man Who Unknew Himself." In it, Paz argues that Pessoa, through his artfulness, hid a crucial creative fact that characterized art in general: Artists use their work to find themselves, but seldom reach the right conclusion. Pessoa's approach was different: He recognized that the self is a void and decided to build a labyrinth around it, a game of mirrors in which the self is multiplied infinitely, thus postponing any concrete answers about what its essence is.

Some may be tempted to compare Pessoa to Borges, who enjoyed his own games with time, the self, and the infinite. Borges's essay "Borges and I" is an astonishing exercise in self-reconfiguration, in which Borges the person surrenders himself to Borges the author, or maybe the other way around. Yet neither of Borges's versions of himself can be more dissimilar from Pessoa's. Every single line by Borges – even the baroque ones he composed in his youth – seems deliberate, seeking syntactical perfection. Pessoa and his family of half-selves were anything but categorical; instead of revealing themselves in their work, they sought to disappear.

The writer in my view who more closely parallels Pessoa in his capacity to dissolve his own personality in those of his characters is Shakespeare. I don't intend to belabor here the trope of there having been a non-Shakespeare, as Freud, Henry James, Charlie Chaplin, Daphne du Maurier, and Helen Keller have suggested at various times. But what I think Shakespeare and Pessoa have in common is their dedication to character creation: Each produced a miscellany of heroes and villains, all with their own complex and contradictory inner universes. But more than that: Like Shakespeare's characters, Pessoa's were in many ways aspects of himself; to create them, he had to explore the very depths of his being.

To tell the life of any person takes more than patience. It requires sacrifice – the biographer must live vicariously through his subject. In reading *Pessoa*, I frequently had the impression that Zenith, to offer that much detail, had to disappear, to become Pessoa for a time. He divides the book into four parts. The first tells the story of Pessoa's early life. He was born in Lisbon in 1888 to a middle-class family. He lost his father at the age of 5 and soon after a brother, and by 1895 his mother had remarried a ship captain who was later named Portugal's consul in Durban, the capital of the British colony of Natal (later South Africa) – where, as it happens, Mahatma Gandhi was also living at the time. Pessoa and his mother followed the ship captain to Natal, where Pessoa attended the University of the Cape of Good Hope before returning to his native Lisbon in 1905.

In these early years, Pessoa took an interest in writing and created several of his best-known heteronyms: Ricardo Reis, who was supposedly born a year before Pessoa (José Saramago, the Portuguese Nobel Prize winner for literature in 1998, wrote the novel *The Year of the Death of Ricardo Reis,* focused exclusively on him); Alexander Search, who emerged as a writer of poems, essays, and stories in 1906; and Alberto Caeiro, whose first poems appeared in 1914, a couple of months before the appearance of yet another heteronym, Álvaro de Campos, and the initial odes of Reis. The beginnings of Pessoa's multilingualism (he knew French, English, and Spanish as well as Portuguese) stem from this period. It might be argued that the unfolding of alter egos was an unwrapping of tongues. That's what happens to polyglots: Different languages give place to a throng of personalities.

By 1918, Pessoa started publishing chapbooks of his English poems, which were favorably reviewed in the British press. This led him to the belief that he might be a successful publisher. His adventures on this front were disastrous. Of course, a disaster is sometimes more valuable than a triumph. For a while, Pessoa seemed to be constantly engaged in unsuccessful businesses, such as the publishing house Olisipo, founded in 1921, using family money without acknowledging his debt, and escaping all sorts of complicated personal situations that forced him to move from one apartment to another. Pessoa's *Luftmensch*-like life – tottering, embarking on one quixotic endeavor after another – was often that of a loner, although he was in love with a secretary, Ophelia Queiroz, but the relationship never quite reached consummation.

Pessoa's politics are hard to pin down. At times, as Zenith portrays him, he appears to have embraced the new right-wing politics that defined Salazar's Portugal and also Germany under Hitler. Yet these loyalties also seem feeble. At best, Pessoa was wishy-washy, switching ideological modes and psychological moods with ease. What is most relevant is that he was interested in occult topics: cabala, Rosicrucians, mysterious objects, spiritism, concocting lines of communication with specters whose cockamamie notions he and a few of his heteronyms adopted as a kind of creed. He had an obsession with symbols, linguistic formulas, conspiracies, mind reading, and clairvoyance. And he believed that all reality is dual in nature and that aspects of the world were only accessible to an elite group of people initiated in special practices.

This, to me, is Pessoa's most decisive side: his belief in supernatural forces. His support for certain fascist ideas was a symptom of his conviction that inner forces rule us and that, as a result, free will is sheer fiction. In his poetry, he articulated the conviction that spirits would visit him, a symphony of them, that he as a writer died in his own work. "I no longer include me in myself," he wrote in the poem "The Mommy," written in 1914. The various spirits had their own ideological systems, at times in opposition to Pessoa's.

Among Pessoa's most disturbing facets were his brushes with anti-Semitic texts as well as fascism. Again, Zenith, adoring as he is of his subject, walks a delicate line on this topic, though he does not flinch from confronting this aspect of Pessoa's writings. Under the aegis of Olisipo, Pessoa entertained the idea of publishing, in Portuguese translation, *The Protocols of the Elders of Zion*, a nefarious, fraudulent document that first circulated in Russia and purported to show that a global Jewish cabal was intent on controlling governments, business, and the media. Pessoa commissioned someone with the initials A.L.R., a writer about whom nothing else is known, to do the translation. In the end, nothing came of it.

The episode, however, was only one in a series in which Pessoa toyed with xenophobic, jingoistic literature, such as a booklet called *The Interregnum*, in which he defended military dictatorship as advisable for Portugal to find political stability. Yet part of Pessoa's mystery is that he was also said to be a direct descendant of Jews, and among his publishing adventures, he planned to issue a pamphlet – in Portuguese, English, and French – titled *The Jew Sociologically Considered*, because, in his view, Jewish themes were not sufficiently pondered in Portugal. The pamphlet never materialized either. If it had, it is possible it might have been anti-Semitic.

Arguably, Pessoa's golden period as a writer started in 1927, thanks to his collaboration with the arts and literary review *Presença*. His best work was produced in this period, including some of the most inspired passages of *The Book of Disquiet*, published in periodicals between 1929 and 1932. A few of his poems were translated into French, and his book *Mensagem* – the only volume of his Portuguese poetry to appear during his lifetime – was released in 1934. He was experiencing the type of success he had dreamed of for a long time. But this success was short-lived: In November 1935, he suffered from abdominal pain, was interned at a hospital in Lisbon, and died, likely of intestinal obstruction. His last words were in English: "I know not what to-morrow will bring." At the time of his burial, in Lisbon's Prazeres Cemetery, Pessoa was largely unknown, and so were his imaginary cohorts. In 1985 he would be disinterred, his remains set to rest in the nation's prime holy ground, the Cloister in the Jerónimos Monastery. It is fitting that he felt a kinship with Walt Whitman, whom, according to Zenith, Pessoa discovered in 1907 and to whom he "hardly knew how to react."

"Song of Myself" (1855), in its vision, is Pessoan. Or perhaps more accurately, Pessoa was Whitmanian. Whitman's straightforward exuberance was the opposite of Pessoa's baroque disguises. Still, Whitman – himself a larger-than-life personality – was delighted, as he put it, to resist any effort at being constrained. The same is true of Pessoa.

– *The Nation*, June 15–22, 2022

On Borges' Blindness
(with Max Ubelaker Andrade)

MAX UBELAKER ANDRADE: Jorge Luis Borges opens his poem "Yo" ("I," *La rosa profuna*, 1975) with a list of various parts that might be imagined as "his": "La calavera, el corazón secreto, los caminos de sangre que no veo, / los túneles del sueño, ese Proteo, / las vísceras, la nuca, el esqueleto" (The skull, the secret heart, / the paths of blood that I do not see, / the tunnels of dreams, that Proteus, / the viscera, the nape, the skeleton). The poem affirms: "Soy esas cosas" (I am those things).

It can take a moment for the sighted reader to notice how all of these words refer to parts of their own self that exist (for them) always out of view: unseen, in any direct way, they must be imagined into existence. It is a poem that can serve as a gentle reminder of how effortless and natural it is to not see, how normal, even when it comes to parts of ourselves that are incredibly familiar and intimately close. The poem expands on this idea to include memories that the mind must compose (non-optically) as well as an evocation of gazing out at ships from a port (perhaps as a memory, when Borges could see them, or perhaps at the time of writing the poem, when he could not). It suggests, finally, that while it is strange that the self would be composed of so many disparate, imagined elements, stranger still is being someone who weaves words together in the room of a house.

The profound strangeness of reading and writing (two acts which seem to overlap or overtake each other in Borges' work) is a central dimension of his stories. I believe that, for him, the transformative potential of literary experiences is often in subtle conversation with his own relationship with sight, blindness, and imagination.

ILAN STAVANS: My mother lost her memory in her last years of life. Without it, she was no longer my mother. I often imagine myself in a similar situation. Who would I be without the capacity of remembering my name, my childhood, the dreams I had last night? And the sense of hearing almost completely disappeared for my brother, a musical composer, during the COVID pandemic. It is slowly returning on the left ear but he has lost the ability to register sounds in quality and quantity on the right ear. His sadness is enormous. He has decided to sell his piano.

I also *visualize* myself without sight; I wouldn't be able to read. And without my two hands, I wouldn't be able to write, to type. Cervantes lost mobility of his left arm during the Battle of Lepanto in 1571; it didn't stop him from composing, more than three decades later, *Don Quixote*. Borges lost his sight around the age of fifty, although not altogether. In his lecture on blindness, which he delivered at Teatro Coliseo in Buenos Aires in 1977 and is part, with six other lectures, of the book *Siete noches* (*Seven Nights*, 1980), he talks about his loyalty to certain colors: "yellow, blue (except that the blue may be green), and green (except that the green may be blue)." He adds: "White has disappeared, or is confused with gray. As for red, it has vanished completely. But I hope some day – I am following a treatment – to improve and to be able to see that great color, that color which shines in poetry, and which has so many beautiful names in many languages."

Borges doesn't want pity from anyone. The blind, in his view, are just like everybody else. He says that "people generally imagine the blind as enclosed in a black world. There is, for example, Shakespeare's line: 'Looking on darkness which the blind do see.' If we understand 'darkness' as 'blackness,' then Shakespeare is wrong." He says that one of the colors that the blind –at least in his case – do not see is black. I find this disquisition enlightening: being blind, Borges stresses, doesn't mean *not* seeing; it means seeing differently. Borges' paternal lineage includes a number of blind relatives, including his father, who at an older age could still see but in a limited fashion. He talks of the enormous privilege he felt at having been director of Argentina's National Library for eighteen years and the inherent contradiction in him accepting the job at a time when he could no longer read. Two other directors of the library were also blind: Paul Groussac, whom Borges admired (and who, like him, adored *Don Quixote*), and José Mármol. He quotes from his own "Poema de los dones" (Poem of the Gifts, 1959). This is Eliot Weinberger's translation:

No one should read self-pity or reproach
into this statement of the majesty
of God; who with such splendid irony
granted me books and blindness in one touch.

In other words, blindness is a gift. Other blind writers include Homer, about whom Greek tradition tells us next to nothing but has granted us his two extraordinary epic poems; John Milton, who, like Borges, imagined the loss of paradise (in his lecture on blindness, Borges says "I had always imagined paradise as a kind of library); and James Joyce, who rewrote Homer. In photographs of his youth, a myopic Borges is occasionally seen wearing heavy glasses, but, according to several biographers, shied from using them in public. But in old age, he is seen in portraits without glasses, his sight lost in space.

In my mind, I see him at Teatro Coliseo in front of the crowd, sitting on a wooden chair, a table with a glass of water to his right, his hands suspended while holding a cane, his eye projecting into the darkness before him. An admirable profile.

MUA: Borges' lecture on blindness, for me, is crisscrossed with important tensions and contradictions. At one level, the lecture does three things: it works to acknowledge and challenge some of the stereotypes that sighted people often associate with blindness; it suggests that being blind has joined Borges with a new community (and a new tradition) of blind writers; and it offers examples of how blindness (which is often framed as a kind of loss) can be additive, creating the conditions for new discoveries, projects, and practices. Yet each of these dimensions of the text double back on themselves in different, contradictory ways.

Despite announcing that he is speaking from his own personal experiences, when Borges dispels the myth that every blind person is "enclosed in a black world," his text makes statements about "el ciego" (the blind person) that can lead readers to assume they are learning about blind people's visual experiences in general. It can, in a contradictory way, replace one generalization with another, despite the diversity of experiences of blindness (which, as Kenneth Jernigan has written, can involve a total lack of visual stimuli, cascading colors, narrowed fields of sight, blocked fields of vision, and also "perfect" 20/20 sight when it is paired with a high sensitivity to light ... all of which *become* "blindness" within social and cultural contexts designed for and by sighted people).

I find it particularly important that while Borges describes his own personal experience of blindness (and sight) as that of a slowly building twilight – a process that began the day he was born and continued up until the moment of writing his text – he also suggests that audiences prefer a more dramatic version of things. Borges, crucially, uses the word *patético* (pathetic) to describe what his listeners might want. He then proceeds to *cater to* these preferences, telling the story of being named as the director of the National Library without being able to read even the titles of the 900,000 books it houses.

This story of loss is complicated by the last part of the essay. Despite writing that he *could not read the books* that he was in charge of, Borges, in the very same essay, describes the experience of *reading as a blind person* as he began his study of Old English literature with a group of students. Borges, of course, read while listening, as do many people (now often with screen readers), which made it, for him, a far more collaborative experience. Writing, too, would now involve other people in a new way. "I had replaced the visible world with the auditory world of the Anglo-Saxon language," he writes, after describing the joyous social experience of collectively discovering the definition of a few key words, which to him and his group were like "talismans." He is working more slowly now, but also with others, and remembers how they all spilled out into the street afterwards happily yelling "Lundenburh" and "Romeburh."

What is most striking to me is that after catering to the desires for a "pathetic moment," where he cannot read the books he is surrounded by, Borges subverts those same expectations with a description of a new form of writing and reading. Repeating the same word from before, he writes that blindness should not, in fact, be approached with the expectations of a pathetic story: "no se la debe ver de un modo patético." Instead, he writes, it should be understood as one of the different ways that people live, a style of life with its own set of challenges, strengths, and creative opportunities.

15: The other six lectures in *Seven Nights* are all about passions Borges engaged in: *The Divine Comedy*, the Kabbalah, nightmares, poetry, *The Thousand and One Nights*, and Buddhism. "Blindness" is the only one about a condition. I have learned enormously from Borges' impromptu style of lecturing. In old age, as a result of his blindness (but even when he was younger), he lets his mind "wander as it wonders" (the phrase comes from Langston Hughes) in an associative journey nurtured by his voracious reading. The volume we have of *Seven Nights* is a transcription of those rendezvous, likely under the supervision of María Kodama, his second wife, in charge of his literary estate. The Fondo de Cultura Económica edition I have, which I bought in Mexico when it first came out (it is now in my archives at the University of Pennsylvania), features cross-outs and other editing, not from his hand though.

Anyway, throughout Borges' life the act and art of lecturing is essential: Several of his most important nonfiction pieces began as lectures: "El escritor argentino y la tradición" (The Argentine Writer and Tradition, "La inmortalidad" (Immortality), "El enigma de Shakespeare"

(The Enigma of Shakespeare), "El concepto de la academia y los celtas" (The Concept of an Academy and the Celts), and so on. It is far different to sit down to write a personal meditation on blindness than to sit in front of hundreds of people and improvise. To accomplish the latter, especially about such an intrinsically intimate topic, you need to be confessional, to bring down your defenses, to eliminate all kinds of subterfuges. It is astonishing what Borges accomplishes at the psychological level. He seems free of anger and recrimination, which are often side effects of our human limitations.

MUA: When you read *Seven Nights*, do you think about your own practice of lecturing?

IS: I do. It is an enormously stimulating exercise. I know roughly where I want to go but not how I will get there. As soon as I introduce the topic, I feel a rush of adrenaline. I find myself at the crux where memory and improvisation meet. I hear the clock ticking and that grants me rhythm. If I have notes in front of me, I get distracted. Comparatively, it isn't that different than crafting an essay, except that in a lecture you're thinking aloud. That, indeed, is the joy: mapping your thoughts in front of a large crowd.

MUA: Borges, I think, brings down the defenses of his audience at certain moments, but also finds ways of challenging their expectations, desires, and ideas. Maybe he is doing the same thing with his own thoughts and feelings about blindness, which are by no means static. In a lecture at Boston University, Aravinda Bhat described Borges' approach to blindness as a "wavering aesthetic," which might move between acceptance, regret, celebration, and sorrow at different moments. Kevin Goldstein has written that Borges' shifting ambivalence about his blindness allows him to present it as a path to knowledge in certain moments, while at others subverting the "blind seer" trope by expressing everyday bitterness, annoyance, and boredom. Goldstein suggests (and I agree) that it is important to frame these tensions within a social model of disability, which differentiates between physical impairment and disability, the latter being produced by the complex encounter between a society and an individual with specific impairments. This allows for the understanding that societies produce disabilities by how (and for whom) they are organized and built. It also points us in the direction of progress by focusing attention on barriers to be removed and questioning implicit ideas about who a "normal" person is. This allows for a key shift: instead of always approaching blindness as a source of suffering or misfortune, it suggests that it can often be more helpful to identify the origin of that discomfort in buildings that are inaccessible, social practices that are exclusionary, and a lack of interest in complicating conventional normative thinking.

I wonder if there was something special about the dynamic between Borges and a live audience that allowed some of these contradictions and tensions to emerge.

In your book *Borges, the Jew* (2016), you write that Borges' approach to blindness was informed by his love of Jews and their countless ways of turning suffering into insight. It makes me think of how Borges pushed back against the notion of his own peripheral position as a Latin American writer by asserting that the margin is simply a less obvious center: he writes that the tremendous cultural impact of Jewish writers arises in part from being at once within the Western tradition and simultaneously at a (critical) distance from it. Borges' relationship with blindness might involve a similar exploration of the possibilities that arise from a de-centered (or re-centered) position – his work often subtly explores the fault lines of a culture built around seeing and sightedness. Especially in the dimension of literature – where no one can rely on eyes to directly perceive reality.

IS: You remind me of Beatriz Sarlo's argument, in her book *Borges: A Writer on the Edge* (1993), that Borges wasn't only interested in *orilleros*, e.g., a 19th-century Argentine slum type living on the urban edge, surviving on criminality. Etymologically, the word comes from *orilla*, edge. Sarlo believed Borges decentralized not only Argentine but Western culture by writing from Argentina, that is, from the most distant cosmopolitan metropolis vis-à-vis Europe, but also from an off-kilter location in Argentina itself, the Buenos Aires slums, where *compadritos*, *orilleros*, and *tangueros* shaped the nation's culture. I empathize with this view. Borges' blindness both confirmed and contributed to that off-centerness. The concept of the edge also related to Borges' myopia. He therefore needed to be "close" to the action.

MUA: One of the most dramatic examples of Borges' relationship with visuality is his most famous story: "El Aleph" (The Aleph, 1945).

IS: Almost everything in "The Aleph" is about seeing. At the beginning Borges arrives to Beatriz Viterbo's house and sees old photographs hanging on the wall. He then reflects on a billboard about cigarettes on Constitución Plaza that has recently changed. His visit to Beatriz Viterbo's cousin Carlos Argentino Daneri is quite visual. And, of course, Borges' exposure to the Aleph itself, "a small iridescent sphere of almost unbearable brilliance," its diameter "probably little more than an inch, but all space was there, actual and undiminished." Then comes that extraordinary list of items he sees – concurrently – through the Aleph, and the word *ví* (I saw) are repeated time and again, as if to emphasize the act and art of seeing as an epistemological condition.

MUA: For me, this story is about the tensions between sight and imagination: both are involved in vision, but in the context of literature I believe that Borges is most interested in our inner capacity to compose a complex, subtle reality (with room for contradictions or paradoxes) in relation to language. And sometimes an excessive attachment to seeing (and the conventions of everyday sight) can get in the way.

For example, after the building, ecstatic celebration of seeing that the narrator describes, he is surprised to note the feelings of indifference that follow and worries that he will no longer able to experience surprise, or the sensation of newness. After a few sleepless nights, he is grateful and happy for the process of *forgetting* that begins to erase his experience. It is worth noting that the owner of the Aleph is an arrogant, unskilled poet who has used it all his life; an obsession with perfect, total sight fuels his less-than-appealing literary project. Perhaps the most striking (and confusing) rejection, however, is when the narrator states that this Aleph was a false Aleph.

The statement arrives with a list of mythical objects (from an invented manuscript) that are also rejected for being "mere optical instruments." It is not made clear why being optical would render this Aleph false, as it was only ever described as a visual instrument. One object mentioned in the list, however, is kept apart: a column in the Amr Mosque of Cairo that is said to contain the entire universe. Here, however, the Aleph buried in the stone column cannot be seen – its distant hum allows only for it to be indirectly imagined into being, through touch and through hearing. The narrator insinuates that this might be the true Aleph.

While there are many ways to work through this story, it is worth considering how Borges – understanding that he would one day be blind – fashioned an object that delivers perfect, total sight only to enigmatically mark it as false. We should notice that the person who views this optical Aleph does not have to expend any energy or effort: they are passive, instantly gratified consumers of the (visible) world. In fiction, however, everything must be created through effort, through the generative creativity of the reader who invests time and attention in the experience; nothing is "seen" in an optical sense, only imagined, heard, or sensed internally. It is the Aleph in the column of the Amr Mosque which requires its visitors to actively and internally create a universe that corresponds to the distant rumble that they hear, or touch. In this way it is compatible with the context of fiction – and is marked true – in a way that stands in contrast to the falseness of the optical Aleph. While Daneri's project was, truly, all about seeing, Borges points to a different aspect of visuality in literature: the way it is composed in the mind. Note how Daneri's Aleph only works for the sighted; the Aleph in the Amr Mosque relies on touch, on hearing: the senses that blind readers of the story are using to read it.

136   Part I: Language on Fire

IS: Sight and imagination go hand in hand at all times. What we see with our eyes is what is in front of us, objectively, but what also what perspective, subjectivity add up. "The Aleph," particularly given the narrator's tension with Carlos Argentino Daneri, isn't impartial; on the contrary, it is infused by what Borges *wants* to see.

Keep in mind that aleph is the first letter of the Hebrew alphabet, which is derived from its Phoenician and Babylonian counterparts. Naming the object with that letter – he could have named it in countless other ways, even though he states, in the appendix, that the Aleph isn't his creation since there have been other examples (sightings?) of Alephs elsewhere – points to both sight and sound, since a letter exists in those two dimensions. There is a beautiful anecdote in *Sefer Yetzirah*, one of the canonical books of Jewish mysticism. Its date of composition is the subject of debate: some trace it back to the Talmudic period, while others believe it was composed in the Middle Ages. In it we are told that before the world is created, the letters appear before the divine, requesting a place in the alphabet. Aleph and Bet, the first two letters, both make a convincing argument to be the first. God listens to them patiently and seems unable to decide. Finally, he places Aleph as the first letter of the alphabet and Bet as the first letter of the Torah, explaining his decision to each of them.

The image is inspiring. Letters, in the Hebrew tradition, have personalities. There is tension between them. They might be reactive or ambitious, bright or submissive.

MUA: I agree. I think that Borges often evokes Jewish mysticism to open readers to the strange magic of language, to defamiliarize it, asking his readers to contemplate its letters, sounds, and powers with curiosity and awe. Using the word Aleph to name this aperture to the world (be it optical or not) brings its mystery in conversation with the words on the page, the letters used to form them. Language is his medium for investigating the world and inventing new ones; theologies that position language as preceding the universe, I think, hold special significance for him.

Another name that Borges chose for this magical object was "mihrab" – it appears (instead of the word "Aleph") crossed out in the original manuscript of the story. A mihrab is an object that, in a mosque, points in the direction of Mecca. Often it is a concave, empty space. Like the unseen Aleph in the mosque that Borges mentions at the end of the story, it invites contemplation without providing an image or an icon.

As it turns out, the Amr Mosque in Cairo was known for its mihrab. In a striking echo of Borges' story, it was destroyed due to an architectural expansion in the year 711. (Daneri's landlords Zunino and Zungri end up demolishing his house and burying his Aleph due to their own architectural expansion of a modern *confitería*.) The original mihrab, however, was not forgotten. Instead, the space in which it once resided was marked off by *four columns* with gilded capitals. In that sense, the "true," non-optical Aleph in Borges' story is also (literally and figuratively) an unseen mihrab.

IS: Intriguingly, perhaps with the exception of *El hacedor* (The Maker, 1960), in general almost none of Borges' protagonists are blind, at least anatomically, although here and there a few passing figures – like the librarian in "El milagro secreto" (The Secret Miracle, 1943) and a passing character in "Utopía de un hombre que está cansado" (Utopia of a Tired Man, 1975) – who are. But I want to go back to *la sombra*, the shadow, also rendered as darkness in Borges' oeuvre. The motif, obviously, is ubiquitous. You mention the link between sight and imagination. In his poem "In Praise of Darkness" (1969), he expands on his portrait of what blindness is by relating blindness to memory. He also opens a psychological window. This is a translation by Hoyt Rogers:

> My friends have no faces,
> women are what they were so many years ago,
> those corners could be other corners,
> there are no letters on the pages of books.
> All this should frighten me,
> but it is a sweetness, a return.
> Of the generations of texts on earth
> I will have read only a few –
> the ones that I keep reading in my memory,
> reading and transforming.

MUA: While in English it might seem contradictory that Borges would use the word "darkness" to title this book of poetry after challenging its association with blindness, in Spanish the original word "sombra" has a lot more luminous potential: one can imagine clouds creating shadows without necessarily removing all light and color.

If there is always a balance between sight, memory, and imagination in the everyday experiences of sighted people, Borges tips the balance in the poem you cite, pushing his readers to sense what they project onto the world (the faces of their friends, the familiar street corners that they walk past). It is as though, at the end of his life, he describes blindness as an invitation inwards, to explore and transform the depths of his life: everything that holds up the coherence (or incoherence) of his world and identity. This life is richer, in this telling, than one lived with the belief that the eyes faithfully transmit reality to those who see.

It directly recalls the argument of his story "El hacedor," which describes a man who can see but is unaware of the stories, myths, and histories that give his life urgency. When he becomes blind, the visible world recedes, but he slowly becomes aware of the stories that were always operating in the background of his life. The text hints that this man is Homer, positioning the generative power of blindness near one of the mythical origins of literary imagination.

IS: Or "Las ruinas circulares" (The Circular Ruins, 1940), about a magician who, through dreams, has a child. The story is about the power of seeing in one's imagination and the capacity to dream one's own descendancy. Clearly, Borges' blindness opens up alternative forms of perception.

A confession: on occasion, I imagine him drinking ayahuasca, a hallucinogenic used by indigenous tribes in various places of Latin America. I was part of a mind-bending shamanic ceremony in the Colombian Amazon that featured it. I turned the experience into a one-man play, *The Oven: An Anti-Lecture* (2016), which I performed nationwide. It also came out in book form. Although Borges' mind, in and of itself, is already extraordinarily malleable, it is delicious to think of him as not being in control of that elasticity.

MUA: A few newspapers reported that María Kodama, in a 1993 lecture, shared how Borges had enjoyed ingesting hallucinogenic mushrooms called "pajaritos del monte" – though I am not sure if this is true. I wonder if any of us are that in control of our minds, with or without the influence of ayahuasca.

I love how "The Circular Ruins" – by borrowing key words and phrases – signals strong connections to Miguel de Cervantes' 1605 prologue to *Don Quixote*. This text *also* describes (in contradictory fashion) how Don Quixote the character and *Don Quixote* the book (they are purposefully confused) are and are not the "child" of the author. It is eventually suggested that the book (or its protagonist) have emerged out of a central rule of nature: that "like engenders like" – people are born of people and books are born of … other books. Cervantes soon presents himself as the *stepfather* of the book (or the character), who/which properly emerges out of a strange convergence of other texts, of language. Literary existence is, in this view, deeply contradictory: at once sensory and textual, artificial and intimate. The same questions echo within the pages that follow, as Alonso Quijano/Quesada/Quijada "becomes" Don Quixote, "seeing" through a literary lens (which is comedic at certain moments and revelatory at others, given that he is, in fact, a character in a book).

Both texts remind me of Robert Burton's ideas about writing and influence in *The Anatomy of Melancholy* (another book that Borges turned to); he stated that all writers are thieves, borrowing words in ways that connect them to a vast tapestry of influence: an infinite series of writers and readers. At first, the dreaming magician might appear to suggest a writer of sorts who has "created" a character in his mind … until we realize that the writer, too, is a strange creation of his tradition, of the books he has read. It is a story that welcomes us, in its way, into the circular ruins that it reveals. In the preface to *El informe de Brodie* (Brodie's Report, 1970), Borges writes that "por lo demás, la literatura no es otra cosa que un sueño dirigido" (literature, in other respects, is nothing but a directed dream). Maybe it could also be described as guided hallucination.

IS: Borges on mushrooms – a perplexing image. Anyway, I agree that all writers are thieves: we steal in order to survive. Cervantes, in that sense, was a consummated burglar. Don Quixote, after all, is a parody of chivalry novels, e.g., he rewrites the tradition in order to subvert it.

Borges ends his lecture on blindness with a quote from Goethe: "Alles Nahe werde fern" (everything near becomes far). Although he says that Goethe is referring to the evening twilight, the image inspires him. In fact, he sees it as an image that refers to life: "All things go off, leaving us. Old age is probably the supreme solitude – except that the supreme solitude is death. And 'everything near becomes far' also refers to the slow process of blindness, of which I hoped to show, speaking tonight, that it isn't a complete misfortune. It is one more instrument among the many – all of them so strange – that fate or chance provide."

How Yiddish Changed America and How America Changed Yiddish (with Josh Lambert)

We have to believe in free will. We have no choice.
– Isaac Bashevis Singer

Celebrated and marginalized, lionized and trivialized, Yiddish is so deeply woven into the fabric of the United States that it can sometimes be difficult to recognize how much it has transformed the world we live in today. It's a language and culture that's as American as bagels and Rice Krispies, Hollywood and Broadway, Colin Powell and James Cagney (and connected to all of these, in one way or another). Yet many Americans think of Yiddish, when they think of it at all, as a collection of funny-sounding words. Oy gvald, indeed!

The aim of this book is to present a very different picture of Yiddish, true to its history, as a language and culture that is – like the Americans who spoke, read, and created in it – radical, dangerous, and sexy, if also sweet, generous, and full of life. Its inception is embedded in a radical shift. Some see Yiddish not only as a language but as a metaphor. They note that, unlike most other tongues, it doesn't have an actual address – a homeland, so to speak – or claim, as Isaac Bashevis Singer did when accepting the Nobel Prize in Literature, that it doesn't have words for weapons. And because of its history, it awakens strong feelings of nostalgia. But others see this as an ongoing problem. In particular, it irritates Yiddishists that the language is fetishized, especially by people who don't speak it.

Since the Second World War, many valuable anthologies have helped American audiences understand the gamut of Yiddish possibilities. Arguably the most influential has been *A Treasury of Yiddish Stories* (1954), edited by Irving Howe and Eliezer Greenberg. It concentrated on the Yiddish literary outpouring from figures like the three so-called classic Yiddish writers, Mendele Moykher Sforim, I.L. Peretz, and Sholem Aleichem, and served as a conduit to connect an American Jewish audience to the pre-Holocaust civilization. Its publication was certainly a watershed: the volume was the manifestation of a collective longing. That anthology looked at the *shtetlekh*, or small towns in which Ashkenazi Jews lived for centuries, through an American lens; they were seen as noble, even idyllic, and with a sense of homesickness, but also as a site of contradictions, violence, and unfaithfulness. Readers simultaneously idealized what Israel Joshua Singer called "a world that is no more" and sought to understand themselves as a continuation, as well as a departure, from it.

Other anthologies of Yiddish literature in translation followed suit. Each concentrated on either a region (the USSR, for instance) or a particular literary genre (such as poetry). These volumes include *Ashes Out of Hope: Fiction by Soviet-Yiddish Writers* (1977), also edited by Howe and Greenberg; *The Penguin Book of Modern Yiddish Verse* (1987), edited by Howe, Ruth Wisse, and Khone Shmeruk; Benjamin and Barbara Harshav's *American Yiddish Poetry* (1986); and *Yiddish South of the Border: An Anthology of Latin American Yiddish Writing* (2003), edited by Alan Astro. To various degrees, the objectives of these anthologies remained the same.

But in the last few decades, the position of Yiddish in the zeitgeist has dramatically changed. The study of Yiddish thrives in America, among teenagers and senior citizens, the religious and the secular, and everyone in between. Technology has made the language and culture available in wider ways. Young people are studying it. Scholarship related to it is prolific. Its musical rhythms and motifs have been borrowed by other traditions. It is part of movies, television, and radio. And the internet serves up lexicons, memes, recipes, and all sorts of surprising artifacts. Assimilation in the United States has indeed presented Yiddish with challenges, and it has responded impressively, dynamically, demonstrating its flexibility, complexity, and strength.

So what is Yiddish, exactly? First and foremost, it's a language, a Jewish one. Throughout the thousands of years of their history, Jewish people have spoken many languages, their own and the languages of the majority cultures in which they've lived. Hebrew, the language of the Torah (what Christians call the Old Testament) and an official language of the contemporary State of Israel, is one such Jewish language, and many others have arisen in other places and times as means of communications for Jewish communities. For example, Ladino, or Judeo-Spanish, has been spoken by the descendants of the expulsion from Spain in 1492, and Judeo-Arabic has been spoken by Jews throughout the Arabic-speaking world. Yiddish, meanwhile, was the primary Jewish language of Ashkenaz, which is what Jews called northern Europe.

During much of its existence, Yiddish was dismissed as a *zhargon*, not quite a language at all; this was the common fate of many vernaculars, which were seen as less prestigious than scholarly languages like Latin, and the major European languages like French, English, and German, which had state power behind them. But Yiddish was absolutely a language, one that originated somewhere in central Europe about a thousand years ago, with the oldest extant example of a printed Yiddish sentence dating all the way back to 1272. Written in the Hebrew alphabet, and drawing for its grammar and vocabulary on Germanic, Slavic, Romance, and Semitic languages, Yiddish soon became the vernacular spoken by the majority of the world's Jews for more than seven centuries, and over those centuries, a language of increasingly popular books and prayers.

In the nineteenth century, around the same time that languages like Italian and Norwegian evolved into their modern forms, Yiddish hit its stride, flowering into a language not just of commerce and community but of modern theater, journalism, literature, and even national aspiration. At that time, speakers of the dialects of Yiddish – sometimes referred to as Lithuanian, Polish, and Ukrainian Yiddish – constituted large minorities or even majorities in many European cities and in hundreds of European small towns and villages, while many more Yiddish speakers had relocated from Europe to other parts of the globe. The world's total Yiddish-speaking population just before the Second World War is estimated by scholars to have been about thirteen million people.

The language's fate would be entangled with one of the world's most brutal tragedies – millions of those Yiddish speakers were murdered by the Nazis and their collaborators in the Holocaust during the Second World War – but it also flowered almost everywhere that Jews settled, before and after the war: Yiddish newspapers and books were published in Montreal and Montevideo, Cairo and Melbourne, Paris and Cape Town (not to mention Warsaw and New York). While mostly the language has had to survive, unlike most major languages, without a government's backing, Yiddish was briefly an official language of the Soviet Union and today it is one in Sweden. It has been recognized as an irreplaceable treasure by UNESCO, and it is currently spoken, at home and in the street, by more than 400,000 people around the world.

We might never know when the very first Yiddish speaker arrived on American shores, but it's clear that a substantial number of speakers had already arrived by the middle of the nineteenth century, and that they quickly found their way to almost every corner of the developing nation. In the late nineteenth and early twentieth centuries, an enormous wave of European immigration brought hundreds of thousands and then millions of Yiddish speakers. Free from some of the strictures imposed by European governments, American Yiddish speakers created newspapers and theaters, and before long they had built one of the most vibrant centers for Yiddish culture in the world.

At the height of the language's American popularity in the 1920s, a handful of different Yiddish newspapers circulated hundreds of thousands of copies every day, and Yiddish theaters on Second Avenue, in Manhattan, seated thousands of spectators every night. Also, as the primary language of a vast immigrant community of poor laborers and their upwardly mobile children, Yiddish became a crucial part of American politics – at a moment when socialism, anarchism, and communism competed for Americans' votes with more familiar political orientations – and of American business, entertainment, cuisine, and speech.

In short, America, famously a nation of immigrants, was the site of many of Yiddish's greatest triumphs – a Nobel prize, bestsellers, and theatrical smashes, as well as political movements that changed the way people everywhere work. As specific as its history might be, like any language, Yiddish is, for all intents and purposes, infinitely capacious: you can say anything in Yiddish that you want. And of course, in America, all kinds of people have done so: factory owners and communists, Hasidic Jews and Christian missionaries, anarchists and political fixers, scientists and quacks. To dive into the diversity and complexity of American Yiddish culture, as this book invites you to do, is one wonderful way to appreciate the wild possibilities of life in the United States.

This anthology showcases the rich diversity of Yiddish voices in America, and of the American culture influenced and inspired by Yiddish. It is made of poems, stories, memoirs, essays, plays, letters, conversations, and oral history. Many of the authors represented here were immigrants themselves who remained loyal to Yiddish in the new land. Others are their offspring, the so-called *kinder* for whom the language was a link to ancestors and a source of inspiration and provocation, or people from a variety of backgrounds, Jewish and not, who learned the language and made it their own.

Much of the material included here comes from the publications or collections of the Yiddish Book Center, a nonprofit organization working to recover, celebrate, and regenerate Yiddish and modern Jewish literature and culture, which was founded in 1980 by Aaron Lansky, then a twenty-four-year-old graduate student of Yiddish literature (and now the Center's president). In the course of his studies, Lansky realized that untold numbers of irreplaceable Yiddish books – the primary, tangible legacy of a thousand years of Jewish life in Eastern Europe – were being discarded by American-born Jews unable to read the language of their Yiddish-speaking parents and grandparents. So he organized a nationwide network of *zamlers* (volunteer book collectors) and launched a concerted campaign to save the world's remaining Yiddish books before it was too late. Since its founding, the Center has recovered more than a million books, and published *Pakn Treger* (*The Book Peddler*), an English-language magazine that features articles, works in translation, profiles, and portfolios about Yiddish culture. Drawing on that rich archive and the Center's other collections, this anthology offers landmarks and sidelights of American Yiddish culture to give readers a spirited introduction to what Yiddish America has been and can be.

   The book does not attempt to present this material in chronological order or to make a single argument. Like many anthologies, this one is like a smorgasbord. We offer the nexus between American and Yiddish culture, in English translation – with full knowledge of how complex, and also generative, translation can be. This anthology's animating hope is that its readers will make connections between its heterogeneous content, browsing and skipping and finding surprises everywhere.

   To that end, the sixty-two entries have been organized into six distinct parts. The first, "Politics and Possibility," explores immigrants' initial encounters with America. It features scenes of ritual and tradition in the Jewish ghetto of the Lower East Side and explores the ways children of immigrants ventured out into Harlem, the Bronx, and well beyond. The selections reflect how, around the turn of the twentieth century, Yiddish culture in New York emanated from a community whose first concern was survival, and who had to decide what that struggle for survival implied about politics, ethics, and culture. For example, a watershed moment in the history of Yiddish in the United States took place in 1923 when Sholem Asch's play *God of Vengeance* (written in Yiddish in 1906) opened, in English, on Broadway. The play represents a setting that was as shocking to audience members then as it would be today: a brothel operated by a Jewish pimp and offering the services of Jewish prostitutes.

   The realities of Jewish participation in sex work in the late nineteenth and early twentieth centuries are complex and tragic, and what Asch's play captures, with stark symbolism, is the tension between the noble aspirations of Jews of that time to holiness and purity, and the degradations imposed on them by the struggle to earn a living under discriminatory regimes. The play included much that shocked its audiences, including a scene in which a young, supposedly innocent girl is seduced by an older, female prostitute – posing the question of what would happen and what would change when the old authority structures, derived from the rabbis and from Christianity, crumbled away. The second act of *God of Vengeance* appears in this part. So does a letter written in 1936 about a female athlete who successfully transitioned to male, written to the editor of *Forverts*, arguably the most important immigrant publication in the United States, in which readers looked for answers to daily questions about becoming American: In what way is this nation also mine? How much tradition am I ready to sacrifice on the road to gaining new rights?

A central question for Yiddish speakers in America, as for most immigrants, was precisely a question about language. Each one had to answer for herself how much she should depend upon and defend the language of her childhood and tradition, and how much she should embrace a new language – English – with its strange possibilities. Such questions had especially large stakes for writers, artists, and politicians. "The Mother Tongue Remixed," the second part of this anthology, concentrates on the vicissitudes of the Yiddish language as it adapted to the new territory. It features reflections on what happens in the classroom to make Yiddish survive, and the role dictionaries and other authoritative entities play in the continuation of life for the language.

The second part also includes appreciations of figures like Leo Rosten, a humorist who became famous for his efforts to codify "Yinglish" – the blend of Yiddish and English that became common in midcentury America – and some concrete examples of the playfulness with which Yiddish can be deployed, as in the case of Stanley Siegelman's poem "The Artificial Elephant." People often get defensive – or *prescriptive* – about the right ways and wrong ways to speak a language (and of course that kind of attitude has its value), but very often the story of Yiddish in America, even linguistically, has been a story of playfulness and irreverence.

The third part of this volume, "Eat, Enjoy, and Forget," focuses on one of the avenues through which the culture of Yiddish-speaking Jews has had the broadest impact in America: food. In an immigrant culture, assimilation in the culinary dimension is about experimenting with flavors and ingredients in order to satisfy evolving palates. Those experiments quickly moved from Jewish homes out into restaurants. In the twentieth century, delicatessens became staples of every major American city, and bagels triumphed across the country. American companies that produced brands like Maxwell House and Crisco understood that they could profit by serving a hungry Jewish market. More recently, as nostalgia for Jewish cooking has found its way into haute cuisine, dishes such as latkes have fused with other ethnic flavors (say, chocolate-based Mexican mole) to create new tastes that reflect the complex families and histories of Jews in America. Over the decades, classic Ashkenazi dishes have undergone changes in the way they are cooked, in how they are presented, and in what they are accompanied with during a meal. In a 1988, 14-minute short film by Karen Silverstein called *Gefilte Fish*, three Jewish women of the same family, an immigrant grandmother and her American daughter and granddaughter, explain how each prepares the dish. The first describes the labor-intensive process of cooking it, which she learned from her own mother, starting with the purchase of a living fish – "to make sure it is fresh." The last just acquires a bottle of the Manischewitz brand before serving it on the table.

The fourth part, "American Commemoration," focuses on the wide array of Yiddish literary voices in America. It includes translations from the Yiddish of a short story and a lecture by the American Nobel laureate Isaac Bashevis Singer – still the only Yiddish writer to win the Nobel Prize in Literature – and examples of poetry, fiction, and literary essays by many equally talented but less widely celebrated Yiddish writers, including Chaim Grade, Jacob Glatstein, Anna Margolin, Blume Lempel, Peretz Fishbein, and Celia Dropkin. Almost all American Yiddish writers of that generation were born in Europe, and they naturally drew upon European models as well as Anglo-American ones in developing their verse and prose. It's not surprising that their narratives frequently take up the experience of dislocation, whether by explicitly telling stories about being an émigré in a land with little patience for the past, or more implicitly by exploring the complications faced by Jews and others in the twentieth century.

The fifth part of this anthology, "Oy, the Children!," considers the descendants of Yiddish speakers, who went on to roles of increasing prominence in American culture. Inheritors of the immigrants' pathos, their offspring built upon that legacy to make their own marks. In many cases, as in Cynthia Ozick's story "Envy: or, Yiddish in America" (1968) or Joan Micklin Silver's film *Hester Street*, they did so by depicting the experiences of Yiddish speakers; artists who did so include novelist Michael Chabon and playwright Paula Vogel, both of them winners of the Pulitzer Prize. In other cases – for example, Hollywood actors Leonard Nimoy and Fyvush Finkel – they distilled the humor or charm of their Yiddish-speaking families and milieus and transformed them in one way or another for wider consumption. Among many other celebrated artists of recent decades, this section also includes graphic artists and storytellers whose drawings depict an older, Yiddish-speaking generation in unexpected and moving ways.

Finally, the sixth and last section of the anthology, "The Other Americas," explores Yiddish as it flourished not just in the United States but through the American continent, from Canada to Argentina. (The word "America" comes from Amerigo – in Latin, Americus – Vespucci, the Italian cartographer, navigator, financier, and explorer who in 1501–2 sailed to Brazil and the West Indies.) The language thrived in these regions, too, and continued to link Jews who had come from the same communities in Europe but found themselves in very different situations after immigration. These selections help to suggest some of the ways in which the story of Yiddish in the United States wasn't unique but rather part of a larger set of phenomena that involved the establishment of Jewish communities throughout the diaspora.

Each of the entries is introduced with a brief contextual headnote, and a timeline presents some fascinating and representative historical events – but, again, this isn't a history. It's most of all meant to be a grab bag, an opportunity for readers to get a little lost and to discover something that they weren't expecting. It showcases the rich diversity of Yiddish voices in America and of the American culture influenced and inspired by, and created as a result of, Yiddish and its speakers and their descendants. They pushed Yiddish – its sound, its sensibility – to utterly unexpected regions in the continuation of its epic story. By doing so, they have changed America.

– Introduction, *How Yiddish Changed America and How America Changed Yiddish* (2020)

The Anxiety of Translation
(with Robert Croll)

ROBERT CROLL: For me, the act of translation always involves an underlying anxiety: my feeling of responsibility toward the original text, which is bound to the knowledge that my words will be taken to represent the author's intentions, leads to a constant fear of being discovered as an impostor. But can experience in translation destabilize the way we read texts in their original languages?

ILAN STAVANS: It unquestionably does. Translators, out of experience, become extraordinary readers. The adjective "extraordinary," in this case, doesn't mean good. Translators are often terrible readers. That's because they come to understand an author's intention better than most people. They see the hiccups, the imperfections. I'm tempted to call that "the myopia approach." As a translator, you hold the original as close as possible. Personally, while I am translating I frequently bring the source closer to my eye, almost touching my nose, to make sure I am getting the meaning accurately. I do the same with the screen: in dealing with a challenging passage, I enlarge the font. This, of course, is in part a result of my age: I am fifty-seven and therefore my eyesight requires a bit of help. But originals don't want to be read that closely, e.g., they aren't designed to be scrutinized with such care, to be tested as if under a microscope.

That act of destabilization, of course, extends itself to any other work coming before the translator's eye, not only those about to be translated. The same happens to a tailor: she sees aspects in clothing the rest of us miss. Or to those dedicated to political polling. They develop an acute eye about human behavior, enabling them to understand if an issue has traction.

RC: And, when we move from speaking a language that is not our own to translating from it, our native language is not left intact. When we attempt translation, we continue a critical process that many of us experience the first time we study a second language in an academic (rather than immersive) setting: we begin to apprehend elements of our first language that we could not have imagined before, simply because we had no vantage point. We must become aware of languages before recognizing that we inhabit a language – the same as belief.

IS: Learning a second language entails apprehending an entirely new epistemological way of approaching the world. But it also does something else: it pushes us to understand our origins – not only language but place – with a fresh perspective. That's because all learning is comparative: we approach a phenomenon from certain assumptions, meaning with a set of preconceptions.

One of my discomforts with the way translation is often discussed is that it tends to look at languages statically: it is about making the content delivered in language A acquire an outfit in language B. But languages aren't fixed. They are in constant change, not only as semantic codes but in the way individuals approach them. American English today is different from American English a decade ago, or in 1985, when I immigrated from Mexico to New York. And so is my own English: its texture, its granular taste, has evolved within me. I don't speak it the same way as I did a decade ago.

Likewise, my Spanish. I really learned how it functions – syntactically – only when I embraced English as my daily language of communication. That is, I became aware of its metabolism, which I knew little about when, as a native user, I employed it day in and day out in my adolescence.

Of course, this transaction, e.g., the multilingual journey as well as the act of translation itself, makes you feel exposed, in a constant state of loss. In my first years in the United States, I used to wake up agitated in the middle of the night, with the sense that, linguistically, I was not yet a full-blown user of English while I was already rapidly losing my grasp of Spanish. At the time, I remember fixating on the expression "no man's land" as a suitable description of this in-betweenness.

RC: I still recall one of the first times I spoke in Spanish after the untested environment of my (rather homogeneous) high school classrooms. I was speaking with a man in an airport; we could understand each other perfectly well, but he immediately started laughing at my speech, and I soon joined in when I realized that, from his perspective, it was like talking to a book (and, at that time, more of a textbook than a novel). To put it simply, my language then was only ever idiomatic in calculated ways. But we become flexible.

Depending on where we learn a second language, we may acquire regional characteristics, but something that fascinates me is how long we can remain ignorant of the associations that our words will evoke for native speakers. The first time I studied in Spain, teachers asked me if I'd learned Spanish in Mexico, saying it was because I habitually used the word *ahorita*, meaning "right now." You're right: we fixate on expressions. It reminds me of the way people latch onto terms in academia when trying to find their footing – the month or two when everyone uses a word like "liminal" or "multiplicity" until it begins to lose meaning.

But another effect of translation on our own language is that we can acquire various idiolects over the course of working with different authors' voices. Translating a writer becomes easier – or seems to become easier – over the course of multiple texts, as we come to understand the kinks and contours of that writer's language. But there is a danger here as well: the belief of mastery. If we come to think we have reached a point of certainty about a writer or a language, it becomes easy to read our expectations into the text rather than assess it on its own terms and remain open to surprise.

I often think about certain contradictions among the anxieties of translation. I am able to feel that what I'm doing is nothing original, almost to the point that it seems like a kind of plagiarism, even as I worry that I'm producing an inadequate representation. How can we combat these lurking uncertainties?

IS: It is more than possible. In fact, it is de rigueur. Translators, in my view, are usurpers. We are just like actors: falsifiers, impostors. We traffic on unoriginality, that is, on making copies. The copies aren't exactly the same as the original but they are bound by it. We are shadows, ghosts.

RC: Does the anxiety of translation change depending on whether the author is alive?

IS: From a translator's viewpoint (at least, from *this* translator), the best author is a dead author. That absence is a form of freedom. You don't have anyone on your shoulder, overseeing what you do.

The freedom I'm referring to, of course, is a mirage. The moment the author dies, your responsibility shifts. If the original is being translated, it's because it has outlasted the author, meaning that it has a claim for posterity. The quality of the translation depends now on how posterity is being negotiated.

RC: And, when a text outlives its author, it is more likely to see future retranslations. In many cases, classics become Everests (or, in the case of more niche novels, at least regional peaks), drawing translators to their challenge. But I think the act of retranslation – though of course affected by such ambitions – is often a reflection of the unfixed quality of language that you mentioned earlier; novels and their translations do not age at the same rate.

One of your latest projects is the translation of languages you don't know. What are the possibilities afforded by translating from a language you cannot speak, and what are the limits and ramifications of that act?

IS: I find that effort – to translate from unknown tongues – incredibly alluring. On the surface, it could be argued that such an enterprise is foolish. And on the surface, it surely is. But life itself is nothing but matching pairs of socks in the dark. Why then not take the bull by the horns, as we say in Spanish?

There is a long tradition of translators rendering work in languages they are not familiar with: Richard Wilbur translated from Russian, Samuel Beckett and Joseph Brodsky from Spanish, and so on. This isn't the same as translating a text from a language in which it wasn't written. Emma Lazarus translated medieval Hebrew poets from a German text by Heinrich Heine. Isaac Bashevis Singer translated from German novels originally written in French. What I'm talking about is doing translations from originals that you as the translator can't decipher.

Singer, by the way, also translated his own work – alone and with the help of others, often women with whom he might have been involved sexually. He called the translations of his work from Yiddish into English "second originals," often announcing to the world that they, and not the Yiddish versions on which they were based, should be approached as the source. And indeed, with the exception of the translations of Singer's work done into Polish and Japanese, which are based on the Yiddish originals, everything else was based on the English versions he co-produced.

Academics these days talk about the impossibility of translation. Or else, about untranslatability, the recognition that, at its core, translation is a doomed intellectual endeavor. The focus actually reaches further, acknowledging that some texts are de facto untranslatable. This argument, of course, isn't new. Religious debates (I'm thinking of basic Talmudic discussions, for instance) are based on this assumption.

Translating from languages one doesn't know is about delving into the unknown head-on.

RC: You do it alone?

IS: With the support of an "informer," so to speak. It is like spying: while an outsider, you need to get immersed in the local culture. You also need to pass. Since you don't have the means, you depend on someone who, over a glass of whisky, will immerse you in the details of, and about, the original. It is left to you, though, to recreate it.

Strictly speaking, this endeavor isn't a translation per se but an interpretation, though it looks, feels, and acts like a translation.

The insider who isn't a translator gives you the sense of how the original moves. You take that information and re-channel it in the translation. However, I don't call these translations but adaptations.

RC: And that's an important distinction to make. These translations seem like more of a creative endeavor, almost using existing texts as points of departure rather than attempting mimesis with your translations. By working laboriously through an initially incomprehensible text in this way, you may come to fully understand its concrete images and actions but not the intralingual resonances of the words.

But even when working with languages that we understand (or believe we understand), translators are in a unique position to appreciate untranslatability, particularly in the way language is constructed. This leads to a familiar question: What is to be gained in the attempt of translating (supposedly) untranslatable texts?

IS: Again, translation, in and of itself, is an impossible task. Something is invariably lost. Yet translation is a much-needed activity, otherwise each of us would exist in a solipsistic universe. To translate is to approximate, to render in another language a piece whose meaning will invariably be refurbished in another. In that sense, any text is untranslatable.

Obviously, we're talking now about another type of untranslatability: rendering a text from a language the translator doesn't know. The gains, in my opinion, are enormous. They aren't about fidelity but about interpretation. My hope is that readers see them as approximations. And in the age of relativity, an approximation is as good as we might get in terms of appreciation.

RC: I have heard two equally confident declarations: 1) translators will shortly become obsolete figures, replaced by technology, and 2) literature can never be translated by machines; any claim otherwise demonstrates a fundamental misunderstanding of the nature of writing. But the wonderful property of such dichotomies is that, once inspected, they reveal little more than the speaker's opinion. Yet the advent of machine translation – and, more broadly, the proliferation of digital texts – does change the conditions under which translators work.

IS: Machine translation is a joke …

RC: Because it cannot revisit a text. I've often thought that the concern about the effects of machine translation comes from a confusion of the roles of translator and interpreter. Interpreters perform a task with immediate political stakes. Often they do not operate near established borders, where mutual understandings already exist, but rather in sites of new cultural proximity: in cities invaded or among populations displaced (likely because of invasions). Their underlying goal, then, is not to repeat precisely what is said but rather to convey what is intended. But translators work with literary texts whose considerations are not exclusively semantic; they may even be intentionally ambivalent. The task, then, is to recreate the way meaning is expressed – or elided.

Of course, our new access to such a surplus of texts means that it is becoming increasingly difficult to encounter a word or phrase that can't be traced elsewhere. The kind of mistranslation that results from isolation grows scarce. This is particularly true when working with widely spoken and widely digitized languages.

But a constant source of anxiety, for me at least, is the fear of reducing the original in some way. This ties back to the effects of translation on our reading. The way we read becomes prismatic as, over the repeated stages of translation and revision, the text refracts into a series of potential interpretations. We must combat the lazy, violent urge to impose a single, favored interpretation onto a text where the original is ambiguous. We must attempt, in the final translation, to retain the potentials. This is the stage to push against our own egos and try, if nothing else, to vicariously inhabit the ego of the author.

IS: I love how you put it: reading is prismatic. I also like your willingness to remain up to various interpretations while you're translating the original. It is as if you were resisting the fact, unavoidable from my viewpoint, that the translator becomes the authority through which a piece of literature arrives to a targeted reader outside the original realm. Maybe it's generational: millennials resist thinking of their presence as an imposition. There's also the fact that, in the age of hypertexts, we want to give readers as many options as possible. It is an illusion, though. Of course, my own view is also generational. I believe, for better or worse, your translator becomes the entryway to the world it conveys. Since you are the conduit, you might as well assume full responsibility for your actions.

RC: For me, I think an awareness that my presence is an imposition on the text precedes much of my thinking on how to approach translation, and it actually produces and intensifies my sense of responsibility to the original; I want to speak for the text and not for the image I've constructed of its author. Of course, it's impossible for the translation to recreate the same set of possible inferences as the original, but what I fear is representing something intended to be multiple as being monolithic.

But it's also important to note that the role of translation has not been static. Historically, translation has often been associated with empire: translating *from* an imperial language in order to impose a specific political and religious ideology or, more broadly speaking, a cultural canon. On the other hand, there is another mode of linguistic domination that occurs through translating other cultures' texts *into* an imperial language as if to claim them for the imperial canon: a manifest destiny of art and ideas. How can translation fight against or contribute to exoticization and propaganda today?

IS: It should fight, yes, but it's a battle it cannot win. Intrinsic in the act of translation is the unevenness of the two languages, the source and the target. The reader accesses the translation because the original is either unavailable or undecipherable. That exclusion inevitably injects a dose of mystery in the original. And all mysteries, psychologically, are dressed in exoticization.

RC: And this perception of mystery doesn't necessarily begin with the translation – just think of the layers of exoticization and reinterpretation around Carmen as the threads of her story evolve through the words and images of Alexander Pushkin, Prosper Mérimée, Georges Bizet, and Carlos Saura. Nor does it end there: readers, sometimes encouraged by publishers, will read assumptions into the text.

In many cases, at least historically, reviews of books in translation have treated them as fully transparent representations of the original works – this oversight is easy to criticize, yet it is also a deadening experience to constantly include disclaimers that rehash the same basic sense of unknowing that foregrounds any translated text.

IS: I believe this attitude is changing. I have noticed that reviewers of translated books are more sensitive than they used to be. Perhaps this is the result of how globalism permeates everything these days. Rather than simply acknowledging that a book has come from another language, as used to happen, reviewers nowadays champion that fact. But we might be pushing it in the opposite direction. I have noticed, since I launched Restless Books, how reverential reviewers are of translated books. Sometimes that reverence verges on naiveté: because a novel comes from Iran or Chile or Iceland, it must say something unique. That's a trap! There's a lot of bad international literature, just as there is a lot of bad native literature. Knowing how to discriminate the good from the bad takes more than education. It takes courage.

– Asymptote, December 12, 2018

We Are All Drafts: The Erotics of Translation (with Peter Cole)

PETER COLE: This new gathering of your translations contains a remarkably wide range of poets, from multiple languages and distant worlds, known and less-known. How does a given poem get into your blood? Where does a translation begin for you?

ILAN STAVANS: I start by finding out if I feel empathy toward a poet and if I indeed might be able to recreate the rhythm of her original work. That's my principal objective. I'm never literal in my translations though I'm always truthful. I disagree with the view that a translation is like a lover: if it's loyal, it can't be beautiful and vice versa. I strive for beauty, even if beauty is a strange concoction that can't be magically summoned; it happens if the right ingredients are in place. Looking back, I realize it is the poem that chased me, waiting until I paid attention to it, making time for us to get to know each other.

PC: Exactly, in the beginning is rhythm. Texture. Tension. So many arguments over translation zero in almost exclusively on *le mot juste*, which of course matters a great deal: but that isn't where good translations come from. They come from a much more physical sort of encounter with the language of a poem or piece of prose – and with a feeling for its shape and movement through us. Empathy is one way of putting it, and a complex experience of beauty certainly enters into play in a major way. At least at the start, I tend to see it more as a matter of *sympathy* – in the way that physics or music uses the term in relation to the vibration of adjacent surfaces. The erotics of translation is much undervalued! Richard Zenith has a marvelous essay about that, where he talks about the "risk-taking attitude crucial for getting close to the text, in the same way two people get close."

IS: "Erotics" is the right word, since what I engage in is a sensuous relationship with the poem. When I translate – and not only poetry – I feel as if I'm in another dimension. In part this is because rather than originating the text from scratch, as I do when I'm writing a piece, say an essay or a story, as a translator I'm following someone else's lead, which means I trigger a more reflexive part of my language. Through translation, I redress a poem. Its body is the same in the original and in my version; only the presentation is different.

PC: "Redress" is an interesting way to put it, since it also suggests righting a wrong, coming up with a remedy or compensation. That seems to apply to the situation of translation, no?

IS: I like the associations you're making. A poem in translation remedies its isolation in the language into which it came into the world. But it does more: it recalibrates the poem, making it a fresh creation and bringing it into other horizons, so both worlds are changed – where the poem came from and where it's going.

PC: Let's get back to slightly brassier tacks. The poem has caught your attention. You're inside it and it's in you. Where does revision come into this dance?

IS: All writing is rewriting. The first draft is like making a sketch on a piece of white paper. Once the sketch is done, I know what I'm creating. But that is only the first approach. I will return a half dozen times, maybe more, before I begin to be satisfied with what I've written. Each time I'm able to see more clearly what I'm striving for. A finished piece is 10% writing and 90% rewriting. The same process takes place with translation. A translation of mine goes through countless versions. Often after it has been published I still see it as a work-in-progress. I must have four or five versions I've done of José Martí's "Dos patrias" in circulation, all titled "Two Homelands." The best one, in my opinion, is the one I'm yet to do.

PC: Well, that comes to "Ten Homelands," but we all know the feeling, about so-called original work too – as Beckett and scores of illustrious others have made painfully and refreshingly clear. ("Fail again, fail better …", etc.) With translation the situation is somehow exacerbated by all the clichés about compromise that flutter around works like tiny white flags of surrender. The translator's halo. How do you deal with the frustration of sensing that what's "out there" isn't finished?

IS: My way may be solipsistic: I ignore that a piece is in the world already; or worse, I tell myself the real world is only a dream and that a better version will inhabit another dream.

PC: Where does that leave the reader?

IS: In the same position I'm left when reading others in this Leibnitzian reality: we're all drafts – a declaration of love is a draft, a grocery list. What we read as readers are versions, just as we readers are versions of ourselves.

PC: Beautiful – a high-resolution imperfection, in all senses of the imperfect, and translation as a paradigm of receptivity and vital movement. That said, I do believe – and feel that I *have* to believe – that I'm working toward a, or even *the*, ping-perfect translation of what I'm translating. One could call that a false proposition, but it might be more accurate to say that it takes us into the realm of fiction, and that I'm translating my experience of a given work, not the work itself in some pure or objective sense. We each have our methods of tricking the translation out of ourselves. In the preface to this new book you explicitly say that you see translation as something akin to "immigration," and "approach translation as hallucination." "Liberation" is also in that mix for you. Are they related?

IS: For me translation is intricately linked to my immigrant life, mine and that of my ancestors and successors. I come from a line of Yiddish-speaking Jews from the 'Pale of Settlement." I can't trace their lineage more than two or three generations, though it is likely others before them migrated too. My family, in other words, never had a permanent address. The fact that I was born into Spanish was an accident of history. Translation is a mechanism of survival: you learn as many languages as possible in order to cope with the circumstances. In my case, I've turned that mechanism into a craft – a means of becoming in a new landscape.

As for hallucination, let me tell you a brief anecdote. A few years ago, I participated in a shamanic ceremony in the Colombian Amazon in which I ingested Ayahuasca, an ancient hallucinogenic. The ceremony lasted several days but it seemed closer to a week, maybe a month. I experienced the texture of things through a different lens. And words – they were like knives. Somehow, I felt as if I had reached the meaning of things in a way I didn't know existed. The closest I've ever come to what happened to me there is in my daily life as a translator. Because when I translate, I'm at the mercy of words: their edge, their weight, their power; I am also in another dimension. My intellect is at work but so are other ways of knowing that are experiential rather than rational.

PC: In short, trance-lation! And where is liberation here? Most people think of translation as The Great Constraint.

IS: Liberty isn't the capacity to do whatever one wants but to do what one wants within the constraints set by the political, economic, social, and cultural ecosystems in which we live. Translation is a ripe example of that: freedom is plentiful within the parameters offered to us by the original poem. A translator will always be aware of limitation, but when I translate I sense the joyfulness of liberation. By the way, I would say the same of any work of the imagination: as artists we can't imagine anything we want; we can only imagine that which is framed by the possibilities of our circumstance.

PC: A slightly random question, but perhaps a good place to end: One of my favorite poems in this book is your version of Neruda's "Ode to the Dictionary" – "From the dense and sonorous / depths of your jungle, / give me, / when I need it, / a single birdsong, ..." It's a poem about the poet's discovery of all the Spanish dictionary contains and what he'd missed before he came to that realization. Do you think it's also about translation?

IS: It's one of my favorite poems by Neruda. Sometimes, as I prepare myself to translate a new poem with the dictionary at my side, I think that my version is already in its pages; my job is simply to unscramble the words, to arrange them in the right way. Neruda says that when he was young he looked down at dictionaries as tombs but in adulthood he came to understand their value: They're "hidden fire." This poem is one of the most moving tributes to what Neruda calls "the granary of language." And that's where poetry and translation meet.

– LitHub, March 26, 2021

PART II

Dictionaries as Confidants

Notes on Latino Philology

1. On Becoming a Philologist

Words are time codes. In their essence, they contain the DNA of the people that created them.

I think of myself as a philologist, although I am well aware of how out of fashion the term has become. It used to be that anyone interested in the partnership between language and literature was called a philologist. Now these two fields are divorced. We refer to their respective endeavors with fancier terms, such as linguistics and literary criticism. It is a shame that their compatibility is no longer required. We all suffer as a result. In the Hispanic world, lexicography carries little cachet.

According to the *Oxford English Dictionary*, this branch of knowledge "deals with the structure, historical development, and relationships of a language." No language exists in a vacuum: it manifests itself in the act of telling something; to isolate language from content is to forget its true worth.

It is less controversial to become a scholar of major languages rather than of those considered minor. A major language (English, Mandarin, Spanish, French, German, etc.) is standardized; its most ideologically contested quality is that it is imperial, usurping space from other, smaller tongues. Minor languages are limited to a small number of users. They exist like an endangered species in a state of suspended continuity. I love words just as much as I love narrative. This devotion originates from my Jewishness. I grew up in an environment where literacy was at the center of life. The way to connect to the past was through a commitment to books. I do not remember being an avid reader when I was a child; that appetite came later, when I was in my late teens. Still, my parents surrounded themselves with culture: books, plays, film, music. There was not a moment in the day when someone was not in the middle of telling a story.

Narrative is the oxygen that makes culture breathe. Narrative is not only story, though; in other words, it is not only the "what happens" but the "how it is said to happen," meaning that a narrative is always delivered in language and that form and content are one. A successful story not only depends on the sharpness of its plot; the language that plot takes is equally crucial.

Of course, language itself tells a story, too: the story of its subjects and predicates, its verbs and nouns and adjectives, its punctuation, and in equal measure, the blank space – silences – between signs within a sentence. Separating story from language is like divorcing oil from water. Yet people seldom look at the two together. They focus almost exclusively on action.

I am dismayed by the degree to which, after the basics are learned in elementary school, the study of language in all its complexity is abandoned by our education system. I am talking not only of the industrialized nations but of developing countries as well. We would do better in multiple levels if we spent more time looking at words from multiple perspectives. It would make us aware of their limitations as well as their potential. It's a tenet of life that there is much that cannot be said properly; the most challenging intellectual task we have in front of us is *to say things clearly and eloquently.*

Those two characteristics are expressions of refinement. That noun, *refinement*, unfortunately connotes elitism these days. To express oneself in convoluted fashion does not seem to be a sin anymore, although it ought to be. I am not only referring to speakers with limited education but to everyone. In fact, the situation, in my view, is worse among the educated, including academics. Ever tried reading an average literary analysis of, say, James Joyce's *Ulysses* (1920)? Joyce at least was deliberately making language more playful.

All this is understandable. Ours is an age that looks at language in utilitarian terms. Its function is to convey meaning in quick, simplistic fashion. Speaking intelligently, matching image and word, takes experience. The accumulation of that experience is what is known as "maturity." Maturity in language is linked to maturity of mind and vice versa. By the way, I am aware these comments are not politically correct. This does not make them less true.

I am not a nostalgist who believes the past is better. Quite the contrary, I am infatuated with the changes the present offers us. Being clear and eloquent is a requirement of any period. It accelerates progress.

In terms of my own intellectual trajectory, I do not remember being obsessed with words when I was young. I took them for granted. I was born into a richly textured cultural milieu where a variety of languages battled for attention. I cannot quite say how I learned to distinguish between them, to appreciate which words belonged to which code and the kind of loyalty they paid to it. In hindsight, it is easy for me to say that it was all a Babel-like chaos, but it is not true.

It was only when I became an immigrant, in the mid-1980s, that words acquired a different status for me. From Mexico, where I was raised, I traveled around the Middle East and then to Europe until I settled in the United States: New York City, to be precise, which in itself is a linguistic statement. Here, all the languages of the world converged into that small archipelago of humanity. Instead of creating confusion in me, however, I became infatuated with sounds, rhythms, and sentence structure. Surely, I had already been predisposed to such cacophony, but now I was invited to discover the infinite possibilities of every word.

In retrospect, it seems like an act of fate: New York City exists in hectic movement; to think of it as a place of meditation is counterintuitive. But that's exactly what happened to me. The environment alerted me to the labyrinthine paths of semantics. T.S. Eliot, in *Four Quartets* (1943), says: "For last year's words belong to last year's language. And next year's words await another voice." I wanted to understand the etymology of words, to trace their history, to appreciate the way they changed over time. In other words, I have never studied philology in any formal way, mainly because no institution in the United States today offers such programs. (The word marketed in graduate school is "linguistics.")

Needless to say, my arrival to New York City did not just define me as an immigrant. All of a sudden, I also became Latino, inserting myself in a minority culture that was rapidly growing. By 2015, that minority amounted to almost a quarter of the overall population of the United States. Linguistically, this means that there are more Spanish-speakers north of the Rio Grande than in countries like Argentina, Venezuela, and Colombia. Obviously, their crux is unique. Their tongue exists in constant contact with English, forcing it to adapt in obvious as well as unforeseen ways.

One of my first quests was to understand hybrid tongues. I became infatuated with languages in contact: Franglais (French English), Portunol (Spanish–Portuguese), Hebreya (Hebrew–Arabic), and so on. Should these be described as dialects? What is the difference between a language and a dialect? In what way were these manifestations the announcement of a new culture?

Eventually, I settled on Spanglish, the mix of Spanish and English. It was already preponderant in New York when I arrived. I looked into its varieties. Was there a difference between the Spanglish spoken in El Paso, Texas, and the one in Tallahassee, Florida?

My book *Spanglish: The Making of a New American Language* (2002) is in itself a composite. It opens with a lengthy essay exploring the history of Spanglish, comparing it to standardized as well as hybrid tongues. It also features a Spanglish–English dictionary of about six thousand Spanglish terms. And it concludes with a translation into Spanglish of the first chapter of Miguel de Cervantes's novel *Don Quixote of La Mancha* (1605–1615), a book that has defined me in innumerable ways.

There is an assortment of reactions to Spanglish. Since the beginning, my view has been that it's a mestizo language announcing the birth of a new civilization. In that sense, I am not altogether certain that Latinos are an immigrant group like all others before and after. My view is that as a result of a number of decisive factors – among others, a unique history, the proximity of the place once called home, restless immigration patterns, and an idiosyncrasy that keeps families together – Latinos announce a new way of being Hispanic. Any discussion of Spanglish must address this dimension.

In subsequent decades, my fascination with the brisk, still-unformed quality of Spanglish has not diminished. Since the year 2000 and even before, I have seen it flourish. It is ubiquitous in all walks of life, not only in the United States but also in the Americas.

It would not be disingenuous to suggest that my own scholarship has contributed to a more recognized status for Spanglish. While the term might have been used in the 1940s, the earliest studies of it date back to the 1970s. It was not until the first decade of this millennium when Latinos in the United States became the largest and fastest-growing minority that the term "Spanglish" began to be used. Along with it came the recognition of Latinos' presence in every dimension of life: politics, the economy, religion, marketing, law enforcement, incarceration, culture, entertainment, and, naturally, language. That's when Spanglish began to be taken seriously. It suggested that, as a decisive force, the language of Latinos needed to be understood.

Other languages have been equally important to me as a philologist. In *Resurrecting Hebrew* (2008), I explored the way Eliezer Ben-Yehuda orchestrated the revival of biblical Hebrew in the framework of the late nineteenth-century Zionist movement and how that language, after the creation of the state of Israel in 1948, mutated in countless, unforeseeable ways.

I have written about the development of Yiddish in *Singer's Typewriter and Mine* (2011) and *How Yiddish Changed America and How America Changed Yiddish* (2020), and on Ladino in *The Schocken Book of Modern Sephardic Literature* (2005), and *A Critic's Journey* (2013). Although I appreciate the value of what detailed linguistic studies mean for a small cadre of specialists and have recurrently written for those audiences on these topics, my default target is the general audience. The reason, again, has to do with the adjectives I mentioned before: if something can be said clearly and eloquently, there is no reason to do otherwise.

I take this approach from Samuel Johnson, the great English polymath, whose oeuvre I thoroughly admire. Although he is referred to as "Doctor," he did not have what we call a terminal degree to hide behind. Johnson is the philologist par excellence: his essays on Shakespeare and his literary criticism in general are models of hermeneutics; his travel writings, principally those with his biographer James Boswell, are exemplary in the way they marry intellectual and experiential information; his columns for periodicals like *The Idler* and *The Rambler* showcase a mind deeply rooted in his time; and then there is *A Dictionary of the English Language* (1755), arguably the most distinctive (e.g., the most personal) of all lexicons ever published in English.

I wrote about Johnson in *Dictionary Days* (2010). And about English I have written profusely, including a regular column in the *Chronicle of Higher Education* website *Lingua Franca* and in volumes like *A Critic's Journey* and *On Self-Translation* (2018).

Having made my home since the early 1990s in a small town in New England, it is inevitable that English would be a central topic in my philological inquiries. I have always engaged in those inquiries from a comparative perspective. That's because any language that is alive is a language in contact. English is the perfect example. Such is its dominance that its survival is never in question. Yet the tongue changes every day in dramatic fashion. Shakespeare would be amazed by the way we use it today, and I am in awe by how different American English has become since I first arrived in New York in the 1990s. The barrage of youth, technological, and so-called foreign idioms that have been incorporated since then, or that have metamorphosed in plain sight, is dumbfounding.

Since I mentioned awe, consider the word *awesome*. It dates back to the late sixteenth century. Shakespeare is one of the Elizabethan writers credited for using it for the first time. It is used to refer to a quality of the divine in the King James Version (KJV) of the Bible, which was published in 1611. But "awesome" has been co-opted by American adolescents to refer to whatever is "excellent." Consequently, using "awesome" to talk about God feels, well, pedestrian. Some fifty years will need to pass for the term to be refurbished.

Other terms are *woke, gnome, startup, driverless, cyberspace,* and *meme*. English, as the world's dominant tongue, is a bully and a thief. It shamelessly borrows and steals and forces other languages to submit to its needs.

Most of my own philological work, however, has rotated around *el español*. This is because I am more closely linked to that language – the accident of birth – than to any other. Each of its words is a molecule waiting to be scrutinized. When did it emerge? How has it changed? What different meanings has it acquired? How do those meanings change from one landscape to another? I have said it elsewhere: it is harder for me to say I was born in Mexico than to say I was born into Spanish. From Gonzalo de Berceo to *Don Quixote de la Mancha* (1605–1615) and Gabriel García Márquez, I feel a deep connection to its millennial journey.

As I wrote in *Dictionary Days*, my personal library is packed with dictionaries of all types. A few are bilingual. Others are concerned with specific linguistic fields: slang, marketing, medicine, Shakespeare, and so forth. My collection includes many Spanish lexicons, from Sebastián de Covarrubias's *Tesoro de la lengua castellana o española* (1611) to the *Diccionario de Autoridades* (1726–1739) to the volumes edited by María Moliner (1966–1967) and Joan Corominas (1982). I spend sleepless nights browsing through them.

It is of singular interest to me that Covarrubias's thesaurus appeared in Spanish in the same year that the KJV of the Bible was released in English. Those were the two supreme empires of the period, and they were at war with each other. The KJV is a magisterial collaboration that defined the English language forever. Covarrubias's volume was less balanced. The flaws at its core announce the handicap forever cursing Hispanic philology: a derivative, non-rigorous approach to language tainted by the meddling of the Catholic Church and other powerful institutions connected with what *en español* is known as *casticismo*, the stink of Spanish pride, whose subjectivity invariably compromises the finished product.

Scholarship on Spanish philology is biased depending on the researcher's geographical location. Spain remains territorial about the language. Although only about 10 percent of Spanish speakers worldwide are in the Iberian Peninsula, the fact that its origins are there results in a distinctive tint. Hispanic Americans laugh at this attitude. There are close to 450 million Spanish speakers from Mexico to Argentina.

The Real Academia Española, known as RAE, has branches in every country where Spanish is the official or dominant language. Yet the matrix is in Madrid and all legislative decisions come from it. In the former colonies, looking at the RAE with suspicion is a sport. Every time an announcement is made in it, people turn it into a joke.

In comparison with English, lexicographic studies of Spanish lag behind. In the United Kingdom, dictionaries come in different types. The most respected is the *Oxford English Dictionary* (OED), which, as its name suggests, has always been affiliated with a prestigious university. Other lexicons are also invaluable, like the one published by Merriam-Webster, in Springfield, Massachusetts, which has always been a commercial venture. Its roots go back to the eighteenth-century lexicographer Noah Webster.

A history of how these and other dictionaries came to be is well known, not only in academic circles but among general readers. Books like Simon Winchester's *The Professor and the Madman* (1998) make accessible the mythology of the first attempts, in the aftermath of the Enlightenment in Europe, to catalog words.

In contrast, the authority in charge of analyzing how dictionaries came to be in the Iberian Peninsula and its former American colonies – for instance, the *Diccionario de la Lengua Española,* first published in 1780 and reprinted periodically under the aegis of the Real Academia Espanola, and Andrés Bello's *Gramática de la lengua castellana destinada al uso de los americanos* (1847) – remain the domain of a few specialists and are almost totally unknown among lay readers. This is a significant limitation.

Bello is a luminary that ought to be better known. In some ways, he is the equivalent of a Doctor Johnson in Spanish: a renaissance man whose interest, from botany to diplomacy, pushed him in countless directions. My own mind works in similar ways. As much as I admire specialized interests, I am a generalist; that is, I am attracted by a plurality of things and do not see why I should reject any of them. It's the infinite connections among them that appeal to me. Latino studies, as an area of scholarship, has grown at a rapid pace. In its essence it is interdisciplinary, combining efforts coming from history, political science, literary studies, sociology, anthropology, economics, and other established fields. Philology is the ugly duckling. On the surface, it does not appear to have any pragmatic value in the age of capital-investment education. This is nearsighted. It deserves a broader reconsideration, since just about every aspect of life can be understood through the study of the language of Latinos.

I fear Latino studies is becoming a discipline rife with sportsmanship devoted to cultural pride. Knowledge is not satisfying but perplexing. And there is no honest pursuit of knowledge without the recognition that the language it is conveyed through in is in itself complex.

2. A History of the Spanish Language in Five Sentences

Knowledge is always about perspective matters, of course: we do not know things as they are but *as we are*.

Most histories of the Spanish language have been written by Iberian scholars, offering naturally disjointed views of *el español americano*. Only a few of them are in English, and even fewer have been produced in the United States by Anglo academics in the field of linguistics. That is, their target audience consists of specialists.

The only full-fledged history of Spanish written by a Latin American scholar is Antonio Alatorre's *Los 1001 años de la lengua española* (1989). Other intellectuals and scholars from the Americas have produced superb philological studies with the region's perspective that seek to correct the imbalance created by an overabundance in Iberian perspective. These include Pedro Henríquez Ureña from the Dominican Republic; Fernando Ortiz and Lydia Cabrera from Cuba; Ángel Rosenblat from Venezuela; Raimundo Lida and María Rosa Lida de Malkiel from Argentina; and Alfonso Reyes and Gutierre Tibón from Mexico. Collectively, their pursuits have opened exciting new intellectual paths and serve as models to emulate.

To this day, no Latino (e.g., a person of Hispanic background in the United States) has ever put together a full-length volume on the subject. After Mexico, the United States has the largest concentration of Spanish-language speakers in the world. It is time for a history of global Spanish to be produced from this perspective.

I envision this history in the form of an accessible, engaging book called *A History of the Spanish Language in Five Sentences*. While the highlights of such history would remain more or less the same, the overall approach would be different: a two-millennia chronological survey, from the Roman period of the Iberian Peninsula to the ascent of the Americas as the driving force of culture. My lifelong passions, from the *Diccionario de Autoridades* to *One Hundred Years of Solitude* (1967), serve as roadmap. And philology – language plus politics, religion, and culture (literature and the arts) equals knowledge – is the driving force.

The central thesis is that Spanish, in and of itself, is a tongue in eternal mutation. In its inception it was not unlike Spanglish, a hybrid used in central Spain, in the regions of Castile and La Mancha, derided by scholars who favored Latin as the language of education. It eventually evolved into a national language when the Catholic King Ferdinand and Queen Isabella consolidated their power by joining forces. From there, Spanish has evolved through imperial conquest, lending to and borrowing from other regional and international languages. Why in five sentences? The answer is simple: why not? A dozen, eighteen, twenty-five – all numbers are random. I have opted for *cinco frases* because it is a compact, accessible number. (We use a decimal system because we have ten fingers, five on each hand.) But it's a gimmick, obviously. Each of these sentences is an excuse to reflect on another period in history, all of them interrelated.

The narrative is built around miscegenation – how disparate elements, in the proper circumstances, combined to form what Spanish is now. The first sentence in the book, "Ya mamma, mio al-habibi" (Your mother, my friend), symbolizes the emergence of the language as a way to orally communicate in thirteenth-century Spain. It uses a heavy dose of Arabic. It is crucial to keep in mind that for a long time the oral use of the word prevailed over its written counterpart. The *Iliad* and *Odyssey* are examples of oral tradition. In all honesty, we are uncertain who Homer was and whether indeed he was even a man. We call Homer the author of those two chronicles of Odysseus's journeys because tradition has attached them to such a name. But those tales lived for centuries in the minds of its tellers: a collective author who used memory, not parchment (let alone paper), to deliver its message.

In this section, the concept of the book as we know it (a rather recent phenomenon) is explored in the framework of Iberian history. It dates back roughly to the codification by Ezra the Scribe in the second century before the Common Era of what has come to be known as *The Five Books of Moses*. Until then, the oral word reigned unchallenged, to the extent that writing things down was understood as a means of impoverishing words. Most of what is known of the Spanish language from the moment the Romans brought Vulgar Latin to the Iberian Peninsula in the year 210 BCE, with the Second Punic War (until the *Glosas Emilianenses* in the ninth century), is open to conjecture since it existed mostly in oral fashion.

The narrative in *A History of the Spanish Language in Five Sentences* would reach further back, though. It would start in 218–201 BCE, as the Second Punic War takes place, in which the Romans defeat the Carthaginians and acquire the Iberian Peninsula. This is generally considered the historical moment, followed in 206 BCE with the Roman invasion of the Iberian Peninsula, when the region comes to be known as *Hispania* in the fourth century. All accounts of the development of the Spanish language, regardless of who is behind them, need to start with this beginning. The difference is in the approach. Mine would talk about invasion as a theme that is present from the start and becomes a leitmotif across centuries. The difference among imperial quests and colonial enterprises needs to be understood while also establishing an essential connection among them.

It is in 197 BCE when Hispania is officially declared a province by the Romans following the conclusion of the Second Punic War. Soon after, in 552, Andalusia, called *Spania*, becomes part of the Byzantine Empire until 624. It is important to stress that the Roman domination of the Iberian Peninsula lasted for about four hundred years. It concluded in the 600s, leaving behind heavy traces in the region's language and culture. They are palpable in the way Latin ultimately became the source of Spanish as one of its outgrowths. As in the case of French, Portuguese, Italian, and Romanian, all Romance languages, the syntactical patterns of Spanish have a foundation in the language used by the Romans in the region.

The Roman Empire was followed by Arab invasions, including, in 711, the major one led by Umayyad general Tariq ibn Ziyad; he conquers Hispania, resulting in the Umayyad Caliphate, which lasted until 718. The Arab presence would ultimately become quite important as well in the shaping of Spanish. Words like *alhambre* (wire), *azotea* (rooftop), and *zanahoria* (carrot) all come from the Arabic.

It was in Castile where the earliest manifestations of a dialect that would become Spanish emerged. It is there where the language transitions from oral to written. Some of the earliest Spanish ballads are the *Las Jarchas*, medieval lyrics, written in colloquial Arabic, and inserted at the end of poetic compositions written by Islamic and Jewish troubadours. These texts, which began to flourish around 975, are considered early manifestations of the language that evolved over centuries into Spanish. Then in the 1100s comes the emergence of *Glosas Silenses* and the aforementioned *Glosas Emilianenses*, glosses written as marginalia in manuscripts during the Middle Ages in what is known as Vulgar Latin, a variation on the Roman Empire's language, which ends up fragmenting into Romance languages. Along with *Las Jarchas*, these are early vicissitudes of Spanish. These are followed by the *Libro de Alexandre*, a medieval Spanish epic poem about Alexander the Great, written around 1178–1250. Consisting of 10,770 lines and 2,675 stanzas, it is an example of *mester de clerecía*, comprising early anonymous works written by authors from within the clerical echelons of the Catholic Church whose language is a forerunner of modern Spanish.

The message is that, like Spanglish, *el español* underwent a series of mutations. The first major figure, political as well as scholarly, that shapes Spanish was Alfonso X "El Sabio," who became king of Castile in 1252 and began his project to standardize and elevate Castilian from a vernacular to a language of knowledge and prestige. It was Gonzalo de Berceo, the first named poet of the Spanish language (d. *c.* 1264), who produced sonnets and other verses that began the standardization of the language, exercising enormous influence not only in the thirteenth century but across history. In terms of written material, Berceo's works were followed by the *Cantar del Mío Cid* written 1195–1207. It celebrates the crusade by Rodrigo Díaz against the Arabs. And Marrano poet Juan Alfonso de Baena composed the *Cancionero de Baena*, an anthology of lyrics dedicated to King John II and Constable of Castile Álvaro de Luna. The full title was *Cancionero del Judino Juan Alfonso de Baena*. It was composed *c.* 1426–1430. In retrospect, these linguistic artifacts were not just important historical documents; they also set the stage for a formalized grammatical structure.

The *annus mirabilis* in Hispanic civilization is 1492. A phrase from my book's second sentence, "La compañera del imperio" (the companion of empire), comes from that year. It is included by grammarian Antonio de Nebrija in the preface to the first *Gramática de la lengua castellana*, which is considered the first attempt to look at Spanish from a serious academic perspective. Nebrija's sentence has come to be seen as an emblematic announcement of the role Spanish would take in the period of colonization, when Spain went outside itself and took control of the Americas. Nebrija, for whom I feel enormous admiration, helped consolidate a sense of pride in *castellano*, one of the peninsula's regional languages, as a unifying force in what was then known as *La Reconquista*: the attempt to unify the kingdom under one monarch, one religion, and one language. Nebrija's sentence is most controversial in its location of Spanish as a sister, a spouse, and a companion to empire.

In that crucial year, 1492, the Jews were also expelled from the Iberian Peninsula as a result of the Edict of Expulsion, and Christopher Columbus sailed across the Atlantic, stumbling upon a new continent. Around that time, Hispania became known as *España*. But *España* was a potpourri of influences: aside from Roman, Jewish, and Arabic, the colonies, at first a source of imperial pride, would come to haunt it. In a new edition of 1496, Nebrija included the first American word known to have entered the Spanish lexicon: *canoa* (canoe). Less than four decades later, philosopher and philologist Juan de Valdés, exiled in Italy, would write his *Diálogos de la lengua* (1533), a series of conversations on the parameters of language change. Valdés's argument is indeed similar to mine: the most constant quality of language is change, he believed; and through the Spanish language one is able to understand how the Renaissance was changing at its heart.

In this sentence, I myself engage in conversation with Valdés, then move in full to the so-called Spanish *siglo de oro* (golden age), the illustrious period – in the arts as well as architecture – that, as is commonly said, was not quite golden, did not last a century, and was about Spain pillaging its subsidiaries in the Americas. The period is partly connected to the Spanish courts moving in 1561 from Valladolid to Madrid before it becomes Spain's official capital. Figures like Lope de Vega, Francisco de Quevedo, and Luis de Góngora wrote sonnets in precise, mathematical *español*. Lope de Vega was the most prolific *comedia* playwright of the Spanish Golden Age. He left behind countless sonnets and other poems as well as close to three thousand plays, the majority of them lost to posterity. Those that survived became examples of how the language had already achieved tangible refinement.

Quevedo and Góngora represent two diametrically opposed aesthetic views: *culteranismo* and *conceptismo*, one looking at language as an artifice, the other employing it as a tool to explore philosophical issues. Then came the most influential work produced in that epoch and one of my two favorite Spanish-language books: Miguel de Cervantes's parody of the chivalry novels, *Don Quixote*, and Gabriel García Márquez's *One Hundred Years of Solitude*. For many, *Don Quixote* is the apex of Spanish as an artistic, philosophical, and political language. More or less at the time Cervantes was considering writing the second part of his novel, Sebastián de Cobarruvias published his *Tesoro de la lengua española o castellana*, the first official lexicon of the Spanish language. He assembled it under the aegis of the Holy Inquisition, which, needless to say, makes it a peculiar artifact. Yet this is a record of the way Spanish was used in Cervantes's time. The two works, Cervantes's and Covarrubias's, are studied in this sentence of *A History of the Spanish Language in Five Sentences* as gateways to understanding the malleability of the language. In *Don Quixote* in particular, Sancho Panza communicated through innumerable sayings that allow a glimpse of the parlance of the poor and illiterate in the seventeenth century.

From its humble beginning as the way of communication of a small regional group in Castile, in the central part of the Iberian Peninsula, *el español* grew to be a colonizing tongue used in navigation, a tool of cultural subjugation, a conduit for literature and the arts, and a technological device essential for politics, commerce, and marketing. Sor Juana Inés de la Cruz, a Mexican nun and poet who died in 1693 in a convent where she lived most of her adult life, left behind sonnets, *redondillas*, a defense of the rights of women, and an epistemological poem called *Primero sueño*. Along with her, a number of crucial colonial writers in the Spanish colonies produced a literature that showcased what *mestizaje* could foster: the mixing of European and aboriginal themes. When the Spanish conquistadors arrived in the Americas in the early sixteenth century, what took place was not only a clash of civilizations but an encounter between structurally heterogeneous linguistic systems. Needless to say, that encounter was uneven. Of the two thousand or so aboriginal languages in existence on this side of the Atlantic Ocean at the time, just a handful survive today in a way that might be described as vigorous. Indigenous words in Spanish include *escuincle* (child), *compadrito* (pal), *cacahuate* (peanut), *tango, ningunear* (ignore), and *hamaca* (hammock). Some come from aboriginal languages like Nahuatl, Mayan, Quechua, and Aymara.

"Limpia, fija y da esplendor" (Clean, fix, and grant splendor), the third sentence in the volume, is in good measure about the origin of dictionaries in the Hispanic world, although it also focuses on pop culture. The line is the motto of the Real Academia Española de la Lengua, known by its acronym RAE, an institution founded in 1713, in part to compete against the Academie française. The motto has been the subject of much debate. In my own case, the function of the RAE is muddled by an inflexible, authoritarian approach to language that often refuses to recognize its ever-changing nature. Over the years, I have been a stern critic of the institution. That critique, handsomely articulated in these pages, starts from a simple premise: does a language need an institution to defend it? In my exploration, I also meditate on the role of dictionaries in the evolution of language in general and of Spanish in particular. The center of my attention is the *Diccionario de la Real Academia*, a proselytizing organ of the RAE.

The Royal Academy of the Spanish Language remains the most conservative institution in charge of legislating the health and continuity of the language. The *Diccionario de Autoridades* was the RAE's lexicographic foundation. Intended to purify and prescribe the use of Spanish, the *Diccionario* was started in 1726. Completed in 1739, the "authorities" of the title are an assortment of historical sources on which the lexicon builds its legitimacy. Most of them are Iberian in status; in other words, the perspective is almost anticolonial. Of course, by the beginning of the eighteenth century, ideological and cultural agitation was already taking place across the Atlantic Ocean. A period of independence fervor officially began in Latin America in 1810, in which countries seceded from Spain to become autonomous nations. Andrés Bello, the most important foundational philologist of the Spanish-speaking Americas, completed in 1847 his influential *Gramática de la lengua española para el uso de los americanos*, the first and still most complete grammar of Spanish ever produced in the Americas. Bello suggested simplifying the grammar of *el español* as well as adapting its syntax to the various linguistic realities in Argentina, Colombia, Mexico, and the Caribbean.

The Hispanic world in the nineteenth century is marked by the ultimate collapse of the Spanish Empire. But first, another empire needed to emerge: the United States. The Treaty of Guadalupe Hidalgo between Mexico and the United States was signed in 1848. It concluded the Mexican-American War, with Mexico capitulating and being forced to sell two-thirds of its territory for $215 million dollars. Most of this territory is known today as the American Southwest. The treaty was about the transfer of land. This is an important historical moment because the Spanish-language speakers in those lands (New Mexico, Arizona, Idaho, Utah, Nevada, etc.) suddenly became Americans, meaning they needed to start using English as their lingua franca. This marks the arrival of Spanglish.

Less than fifteen years later, in 1872 José Hernández published *El Gaucho Martín Fierro*. It became Argentina's national poem. The sequel, *La vuelta de Martín Fierro*, appears in 1879. For purposes of *A History of the Spanish Language in Five Sentences*, and for Hernández and other gaucho and *gauchesco* authors; the difference between the two has to do with the perspective the author takes. Hilario Ascasubi, Benito Lynch, Bartolomé Hidalgo, and Estanislao del Campo would use an idiosyncratic, localized Spanish that reflected life in the pampas among the gauchos. It is an important chapter in the development of Spanish in the Americas.

The emergence of gaucho literature and its attempt to reflect the parlance of that population was followed by the publication in 1885 of Nicaraguan *hombre de letras* Rubén Darío's *Azul ...*, a collection of poems and prose pieces. It fostered the *modernista* movement, lasting until 1915, the year before Darío's death. The *modernista* worldview was shaped, in 1898, by the Spanish-American War, when Spain lost control of its last colonies: among these were Cuba and Puerto Rico in the Atlantic Ocean and the Philippines in the Pacific. Darío, José Martí, Leopoldo Lugones, Delmira Agustini, and other *modernistas* sought to make Spanish more like French at the beginning of the twentieth century: refined, politicized, and aware of the excesses of European colonialism. The *modernistas* introduced a lexicon – about *cisnes* (swans) and *princesas* (princesses), among other foreign items – still in vogue today.

Important subsequent highlights in the development of the language are Cuban ethnographer Fernando Ortiz's *Un catauro de Cubanismos*, a lexicon of Afro-Cuban words, in 1923, which analyzed African influences in Caribbean Spanish. Likewise, Amado Alonso, working in Argentina, published *Gramática castellana* in 1938, in collaboration with Dominican essayist Pedro Henríquez Ureña. These are influential works seeking to evaluate the way Spanish in the Americas was in itself already the most powerful verbal norm, surpassing in influence what was coming from Spain at the time. At the level of folklore, in the mid-twentieth century Mexican *carpero* (stand-up comedian) Mario Moreno, better known as Cantinflas, appeared in the movie *Allí está el detalle* (That's the point!) in 1940. It was not his first film, but it would become his most successful. He would make close to sixty movies during his prolific career. *Cantinflismo* is a style of oral Spanish that deliberately confuses grammatical structures. It has been seen as a rebellion against Iberian, upper-class Mexicans, as well as Iberian linguistic patterns. Less because of what he did himself than as a result of his influence on millions, it is hard to imagine a more significant force than Cantinflas in the development of Spanish in the Americas.

The fourth sentence in the book, "Lo bueno ya no es de nadie" (what is good no longer has an owner), belongs to Jorge Luis Borges. It is included in his essay (or is it a poem?) "Borges and I," originally included in his collection of poems *El hacedor* (1960). It reads in full: "Lo bueno ya no es de nadie sino del lenguaje y la tradición" (That which is good belongs to no one but language and tradition). In pondering this fourth sentence, my argument is that centuries of distillation culminated in a crystalline sentence in which individual ownership of words is finally renounced. This section includes meditations on Amado Alonso's *Castellano, español, idioma nacional: Historia espiritual de tres nombres*, an influential 1943 volume on the distinction between Castilian and Spanish. Alonso's book offers an intriguing argument on how Spanish went from a local language of Castile to a global tongue.

That transition is at the heart of Pablo Neruda's *Canto General* (1950), an epic poem about Latin America that juxtaposes history with economics, psychology, and religion. From Chile to Argentina, from Mexico to Spain, the language used by Neruda, who was awarded the Nobel Prize for Literature in 1970 and was a close friend of Iberian poets like Federico García Lorca and Miguel Hernández, seeks to represent a transcontinental drive toward a common verbal force. Conversely, emphasizing the local rather than the universal, in 1950 Mexican poet and essayist Octavio Paz released his study *El laberinto de la soledad* in book form (it is a collection of previously published essays), in which he studied the Mexican collective psyche. In his book, Paz examines how *el peladito*, the Mexican streetwise guy, adapts the language to specific needs, using terms like *chingar* (to fuck), *cabrón* (badass), *pendejo* (asshole), and so on.

This fourth part of *A History of the Spanish Language in Five Sentences* discusses the proliferation of dictionaries in the twentieth century. Joan Corominas began publishing his *Diccionario crítico etimológico de la lengua castellana* in 1954. Along similar lines, Spanish housewife María Moliner begins publishing her *Diccionario del uso del español* in 1972. Eventually known as *Diccionario Moliner*, it became the most popular nonofficial lexicon of the Spanish language. Another lexicon is *Diccionario Clave* (2005), a popular descriptive dictionary comprising an assortment of neologisms.

The section also looks at the linguistic contribution of Colombian writer Gabriel García Márquez's *Cien años de soledad*, which becomes known as "the Bible of Latin America," as well as the verbal pyrotechnics of Cuban movie critic Guillermo Cabrera Infante's *Tres tristes tigres*, Guatemalan novelist Miguel Ángel Asturias (another winner of the Nobel Prize for Literature), and Peruvian writer José María Arguedas, author of the novel *El zorro de arriba y el zorro de abajo*, in which there is an indigenous undercurrent. The lexicon these three authors use in the oeuvres is either region-specific or transcontinental. In some cases, it looks to replicate the jargon of specific segments of the population while in others it aspires to find a common tongue that erases differences.

In countless ways, the evolution of Spanish in the Americas is the result of migration (Italian, German, Jewish, Russian, Japanese, etc.), which became a feature of national and foreign policy in the last decades of the nineteenth and the early twentieth centuries. After the arrival of the Spanish conquistadors, missionaries, and traders, the spread of the language came about from transactions across large expanses of land. And, as time went by, other migrants came to the Americas, reinvigorating Spanish with their own tongues. *Lunfardo* and *Cocoliche* are dialects devised by Italian immigrants used in Argentina. José Hernández, Leopoldo Lugones, and Borges were among the many writers who used them in their work. There are also variants linked to Yiddish, Swedish, Japanese, Ladino, among other languages. The study of the influence of immigrant languages on Spanish is long overdue for more scholarly attention.

Those immigrant languages become essential in the last section of the book. "In un placete of La Mancha" (In a place of La Mancha) is from the fifth sentence. It is the first line of my translation of *Don Quixote*, Part 1, chapter 1. This one reads in full: "In un placate of la Mancha of which nombre no quiero remembrearme." Over a thousand-year history, the Spanish language has fostered a considerable number of variations, let alone Creolizations, from Ladino to Lunfardo and Cocoliche. Arguably one of its most significant variations is Spanglish, a driving force at the beginning of the twentieth century. Spanglish is the hybrid that results from the mixing of English and Spanish. It is used in a variety of ways by millions of people, predominantly in the United States. This last section elucidates the tension between linguistic unity and fragmentation.

There are two paths to navigate the changes the Spanish language has gone through since Antonio de Nebrija published his *Gramática* in 1492, which was the first and arguably the most influential early lexicographic study of its kind. One path is to focus on phonological, morphological, and syntactical changes – say Alphonsine orthography, the cacophony of pronoun combination, and so on – as they take place over time. The other is to look at how the language responded to the social, economic, and political changes in Hispanic society. I have taken the second path in this book, without forgetting the first.

As I have made clear, I do not believe in purity – linguistic, racial, cultural, or otherwise. Like everything else, words exist in a state of cross-fertilization. They sharpen their appeal by interacting with others. In doing so, the resultant change sharpens their value, which goes up and down like capital depending on the intercourse they participate in. In short, *A History of the Spanish Language in Five Sentences* is a people's history of the language: how people talked, how singers sang, how actors acted, how writers wrote, and how politicians legislated. It looks at how myriad groups use and abuse the Spanish language without causing it to completely disintegrate.

Seen as a force that travels across time and space, Spanish is a hodgepodge. To talk about unity in the language is to look for commonalities in a landscape also defined by decisive differences. No matter where they find themselves, Spanish speakers miraculously understand each other: yet each of them belongs to a specific location. Such nuances are the purview of philology.

– The Oxford Handbook of Latino Studies, 2020

The Miasma of Order; or, Why Dictionaries Ought to Be Seen as Literature

> The struggle of literature is in fact a struggle to escape from the confines of language; it stretches out from the utmost limits of what can be said; what stirs literature is the call and attraction of what is not in the dictionary.
> – Italo Calvino, *Six Memos for the Next Millennium* (1988), translated from the Italian by Patrick Creagh

I. The Why of Lexicons

Calvino is right: literature is what happens *after* words find their right place on the page. But the quote fails to acknowledge that dictionaries are narratives too. Without an obvious plotline, for sure, even disjointed, a list of words alphabetically organized, followed by their respective definition; yet each of those definitions is a story unto itself: not only about what that word says but about what it means and how it came to be that way. The definition of "love," for instance, is in constant flux in dictionaries; the same goes for "bad," "patriotism," and "home." In their aggregate, the definitions for all these words and others represent a massive and methodical undertaking: to explain not only the vocabulary of a people at a specific time and place, but their *weltanschauung*, too. Hence, any edition of the dictionary is a cultural snapshot – ephemeral, limited, and practical in its functions, just like the *White Pages* used to be: as much a glimpse of those who produced it as it is of those who use it.

The pitch I'm making isn't a recent conception. While the voraciousness of the postmodern imagination, which looks at any artifact as a metaphor, has transformed dictionaries from reference tools to symbols of wisdom and even literary motifs, our predecessors were there already. Victorians, for instance, read the *New English Dictionary* like a journal, maybe not literature in the sense of "imaginative" literature, but not reserves or repositories of language either. Likewise, paratexts of earlier dictionaries suggest intertextual reading, admittedly on the part of the few. And modernists like Eliot and Auden spoke of dictionary reading, and, in Auden's case, of words themselves as poems.

Plus, dictionaries are characters inside literature, which is again proof of Calvino's nearsighted quotation: they show up in memoirs, novels, stories, poems, theater, and other genres, sometimes as passing references, other times as characters or as scaffolding that makes stories come alive. And they play another function: they are nation-building machines. It is impossible to imagine a nation without them simply because all nations coalesce around a language and dictionaries serve as the mechanism to catalog that language. Indeed, dictionaries are gravitational forces around which literature, and culture in general, congeals; and the other way around, a national literature needs dictionaries to consolidate its existence as well as to test it. In other words, without a dictionary a nation is somewhat soulless. Freestanding dictionaries of the fully modern period are so implicated in nationalism that one can't be without the other. That is the case with Cawdrey, Cockeram, Blount, and the glossaries at the ends of Renaissance books, etc. It might be said that as documents they aren't dependent on an idea of "nation" in order to be written; still, they exude a national – and even nationalist – ethos. One can't have dialect dictionaries until there's a unifying identity against which to pose the dialects. Slang works somewhat the same way. Slang isn't exclusively modern, as some claim, because it must argue against a standard language, but slang dictionaries are counterpoised to the standard, which means they react to the national. Wherever a people come together as a nation, a dictionary is required to validate the intention. And it also becomes the symbol of amalgamation.

II. Snapshots

God, as Maimonides argued, is the sole possessor of *all* knowledge. Every word past, present, and future is within the almighty. For humans, there is no such thing as an unabbreviated dictionary. We are all trapped in our own narrow linguistic universe. Multilingualism is a way to escape that trap, but even the most expert of polyglots is limited. I'm family with the lexicographic enterprises of about a dozen traditions; Czech, Hungarian, Russian, Swahili, and Urdu, to list just a handful of important examples, are beyond my scope. The purview that follows is inevitably narrow.

Arabic philosophers and philologists in the Middle Ages, like Avicenna and Averroes, were interested in the study of alphabets. Al-Khalil ibn Ahmad al-Farahidi composed his *Kitab al-'Ayn,* believed to be the first Arabic lexicon and arguably one of the first in any language, in the 8th century. Yet dictionaries aren't a theme in them. Nor are they present in the poetry of Hebrew poets of Spain during La Convivencia, such as Samuel ha-Nasi, Yehuda ha-Levi, and Shlomo ibn Gabirol, even though the first lexicographic reference in Hebrew, Saadia Gaon's *Agron,* dates back to the 10th century. (It also includes Arabic word translations.)

In France, Montaigne, in crafting his personal essays in the 16th century, patiently calibrates each of his words, often pondering their meaning. He will carve the way for Flaubert's concept of *le mot just,* but again, as such the dictionary is in the background. In Merriam-Webster, "Montaignesque" is defined as "of, relating to, or having the characteristics of the essayist Montaigne, his literary style, or his thought." Today there are dictionaries in French that survey Montaigne's usage. His early education was in Latin. And he filled his *Essais* (1580) with foreign-language quotations. And he asserted that he had created a "dictionary all [his] own."

Shakespeare might have invented around 1,700 English words ("gossip," "kissing," "lament," "undress," and "zany"). And the King James Version of the Bible, published in 1611, is a statement of his language. But the fact that the Bard makes no mention of dictionaries is in part due to the synchronisms of history. Ben Jonson's words in "To the Memory of My Beloved the Author, Mr. William Shakespeare and What He Hath Left Us" argue in favor of a vast, sponge-like intellect with a limited education. There also weren't any English dictionaries available at the time until after *Measure for Measure,* which was probably written in 1603 and first performed in 1604. (It was published in the First Folio in 1623.) That leaves still a generous period of prolific output, since Shakespeare didn't leave London until 1611. It's possible, therefore, to think of Shakespeare as culturally uninterested in the useful if obnoxiously limited lexicons in circulation. Or else, that he used them but didn't leave a record of it.

Miguel de Cervantes was also the creator of neologisms. In Part I of *Don Quixote* (1605), the priest and the barber visit Alonso Quijano's personal library. The reader gets a glimpse of its content: mostly poems and plays. There is no dictionary, in part because, again, the first extensive one, Sebastián de Covarrubias' *Tesoro de la lengua castellana o española* (1611), was still in the future. In Part II of the novel, published in 1615, the knight and his squire enter a print shop during their visit to Barcelona. They find numerous works translated from foreign languages as well as an assortment of other books. But, alas, no reference to dictionaries here either.

In any case, it would not take long for European thinkers to conceive of the dictionary as a center of gravity. During the European Enlightenment, particularly among the French *Encyclopédistes*, the idea of corralling human knowledge, and then cataloging it in accessible fashion, became an obsession. Voltaire, Diderot, Rousseau, Jaucourt, and others were behind such universalist views. The universe, of course, was always being seen through strict European – and Europeanizing – eyes. It is noteworthy that the distinction between a glossary, a dictionary, and encyclopedia, employed at times as synonyms, is a confusion ratified by this age: they are all efforts at zooming in on information; the decision how to organize that information is still ambiguous. The admirable dream of the *Encyclopédistes* was to look at words as implements to organize information, to bring the miasma of order into our chaotic surroundings.

Samuel Johnson, their contemporary and a magisterial man of letters, took the lead in ways still astonishing to us. No other lexicographer, regardless of the language, single-handedly embarked on the effort to compile a dictionary of his own native language and largely succeeded. Johnson was also a literary scholar and Shakespeare specialist, a cultural critic, a travel writer, a novelist, and a poet. Interestingly, dictionaries don't play an important part in his fiction. Perhaps this is because, as he famously put it in *A Dictionary of the English Language* (1755), lexicographers, by his account, are "harmless drudges." He was neither.

Johnson turned quotations from literary authors, most prominently Shakespeare but also many others, into a validating tool. That strategy had been used in other European dictionaries, among them the six-volume *Diccionario de autoridades* (1726–1739), composed during the reign of Felipe V, which made frequent reference to Spanish Golden Age authors like Cervantes, Lope de Vega, Góngora, and Quevedo. This strategy, among other things, consolidated the marriage between lexicography and literature: to be taken seriously, and for a nation to manifest its pride, lexicons showcased their respective writerly traditions.

In chapter 1 of William Thackeray's *Vanity Fair* (1848), set during the Napoleonic Wars, Johnson makes a cameo appearance. "This letter completed, Miss Pinkerton proceeded to write her own name, and Miss Sedley's, in the fly-leaf of a Johnson's Dictionary – the interesting work which she invariably presented to her scholars, on their departure from the Mall. On the cover was inserted a copy of 'Lines addressed to a young lady on quitting Miss Pinkerton's school, at the Mall; by the late revered Doctor Samuel Johnson.' In fact, the Lexicographer's name was always on the lips of this majestic woman, and a visit he had paid to her was the cause of her reputation and her fortune."

In the 19th century, Flaubert led the way in looking at the structure of dictionaries as tools for literature. His *Le Dictionnaire des idées reçues*, compiled in the 1870s in journals in which he lampooned figures of his time, wasn't published until 1911. Known in English as *The Dictionary of Fixed Ideas*, it is a kind of spoof encyclopedia through which he made fun of some of the platitudes of the Second French Empire. At some point, it appeared as if he intended his compilation to be an appendix of his posthumous novel *Bouvard et Pécuchet* (1881), which, somewhat like Diderot's *Jacques the Fatalist* (1796), uses narrative devices to tackle philosophical questions. This is one of the first instances in which the dictionary is presented as the structure to satirize an epoch.

It was in the late 18th and throughout the 19th century, the age of cosmopolitanism, that the dictionary was placed at the center stage of culture. Writers no longer used it to consult; they now read it tirelessly, and wrote about it as a subject of adoration. In America, Emily Dickinson's niece Martha Dickinson Bianchi reminisced that that her aunt read the dictionary (notably Noah Webster's *An American Dictionary of the English Language* [1844]) "as a priest his breviary." And essayist Ralph Waldo Emerson, a lover of dictionaries, approached them as the inspiration for any literary work worthy of lasting across time, though in his work Emerson never turned them into raw material, at least not extensively. Emerson argued once that dictionaries are a good read. "There is no cant in it," he stated, "no excess of explanation, and it is full of suggestion. The raw material of possible poems and histories." While compiling the *Oxford English Dictionary*, James Murray, in 1895, used the comment as an illustrative quotation in the entry for the word *dictionary*.

Arguably one of the feistiest American writers, and a devotee of dictionaries, was the Civil War poet, fiction writer, journalist, and war veteran Ambrose Bierce, known today for the extraordinary story "An Occurrence at Owl Creek Bridge." Among his most famous volumes is *The Devil's Dictionary* (1909), a lexicon in which Bierce sarcastically organizes knowledge alphabetically and as dictionary entries in order to criticize the mores of his time. Politicians and lawyers were Bierce's principal target. A capital was, in part, "The seat of misgovernment." A lawyer was "one skilled in circumvention of the law." And a liar was "a lawyer with a roving commission."

The celebration of the dictionary as a linguistic fountainhead was, in Bierce, transformed into a cautionary tale. From the human cost of the Civil War to the upheavals in Russia and elsewhere, his was an age of skepticism toward politicians as benign leaders. Sarcasm spilled into other human endeavors, such as the objective compilation of knowledge. Bierce defines dictionary as "a malevolent literary device for cramping the growth of a language and making it hard and inelastic." But he adds: "This dictionary, however, is a most useful work." A lexicographer is "a pestilent fellow who, under the pretense of recording some particular stage in the development of a language, does what he can to arrest its growth, stiffen its flexibility and mechanize its methods. For your lexicographer, having written his dictionary, comes to be considered 'as one having authority,' whereas his function is only to make a record, not to give a law."

Ezra Pound, an American expatriate who loved languages (aside from English, he knew Latin, Greek, French, Italian, German, Spanish, Chinese, Provençal, and Anglo-Saxon) and also dictionaries, published the volume *ABC of Reading* (1934), which uses the dictionary as a kind of structure. Despite its title, it isn't about reading as such but about how to write poetry. He had tried the approach before. A year earlier, he published a collection of essays called the *ABC of Economics*.

In 1940, T.S. Eliot, Pound's friend, who was also born in the United States but became a British citizen, was asked if a great nation needed to have a great language, and if so, if it was the business of the writer as artist to help to preserve and extend the resources of that language. Eliot replied that "the dictionary is the most important, the most inexhaustible book to a writer. Incidentally, I find it the best reading in the world when I am recovering from influenza, or any other temporary illness, except that one needs a bookrest for it across the bed. You want a big dictionary, because definitions are not enough by themselves: you want the quotations showing how a word has been used ever since it was first used." Eliot wasn't thinking of the *OED* but of the *Shorter Oxford*.

As the various successive editions, as well as the supplements, of the OED appeared over time, the database of contemporary writers was updated. Authors like George Bernard Shaw, W.H. Auden, Virginia Woolf, and George Orwell were quoted. Conversely, these writers occasionally reflected on the dictionary as a source of control and as a receptacle of collective memory. Orwell (whose adjectivized last name, "Orwellian," is defined as "characteristic or reminiscent of the world of *Nineteen Eighty-four* [1949], a dystopian account of a future state in which every aspect of life is controlled by Big Brother, by the British novelist George Orwell [1903–50])," turns the dictionary into an image in his dystopian novel. In the back matter, he includes an extraordinary section on Newspeak, defined as "a language that sounds impressive but deliberately hides the truth and tries to change people's traditional views about something." However, *Nineteen Eighty-Four* doesn't include a lexicon per se.

By the second half of the 20th century, the idea used by Pound and others to organize one's thoughts and even one's own life experiences in the manner of dictionaries took hold. Polish essayist and poet Czeslaw Miłosz also wrote a couple of autobiographical volumes, *Miłosz's ABC's* (1997) and *A Further Alphabet* (1998), in which he organized his life using the alphabetical sequence. So did Carlos Fuentes in *This I Believe* (2002), a dictionary of his ideological preferences. I'm not sure these narratives are actual tributes to dictionaries as such or to encyclopedias, which proves, in any case, that the line between these two formats remains muddled. And in the word-playing young adult novel *The Phantom Tollboth* (1961), by Norton Juster, Milo, the protagonist, travels to all sorts of philological demographies, such as the Lands Beyond, where he is in a quest to rescue Rhyme and Reason. Figuratively, in the novel the dictionary is both a labyrinth and a map.

While Jorge Luis Borges believed that "the dictionary is based on the hypothesis – obviously an unproven one – that languages are made up of equivalent synonyms," dictionaries don't occupy a prominent space in his oeuvre. Encyclopedias do, as in the case of the encyclopedia of Tlön, of which it is said, in the story "Tlön, Uqbar, *Orbis Tertius*" (first published in the magazine *Sur* [1940] and reprinted in *Ficciones* [1944]), that it is an idealized territory that exists only in the minds of a few initiated followers. Elsewhere, Borges writes about alternative languages, some of them created ex nihilo, for instance in "The Analytical Language of John Wilkins" (*Other Inquisitions: 1937–1952*). In Wilkins's arbitrary language, Borges states, he divided the universe "into forty categories or classes, which were then subdivisible into differences, subdivisible in turn into species. To each class he assigned a monosyllable of two letters; to each difference, a consonant; to each species, a vowel. For example, *de* means element; *deb*, the first of the elements, fire; *deba*, a portion of the element of fire, a flame," and so on. Yet Borges doesn't offer a dictionary of Wilkins' enterprise, which would showcase its symmetrical structures.

In chapter 3 of Gabriel García Márquez's *One Hundred Years of Solitude* (1967), an epidemic of insomnia sweeps over Macondo, the mythical town where the action is set. Soon the lack of sleep leads to another equally troublesome symptom: the loss of memory in the town population. José Arcadio Buendía, the founder of Macondo, devises a method made of tags – a kind of Montessori system – that allows people to remember what objects are for: "This is the cow. She must be milked every morning so that she will produce milk, and the milk must be boiled in order to be mixed with coffee to make coffee and milk." José Arcadio Buendía's idea is successful; it then leads him to his next invention: the memory machine: "The artifact was based on the possibility of reviewing every morning, from beginning to end, the totality of knowledge acquired during one's life." And here's the pertinent aspect of it: "He conceived of it as a spinning dictionary that a person placed on the axis could operate by means of a lever, so that in very few hours there would pass before his eyes the notions most necessary for life."

One of the most beautiful literary tributes to dictionaries is by Chilean poet Pablo Neruda. His "Ode to the Dictionary" is one of the 250 odes he wrote in the middle period of his career. He describes the ambivalent relationship he had with the dictionary when he was young and how, as years went by, it became an invaluable companion. I included my English translation in my book *Selected Translations: Poems 2000–2020* (2021).

Postmodern games with the alphabet, and sometimes with the dictionary as well, were common in the sixties and beyond. Among the most famous is Georges Perec's novel *La Disparition* (1969), known in English as *A Void* (1994). Perec writes the entire narrative without the letter "e," quite a challenging feast given its invaluable status as one of the five most important letters of the alphabet. Needless to say, any translation of it – the English one was done by Gilbert Adair in 1984 – is equally difficult, as much a jigsaw puzzle as a full-fledged narrative. It isn't surprising that Perec loved dictionaries. But as a presence the dictionary isn't quite a character in his oeuvre.

A bit closer perhaps, though still resisting the presence of the dictionary as such, is another postmodern novel, *Alphabetical Africa* (1974), by the Jewish-American writer Walter Abish, follows what has come to be known as an alliterative approach to literature. The architecture of the volume is interesting: each of the first 25 chapters is devoted to another letter, containing only words starting with "a," or "b," and so on. Then the flow is reversed, letters are removed in the reverse order. The idea is intriguing, but is it good? Milorad Pavić's *Dictionary of the Khazars* (1984), written in Serbian, is built as an encyclopedic dictionary about the Khazars, who supposedly converted to Judaism at the end of the 8th and beginning of the 9th century. The three sections in the novel are each written from another perspective from the viewpoint of the three Abrahamic religions: Judaism, Christianity, and Islam. Though it purports to be a historical game, all the characters in the book are fictional.

Likewise, the use of the dictionary as a manual for specific emotions became a standard trope. Han Shaogong's *A Dictionary of Maqiao* (1996), set in a small Chinese village in Hunan province, is compiled as a dictionary composed as 115 articles in a dictionary written by a student sent by a policy institute in the 1960s in the People's Republic. The author was accused of imitating Pavić and went to court to defend himself. And Xiaolu Guo's *A Concise Chinese-English Dictionary for Lovers* (2007) is a novel about a Chinese woman who has an affair with a British man. As she struggles to make sense of her emotions, she puts together a dictionary.

One of the writers fascinated with dictionaries, encyclopedias, and with language as a semiotic code is the Italian scholar and novelist Umberto Eco, author of the thriller set in the Middle Ages, *The Name of the Rose* (1980). Eco spent his life thinking about language as a system to organize reality. He published encyclopedias of various kinds, including one called *On Beauty* (2004) and another *On Ugliness* (2007). In *Serendipities: Language and Lunacy* (1998), he said that "the cultivated person's first duty is to be always prepared to rewrite the encyclopedia," which, again, was a synonym of *dictionary*.

I have left for the end literary explorations that have dictionaries at their heart. The business of lexicography, the ins and outs, has spilled into mainstream culture. At the dawn of the new millennium, explorations of how words change, who is behind the adoption of any of them into the OED or Merriam-Webster's dictionaries, and how dictionaries have come to occupy a privileged place in society are frequent topics of nonfiction books. Among the best is British journalist Simon Winchester's *The Surgeon of Crowthorne: A Tale of Murder, Madness and the Love of Words* (1998), a history of how the OED was put together by professionals as well as laymen contributors, one of whom was William Chester Minor, a surgeon in the US army who lived at the Broadmoor Criminal Lunatic Asylum, in Berkshire, England. Other literary explorations include my own *Dictionary Days: A Defining Passion* (2005) and Ammon Shea's *Reading the OED: One Man, One Year, 21,730 Pages* (2008).

Along the same lines, there are excellent volumes on how Johnson or Webster came to compose his dictionary. Notable are Joshua Kendall's *The Forgotten Founding Father: Noah Webster's Obsession and the Creation of an American Culture* (2012), Winchester's *The Meaning of Everything: The Story of the Oxford English Dictionary* (2018), and Peter Martin's *The Dictionary Wars: The American Fight over the English Language* (2019).

These meditations emphasize the centrality of dictionaries as literary themes. There is an insatiable need to understand them as engines of nation building. That need turns them into magnets but also into targets: they codify words as much as they prescribe what is and isn't accented, thus becoming enemies of freedom, at least a romantic conception of it.

– Cambridge Companion to the Dictionary (2023)

Is American Spanish Healthy?

How does one measure the health of a language? By means of looking at its diversity and by attentively exploring the way it reacts to the challenges it faces.

With approximately 400 million speakers worldwide today, Spanish is the second most widely spoken native language in the world, after the sum of varieties of Chinese (1.3 billion), and before English (about 379 million). Internationally, English is the most popular second language, which means there are far more non-native (approximately 1.5 billion) than native speakers, at a ratio of roughly five to one. Some twenty countries have Spanish as either their official language or, as in the case of Bolivia and Paraguay, as one among several. All of this is a statement of global dominance but not about fitness. The Spanish-speaking Latin American countries with the largest populations are, in descending order, Mexico, Colombia, and Argentina. (Spain comes after Colombia, with 47 million speakers.) In each of them, the language is used in pluralistic, idiosyncratic ways, to such a degree that talking about a "national language" is pertinent only insofar as the designation accommodates the nonstandard varieties encompassed within a specific territory. There is Lunfardo in Argentina, for instance; elsewhere, there are also hybrid tongues like Frespañol (French and Spanish), Portuñol (Portuguese and Spanish), Tanglañol (Tagalog and Spanish), and Casteidish (Spanish and Yiddish). In general, Spanish doesn't recognize these mixed forms. Yet the second-largest concentration of Hispanic people in the globe is in the United States, with over 60 million, of which close to 45 million use some type of Spanish. Nowhere else does it face more substantial hurdles in its daily interaction than it does with English, resulting in an assortment of communication strategies as well as – and prominently – Spanglish, a mestizo form that, although controversial, is increasingly recognized as a legitimate form of communication. Spanglish is the elephant in the room, meaning that it does not cease to exist because one works hard at ignoring it.

Iberian and American Spanish exist in a state of inequality. For starters, the tension between standard Iberian Spanish and the American varieties poses a number of important questions, not only what is "normal" in a particular type of Spanish and what is deviant but to what extent "normality" should be defined in Spain. How does the language negotiate the balance between a standardized form in one corner of the Hispanophone world vis-à-vis the other? What number of words is it acceptable to loan from other languages in one country, and how many should that national Spanish loan to others? Does the Spanish of Mexico affect the Spanish of, say, Argentina or Venezuela or Costa Rica?

Arguably the most sensitive thermometers of a language are writers. Writers experiment with words, turning them upside down and inside out. Their relationship with the lexicographic archives is ambivalent at heart: they discard what they deem unnecessary and invent what they feel is needed. Among the most fertile of writers – such as Alejo Carpentier, Julio Cortázar, Gabriel García Márquez, and Elena Poniatowska – reshape syntax in their own image. Of course, there are a number of other significant keepers of a language, such as the makers of dictionaries and the members of academies, and maybe a cohort in the media (bloggers, commentators, and newspaper columnists). But overall they tend to be more solemn, less playful. Writers are clarions. They get dirty with words, so to speak. Writers not only embrace linguistic change; they even take a lead in bringing about that change. On the opposite end are academies, largely non-educational institutions in charge of safeguarding a language, a task that takes all sorts of strategies to accomplish, which function differently depending on the culture in which they are located. Academies tend to be less permissive, more conservative. Their responsibility is to maintain the status quo; to that end, they become self-proclaimed fortresses against change. Language on the street often moves at a rhythm different from that of the academy.

In the case of Spanish, speakers in the Hispanophone world nurture a love/hate relationship with the Real Academia Española, the Royal Spanish Academy, originally founded in 1713. In part this is because of the anarchic emotions ingrained in the DNA of the culture, but also because of the aloofness and datedness the institution maintains, at least on its facade. Apparently, none of the academies in other imperial languages – such as French, Italian, and Portuguese – projects such snootiness, such pomposity as the one based in Madrid. (English doesn't have the equivalent of a royal academy, although at different times in its history there have been attempts to establish one, either in London or in Washington, DC, or New York.) The embarrassing institutional motto, "limpia, fija y da esplendor," is frequently derided as paternalistic, not to say colonizing. (For decades, if not centuries, there have been fruitless petitions to the RAE to change it.) Almost every Spanish-speaking country has its Academia Correspondiente (altogether, there are twenty-two), which, at least according to lore, are extremities of the Spanish matrix endowed to arbitrate what is proper in their respective habitats; yet, when it comes to the nitty-gritty, they have a subaltern position vis-à-vis Madrid. At any rate, the RAE decides what words go in the official *Diccionario de la Lengua Española*, a tool fitting the language to the Iberian taste. Variants emerging in the Americas are said to take years to reach the academy and only a few are deemed acceptable for inclusion in the lexicon. This creates a centralized structure that is at once stifling and unidirectional. Change happens all the time in Spanish; it is just that officialdom isn't prone to accepting it.

Among the assortment of books under review, the one in which the love affair with Spanish is most creative is Daniel Balderston's lavishly illustrated edition of *How Borges Wrote* (2018). (Curiously, the title is in past tense, although dead writers exist in an eternal present.) Heavily illustrated, the volume is made of photographic and textual reproductions of a large number of Borges's manuscripts. Balderston, who teaches at the University of Pittsburgh and has devoted his whole career to the Argentine author of *El Aleph*, studies, with meticulous care, the artistic development of a writer who, with little doubt, is among the best of the twentieth century. It is possible to count on one hand the writers in Spanish who, aside from being extraordinarily eloquent in their oeuvre, have a deep knowledge of, and influence on, the ins and outs of the language. Even among them, Borges is on top. A polyglot, he wrote in Spanish, English, and French, and knew, among other tongues, German, Latin, and Hebrew. Of him one might say what is often ascribed to Flaubert: he was about *le mot juste*. There is a mathematical precision in his best work – say, the poem "Spinoza," the story "Tlön, Uqbar, *Orbis Tertius*," and the essay "The Argentine Writer and Tradition" (which began as a lecture in Buenos Aires and was first published in 1951) – that gives the impression of complete control over language. But there is something more: Borges was attuned to the undulations of Argentine Spanish in a unique way. His early oeuvre, especially as seen in "Man on Pink Corner," displays an interest in Argentine slang and even in Lunfardo. This is because Borges was attracted to the language of *orilleros* and other urban social types, just as he was attracted to the world of the gauchos from the pampas. Among his innumerable contributions to gaucho literature, for instance, was the distinction between what was gaucho and *gauchesco*, the latter an artistic recreation of gaucho life not written by those who experienced it. In other words, Borges was drawn to degrees of experiential knowledge and the way an individual or work of art represented, genuinely and otherwise, a particular archetype of Argentina's identity.

How Borges Wrote is about how Borges became an Argentine writer and, along the way, how he transformed himself into the most universal of American writers in Spanish. The book benefits from a couple of crucial factors. One is the accumulated research done by dozens of scholars over the last half century or so on the author's evolution, his aspirations, and his pantheon of myths. The details of these affinities are quite granular. I myself recently published *Borges, the Jew*, a short book/long disquisition on Borges's interest in Jewish themes.[1] In it I go so far as to describe him as a Jewish author, so nuanced was his knowledge of symbols and motifs from the Kabbalah, the Talmud, and modern Jewish literature, including Franz Kafka, Martin Buber, and S.Y. Agnon. The other factor is the surfacing of Borges's manuscripts, frequently coming from suspicious collectors and misguided dealers. The abundance of such items makes it possible to compare versions. This allows for a refreshing take on the oeuvre: to what extent did Borges edit (that is, "correct") as he shaped several versions of the same text? Did he alter material even as he was reading proofs? Are all the changes visible in the manuscripts coming from his own hands?

The result is a window into the Argentine writer's inner and outer drive. In analyzing various versions, Balderston allows the reader to see the superciliousness with which Borges approached writing. Like the nineteenth-century French poet and essayist Paul Valéry, Borges believed that a work of literature is never really finished; it is only abandoned. What comes across is a supreme devotion – one might even talk of a religious fervor – toward Spanish as an inexhaustible verbal reservoir and Borges as its supreme keeper. Without being too rigid, he looks for the syntactically correct sentence. But often he does something else. Since he learned to read in English (in a famous anecdote included in "An Autobiographical Essay," published in co-authorship with Norman Thomas Di Giovanni in the *New Yorker* in 1970, Borges said he first read *Don Quixote of La Mancha* in Shakespeare's tongue;

---

1 Ilan Stavans, *Borges, the Jew* (Albany: State University of New York Press, 2016).

when he later encountered the Spanish original, he thought it was a poor translation), it is possible to detect an English-language grammatical base in his structure. So much so that a number of translators of his work – myself included – have said that bringing it from Spanish into English is less about structure and more about everything else. The fact that Borges polished his works with such intensity creates a feast for language lovers. It serves as a reminder that the health of a language lies in the infinite possibilities it allows.

Another way of attesting how a language functions is by looking at its dictionaries. Unfortunately, the dominant dictionaries of the Hispanic world – where lexicography is recognizably several steps behind that of other ecosystems – reflect this pseudo-federalist approach. A recent edition of the *Diccionario Panhispánico de Dudas (DPD)* is a perfect example. Reviewing a dictionary, needless to say, is a daunting task. The key markers indicate not only if it is complete but how it defines the very concept of completeness, if it is clearly and accessibly designed, if it addresses a tangible overall need, if it contains typos or mistakes, and if it proposes definitions that are either misconstrued or contain implied biases. Finding mistakes in dictionaries, it should be added, is occasionally the sport of writers like Guillermo Cabrera Infante, García Márquez, and Rosario Ferré. For instance, García Márquez, in a column in the Spanish newspaper *El País* (May 19, 1982), pointed to the word *perro*, which used to be defined as "Mamífero doméstico de la familia de los cánidos, de tamaño, forma y pelajes muy diversos, según las razas, pero siempre con la cola de menor longitud que las patas posteriores, una de las cuales levanta el macho para orinar." The author of *Cien años de soledad* was a fan of María Moliner, but this didn't stop him, in the same article, from criticizing her definition of *día*: "Espacio de tiempo que tarda el Sol en dar una vuelta completa alrededor de la Tierra." The mistake, it appears, was rooted in the *Diccionario de la Lengua Española*, which defined *día* as "Tiempo que el Sol emplea en dar, aparentemente, una vuelta a la Tierra." As a discipline, lexicography constantly borders on plagiarism.[2]

Since the publication of its first printed edition in 2005, the mission of the *DPD* has been to resolve "las dudas lingüísticas más habituales

---

2 In his *The New Discoverer Discover'd* (1659), Thomas Pierce writes: "It is not certainly for nothing, that the word Plagiary should signifie (in Classick writers) a stealer of other folkes children, and of other folkes Wit; the fruit of the body, and of the brain." The *Oxford English Dictionary Online* (2012), offering a historical definition, describes a plagiarist as "person who abducts the child or slave of another, kidnapper, seducer, also a literary thief."

(ortográficas, léxicas y gramaticales) que plantea el uso del español." The 2015 edition updates those definitions and expands the lexicon's database. How does one accomplish such a task in such a vast, heterogeneous milieu? Is *vosotros* better than *vos*? Is *con tal que* right and *con tal de que* wrong? Is *bicho* a bug or a sexual organ? In principle, the lexicon isn't only orthodox but Iberocentric; it settles questions according to the mode used in Spain, in spite of the fact that only one out of every nine users of the language lives in the Iberian Peninsula. And while it purports not to impose but to persuade, its 888 pages, in this age in which the legacy of the colonial enterprise is thoroughly being questioned, do come across as paternalistic.

It is useful to distinguish between two types of dictionaries: descriptive and prescriptive. English-language lexicography endorses the former; that is, the purpose of the *Oxford English Dictionary* or *Merriam-Webster Dictionary* is to describe how the language is used at a specific time. For better or worse, English is a language "of the people, by the people, and for the people," a line, by the way, first used by John Wycliffe in 1384 in the prologue to his translation of the Bible. In the Hispanic world, in contrast, there is a preponderance of prescriptive lexicons, that is, manuals that purport to tell people how to use the language properly. The very idea of a *diccionario de dudas* already unmasks the objective behind it: the dictionary doesn't collect words for users to ponder at will; instead, it resolves doubts; that is, is legislates what is right and what isn't.

The general state of lexicography in Spanish, in my view, is rather sleepy. It doesn't have the sort of grip that builds on critical analysis. The *DPD* prolongs the approach established by the *Diccionario de americanismos* (2010), spearheaded by Humberto López Morales, who for years coordinated the Asociación de Academias de la Lengua Española in the Hispanic world. While recognizing plurality, it quiets diversity. It reduces the number of loan words, especially from English, to a minimum. It is no surprise that noninstitutional lexicons like *María Moliner* and *Clave*[3] feel spongier, more accepting, in the spirit of the polemical *Webster's Third*.[4] They aren't forced to fit any political

---

3 María Moliner, *Diccionario del uso del español*, 3rd ed., 2 vols. (Madrid: RBA & Gredos, 2007); and *Clave: Diccionario del uso del español actual* (Madrid: Ediciones SM, 2006).
4 Published in 1961 by G. & C. Merriam & Co., *Webster's Third New International* (unabridged) was called the most progressive of English-language dictionaries. See David Skinner's "Ain't That the Truth: Webster's Third, the Most Controversial Dictionary in the English Language," *Humanities* 30, no. 4 (2009): https://www.neh.gov/humanities/2009/julyaugust/feature/ain%E2%80%99t-the-truth.

agenda like those of the Royal Spanish Academy. The *DPD* places emphasis on the term "pan-Hispanic," which, ironically, it doesn't define. Still, in attempting to look at normative language across the entire Hispanic world, it relates "norma" to the "standard form," by which it means "norma culta." Except that, in establishing that norm, it is aspirational rather than scientific. In the front matter, this is how it explains its purpose:

> El español no es idéntico en todos los lugares en que se habla. En cada país, e incluso en cada zona geográfica y culturalmente delimitada dentro de cada país, las preferencias lingüísticas de sus habitantes son distintas, en algún aspecto, de las preferencias de los hablantes de otras zonas y países. Además, las divergencias en el uso no se deben únicamente a razones geográficas. También dependen en gran medida del modo de expresión (oral o escrito), de la situación comunicativa (formal o informal) y del nivel sociocultural de los hablantes.
>
> Por su carácter de lengua supranacional, hablada en más de veinte países, el español constituye, en realidad, un conjunto de normas diversas, que comparten, no obstante, una amplia base común: la que se manifiesta en la expresión culta de nivel formal, extraordinariamente homogénea en todo el ámbito hispánico, con variaciones mínimas entre las diferentes zonas, casi siempre de tipo fónico y léxico. Es por ello la expresión culta formal la que constituye el *español estándar:* la lengua que todos empleamos, o aspiramos a emplear, cuando sentimos la necesidad de expresarnos con corrección; la lengua que se enseña en las escuelas; la que, con mayor o menor acierto, utilizamos al hablar en público o emplean los medios de comunicación; la lengua de los ensayos y de los libros científicos y técnicos. Es, en definitiva, la que configura la norma, el código compartido que hace posible que hispanohablantes de muy distintas procedencias se entiendan sin dificultad y se reconozcan miembros de una misma comunidad lingüística.

Expressed differently, the *DPD* establishes what is correct and what isn't according to an educated criterion that is established by a community of Iberian linguistic legislators who, while paying attention to multiple variants, reach their final decision in Europe. Centralism supersedes demographic representation.

Periodically, a history of the Spanish language is published to assess the historical development of the language over the centuries. Here, again, the quality of explorations is an expression of the type of thinking on language that goes on in the culture at large. The most distinguished figures in the field, including Ramón Menéndez Pidal, Amado

Alonso, and Rafael Lapesa (with rare exceptions, such as María Rosa Lida de Malkiel, this is mostly a men's club), tend toward static, revisionist accounts that analyze the development of Spanish in a suffocating fashion. They come from a Germanic philological tradition that focuses on morpho-syntactical patterns rather than on large cultural waves. The result are historiographies that tend to be triumphalist in their vision, of the type that argues that Spanish is an astonishing language because it has survived more than a million years. In my view, less methodical but more compelling is a book like *The Story of Spanish* (2013) by the Canadian couple Jean-Benoît Nadeau and Julie Barlow. While chatty and lighthearted, it is far more enlightening, in part because the authors provide a larger comparative context against which to understand the development of the Spanish language. (They have also written *The Story of French* [2008].)[5]

At the time of his death in 1968, Menéndez Pidal left unfinished a history of the Spanish language, two volumes of which were published posthumously. In spite of his narrow focus, it would have been enormously useful to see the project in toto. Useful books by John M. Lipski,[6] Ralph Penny,[7] and David A. Pharies,[8] among others, have followed the historical arch of the language. Francisco Moreno Fernández, who

---

5 Jean-Benoît Nadeau and Julie Barlow, *The Story of French* (New York: St. Martin's Griffin, 2008), and *The Story of Spanish* (New York: St. Martin's Griffin, 2014). Nadeau and Barlow are idiosyncratic essayists. More than straight arguments, their books feel like accumulations of anecdotes. *The Story of Spanish* is made of disparate sections about topics like Alfonso X ,"El Sabio," the Real Academia Española, and the syncopated relationship between dialects and standardized languages.
6 John M. Lipski, *Latin American Spanish* (New York: Longman, 1994).
7 Ralph Penny, *A History of the Spanish Language*, 2nd ed. (New York: Cambridge University Press, 2003). The historical emphasis in this volume isn't on social changes but on how phonology, morpho-syntax, and semantics, among other dimensions, have evolved over time. In that sense, it isn't a history of the Spanish language as much as a compendium of linguistic evolution. This makes for a dry, obtuse reading experience. Only chapter 6, "Past, Present, and Future," lives up to the volume's title.
8 David A. Pharies, *A Brief History of the Spanish Language*, 2nd ed. (Chicago: University of Chicago Press, 2015). At 314 pages in a volume with a small trim size, this is a "brief" history. Unfortunately, the sections on American and US Spanish are minuscule. Divided into nine chapters, the book explores language change in sweeping ways, looking into, among other things, language families, bilingualism and diglossia, the Visigothic and Muslim invasions of the Iberian Peninsula, the so-called Reconquista, Latin syntax, Alphonsine orthography, the Jewish dialect known as Sephardi, and American Spanish. The book also includes excerpts from important texts, which are accompanied by questions designed for students to engage with the material. This pedagogical component feels like an afterthought, however. Pharies is also the editor-in-chief of the *University of Chicago Spanish-English Dictionary/Diccionario Universidad*

teaches at the Universidad de Alcalá, is a member of the evangelical Cervantes Institute, and recently published the rather unsatisfying *Diccionario de anglicismos del español estadounidense* (2018), has embarked in such a quest in *La maravillosa historia del español*.[9] It is a bizarre, disjointed, and mechanical examination that shows little by way of insight.

Moreno Fernández's approach is rather conventional. He divided his narrative into three major parts, each subdivided into six chapters. The first section, "De los orígenes a las navegaciones," reaches the age of Columbus. "Del imperio a las revoluciones," the second section, looks at the falling Spanish Empire and its colonies, exploring the Enlightenment and its approach to science, religion, and language. And the third and last section, "De las independencias al siglo XXI," is a sweeping account of the age of independence and the challenges Spanish faces in modernity, in particular on social media.

As in other ambitious undertakings of this type, Moreno Fernández must go fast in order to cover as much terrain as possible. The problem is that his style is stilted (he writes in a *castizo* voice, an affected Castilian trait that feels outdated) and his insights are uninteresting. For instance, the part on the colonization of the Americas is delivered without a hint of regret for what was lost in the Iberian imperial quest. Andrés Bello, arguably the most influential thinker on language and a Renaissance man in his own right, gets a summary profile. Borges barely gets a mention. Regrettably, essential scholars Amado Alonso, Miguel Antonio Caro Tobar, Rufino José Cuervo Urisarri, Rubén Darío, Américo Castro, Pedro Henríquez Ureña, and Alfonso Reyes just don't exist. It should be said that the vast majority of histories of the Spanish language that are available are the product of Iberian authors. This inevitably situates them in a mindset that looks at Spanish as a centripetal exercise. Moreno Fernández doesn't appear to be aware of his own viewpoint. A counterpoint to his stand is Antonio Alatorre's *Los 1001*

---

de Chicago Inglés-Español, 6th ed. (Chicago: University of Chicago Press, 2012), which, at 626 pages, is also relatively concise. For a different historical and lexicographic approach than that of Nadeau and Barlow, Lipski, Penny, and Pharies, see my essay "Notes on Latino Philology," in *The Oxford Handbook of Latino Studies*, edited by Ilan Stavans (New York: Oxford University Press, 2020), 267–83. The latter also appears in this volume.

9 Antonio Alatorre, *Los 1001 años de la lengua española*, 3rd ed. (Mexico City: Fondo de Cultura Económica, 2002). Alatorre (1922– 2010) is an insightful thinker awaiting recognition. Aside from his studies on language and literature, he translated, among others, Marcel Bataillon, Jacques Lacan, and Machado de Assis into Spanish, edited the complete works of Sor Juana Inés de La Cruz, and led El Colegio de México between 1953 and 1972.

años de la lengua española (1989). Written in Mexico, it looks at Spanish reverentially while also recognizing its oppressive, undignified nature as it reached beyond its immediate confines in the Iberian Peninsula. This attitude – the perspective of the coerced – is palpable in every sentence.

Another vantage point from which to appreciate how a language relates to the world is translation. It is the mechanism whereby what occurs outside one's language is verbally reconstructed.

Without translation, we would exist in total isolation. But translation also poses challenges when it comes to understanding one's own habitat and that of others. While the number of books translated into Spanish in the nineteenth century was far lower than the equivalent in German, French, English, or Italian, a vigorous effort to bring other literatures to the heart of Hispanic culture has greatly expanded the reservoir of possibilities. Still, a number of important issues have emerged. Since the fact that many of the translations are made – paid and published – in Spain, and given that the syntax is often Iberian, does this endeavor amount to a perpetuation of the colonial relationship between Spain and the Americas? Is this another way to make Iberian Spanish the default normative variety? Obviously, the outpouring of translations from Spain to the rest of the Hispanophone world is a legacy of the economic dependency of past centuries. Shouldn't there be active ways to address this dilemma?

There is also the issue of loyalties. In an epoch in which popular culture, traveling fast through broadcast and social media, allows English to remain a global conqueror while also opening doors to other tongues, purity is actually impossible to imagine in concrete terms; so is the penchant for verbal contamination. Vicente L. Rafael's *Motherless Tongues: The Insurgency of Language amid Wars of Translation* is, among other things, an exploration of identity in the Philippines, an invaluable case study when it comes to understanding the adventures of Spanish since the Spanish-American War of 1898. A professor of history at the University of Washington, Rafael focuses on the clash between Spanish and English and on what he calls "the vexed relationship between language and history."[10] In the early pages, Rafael offers an insightful

---

10 Rafael wrote the introduction to Nick Joaquin's *The Woman Who Had Two Navels and Tales of the Tropical Gothic* (New York: Penguin Classics, 2017), a classic of Filipino literature that is fascinating not only for its content but for the English in which it is written, showcasing the "doubleness" of his postcolonial worldview. That "doubleness" is at the heart of translation as an intellectual endeavor, especially when the source comes from the misnamed "Third World."

autobiographical meditation on his own journey. Born in the mid-fifties, he talks about his various languages in private school, how English ruled and Spanish was taught badly so that students wouldn't learn it properly, as well as other tongues that connected him with several segments of Manila. On page 5, he offers a portrait of how Spanish lost its dominance in the Philippines and even English stopped being enforced by outside powers (nearly half a century of US colonial rule came to an end in 1946), giving place to a Babel-like plurality of options:

> Such is a condensed inventory of my linguistic legacy: the privilege of American English punctured and punctuated by a variety of vernaculars: Tagalog, Ilonggo, Kapampangan, bits and pieces of Hokkien, Hakka, Spanish, and Latin. The garrulous and swiftly changing idioms of creole Tanglish, gay-speak, private school talk, and Marxist-Maoist jargon woven into the black vernacular and bohemian lexicon of American pop culture of the 1960s – all of which were pronounced with different regional accents – further added to this dizzying density. Hence, whenever I am asked what my native language is, I always hesitate to respond. I cannot point to a single one without feeling that I might be betraying the others.

Is the eclipse of Spanish, as Rafael describes it, a concession of misbegotten imperial dreams? In what sense is the experience in the Philippines the opposite of what took place in Spain's former colonies in the Caribbean Basin, such as Cuba and Puerto Rico? Does the eclipse of Spanish fully explain why the Philippines are frequently excluded from general accounts of Latin America?

In a volume in which I found much to admire, perhaps Rafael's most inspiring sections deal with war: translation in war and translation as war, as well as the battle for the soul of the Philippines from the perspective of the receding Spanish Empire, which lost the 1898 war, and the arrival of English as a language of instruction and also of submission soon after, and, in the middle of this, the role of Tagalog as a conduit of insurgency. Rafael's disquisitions are fascinating, in part because in the spectrum of Hispanic civilization the Philippines remains a marginal, eclipsed space. There is an astute section on Renato Rosado ("Contracting Nostalgia") and another on Reynaldo Ileto ("Language, History, and Autobiography"). War, tacit or concrete, is, for Rafael, the natural state of the Philippines. And language is the field in which insurgency and consent are played out. He is a perspicacious observer of culture whose discernments constantly open up new vistas.

Rosina Lozano's *An American Language: The History of Spanish in the United States* has breadth and vision. Its focus isn't really the present, although the implications of its findings surely reach to our day. Lozano, who teaches at Princeton, focuses on approximately a century, from the end of the Mexican-American War of 1846–1848 to the end of the Second World War in 1945. She breaks this period in two, with the immediate aftermath of the Guerra del '98 as the parting of the waters. It was at that time that Spain finally receded from the Caribbean Basin and the Philippines, and the United States became the new ruling imperial power. The division is productive. The territories that are known now as the Southwest entered the US constellation after the Treaty of Guadalupe Hidalgo was signed. The population in them, including Nevada, Utah, and New Mexico, diverse as it was, was suddenly asked to communicate in English, with Spanish becoming a subservient tongue. This linguistic imposition created an identity among Spanish speakers whose scars are felt to the present day. Likewise, the use non-Latinos made of Spanish in those lands underwent a series of dramatic transformations, syntactical as well as cultural. Then, in 1902, Puerto Rico officially entered the liminal condition it still finds itself in: neither a fully independent nation nor a full-fledged state of the union. This duality again played itself out at the level of language, in the island's labyrinthine negotiations between Spanish and English. Scores of Mexicans in the United States and Puerto Ricans in the mainland enlisted in the military in the 1940s, displaying their patriotism. The way Spanish was employed in their ranks, and the vitality it displayed on the home front in politics, education, media, and advertising are superb channels to understand the vicissitudes the language underwent in the early half of the twentieth century.

Lozano isn't a linguist; she isn't a philologist, either. Her academic field is history. This is palpable everywhere in her approach. *An American Language* (the title echoes H.L. Mencken's invaluable multivolume *The American Language*)[11] looks at empirical data coming from social fields rather than zooming in on grammar, syntax, and other verbal devices. Although Lozano is a savvier, far more accomplished interpreter of reality than Moreno Fernández, this absence produces a picture that isn't unlike Francisco Moreno Fernández's: a view of the ups and downs of people and artifacts but not enough analysis of the actual transformations, that is, how verbal conjugations, nouns, adjectives,

---

11 H.L. Mencken, *The American Language: An Inquiry into the Development of English in the United States*, 2nd ed. (New York: Alfred A. Knopf, 1938; first published 1919). This is an extraordinary work through which it is possible to appreciate the immigrant waves defining American society through the prism of language. Mencken's erudition is admirable, as is his witty, irreverent style.

adverbs, and punctuation have changed over time. The reader finishes Lozano's book with a clear sense of how Spanish was besieged across those one hundred years, but the adventures of its grammar are barely mentioned.

Spanglish, in my opinion, was the real outcome of the debacle. The term wasn't used in full until the 1970s by Nuyoricans, whose pugilistic search for place on the East Coast connected them with the freedom fighters of the Civil Rights era. At first, the sense of a common hybrid language that took from both Spanish and English was split into subgroups: Mexican-Americans, Puerto Ricans in the mainland, and Cubans in Florida. However, by the 1990s there was a growing sense that these diverse national entities had come together in a larger whole and that the mixed tongues they used had much in common. It was then that the word *Spanglish* gained currency. Is the use of Spanglish a sign that Spanish is in retreat? Does Spanglish represent a defeat for English-language instruction in schools? Is Spanglish evidence that Latinos aren't assimilating to the so-called melting pot (or, in the jargon of other sociologists, the mosaic) the way other immigrant groups have?[12] This is why, in spite of its rigid, scientific structure, *Educating across Borders: The Case of a Dual Language Program on the U.S.-Mexico Border*, by María Teresa de la Piedra, Blanca Araujo, and Alberto Esquinca, is important. The first and third authors teach at the University of Texas at El Paso and the second at New Mexico State University. Their book is an ethnography by three researchers of the lives of bilingual students on both sides of the border. This population is called "transfronterizxs." They not only cross the border regularly but they exist in a state of permanent language switch. The traditional view is that such back-and-forth ends up being detrimental to those who engage in it. Worse, there are preconceived assumptions that the people on the border suffer from an educational deficit and that such a deficit delays them in comparison with monolingual populations on either side of the divide. What de la Piedra, Araujo, and Esquinca find is altogether different.

Perhaps this is the appropriate place to offer a brief reflection along the lines of an op-ed I wrote in the *New York Times en Español* on the

---

12 I have debated these questions in "For the Love of Spanglish," *New York Times*, July 20, 2017, https://www.nytimes.com/2017/07/20/ opinion/puerto-rico-spanglish.html. Among other examples, see my translation of *El Little Príncipe* by Antoine de Saint-Exupéry (Neckarsteinacher, Germany: Edition Tintenfass, 2016) and the essay "*El Líttle Príncipe* –Translating Saint-Exupéry's Classic into Spanglish," *Words Without Borders* (January 25, 2017): https://www.wordswithoutborders.org/dispatches/article/el-little-principe-translating-saint-exuperys-classic-into-spanglish.

recent scholarly prevalence of using *x* in gender-based words.[13] While the intention is honest and legitimate – Spanish, one of the Romance languages, is a child of Latin in its gender-defined formations – the effort is misguided. Unlike, say, Arabic, the equality between oral and written languages is of one the prime reasons Spanish remains vital. The *x* is impossible to pronounce across all syntactic constructions; it also undermines the health of the language overall. The insistence with which the form is used in *Educating across Borders* makes a political statement that is less about scholarly rigor than it is about precision. Nevertheless, the volume offers a valuable contribution. They write on page 164, "we are sickened about the damaging false rhetoric about the border as a lawless land and a war zone, and about border residents characterized as violent criminals." Although the group they studied included upper-middle-class as well as working-class people, the majority belonged to the latter. The authors insist that further explorations on a more heterogeneous sample would offer more detailed findings. Still, the findings point to a singular asset: speakers who code-switch, when encouraged to be translingual without being penalized, display confidence and admirable depths of knowledge. To put it bluntly, *mestizaje* of languages as well as cultures should be welcomed. After all, it is a statement of the way things are among large portions of the border population.

In truth, these are also characteristics of a large number of Latinos who don't live along the US-Mexico line. *Mestizaje*, indeed, is the key word here. It is what characterizes the entire minority, all 60 million or more who live in every corner of the country. The dual identity among a large number of them, feeling loyal to Spanish but welcoming English as the lingua franca, is evidence of a new civilization rising in front of our eyes. That ascent, categorically, is one of the most significant transformations of Hispanic civilization in the last hundred years, one that, as a result of political clout and financial prowess, will surely define the future for all of the Hispanophone world. How Spanish, as a language, at the very least acknowledges that change is an indicator of where Hispanic civilization, and its language along with it, are likely to go in the future. It is emblematic that there are few books of value in Spanish on how to write well. Likewise, learned yet accessible meditations on how the language has evolved are few and far between. English has no linguistic police, yet there is a plethora of forums on how the language functions, who uses what strategies, what the histories of a

---

13 "El significado del 'latinx,'" *New York Times en Español*, November 14, 2017, https://www.nytimes.com/es/2017/11/14/el-significado-del-latinx/.

certain modality are, and so on. In contrast, in Spanish there is poverty in this regard. No doubt Spanglish represents the biggest challenge Spanish faces nowadays. Yet let us not forget that Spanish itself, since even before 1492, is constituted as a hodgepodge of elements in constant change. Latin is the original foundation, on top of which French, Arabic, English, German, and many other sources have left their mark. To survive, Spanish has needed to adapt to the circumstances, absorbing these ingredients in an ever-changing movement that keeps it spinning all the time. In the Americas in particular, that spin is frantic. The way Spanish has resolved the tension between unity and diversity highlights is in its versatility. This is to say that change is the most constant aspect of language, as it is of nature as a whole. Will it be capable of retaining its center as it continues to evolve? Will Spanglish, rejected for what it represents, be an autonomous, self-sufficient spin-off, a language in its own right? And will that loss leave Spanish limping?

– *Latin American Research Review*, volume 55, issue 1 (2020)

On Decidophobia (with Haoran Tong)

HAORAN TONG: The complex relationship between language and thought is a topic that has long intrigued poets, linguists, and philosophers. As philosopher Ludwig Wittgenstein famously proposed, "The limits of my language mean the limits of my world." While he faces challenges from some linguists and neuroscientists, generations of poets have followed his lead to explore the dialectic between language and thought through their own literary experiments. Translingual poets, for example, expand the scope of "poetic thoughts" by adding elements of multiple languages.

If we adopt a strict definition of "translingualism" – "trans" means "across, over, and beyond" – conversations across different languages may seem quite effortless. But the purpose of translingual poetry centers on "going beyond," that is, transcending the barriers of certain languages and therefore the thoughts and ideas they constrain. This nebulous process involves death and rebirth of mother tongues, confusion and epiphany of language-specific expressions, struggles of local and cosmopolitan identities. Do languages converge or compete in a multilingual poet's mind? Or must there be a dominant language?

ILAN STAVANS: The question has been with me ever since I have had memory. I grew up in a multilingual environment. On an average day, I would switch languages – Spanish, Yiddish, Hebrew – depending on the circumstance: in school I would use one, on the street another, with a particular set of relatives a third or fourth. Astonishingly, I don't remember ever getting confused. What's more, these languages, unless I'm mistaken, never intermingled. Years later, when I immigrated to New York City, I discovered what I would later recognize as "hybrid tongues," the mixing of Spanish and English (aka Spanglish), English and French (Franglais), English and Chinese (Chinglish), and so on. To the extent possible, the Spanish of my childhood was pure, and so was my Yiddish and Hebrew.

Therefore, languages do converge, though only on occasions defined by socio-economic circumstances. Conversely, languages also keep themselves apart, retaining their respective consistency. And, of course, they compete. That competition, in my view, is shaped by Darwinian forces. In a certain period, Yiddish was my dominant language. But at some point, Spanish took over. I wasn't interested in writing at that stage, but had I been, Yiddish would have come first and Spanish second. This competition also depends on one's audience. In Yiddish, my audience would have been negligible: my family elders, my teachers, a few schoolmates … Spanish, on the other hand, was Mexico's *vox populi*.

I confess to having been rather impatient, even upset, with my parents, for teaching me more than one language. Life as I understood it at an early age would have been simpler had everyone communicated in the same tongue. I only understood the advantages of multilingualism when I left home and became an immigrant to the United States. Suddenly, what I had understood as a handicap became an asset. This asset led me to become an essayist, a cultural commentator, and a translator. Today I believe that living in two or more tongues is a way of multiplying one's perspectives. And I think to myself: does a particular language foster a specific kind of thought mode? Does my mind function differently depending on the language I'm using?

HT: My experience of being translingual is a bit different from yours, Ilan. I was born in a Chinese-language environment and acquired English later. For me, there is certainly competition, or, to employ a more aggressive word, war (invasion and defense), between the languages in my poetry. I had my first encounters with Chinese poetry at the age of 3, when I sat on my grandma's lap and heard her recite Tang-dynasty poems. Since then, the seed of Chinese poetry – its rich history of civilization and cultural inheritance – has been planted in my mind and tongue, and my immersion in Chinese culture and language has engendered in me an identity as a Chinese poet. Chinese language, culture, and society are undoubtedly my anchor.

My English education, in contrast, focused more on practical dialogues than on literature. English was taught to me as a useful tool to acquire more knowledge, but Chinese was *me*. This probably explains my initial reluctance to use English elements in Chinese poems, or vice versa. Moreover, I seriously scrutinized my poems, out of guilt, for any "latinized" syntax that sounded "unChinese." I defended the language against "mother tongue corrosion," as Yu Kwang-chung, a cultural critic and poet, asserted. More nuanced encounters with English literature made me realize that any language gains its strength from inclusive and selective absorption from others.

My inspiration for a translingual poem often comes from the collisions in "wave-crossing": different languages superpose like waves in different directions crossing at a fixed point. For some parts, the languages I learn cancel each other; for others, they enhance. Translingualism gives rise to more signals and greater noise. I have become more careful, as a translingual poet, to ground my ideas and images in a specific cultural context.

I'm reminded of *Poetry, Language, Thought* (1971), a book by Martin Heidegger in which he links language to the pursuit of truth. The more languages you speak, the closer you are to the truth; this is an intriguing statement. How does a poet embrace or resist such confusion or complexity? Does a poet have certain faith, or perhaps loyalty, to one language over the other?

IS: First, let's remember that linguistic confusion is a sine qua non of life. All monolinguals experience it. Is the confusion different among multilinguals? Different, yes, but not worse. Simply put, a multilingual poet has more offerings at her disposal from which to choose.

When I'm writing in it, it isn't that I love Spanish more than Yiddish, Hebrew, or English; it is just that I have chosen it over the others in order to deliver my message. At other times, I will do the same with any of the other languages I live in. Being a rather recent arrival to the English-speaking milieu, maybe you haven't experienced this "faith."

HT: Perhaps linguistic confusion is exactly what makes translingual writing a fascinating literary phenomenon; it can create space for surprising cultural connections. For example, if I were to write a Chinese poem constructing an image of the moon and the willow tree, most audiences would guess it relates to reminiscence, departure, or reluctance to leave home, since "The Moon" has become a common metaphor for home. "The Willow," pronounced 柳"liǔ" in Chinese, is a quasi-homophone character to 留"liú" (stay). If I transplant the two symbols into an English poem without much context, few readers would grasp my message. Writing translingually allows me to transform the Chinese-specific symbols into the English scene without destroying their mystic beauty. The process results in synesthesia: one might see the flower in one language and smell its scent in the other.

I agree with you that translingual writing isn't about loving one language more than the other. However, I do believe that some poets choose an "anchor" language even though they hold the same level of passion for other languages. Like you said, the anchor might shift from poem to poem, depending on cultural connotation, message, audience, etc. If a poet's home is their language, then a multilingual poet owns several homes. A translingual poet, I think, resides on the train that constantly travels back and forth from one home to another. For you, a mature polyglot who has been writing translingual poetry for years, the trips make perfect sense. For me, who's still exploring the expressive capacities of an acquired language, the trips make me feel "homeless," in diaspora. I often trap myself in the decidophobia, fearing I have chosen the wrong anchor language and, therefore, weakened my message. Maybe I still need to cultivate my faith.

IS: Decidophobia is a common social trait, especially in capitalist societies: we are constantly demanding ourselves to make a choice. This, obviously, comes with the fear of making the wrong one. Is it possible to have too many choices before us? Should one try to avoid such a situation? Probably not. It is important to distinguish between translingualism and hybrid languages. Translingualism, as you defined it, is the travel from one linguistic code to another. Hybrid languages, in contrast, are built through combination. Spanglish, which I adore, is a prime example; it has its own rules. I recently translated *Alice['s Adventures] in Wonderland* (2021) into Spanglish. If you are either a Spanish or an English speaker, you only get a portion of it, as you might when as a Spanish speaker you read Portuguese. Every poet creates her own language – and translingual poets do so by absorbing elements from whatever languages they have at their disposal. But they must choose one of them as their prime vehicle.

HT: I wonder if the "prime vehicle" you describe is the same as "the anchor language." Would different "prime vehicles" create different mindsets, even if elements are collected from the same set of languages? Xu Yuanchong, who was known for translating Tang poems into English, told his students in 2014: "English is a more scientific language and prioritizes logical coherence between scenes, but Chinese is picture-oriented and emphasizes formal beauty among images."

IS: I agree with Xu Yuanchong. English is precise, even methodical, maybe even to a fault. I enjoy channeling thought in it, but when faced with emotional explorations, I often find it constraining.

HT: Xu Yuanchong's words resonate with me too. When I develop a poem using English as the prime vehicle, I think first about a central idea and arguments, then the narrative arc to unveil them. Using Chinese, I come up with a set of images, then connect them – sometimes through purely aesthetic expressions. I often don't even have a message until I assemble the language. Of course, if I were not multilingual, I wouldn't even realize the difference in the process. Is this discovery of linguistic phenomena enough to make poetry truly translingual? Should translingual poets treat the languages as *the end*, instead of *the means* to expressing transcultural ideas? There are poetry critics who believe that translingualism makes poetry weaker, seeing it as "counterfeit" or as a "betrayal." Can we view translingual writing as a process of translation, re-translation, and pseudo-translation of works in one particular language?

IS: I'm well aware of this criticism. I remember listening to Stanisław Barańczak, the translator of Polish poet and Nobel Prize winner Wisława Szymborska, make the same argument. His thesis was that translingual poets have a more limited lexicographic reservoir. My initial reaction to Barańczak was that he was right. For a long time, I nurtured an inferiority complex vis-à-vis natives, sensing that they had and always would a far vaster, more robust vocabulary. But I've lived in the English-language habitat now longer than in other linguistic realms. I see myself as a religious convert who, after a long period of studying, knows more about the new faith she has embraced than those born into it, simply because she chose it. The natives take their language not as a gift but as given. I now believe a non-native poet, and particularly a translingual poet, makes poetry stronger.

HT: In the American context, being non-native and particularly translingual screams politics to me. Writing translingually challenges the presumed centrality and "nativity" of a language in a nation. Lydia H. Liu and Ruth Spark describe translingualism as a practice that encodes processes of domination, resistance, and appropriation. Translingual poets in the US actively resist settler colonialism by displaying the diversity of their mother tongues on top of English – "the American language."

IS: I disagree with Liu and Spark. I don't believe translingualism is a subversive praxis. There are scores of places on the planet where the vast majority of speakers are polyglots. In fact, one could argue that monolingualism in such locations is rebellious. I also don't believe translingualism is anti-colonial. Colonialism thrives through polyglot strategies. I want to go back to Xu Yuanchong. One of his theses – rather controversial, in my view – is that a translator competes with the poet in making the best possible version of the poem. Of course, there is a second competition: between the translation and the original. I won't argue with the idea here. Instead, I want to link it to our conversation about translingual poets. The translingual poet, in choosing the appropriate language in which to write a piece, competes with herself – that is, with avatars of herself.

HT: To me, the most fascinating part of translingualism is ultimately not what is translated but what is untold or needn't be told. A translingual poet legitimizes the "misuse" of language(s): the organic, creative engagement of possibilities unforeseen through the lens of any single language. Competing with herself in a poem of different languages, she detects and derails from constrained patterns or clichés. While she isn't literally translating, she is transplanting the syntactic, dictional, or symbolic advantages of that language into an otherwise underwhelming monolingual poem. And she simply leaves the translingual complexity there for the audience to explore. Whereas translation tells, explains, or instructs, translingual writing shows, infuses and liberates.

IS: Translation and translingualism in poetry are two categorically different endeavors. The first one seeks to bring to the target language a text that originated in another linguistic realm. Translingual poetry might play with various linguistic realms but ends up privileging one. The translingual poet does some translation but only to achieve certain creative effects. Let me ask a final question: if language shapes thought, does a multilingual poet have alternative ways of thinking that differ from those of a monolingual? To me this goes to the heart of the matter. A translingual poet does think in different modes. Understanding those modes takes substantial time. They come after years of getting acclimated to the essence of a language.

HT: I do believe multilingual poets have the capacity to think in different languages, which helps them produce more creative and imaginative poetry. I would characterize translingual poetry writing as a meaningful detour from a set path. It aims to inspire, not foreclose; to pose questions, not dictate answers. As long as one gains faith from confusion and rescues her voice from noises, one would find her mission.

– *The Common*, August 17, 2021

"'Clean, Fix, and Grant Splendor'":
The Making of *Diccionario de autoridades*

The most colossal lexicographic exercise ever assembled in the Spanish language might be the *Diccionario de Autoridades* (1726–39). More recent projects, including the ubiquitous *Diccionario de la Lengua Española*, which supplanted it and is about three times the size, as well as the dictionary of María Moliner, a librarian in Zaragoza who in 1966–67 published the *Diccionario del Uso del Español*, a lexicon based on intuition that took fifteen years to complete, are far more comprehensive. Yet considering the tools at the disposal of the compilers of *Autoridades* and the fact that they inaugurated an orthographic tradition based on an etymological criterion that survives to this day in Spanish, there is little debate about which deserves the accolades.

A product of the long-delayed arrival of Enlightenment ideas in Spain, *Autoridades* was conceived to make the nation look modern vis-a-vis its European counterparts, particularly Italy and France. Long considered a precious relic among collectors, it contains a total of 37,000 entries. A handful of curiosities, some humorous, others poetic, serve as windows through which to appraise its sensibility. One of my favorites is the definition to *besar* (to kiss) on page 598 of volume II: "v. a. Poner la boca sobre alguna cosa, y frunciendo y apretando los labios pronunciar la letra B tacitamente, con cierta especie de reverencia en se~na´ l de amór y obséquio" (to place the mouth upon something, and puckering and tightening the lips to pronounce the letter B tacitly, with a certain type of reverence signaling love and obsequiousness).

Or *día* (day) in volume III, page 254: "Se llama tambien el efpácio de tiempo que el Sol gatta con el movimiento diurno, desde que sale de un meridiano, hafta que vuelve al mifmo, dando una vuelta entera à la tierra" (also the name of the space of time the sun employs in its diurnal movement, from coming out in one meridian, until it returns to it, giving a full circle around the earth). The definition is amusingly unscientific – poetically so, not to say stubbornly out-of-date for the time. Copernicus developed his heliocentric system in 1543 and Galileo died in 1642. Or *hombre* (man) on page 168 of volume IV: "f. m. Animal racional, cuya eftructura es récta, con dos pies y dos brazos, mirando fiempre al Cielo. Es fociable, próvido, fagáz, memoriofo, lleno de razón y de conféjo. Es obra que Dios hizo por fus manos à fu imagen y femejanza" (rational animal, whose structure is erect, with two feet and two hands, looking always to heaven. Is sociable, cautious, sagacious, memorious, full of reason and advice. It is a work made by God with his own hands in his own image).

Autoridades was an endeavor spearheaded under the regime of King Felipe V (1683–1746), not a particularly progressive leader. Still, he was known for his reformist instinct to centralize power around the monarchy. In order to compile the lexicon, a cadre of philanthropists and other influential figures relied on the king to sponsor an intellectual gathering that could aspire to collect words in the way the Academia della Crusca, founded in Florence in 1583, and the Académie française, founded in Paris in 1634, had done.

In my hefty personal collection of dictionaries from different languages and national traditions, I own a three-volume facsimile of *Autoridades* published by Editorial Gredos in 1990, in the series Biblioteca Romántica Hispánica created by the philologist, poet, and literary critic Dámaso Alonso (1898–1990), author of studies on Spanish baroque poetry, especially Luis de Góngora. I got my set in an antique bookstore in Madrid. The first volume covers A to C, the second D to Ñ, and the third O to Z. It runs to 4,143 pages. The compilers' emphasis on each of the letters of the alphabet immediately becomes tangible: the first three letters take 1,437 pages; the next twelve, 1,512; and the remaining eleven, 1,194. Although the font is puny, it is a joy to let myself loose in its two-column pages. Volumes I and II were printed by Imprenta de Francisco del Hierro. After Francisco de Hierro passed away in Madrid in 1730, the rest of the volumes appeared under the aegis of Imprenta de la Real Academia Española por la viuda de Francisco del Hierro. The best appraisal I know of *Autoridades* is still Fernando Lázaro Carreter's "discurso" on June 11, 1972, upon being accepted as a full member into the RAE. Carreter, an admirable scholar and literary critic as well as a sharp, incisive columnist for the newspaper *El País*, depicted, in his nationalist acceptance speech, *Autoridades* as an instrument of linguistic centralization, failing to understand its nearsightedness in terms of appreciating the rich linguistic variety of the Hispanic world. He egregiously failed to recognize the value of contributions such as Andrés Bello's *Gramática de la Lengua Castellana: Destinada al Uso de los*

Americanos (1847), which sought to adapt Spanish to the realities of the Americas in what came to be known as "the age of independence." As comprehensive as his study is (far more nuances that I could dream to achieve in this review), Carreter ended up producing a rather narrow-minded picture that, in an age like ours fascinated with colonial iterations, feels rather parochial.

In the Americas, among the last references I've seen to the lexicon are by Octavio Paz, the Mexican poet and essayist and winner of the Nobel Prize for Literature in 1990. In his biography of Sor Juana Inés de la Cruz, published in 1982, Paz quotes from it with assiduity. It makes sense: the language in *Autoridades* was the one used by Sor Juana, who died in 1695 and is possibly still the best poet from Latin America. Her sharp, astute, versatile linguistic reservoir is obvious in *Carta Atenagórica* (1690), her sonnets and other poetry, her plays, and *Respuesta a Sor Filotea* (1700). I have also seen it quoted by Carlos Fuentes and Mario Vargas Llosa. Mentions of it by writers and academics in Spain today are more frequent (Camilo José Cela, Antonio Muñoz Molina, et al.), although always as the vestige of a foregone era.

As was common in the 18th century, not only in Spain but in England, France, Germany, and Italy as well, the line between a lexicon and an encyclopedia is amorphous. For instance, the dictionary opens with a definition of the letter A that runs for almost two full pages. It describes the history of the letter, its vicissitudes in Hebrew, Arabic, and Latin, its phonetic profile, its grammatical function, and so on. This entry is followed by "aba," a small linear measure, with a definition comprising barely twelve lines; and "ababol," a kind of herb, comprising six.

Entries in *Autoridades* quote from famous and lesser-known authors, thus the term *Autoridades*. Popular sayings form part of numerous entries too. Greek, Latin, and Hebrew etymologies are listed. The general tone is rather suffocating, though, at least in today's terms. In the first half of the 18th century, the scope of the Spanish language in the Iberian Peninsula was constrained to linguistic varieties in Spain. While in demographic terms the colonies across the Atlantic already had a larger population than "la madre patria," and, consequently, there were more Spanish-language speakers across the Atlantic, their parlance is barely noticed by *Autoridades*. Only a handful of entries might be described as Americanisms: *canoa* (canoe) and *mestizo* (person of mixed race) among them. But thousands of others – terms like *azteca*, *inca*, and *mexica* – which were ubiquitous in Nueva España, as Mexico was known – are absent. The word *maya*, which more aptly refers to the Mayan people, is defined as "a Spanish girl who intends to marry in *mayo* (May)."

Naturally, *Autoridades* is prescriptivist in its scope. Susana Rodríguez Barcia portrays it as "el germen de la entronización de lo prescriptivo desde una posición institucionalizada" (the seed of the crowning of prescriptivism from an institutional perspective). In her view, *Autoridades* initiates the eternal tension, in the Spanish-language ecosystem, between norm and usage, between an acculturated language and that which is colloquial or vulgar, which means this lexicon is always related to certain elites within Iberian society. Accordingly, one of the objectives is to legitimate Spanish literature, to grant it gravitas. From its front matter to the tone of its entries, it is unapologetically, furiously jingoistic: no matter what, its agenda is to prove that the Spanish language is splendrous, i.e., as capable of depth and complexity as Italian and French. In other words, an inferiority complex palpitates at the core of the project.

This isn't surprising. Spanish civilization is built around *el qué dirán*, the tyranny of an outsider's perspective, the way appearances at times override substance. The persecution of Jews who had converted to Catholicism, known as *conversos*, as well as heretics, and sexual and other deviants, by the Holy Office of the Inquisition established a merciless division between the public and private realms. *Autoridades* is a prime example of that imbalance. Spanish lexicography is known for forever moving at turtle speed. Before *Autoridades*, the two most significant lexicographic publications in the language were by two philologists, Antonio de Nebrija, who died in 1552, and Sebastián de Covarrubias y Orozco, a contemporary of Miguel de Cervantes, whose contributions are separated not only by a hundred years but by enormous cultural mileage.

Probably of *converso* ancestry, Nebrija was the first scholar to formally endorse *castellano* as the language of the Spanish Empire. He put together a grammar of the Spanish language, published in 1492, the same year Columbus stumbled upon what he called Hispaniola, the island known now as Haiti and the Dominican Republic. That same year he published a bilingual Latin-Spanish dictionary, known as *Lexicon hoc est Dictionarium ex sermone latino in hispaniensem*, which contained approximately 28,000 entries. (He referred to the language as *castellano* in the grammar and as *español* in the dictionary; the two terms are still in use, in quiet competition.) In the second edition of his bilingual dictionary, known as *Dictionarium ex hispaniense in latinum sermonem*, released in 1495, Nebrija was the first to introduce an American word into a Spanish dictionary: *canoa*, which replaced *barco* (boat). Nebrija was a Latinist as well as the author of the first Spanish grammar. Before him, Alfonso de Palencia, who died in 1492, beat him with the first *Vocabulario Romance Latin*.

Covarrubias pushed Nebrija's contribution noticeably forward. In 1611, six years after the publication of Part I of Cervantes's *Don Quixote de la Mancha*, he brought out his *Tesoro de la Lengua Española o Castellana*. His was the first European effort to catalog a language. The second was the *Vocabolario degli Accademici della Crusca* (1612). For Covarrubias, the word *tesoro* (thesaurus) appears to be a synonym of dictionary. This is the first significant monolingual lexicographic effort in Spanish. Covarrubias, a former priest, codifies language with a couple of clear-cut objectives: to establish the linguistic strictures of the language at a time of prolific literary production – the Spanish Golden Age was at its apex – and to promote a series of orthodoxies the Catholic Church was intent on safeguarding.

While the compilers of *Autoridades* mention Nebrija in the front matter to volume I, it is Covarrubias they feel closest to. They cherish his linguistic acumen; they also endorse his chauvinistic views. The definition of *judío/día* (Jew) (volume IV, page 325) is barely less anti-Semitic than that of Covarrubias's *Tesoro*: "f.m. y f. El Profeffor de la ceremónicas y ritos de la Ley Antigua de Moifés ... Ningun Judío ni Judía que fea ofado de criar fijo de Christiano ni de Christiana" (the professor of ceremonies and rites of the ancient law of Moses ... No Jew or Jewess ought to be allowed to raise a Christian son or daughter).

Each of the six volumes starts with an erratum, followed by a list of the *académicos*. Their place and date of birth and, when necessary, death, is summarily provided. The majority are priests and scholars based in Spain, although occasionally there are some in Peru and Mexico. Personally, I'm unaware of any historical archive, in Madrid or anywhere else, detailing how each of these individuals worked on canvassing the language to create *Autoridades*. Assignments were likely handed out to each of them. No effort appears to be made to invite non-academics, as in the case of the *Oxford English Dictionary* for instance, to contribute to the reservoir. The effect, obviously, isn't only anti-populist but also anti-democratic. Although it requests readers to submit errata, it is evident that cataloging the Spanish language is the domain of a deliberately convened elite.

Another challenge is that the compilers don't appear to have coordinated their efforts. Some entries are notoriously lengthy while others are short. Indeed, the gravest handicap of *Autoridades* is that it doesn't appear to have a centralizing editorial figure coordinating the effort. A unifying copy-editing style surely permeates the six volumes; but the length and purpose of the entries, their oscillation between creating lexicographic and encyclopedic entries, often baffles the user. This, however, is a result of the epoch in which it came to be. The *encyclopédistes* in

France, starting with Diderot, whose task it was in 1747 to translate into French the English *Cyclopaedia* by Jean Paul de Gua de Malves, ending up with an ambitious project to corral all human knowledge, might be accused of the same excesses. When seen in toto, the 37,870 entries they produced were uneven, not to say Quixotic. (Diderot famously said of his team: "Among some excellent men, there were some weak, average, and absolutely bad ones. From this mixture in the publication, we find the draft of a schoolboy next to a masterpiece.")

I don't know the total number of compilers, official and unofficial, behind *Autoridades*. The majority seemed to be in or connected with Madrid, where the dictionary headquarters were located. The Academia members are listed on pages xxx to xxxiii of the section "Historia de la Academia." They are about two dozen. It looks as if a handful of individuals, some of them *académicos* and others not, were assigned the task of compiling full letters according to certain stylistic parameters (the letter E to Don Adrian Connink, F to Don Vincencio Squarzafigo, G to Don Juan de Ferréras, H and L to Don Fernando de Bustillo, etc.), although judging from the description those parameters are somewhat elusive.

An explanation is given about the lack of editorial cohesion, the overabundance of entries in some letters and not in others, and the urgency with which the enterprise needed to be validated, even before the entire alphabet was completed, by publishing the initial volumes first and not waiting for the whole manuscript to be approached integrally. It is also stated that while the early years of research the enthusiasm was enormous, it dwindled as time went by, to the point that compilers needed to be pressured, in various ways, to fulfill the obligations they had committed to.

For years I have been drawn to the ninety-six pages that constitute the front matter of volume I. To me, it is the map through which to value the overall undertaking. It starts with a rather formal two-page letter by the Academia to the king, followed by an equally stilted response by the king. It contains an erratum as well as approvals by inquisitorial figures, such as Don Fernando de Luján y Sylva, Marqués de Almodóbar, and by censor Don Balthasar de Acevedo. It then presents an eight-page prologue in which it is stated that the principal objective in the creation of the Academia is the compilation of the *Diccionario*, "copiofo y exácto, en que fe vieffe las grandéza y poder de la Léngua, la hermoffura y fecundidd de fus voces, y que ninguna otra la excede en elegáncia, phrafes y pureza: fiendo capáz de expreffarfe en ella con la mayor energyía todo lo que pudiere hacer con las Lenguas mas principales, en que han florecido las Ciéncias y Artes: pues entre las Lénguas vivas es la Efpañola, sin la menor duda, una de las mas compendiofas y exprefívas, como fe reconoce en los Poétas Cómicos y Lyricos, á cuya viveza no ha podido llegar Nación alguna" (copious and exact, in which the grandeur and power of the language can be seen, the beauty and fecundity of its voices, and none other exceeds it in elegance, phrases, and purity; being able to express with it with maximum energy everything that can be done in the more principal languages, in which Arts and Sciences have flourished; because among the living languages it is Spanish, without any doubt, one of the most compendious and expressive, such as it is able to recognize in the comic and lyrical poets, in whose liveliness no nation has arrived).

The prologue in the front matter of volume I proceeds to explain the methodological approach used to compile *Autoridades*. It explains the usage criteria, showcasing the historical breadth of the endeavor. The lexicographers explain the choice of words in alphabetical order, the use of synonyms, diminutives and augmentatives, the scope of reaching back to 1555, establishing a rationale for the inclusion of the *dichos* and other popular sayings. It emphasizes that the goal is to make definition simple and easy to handle. It stresses the value of verbs in the infinitive and elaborates on the confusion between B and V.

The next section in the front matter is a history of the Academia. It states that the institution dates back to 1713, naming its first author Don Juan Manuel Fernandez Pacheco, Marqués de Villéna, Duque de Escaóna, Mayordomo Mayor del Rey and Caballero del Toisón de Oro. Shortly before his death, the Marqués de Villéna, *Autoridades* recounts, requested the formation of the Academia. It then lists other "autores" enlisted in the effort, the general purpose to "fijar la lengua" (to fix the language), which, "(haviendo tenido à la Latina por Madre, y despues con la variedad de domínios padecido la corrupció que es notoória) se havía Pulido y adornado en el transcurso del tiempo, hasta llegar à la última perfección del siglo pasado: y no era decente à nosotros, que logrando la fortuna de encontrarla en nuestros días tan perfecta, no eterniffemos en las prensas su memoria, formando un *Diccionario*" (having had Latin as its mother, and after the variety of domains in which it suffered the corruption that is noticeable) had been polished and embellished with the passing of time, until arriving to the ultimate perfection of the last century; and it wasn't decent for us, having been fortunate to find it in our time in such perfect state, not to make its memory eternal through the printers, creating a dictionary).

The compilers seem to be in search of elegance and "good judgment." The method used by the compilers seems to have been straightforward. There was an effort to collect all *worthy* Spanish words in alphabetical order. Each voice was cataloged with an abbreviation describing a noun, adjective either masculine or feminine, active or passive verbs, and other parts of the sentence. There is also evidence of a desire to include the etymology, follow adverbial patterns, trace the usage of "primitive" voices (e.g., Latin formations), and annotate whenever a word derives from French, Italian, and other European languages. If such foreign origin is established, then *Autoridades* simply refers to it, excluding any etymology.

The line "limpiar, purificar y fijar la léngua" is mentioned for the first time on page xviii of volume I. This eventually became the motto of the Academia. *Autoridades* adds: "Es obligación precifa que la Acadeémia califique la voz, y manifiefte los méritos de fu juício; pues con efte méthodo mueftra la moderación con que procéde, y defvanece las inventadas objeciones de querer conftruírfe maeftra de la lengua: porque calificada a la voz por limpia, púra, caftiza y Efpañola, por medio de fu etimología, y autoridades de los Efcritores; y al contrario, caftigada por antiquada, ò por jocófa, inventada, ò ufada folo en estílo libre, y no ferio: viene à falir al público, con notoriedad de hecho, que la Academia no es maeftra, ni maeftros los Académicos; sino unos Jueces, que con su eftúdio han juzgado las voces: y para que no fea libre la fentencia, fe añaden los méritos de la caufa, propueftos en las autoridades que se fitan"(it is the precise obligation of the Academia to qualify the voice, and to manifest the merits of its judgment; since with this method it shows the moderation it proceeds with, and it erases the invented objections of pretending to be a teacher of the language; because once a voice is qualified as clean, pure, *castiza*, and Spanish, through its etymology and the authorities of the writers; and, on the contrary, castigated for being antiquated, or humorous, invented, or used at random, and not serious; it emerges in front of the public, with gravitas, that the Academia is not a teacher, nor are the académicos teachers, but judges, who, with their study have judged the voices; and in order for their decision not to be random, they offer the merits of the cause, presented with the authority they based their quotations on).

This argument is, in fact, the cornerstone of the entire apparatus that sustains *Autoridades*. The thesis of its compilers is that the Academia isn't a teacher whose purpose is to impart knowledge on the speakers of the language; instead, it represents itself as a referee, adjudicating decisions on what is accepted and what is rejected. Obviously, while the distinction between teacher and judge is straightforward, it confounds its mission. For does not a teacher also assess, arbitrate, and recommend to its students that which is proper? Therefore, the prescriptivism of *Autoridades* is built on its ambition to establish tangible parameters of

Spanish: how it should be used, what is acceptable, and where Spanish becomes muddled.

The key word in the argument is *castiza*, a term difficult to translate. Volume II, page 225, defines *castizo*: "Adj. Lo que es de origen y cafta, de cuyo nombre fe formó" (that which has its origin and caste, in which name it was formed). Hispanic society isn't built around castes in the traditional sense. Six pages earlier, *casta* is said to be "f. f. Generacion y linage que viene de Padres conocidos" (generation and lineage that comes from known ancestors). The reference is to the concept of *limpieza de sangre* (purity of blood), around which the Spanish Inquisition constructed its policies of religious cleansing. Caste, hence, is an allusion to a possibly undesirable background, most likely Jewish, among *cristianos nuevo* (New Christians), who, in comparison with the *cristianos viejos* (Old Christians), were recent converts, themselves or their family, into Catholicism.

Unmistakably, the idea of Spanish as a pure language is utopian. Needless to say, no languages are truly "pure"; borrowings and other signs of what pedants call pollution are an inevitable feature of being active and in constant dialogue with other linguistic codes. Yet the 18th-century Spanish Academia defined itself, historically, as a force against unwanted contaminants, especially those coming from either religious backgrounds (say, Jewish) or from geographic closeness (influence of Italian and French over *español*). *Autoridades* consequently endorses the essentialist view that, in order to distill pride among its users, languages need to defend themselves from enemy forces, be they internal or external.

In any case, the motto was slightly edited, becoming *limpia, fija y da esplendor* (clean, fix, and grant splendor). Regrettably, it is still in use today by the Real Academia Española. Especially in the 20th century, countless critics – myself included – have ridiculed it as sounding like a TV commercial for soap. Yet the Academia remains undeterred toward it, exposing it as an ideological weapon to sharpen its mission: to cleanse the language of unwelcome elements. *Autoridades* came about with an unencumbered purpose: in an age of constant European conflict, to protect the Spanish language from foreign intervention. As conflicts with the French came about, Felipe V was frequently criticized for siding with the enemy. Even half-heartedly, the Academia, through its publishing tool, was proof of his patriotic loyalties.

As in the case of English in the 18th century and onward – as with Samuel Johnson's *A Dictionary of the English Language* (1755) and, to a lesser extent, Noah Webster's *An American Dictionary of the English Language* (1828) – the pervasiveness of Gallicisms was seen as a cancer – in

English as well as in Italian, German, and Spanish. From a present-day perspective, "Limpia, fija y da esplendor" is the lens through which exclusions might be understood. *Autoridades* records foreign influence on the Spanish language but insistently discriminates against it, suggesting it adulterates Spanish. Not surprisingly, the RAE, without fully abandoning the motto, has chosen a different, even opposing route: the slogan "Unidad en la diversidad" (unity in diversity). At least nominally, it represents an effort at being inclusive and wide-ranging, recognizing that the plurality of Spanishes in the Americas, for instance, cannot be subsumed to the normative approach of the Iberian variety. This approach is rather deceitful, though. Behind it is a bias that keeps Spain, illusorily, as the gravitational center of a civilization increasingly fractured, not to say regionalized.

The front matter of volume I then presents the Academia's bylaws, divided into five chapters, with one *estatuto* (statute), in chapter 1, six in chapter 2, eight in chapter 3, fourteen in chapter 4, and six in chapter 5. Most of the *estatutos* are about governance: how many members it ought to have and how they are organized (by the letters of the alphabet), how they are elected, what hierarchical structure they fit into, the finances of the Academia and its direct relationship with the king and his monarchy, and so on. Then comes a history of the Spanish language, tracing it to the expansion of the Roman Empire into the Iberian Peninsula in the year 516. It offers a case to appreciate the development of etymology in Spanish, then an approach to orthography, discussing the way to use accents, the use of upper and lower cases, various orthographic rules, pronunciation, duplication of letters (*abbreviar*, *Abbad*, *Collegio*), the concurrence of consonant letters (*producto*, *redempción*), how to divide a letter at the end of a line by syllables (*á-ni-mo*), and various other orthographic rules.

The list of authorities on which the lexicon is based is stunning. The authors are organized by period: prose authors per century starting before 1200, from 1200 to 1300, from 1300 to 1400, from 1400 to 1500, from 1500 to 1600, and from 1600 until 1700. These include Mateo Alemán, Bartolomé Leonardo de Argensola, Pedro Calderón de la Barca, Miguel de Cervantes, Sebastián de Covarrubias, Luis de Góngora, Lope de Vega, Fray Luis de León, Jorge Manrique, Tirso de Molina, Antonio de Nebrija, Francisco de Quevedo, and Conde de Villamedina. The list represents an inventory of Spanish culture from the collapse of the Roman Empire to the 18th century. To say that all the authors are male is to point out the obvious. Misogyny was at the core of Spanish civilization until rather recently and it has begun to recede rather slowly.

To give an example: it has been said that the Siglo de Oro Español, the Spanish Golden Age, is a misnomer in that the period spanned more than a century, wasn't golden but rather ruinous, and what made it Spanish was the pillage of the trans-Atlantic colonies it depended on. The role and portrait of women in art, architecture, music, and literature was minimal if not outright negative. In that sense, *Autoridades* is a nationalistic tool. In creating a dictionary to validate Spanish as its glue, it pointed to the cultural promoters of that language as validation.

But things aren't that simple. It is worth noting that among the authorities listed are several featured in the *Index Librorum Prohibitorum* of the Spanish Inquisition. One of them is *Lazarillo de Tormes* (1554), an anonymous novel about the adventures of a rascal through whose eyes corruption at all levels, ecclesiastic as well as governmental, and the immorality of various social classes are exposed. Another aspect worthy of attention is that the *Autoridades* also refers to translations into Spanish, for instance Antonio Pérez-Singler's poetic reimagining of Ovid's *The Metamorphosis* (1553). This elevates translation – or its cousins, any type of "retelling" – into the canon of worthy literary endeavors. Of course, the art of translation in the Renaissance wasn't far from today's idea of appropriation. Still, the inclusion of such works signals the relevance of translation, whatever its limits might be, as an intellectual endeavor.

Another significant aspect of the *Autoridades*, one to which I made passing reference earlier, is the rejection of works produced in the Americas. An exception is the Peruvian author Garcilaso de la Vega, known as "El Inca," known for *Comentarios reales de los Incas* (1609). "El Inca" was considered one of the earliest mestizo writers in Spanish. But even "El Inca" poses challenges because he spent most of his life – starting in 1561 – in Spain, where he wrote his chronicles of the viceroys of Peru and of Hernando de Soto's doomed expedition to Florida in 1539.

Finally, a revealing aspect of the dictionary is the way it features the work of Miguel de Cervantes, who, obviously, is the most famous Spanish author of all time. There are references to all of his books, from *La Galatea* (1585) to *Voyage to Parnassus* (1614), although the most cited, unexpectedly, is *Don Quixote of La Mancha* (1605–15). It is significant that when Volume I of *Autoridades* came out, a little more than a century had gone by from the completion of Cervantes's masterpiece. In Spain, it was still seen as a popular novel – —a parody of chivalric adventures – without particular aesthetic merit.

It was only at the end of the 18th century, in part because of the accolades the book received in England, France, and Germany, that

Spaniards began to look at it as the centerpiece of their national literature. By featuring Cervantes, and specifically *Don Quixote*, in such prominent fashion, *Autoridades* played a crucial role in his canonization. Nevertheless, as that century reached its end the fate of the lexicon itself was increasingly in question. A second expanded edition of *Autoridades* came out in 1770. As time progressed, the fate of Spain and its empire was uncertain. By the end of that century, a movement by the American colonies to secede coalesced. The earliest independent effort took place in Mexico in 1810. Others quickly followed. In Europe and across the Atlantic, Spain was perceived as awkward, intransigent, and stuck in the past.

By then, Spain was immersed in renewal on numerous levels, from the political to the religious. This also pertained lexicography. Still, that renewal remained attached to etymology as the criterion for orthographic standardization. It pushed away from historical sources as legitimizers of lexicographic value. The first edition the *Diccionario de la Lengua Española* came out in 1780. Once again, it sought to modernize the language, just as *Autoridades* had done, although its course was different. It pushed away from religious zealousness in favor of scientific thinking. The world was in the midst of upheaval at the time: the American War of Independence had taken place a few years prior, with support from Spain to the rebels; simultaneously, the Spanish-Portuguese War had exacerbated Spain's standing in Europe; and, just a few years later, the French Revolution of 1789 would push forward ideals of republicanism, individual freedom, and Enlightenment principles. Modernity had irrevocably been realized. Then, throughout the 19th century, repeated efforts by the many Spanish colonies to achieve their independence pushed the Spanish Empire to collapse. Spanish, in order to catch up with the times, needed to present itself as a more flexible, less intolerant language. It also needed to reflect the changes taking place across the Atlantic.

The *Diccionario de la Lengua Española* only partially achieved these ideals. For instance, it didn't start from scratch; instead, it blatantly plagiarized *Autoridades*. To this day there are still a few remnants of it in its pages: here and there a twist in a sentence, or else a definition inspired by its precursor, like the proposition that a day is the time for the sun to circle the earth, which remained until late in the 20th century. The latest, twenty-third, edition of the *Diccionario* (officially known as the *DLE*), released in 2014, includes over 93,000 entries. Its imperial spread – in Latin America it is perceived as an evangelical tool – resulted in the erasing of the memory of *Autoridades*.

– International Journal of Lexicography, August 2021

Pablo Neruda's "Ode to the Dictionary"

Back like an ox, beast
of burden, systematic
dense book:
young
I ignored you, I was visited
by smugness
and I thought myself complete,
and plump like a
melancholy toad
I proclaimed: "I receive
words
directly
from the roaring Mount Sinai.
I shall reduce
forms into alchemy.
I am a magus."
The great magus said nothing.
The Dictionary,
old and heavy, with its scruffy
leather jacket,
was silent,
its test tubes undisplayed.
But one day,
after having used it
and perused it,
after
declaring it
a useless and anachronistic camel,
when for long months, without protest,

it served as an armchair
and a pillow,
it rebelled, and planted itself
in my doorstep,
it expanded, shook its leaves
and nests,
it moved the elevation of its foliage:
it was
tree,
neutral,
generous,
apple tree, *apple orchard*, or *apple blossom*,
and the words
shining in their inexhaustible cup,
opaque or sonorous,
fertile in the lodging of language,
charged with truth and sound.
I turn
to a single one
of its
pages:
Cape
Cartridge
how wonderful
to pronounce these syllables
with air,
and further on,
Capsule
hollow, awaiting oil or ambrosia,
and near them
Captivate Capture Capuchin
Carousel Carpathian
words
slippery as smooth grapes
or exploding in the light
like blind seeds awaiting
in the storehouse of vocabulary
alive again and given life:
once again the heart is burning them.
Dictionary, you are not
tomb, sepulcher, coffin,
tumulus, mausoleum,

but preservation,
hidden fire,
plantation of rubies,
living eternity
of essence,
granary of language.
And it is wonderful
to harvest in your fields
a lineage
of words,
the severe
and forgotten
sentence,
daughter of Spain,
hardened
like a plow blade,
fixed in its limit
of antiquated tool,
preserved
in its exact beauty
and the immutability of a medallion.
Or another
word
we find hiding
between lines
that suddenly seems
as delicious and smooth in our mouths
as an almond
or as tender as a fig.
Dictionary, let one
of your thousand hands, one
of your thousand emeralds,
a
single
drop
of your virginal springs,
one grain
of
your
magnanimous granaries
fall
at the right moment

on my lips,
the thread of my pen,
into my inkwell.
From the dense and sonorous
depths of your jungle,
give me,
when I need it,
a single birdsong, the luxury
of a bee,
the fallen fragment
of your ancient wood perfumed
by an eternity of jasmine,
one
syllable,
one tremor, one sound,
one seed:
I am made of earth and with words I sing.

– *The FSG Book of Twentieth-Century Latin American Poetry* (2011)

Letter to a Young Translator

Dear Miranda,

Gracias for your recent note. It has taken me longer than expected because your request – to explain why I became a translator and "to grant advice about how to translate in an age of perplexity" where "everything seems to come to us at frantic speed" – needs careful calibration.

    Actually, I never intended to become a translator. It all came to me rather circuitously. I had grown up in a multilingual house, although I didn't pay attention to that richness until much later, when, after I left Mexico, I realized, from afar the gift I had been given. Switching from one tongue to another was natural. Everyone did it. It was only when I became an immigrant, after an itinerant life that took me to many corners of the world, that I realized the extent to which immigration involves translation.

    My recommendation is that, at first, you surround yourself with dictionaries. Dictionaries are what in social media lingo is known as BFF. Through them, the entire reservoir of the language is at your disposal. Some people believe that you're cheating if you look things up. On the contrary, your task is to find a way to look things up without regret. You might not go with what a trusted dictionary suggests to you. But at least you'll know such an option exists. Having dictionaries at your side is a way to feel that translation is an effort done among friends.

    A good translation makes the original text feel comfortable in the receiving language. For that, you need to trust the music you carry inside. We all have an internal rhythm that expresses itself through language. Through practice, you learn to hear the syncopated moves of that rhythm. Allow it to speak to you, to enchant you, to communicate secret truths to you. When that rhythm is fully yours, it will be the glue with which the translation will coalesce.

There is, in my mind, something peaceful about this process. I have said in the past that a translation comes about through hallucination. Whenever I translate, I get transported to a different intellectual realm, on where I am and I'm not myself. I can see what I'm doing as if from a distance. Language flows through my fingers but I also swim in it. There is a mystical aspect to it all.

You ask in your letter when do I know a translation is finished. Honestly, it never is. Even years after I completed it, I feel compelled to make changes. And, if the opportunity arises, I do implement those changes. One's relationship with words exists in a state of endless mutation. What a certain word says to me now might change tomorrow. I like precision in translation but I also enjoy looseness. Perhaps the answer to your question is *death*. Only when I'm dead is a text no longer changeable, at least not by me.

Do I recommend that you, just a few years out of college, devote yourself to translation? Only if you feel it as a calling. Being a translator is a lonesome endeavor. You are alone for hours on end, in front of a text that belongs to someone else. Do you feel the drive to make that text available in one of the languages that is your home? If so, you're a translator. But that's only half the text. The other half is to recognize that, in spite of the fact that translators are gaining more visibility, you will always work in the shadow: in the author's shadow, and in the shadow of the language you're serving. This isn't a punishment. It is rather a form of liberation. Translate not because you want recognition – although you deserve it and will get it one day – but because you love dressing up reality through words. That's the key.

The writers I most admired were also translators. Look them up: Friedrich Schleiermacher engaged in illuminating philosophical investigations, but he also translated works into German. Borges translated Oscar Wilde, Walt Whitman, and William Faulkner, among others. I also like thinkers like Hannah Arendt and Susan Sontag, whose quest was to appreciate culture from multiple perspectives. Borges thought an original can be untruthful to its translation. I think a translation might be better than its source.

In the past few years, I have experimented with translation in ways that surprise me. As you know, I have translated from languages I don't know. I have also created translations – mostly of poems, but also of prose – that don't have an original. My motivation stems from the certainty that translation isn't reactive but active and that texts might read as if they are translations even when they are originals. And I have done something else: I have published a number of translations of texts without originals that are signed by fictional translators. Each of these translators, in the spirit of Fernando Pessoa's heteronyms, has their own theory of translator. You will ask me why I've embarked on such a project. The answer is simple: I feel I'm inhabited by more than one self. These various selves talk to each other, at times agreeing, at times expounding opposing views. In these translations, I have allowed this coterie of selves to take the helm.

Ever since you were my student, I saw enormous promise in you. You were driven to experimentation. Or else, to improvisation. Those two – experimentation and improvisation – are my own mottos. I like that you've kept truthful to these modes. Needless to say, I have seen far too many talented young people surrender their true talent the moment they get a diploma because they doubt they will succeed in the creative realm. You've stuck to your guns. I salute you for that. You aren't alone. I and others who admire you are at your side. Readers will thank you, sometimes by simply enjoying the fruit of your labor.

Translation makes us human. Several times in your letter you talk of translation as a career. And you use the word "career" as an arc, saying that my career inspires you. With all due respect, while I see an arc in what I've done (over time, I recognize I have become more confident in what I do), I don't see what I've done as a career. A career only exists in retrospect, as we look back. When a young person, like you, talks of a career, it appears as if they are talking about a straight arrow traveling in space. Nothing I've done, in translation and in any other field, has ever followed a straight path. Instead, life twists and turns all the time, in unexpected, infuriating ways. Looking back might give you confort if you were courageous.

I guess what I'm saying is that we're all the product of chance. The right time to do anything never really comes; you must do what you must *now*, otherwise it will be too late.

Send me your next draft when it's ready.

Yours,

Ilan Stavans

How Dictionaries Define Us (with Margaret Boyle)

Part I: Language in Crisis

MARGARET BOYLE: It wouldn't have taken any convincing for me to take on the opportunity to collaborate on a course on the cultural history of Spanish dictionaries, teaching alongside a scholar I so admire, engaged in conversation around so many of my favorite things: collecting words, print histories, translation, interpretation, and the larger nexus of language and politics. But there is something especially motivating about contemplating the relevance of dictionaries in the moment we are all experiencing, what we now call the "the twin pandemics." Living with COVID-19 and structural racism has produced an upswell of global activism, inspiring and energizing – massive protests around the world demanding change – but also horrifying in the constant repetition and grappling with violence and suffering: George Floyd's murder in May 2020, racial health inequities, and the physical toll for communities of color unable to access needed medical treatment. And so, when we talk about dictionaries now it is not only the rarified book as object, but the dictionary as a book that can capture or exclude our sense of self. Talking about dictionaries during crisis means exploring how crises motivate us to change the words we use, our definitions, the ways we use language and consequently interact in our world.

ILAN STAVANS: When I was growing up in Mexico, the word "crisis" (from the Greek *krisis*, "decision") was used with obscene ease. It seemed as if every day, for whatever reason, we were at a juncture: in crisis. One of the *Merriam-Webster* definitions is "an unstable or crucial time or state of affairs in which a decisive change is impending." To us then – to me, at least – it felt as if every time was unstable or crucial. Yet the use of the word was turning it into a permanent condition. I bring this up because it seems to me that the connotation of *crisis* has been upended. That is to say, every time, in the way we approach life, feels like a crisis. Still, there are no doubt pivotal moments – I think of the word "catharsis" – that prompt us to act differently, to engage with our circumstances in new ways. The murder of George Floyd, the #MeToo Movement, and the COVID-19 pandemic are a confluence of such moments.

Such pivots require a fresh array of new words. With COVID-19, this is especially clear. The word itself, "COVID-19," according to *Merriam-Webster*, received the fastest acceptance ever in the dictionary's history: it took a record two weeks from when it was first uttered to its appearance on the company's website. The speed is a sign of its urgency: in those two weeks in February 2020, the entire world was at a standstill. Subsequently, the pandemic generated a veritable treasure trove of terms: "Zooming," "anti-vaxrs," "social distancing," "muting," etc. Social upheaval creates its own language, and given the planetary dimensions of COVID-19, without knowing it, we were thrown into a brand-new era such that our own poor lexicon was in quick need of renewal. The same goes for the social justice drive that made terms such as "consent," "rape culture," "male abusers," "consensual," "white supremacy," "systemic racism," "anti-racism," and "police brutality," all no doubt in circulation before, extraordinarily current from one day to another. This vocabulary seems to have moved from the outskirts of culture to centre stage.

Maybe this is how the word "crisis" ought to be defined now: a rupture in the real language that begets a new language.

MB: Fascinating, Ilan. And what I hear you describing are a couple of intertwined relationships: between these kinds of collective experiences (and for our pandemics at a massive scale) and the ability and desire to name and describe. With crisis, you are also pointing at the tie between urgency and innovation. And as with much of the generative word-making as we might find in the dictionary since March 2020, I've also been struck by how our health crises foreground the physical cost of not having access to language. With our attention to racial and ethnic health disparities we are (I hope) slowly but surely attending to removing some of these barriers and thinking more critically about what it means to practice culturally relevant medicine. These already existing inequities were magnified when you added the lack of access to English: a spring study out of Brigham and Women's hospital described that Spanish-speaking patients with limited English had a 35% greater chance of death from COVID-19. Of course, there are so many factors here: all the standard questions of access, paired with lack of translators and interpreters, lack in cross-cultural communication, lack in confidence. But to get us back to the topic of dictionaries, we can also call to mind the bilingual, bidirectional dictionary (allowing translation to and from both languages) and how it could improve treatment.

IS: Dictionaries project an image of loftiness. This is because, in an epoch like ours where no one appears to have enough time, they are produced with stunning care by a professional team whose job it is to monitor a culture's temperature. Consequently, they project authority. Yet what makes culture, particularly in a country like the United States, move is often an anti-authoritarian drive. Rebellion, protests, marches – we like to think of ourselves as having a voice. That voice, in linguistic terms, is in a constant state of unsettlement. We not only like to oppose power; we also like opposing the languages of power.

MB: Part of being able to appreciate nuance and engage with the dictionary as an object of power is to cultivate a more general understanding about lexicography as a field, that is, the hands-on process of making the dictionary and our attending to the individuals that comprise these efforts. And when we begin to see these human beings both as individuals and as a collective, it becomes possible to talk about the standards of diversity, equity, and inclusion as they apply, let's say, to the advisory boards of the dictionaries we use and, more concretely, to how these boards reflect diversity across race, gender, socioeconomic status, ability. Part of why I am so interested in the history of the book, broadly, is that I am curious about the life stories that frame each volume: not just the individuals who produce text, but also binders, printers, vendors, readers – what Michael Suárez affectionately calls "the book as the coalescence of human intention." Every single volume of a dictionary that we handle connects us to this wider community. This makes it possible for us to attend to the people who have made up or currently make up this community, and to think critically about gaps and exclusions.

IS: A dictionary as a community – I love the concept. We could also talk about the doppelgangers. Every dictionary has its own double: one of them features all the words its makers included, and the double features the words that were excluded. Inclusion is power, but so is exclusion. I say this because dictionaries exert a strange allure on us: all want to be complete, but none truly is. And the exclusions, readers know, are a statement about life itself: the words that were left haven't been co-opted; perhaps they haven't even been created. By not yet being cataloged, they still belong to us, its users.

It is a source of constant amazement to me that, unlike other languages, English doesn't have the equivalent of an Académie française. No institution forces us to use our words in a particular way. Yet we do have, of course, mechanisms of authority. For instance, peer pressure: we use the words we hear and vice versa. That is, usage is a mechanism of cohesion. And dictionaries, too, are tools of consent. I say this with absolute reverence. No language, especially no standardized language, is able to exist without a drive toward cohesiveness; otherwise, it would disintegrate rapidly. At the same time, those mechanisms of authority, including dictionaries, need to be questioned. Who is behind them, for example? The majority of lexicographers are people older than forty. Should younger people, known for their verbal acumen, also be at the helm? Are there strategies dictionary makers use to reach out to not only the young but all members of society? In recent years, dictionaries, it is true, have undergone a process of democratization. More voices traditionally seen as marginal are now considered for inclusion. Is the effort enough? Are we satisfied with the dictionaries we have?

MB: In a just a few days, Simon & Schuster are releasing the print copy of John Koenig's *The Dictionary of Obscure Sorrows*. I have been fascinated by the development of this project and the premise of the collection: "original definitions aimed to give a name to emotions we all might experience but don't yet have a word for" and the general idea of inventing language to fill in gaps that we can't yet express in a single word. An example from the collection is the word *sonder*, meaning the realization that everyone has a story "as vivid and complex as your own." Viewing the project over the last 11 years, from the launch of the website to the YouTube web series with 3-minute episodes (viewed more than 11 million times!) to finally the dictionary as book, traces an exciting conversation about process, the relationship of the genre to popular audiences, and the way language is continually adapting to express our lived realities and experiences. For those of us that are already bilingual or multilingual, we may already be familiar with the ways our brains turn to a word in one language that doesn't quite exist in the other, and the kinds of cognitive efforts and creativity that result from this dance between languages.

IS: I love the concept. My initial reaction is to invoke Spinoza's *Ethics* (1677). Prior to it, there were attempts (Aristotle, Galen, Averroes, Maimonides) to study human emotions. But Spinoza is the first, in my opinion, ever to list them. Written in Latin, the language of science in the Renaissance, his book, strictly speaking, isn't a dictionary; instead, it is a philosophical disquisition. But it might also be seen as a lexicon because Spinoza's quest is to make as comprehensive an inventory as possible. How many human emotions are there? No one can say for sure; not even he does. Do all languages register the same amount? Or are there more emotions in one language than in others? Think of joy and happiness. What is the difference between them? And is the number of human emotions stable across history? Or are there more today than say five hundred years ago? Therefore, to compile a catalog of unnamed emotions is an imaginative task. The word "frenemy," for instance, refers to a person who is both a friend and an enemy. Does it announce a new emotion, or it is simply a sum of two previously known one? Should we do with emotions what we do with colors, differentiate between the primary and secondary ones, and maybe even add another layer that mixes primary and secondary emotions?

MB: Pip William's first novel, *The Dictionary of Lost Words* (2021), is another wonderful example of how contemporary fiction shapes our interactions with dictionaries. From my own gender studies perspective, I am intrigued by the novel's premise: using archival research to re-evaluate the role of women in the making of the *Oxford English Dictionary*, crafting an alternative history that centers a young female narrator, Esme. As readers, we observe her assembling a collection of excised words and form attachments to these words as they center marginalized experiences, not only attached to gender norms, but also to race and class. We know these stories do exist in the historical record, but what the fiction does here is allow us to run with our desire to invent and imagine and fully inhabit the re-centered history. I wonder if in this way fiction emboldens us to make change in our present.

IS: Fiction is the great enabler: the moment we dream something, the desire to achieve it becomes tangible. That, for example, is what makes science fiction so essential. It is escapist, for sure, but it motivates scientists as well to dream alternative universes. In my view, without fiction our spiritual life is infinitely poorer. It is enough to invoke *Don Quixote*, in my mind the greatest novel ever written. As a person, Alonso Quijano is pathetic. Yet the moment he becomes *Don Quixote*, Quijano's life is turned upside down. He is now a dreamer, a revolutionary, a usurper. It is enough to dream in order to get out of our imprisonment. That's the beauty of fiction: it offers us alternatives to the mendacity of our immediate circumstance, and, in doing so, to imagine alternatives for ourselves.

As for gender-neutral language in Spanish, while fully endorsing the ideology behind it, I recognize that the Latin morpho-syntactical roots of the language make this a foolish quest. As in other Romance languages, everything in Spanish is gendered: *la luna*, the moon, is feminine, and *el sol*, the sun, is masculine. This, needless to say applies, to human endeavors, too. Is there a patriarchal imposition when we use *nosotros* to refer to a mixed-gender group? There is, but opting for nosotrxs is unpronounceable. The "ex" has been ideologically charged in Latin America since the 19th century. Spaniards spelled present-day Texas "Tejas," whereas for Mexicans (and not *Mejicans*) it was "Texas." The change had to do with an outright attempt at reclaiming the way people were named among newly independent nations. I'm struck by the fact that today Republicans use the word "Hispanic" but Democrats prefer "Latinos," "Latina/o," or "Latinx," though never "Latin," which used to be a favorite term in the fifties. (Ricky Ricardo was "Latin.") The ideological rift is also a semantic divide.

MB: To what extent do you think your own language practices have been "Americanized"? I ask you this knowing about your own work on creating dictionaries for Spanglish. My take is that you've been pulled toward this project of documenting and legitimizing, but you've also been reluctant to claim comprehensiveness because standardization isn't possible in the same way. So, there isn't yet and maybe never will be the Academy of Spanglish or Google Translate to Spanglish, but the popular consciousness and representation of Spanish-English bilingualism in the last years is just extraordinary. We know Spanish is the second most common language in the United States, but there is also projected data for 2050 where the United States is expected to have 138 million Spanish speakers, making it the largest Spanish-speaking country in the world and Spanish a language spoken by 1/3 of its citizens. I have a feeling this is going to impact our dictionaries too.

IS: I'm a sucker for books that use dictionaries – or else, encyclopedias – as structures to build an imaginary universe. Milorad Pavić's *Dictionary of the Khazars* (1984) and Roberto Bolaño's *Nazi Literature in the Americas* (1996) are prime examples. By creating a catalog of fictional books detailing the activities of marginal Nazi groups in South America, Bolaño imagined a chapter of the Third Reich beyond Europe. On the other hand, Pavić explored the spiritual life of the Khazars, a 6th century semi-nomadic Turkish empire that, it has been speculated, might have reshaped the religious landscape of Europe before the Middle Ages. Yehuda ha-Levi, one of the last poets of Muslim Spain, wrote about them in his philosophical treatise *Sefer hu-Kuzari* (1140). And I'm interested in the dictionary – or, again, the encyclopedia – as a work of fiction, as in Borges' encrypted one in "Tlön, Uqbar, *Orbis Tertius*," which supposedly conveys an alternative universe that is the reverse of ours.

MB: You remind me of a piece of fiction that made me fall in love with Spanish literature: Julio Cortázar's "Axólotl" (1964). On the surface the story tells us about a narrator who becomes obsessed with visiting an aquarium and staring through the glass at these tiny salamanders, until the narration breaks down and his identity is destabilized. We know there's so much we can read into this story: about identity, perception and sense of self, the pull between reality and fiction, colonization, mortality (and this is likely why we can read it again and again). But right at the start of this short story our narrator turns to a dictionary to understand these tiny creatures, how to describe them, where they lived and evolved, how they would be translated across cultures. And perhaps most fascinatingly in the context of our conversation, we have another compelling example of turning to dictionaries to understand ourselves.

IS: I had forgotten that Cortázar anchors his narrative in a lexicographic definition. I do that often in my essays: how does the dictionary define a word? Looking at the definition grants me a sense of certainty. Truth might be relative, particularly in democracy, yet we all agree that dictionaries are a kind of "revealed" truth, a truth that is absolute. If the dictionary defines the word in a way, there is no discussion about it. Maybe I'm talking about tyranny here: the word offered by a dictionary is taken for granted, meaning it is unquestioned. This inspired me to reflect on the language of tyrants. Of the habitats I know well, I may list Francisco Franco's Spain, Argentina's Juan Domingo Perón, Chile's Augusto Pinochet, the Dominican Republic's Rafael Leónidas Trujllo, and Venezuela's Hugo Chávez. And, obviously, Donald Trump. They all were dictatorial not only in their actions but in their rhetoric, believing that if they said something then it must be true. Cortázar left Argentina because of Peronism; he just couldn't stand the limits imposed by Perón's conception of the state. His use of a dictionary definition in "Axólotl" is connected to his life in Paris, where the action takes place. Somehow, the perception of dictionaries in authoritarian and democratic regimes, at its core, is different. The same might be said of the Spanish Inquisition in the Middle Ages. As you know, the debate on Jewish identity in Spain from the 15th century onward gave room to a nomenclature of possibilities. On the surface, the difference between "cristiano viejo" and "cristiano nuevo" was semantic. But it could be the difference between life and death. Even more complicated are terms like "conversos," "anusim," "marranos," and "crypto-Jews." Political power is about awareness: the power a party, a leader, or a dictator might have is nothing but the perception of it projected on others.

MB: Awareness is exactly the right concept. And this is part of what is so exciting about our conversation this afternoon, the ability that we have to take part in a kind of consciousness raising through our discussion of dictionaries. Both historically and in our present moment, we can attend to how these perceptions have been shaped by the definitions presented to us and the ways we access information. Even more, we come to a better understanding around the dictionary's role in mediating political power. And to reach back to some of our earlier conversation, how do we grapple with the representations of ourselves in the dictionary?

IS: Change is the one constant of our universe. And change is at the heart of language. Youth these days acknowledge that for the world to change, one needs to start with language because when you question words, what they mean, and how they came to mean what they do, you delve into the meaning of everything.

Part II: Dictionaries as National History

MB: In his seminal *A Dictionary of the English Language* (1755), Samuel Johnson's second definition of "language" was "the tongue of one nation as distinct from others." The first definition was linguistic, language as a particular system for communication. The second is cultural: it defines language in relation to the cultural productions of a particular people or nation.

IS: To my mind, Johnson's is the best dictionary ever made by a single author – in any language. He was a true Renaissance man, a polymath who wrote newspaper columns, travelogues, fiction, literary criticism (I'm still in awe of his introductions to Shakespeare's plays), and all sorts of minutiae. As you know, most dictionaries today are shaped by committee. Noah Webster comes in a far second with his *An American Dictionary of the English Language* (1828). While trying to distinguish American from British English, he shamelessly plagiarized a number of Johnson's entries. At any rate, Johnson's idea of distinguishing one national tongue – say English in the United Kingdom – from another – say English in the United States – is crucial. Remember that George Bernard Shaw, author of that intriguing play, *Pygmalion* (1912), about language and class, said once that our two countries are separated by a common language. The English of the United States is different: more pluralistic, defined by immigration, by Hollywood, monetary and foreign policy, and so on.

Mindful of his European ecosystem, even if also trapped in his Englishness, Johnson's second definition of "language" is comparative. He was mindful of the degree a national language is shaped in relationship to others. For no individual, no group, and no nation ever exists alone, without others. In that sense, nationalism is always a competition, as are national histories. Dictionaries function as engines of those histories: museums of the past and exhibits of the present. They showcase the DNA of a group in tandem with those of other groups. In Johnson's *A Dictionary of the English Language*, it is possible to see how he, and the English, look at the world: famously, he defined a lexicographer as "a writer of dictionaries; a harmless drudge, that busies himself in tracing the original, and detailing the signification of words." Anyway, Johnson, and his dictionary, were surely a product of their time, as all of us are. A nation, let us say, is nothing but the sum of those products.

MB: Out of our collaborations this year, I've been able to work with Bowdoin's special collections and archives to pull editions of special interest. In this context of US English, I want to talk about John Russell Bartlett's *Dictionary of Americanisms* (1848), a pioneering work for its engagement with slang. The Bowdoin copy is a fourth edition from 1877, printed in Boston by Little, Brown and Company. It comes from the estate of Franklin Ripley Barrett (1835–1912) of Portland. This heavily annotated personal copy includes contemporary newspaper clippings from a variety of sources – *The Nation, Atlantic Monthly, The Evening Post,* the *New York Post* – on current debates in language use (letters to the editor on the meaning of words including "banter," "blizzard," "dude," or "Uncle Sam") – and even notes from his personal letterhead at Portland Savings Bank Building, where he worked as director and later president. I read aloud this very intense critique from famed literary critic Richard Grant White, author of the decidedly more conservative manual *Words and Their Uses, Past and Present* (1870), inscribed into the front of Bartlett's copy: "The most of it is mere ephemeral fashion and transient tricks of speech, bad fashion and bad trick, but prevalent only among those who being neither cultivated on the one hand nor on the other the rude product on the soil on which they live, are not properly to be taken as the exponents of language in any way – fashion and trick which will pass away, some of it before Mr. Bartlett's book passes to another edition." And the humor is of course that Bartlett is transcribing this quotation into the 4th edition of the *Dictionary of Americanisms*, evidence that these Americanisms are here for the long haul: words that have changed meaning across England or the US, "newly minted words which owe their origin to the production or to the circumstances of the country," and words borrowed from Black and Indigenous vernaculars, as well as "French, Spanish, Dutch and German."

IS: Bartlett is an important figure in American lexicography. Originally from Rhode Island, he wrote a catalog of books relating to the American Civil War, about the Soldier's National Cemetery in Gettysburg, and other topics. His *Dictionary of Americanisms* has what is, in my mind, a special distinction: it was translated into German in 1866. Dictionaries, for obvious reasons, are seldom translated; this one was because of its innovative qualities but also because, in the middle of the 19th century, German immigration to the United States was at its highest. Like Webster's, Bartlett's enterprise survived him, becoming a staple of the nation's life, although this one, too, mutated in such a way that Bartlett himself would probably have found successive products based on his research unrecognizable. Updated commercial editions of Bartlett, in the format of a thesaurus, are still available today, mostly designed for students. The most recent edition might be the one published by Little, Brown and Company in 2009. Again, I want to stress how unusual it is for a dictionary to go on being published after its author's death. Webster, Bartlett –
these household names continue to play a major role in the building of the nation's linguistic identity. Someone saw financial value in them from the start and that value has only increased with time. Not long ago, I had a conversation with one of the editors in charge of modernizing Bartlett – it's a bit like new authors writing Sherlock Holmes. It was a fascinating dialogue: from behind Bartlett's shadow, a fresh light must be born.

In any case, I'm raising this issue because there's an important difference between a dictionary and a thesaurus. The former offers definitions, the latter synonyms, antonyms, and related words. Whereas a dictionary is epistemological in nature, a thesaurus is content with listing lexical possibilities. Not all languages have thesauruses; French, Portuguese, Italian, and Spanish, for instance, have dictionaries of synonyms, but they are not in wide circulation. English has an industry of thesauruses and Bartlett's is a famous example. This, to me, shows how cultures approach language differently. I remember, upon immigrating to New York in the mid-eighties, coming across, for the first time, Bartlett's volume. I was flabbergasted by the sheer – to me innovative – idea. But of course, it's only innovative to an outsider; in New York, Bartlett's *Dictionary of Americanisms* was, well, a rather pedestrian artifact.

MB: Yes, I love this idea about cultural approaches to language, and it reminds me of conversations we've shared about the ways we narrate stories about lexicographers. For the OED, we've talked at length about narrative and film approaches from *Professor and the Madman* to the child-centered narration we find in *Dictionary of Lost Words*. I'm curious too about how we present these biographies to children in the context of picture books, and Jen Bryant's *The Right Word: Roget and His Thesaurus* is a wonderful place for us to begin – and yes, I'm the parent who was giving this book at birthday parties. In 2014, the *New York Times* reviewed the book with the disclaimer: "Ten years ago, *The Right Word*, a picture-book life of Peter Mark Roget, inventor of the thesaurus, would have been a publishing non-starter – a project 'too special' for the market to bear." Or in 2016 when Robert Macfarlane published the oversized, gorgeously illustrated *The Lost Words*, the ode to natural world vocabulary lost from the 2007 edition of the *Oxford Junior Dictionary*. So we have evidence of the demand for cross-generational stories about dictionaries in the English-language context; and now I'm wondering what it would mean for us to consider the picture book version of Andrés Bello's life and works in the Spanish-language context. Or how we might get to the point in a US context to find market demand for the representation of Spanish lexicography.

IS: If lexicography is in and of itself a limited field in America, Spanish lexicography is so rarified, it makes me think of what the Finns call "a professional sleeper," that is, a professional devoted to trying beds in luxury hotels. You could count the professional sleepers in all of Finland with one hand. Still, they obviously make a good living. For years I've seen myself as a "Spanglish lexicographer," an even more peculiar endeavor than that of Spanish lexicographer in the United States. In my eyes, it is, unquestionably, a very important activity. Even if I often feel like a thief, "stealing" Spanglish words from the people that use them in order to catalog them in dictionaries, I'm proud to do it. In his story "Pierre Menard, Author of the *Quixote*" (1939), Borges says that "*There* is *no intellectual* exercise that is *not* ultimately pointless." I agree with him, although I believe there is pointedness in pointlessness. To compile a lexicon of Spanglish is a way of legitimating this form of communication.

Let's switch to Spanish in order to look at dictionaries through the prism of nationalism. After the wars of independence in the Americas in the 19th century, the educated elite sought to distinguish the Spanish of the former Spanish colonies from that of Spain. Arguably the most revolutionary of all lexicographers – and, mind you, a politician himself who befriended and was an ambassador of sorts for Simón Bolívar, El Libertador – was Andrés Bello. Although a grammar and not a lexicon, his *Gramática de la lengua castellana para el uso de los americanos* (1847), released thirty years after Webster's dictionary, proposes a similar feast: to adapt a colonial language, in Bello's case Spanish, to the "New World." In his prologue, he looks for a way to distinguish Iberian Spanish and American Spanish, arguing for a simplified grammar that would reflect the needs of people in Chile, Colombia, Venezuela, Argentina, and other newly independent nations in South America. Bello had lived in London, where he advocated for Simón Bolívar's revolutionary ideals. Upon his return to the Americas – to Santiago, Chile – he focused his attention on creating both the grammar as well as the *Código Civil*. Yet Bello's simplifications (he wanted to eliminate the needless "h," for example) weren't quite "liberal." He didn't believe the indigenous population, former slaves, *guachos*, and immigrants (Italians and Jews began to arrive in the 1880s) had a say in how the language should be shaped. In Bello's view, the fate of South American Spanish was exclusively in *criollo* hands. It was, in his opinion, a language for the *criollos* by the *criollos*.

MB: We see the intersection between politics and philology in the early unification and imperial project for Spain and the standardization of Spanish. Those famous events of 1492: conquest, expulsion, unification? For me, the stand out is the publication of Antonio de Nebrija's *Gramática*, gifted to Queen Isabel with the now famous dedication "Siempre la lengua fue compañera del imperio," the language was always a companion of empire. And in this moment, we have this explicit fusion between Spanish language and empire, and out of this context a little more than a generation later Sebastián de Covarrubias' publishes his enormous monolingual dictionary *Tesoro de la lengua Espanola o Castellana* (1611), one that I was introduced to as the "Cave of Rubies" as a way to remember Covarrubias' last name. And, of course, this isn't just a pseudonym, but it's also a direct reference to the prologue of the text where Covarrubias develops the metaphor of the cave guarded by multilingual beasts and monsters; accessing the treasure of Spanish language requires knowing and naming Latin, Greek, Hebrew, Arabic, French, and Italian. The user of the Spanish dictionary enters the cave with boldness, acknowledging the risk and danger.

IS: Covarrubias is our Dr. Johnson: the only lexicographer, with the exception of María Moliner in the mid-twentieth century, to have authored his own lexicon. For that reason, and much more than Moliner's, who lived in a more scientific, objective age, Covarrubias' is quite idiosyncratic. For instance (and as Gabriel García Márquez once noticed), he defined love as "being yellow." This is less a definition that a poetic approximation. Similar "deslices," playful twists, are found on almost every page.

Covarrubias' *Tesoro* was produced rather late in his life. It was published in a crucial year, almost right between the first and second volumes of *Don Quixote*. I don't know if Cervantes knew of it. I frequently read that crucial Chapter VI of Part I, in which the priest and the barber go through Alonso Quijana's personal library. Might it be a reflection of Cervantes' own library? There are no references to dictionaries in it. Did he criticize Covarrubias' inquisitorial zeal? Taking about the metaphor of the cave, Cervantes, in Don Quixote, also uses it, in the extraordinary section on the Cave of Montesinos, where Don Quixote gets lost in what could be described as a mystical section. He and Sancho will endlessly debate Don Quixote's genuine or falsified experiences there and this. The cave was a favorite trope of baroque writers of the Spanish Golden Age: a trap but also a depository of treasures (which in Spanish is one word for "thesaurus").

MB: At Bowdoin, we have a 1611 imprint of the *Tesoro*. I will dig into the provenance of this text as a way to think about how this early modern Spanish dictionary found its way to Bowdoin. (I want to thank our incredible team of archivists and librarians, especially Marieke Van Der Steenhoven.) There's no record of purchase or transfer in our paper or digital catalog. But we locate purchasing information inside the book, dating to November 6, 1933, when the volume was purchased for $15.96 with the Lewis Pierce Book Fund. On the front-end pages, there are the initials "C.P.H." and, a few pages later, in a different hand, what appears to read "G.M. Sale." On the following page, there is an official signature from Juan Ximénez. In the second half of our copy, you can find evidence of a single bilingual reader, primarily annotating words in Spanish that do not appear on the page where they should be listed (adding the words like "ultrajar," "unidad," "velocidad," and "viento"), although there are occasional instances of English translation. The hand and content of these annotations makes it possible to speculate that the volume at some point comes from the collection of Scottish-born surgeon John Hunter (1728–1793), which includes an array of early modern Spanish novels and dictionaries. (See James Christie's catalog from February 1, 1794, which exhibits an interest in cross-referencing between volumes.) Our edition of Covarrubias, for example, includes a reference to alternative definitions from Robert Ainsworth's 1773 dictionary.

IS: Dictionaries, as we established, are communities. Their satellites are the authors, editors, illustrators, printers, booksellers, readers, and collectors who rotate around them. It used to be that when you borrowed a book from the library, a card in the back would name all the readers who had borrowed that copy. What an astonishing feast that was: to know that the book you hold in your hand has been touched by all those people before you, and that a similar cadre will follow you one day. With new technology, those cards are gone now, yet the communities, even if unnamed, are still there.

I want go back to María Moliner. In the history of dictionaries, white men, it goes without saying, have been the principal producers. Even though they have sought to be objective, we known their attempts – all attempts – have been inescapably biased. Would the dictionaries we have be different had women been at the helm? Yes, of course. Moliner is exceptional in that sense and in many others as well: a Spanish librarian who decided, in the 1950s, to focus her non-work-related energy in making the *Diccionario del uso del español actual*. Her effort was a reaction to the patriarchal strategies of the Real Academia Española, particularly their *Diccionario de la Lengua Española*. Gabriel García Márquez, in a prologue to the 2007 edition, when the endeavor was called CLAVE, celebrated her as a harvester of "las palabras de la calle." She focused not on what language means but on how words are used. What to me is most attractive is her flexibility in accepting neologisms: her dictionary is a harbinger of my own lexicon of Spanglish, published in 2003. Words like "marketing," "feedback," and "anti-baby" are included in it. As I said, García Márquez was a lifelong admirer of Moliner. He described her as "a writer's lexicographer," and he thanked her not only for her dedication, which went unrecognized during her life, but for standing up to the pretentious "letrados" of the RAE, who didn't think of making room in their own ranks for such a genial figure. This attitude says something about Hispanic machismo.

MB: I'm still marveling at the conversations in class, where we've shared about "anti-baby" (birth control pill). Shortly after Moliner's death in 1981, Gabriel García Márquez wrote an essay about "the woman who wrote a dictionary." In it he describes how Moliner began to write the dictionary, modeled from her own experiences learning English using A.S. Hornby's *Learner's Dictionary of Current English*. There's so much fascinating content about her process: that she wrote on her own, that she wrote from home, that she wrote as a mother, that she incorporated words from newspaper and magazine clippings, that she would water flowers between writing sessions, and how she is described as a language learner and lover, and how the attributes of her life as a woman in Spain in the 1950s intersected with these aspirations.

Let's talk about bilingual and other dictionaries that work across languages. An incredibly compelling example comes from English linguist and lexicographer John Minsheu's polyglot dictionary *Guide to Tongues* (1617). With more than 12,000 entries in eleven languages

(English, Welsh, French, Italian, Spanish, Portuguese, High Dutch, Low Dutch, Latin, Greek, and Hebrew), it is the first book to be published by advance subscription using a printed prospectus, and the first book to include a list of subscribers. Ben Johnson describes Minsheu's "roguishness," which he learned his Spanish while imprisoned in Spain. Before composing the polyglot dictionary, Minsheu authored *Spanish and English Dictionarie* (1599), a paradigmatic example of English-Spanish bilingual and historical lexicography (reprinted in 1623). The catalog's endpaper indicates that the Bowdoin copy of Minsheu was donated by Helen Johnson Chase. Henry Johnson, Helen's father, was a long-time Bowdoin professor of modern languages. The book was likely part of his personal collection. Helen served as college registrar. She married Stanley P. Chase, who was Bowdoin's English literature professor. Most entries do not include definitions (as in the word "dictionary" itself); instead, they include lists of translated words.

IS: In the context of national histories, bilingual and polyglot dictionaries are fascinating artifacts. They allow citizens to relate to other linguistic traditions; or else, they recognize that the national tradition isn't altogether monolingual. The history of multilingual dictionaries goes back to Arab culture in medieval Spain. There are numerous samplers in the English-, French-, and German-speaking worlds from the fifteenth century onward. Given my interest in Latin America, I'm interested in the *lenguas indígenas*, at times known as *lenguas naturales*, which, during the colonial period, were kept at bay by the Spanish colonizers. However, a number of important changes happened during the colonial period, with efforts – quite controversial, of course – to translate the Bible to Nahuatl, Aymara, Quechua, and other indigenous languages. These efforts came with small bilingual dictionaries: Nahuatl/Spanish for instance. The tension between centripetal and centrifugal forces was obvious: should the entire population of the colonies speak only Spanish? Or should there be a recognition of alternative verbal instruments? Centuries later, Latin America continues to thrive in this tension.

MB: As we close, let's return to some of the question of why dictionaries matter. We have discussed tackle the urgency of language to change in response to a global crisis, specifically with respect to COVID-19, racism, and sexism. We also have talked about the history of lexicons broadly and the way the discipline that studies them brings us into contact with so many individual stories that took part in shaping the content of an individual volume, both makers and readers, and how these life stories teach us about illness and survival and discrimination and inclusion. Part of what I hope we've accomplished this afternoon with this new round of archival storytelling is better proximity to all of these life stories. The cultural history of dictionaries is populated with countless dynamic individuals. Getting to know these individuals shapes how we understand both the past as well as our ability to make sense of, and make change in, our present.

– Los Angeles Review of Books, March 30, 2022

PART III

Translation as Home

Sor Juana's Nahuatl

Sor Juana Inés de la Cruz (1648–1695) is an underappreciated translator. The "Response to Sor Filotea," as well as "Allegoric Neptune" and other prose, is full of Latin quotations. She also rendered five *Dísticos* from Latin into Spanish, turning them into *coplas castellanas*. This is one in Latin, which she lucidly reinvented in Spanish:

Nomine materno, mutate parte, Camilla
    dicitur, ut Triviam, digna ministra, colat.
Totum nomen ego, Triados quae Ancilla, Parentis
    muto: tota in Ave vertitur Heva mihi.
Nec mutase satis nomen: mutase Parentem
    gaudeo: me prolem Gratia mater habet.
Namque Annae sum nata, dedic cui Gratia nomen:
    Gratia cui Proles, cui sine labe ganus;
Flos ídem humano generi, vivum Decus. Inde
    pro Ancilla, Matrem me vocat ipse Deus.

El nombre materno tuyo
Camila mudado en parte,
para que la Trivia Diosa
dignamente ministrase.
    Yo, esclava del Trino Dios,
todo el nombre de la Madre
mudo, y todo para mí
el EVA se vuelve en Ave.
    Ni bastó mudar el nombre;
alégrome que mudase
a la Madre, y que la Gracia
por hija me señalase.

> Hija de Ana soy, a quien
> la Gracia dio nombre grande:
> a quien dio Prole fecunda,
> a quien Géenero impecable.
> De aquí me ha venido el ser
> Flor del humano linaje,
> vivo Honor; y que es Esclava,
> Madre el mismo Dios me llame.

Sor Juana also translated in the opposite direction: Spanish to Latin. In her *Obras Completas*, edited by Alfonso Méndez Plancarte, there is a *décima* written by another author, whose name is unknown, that she twice translates into Latin. The second version is infinitely better:

> Ya el Alma al Verbo se ase,
> ya estriba en el Corazón,
> y tirando, de la unión
> rompe el nudo, y se deshace,
> Ya sale… ¡Ay!, antes que pase,
> Labios, pues que sois tan sabios,
> que perdone mis agravios
> pedidle, antes de partir…
> Mas ¡ay!, aquello es morir:
> ya dió su Espíritu.

Version #1:

> Iam Anima Verbo adhaeret,
> iam nitiur Corde puro;
> et Corpori vix casuro,
> unione rupta, non haeret.
> Per vos, o Labia, se ferret…
> Disserta siquidem estis,
> exorare nunc potestis
> veniam tanto nostro errori…
> Sed heu!, aim illud est mori:
> iam dedit Spiritum.

Version #2:

> Iam cupit Anima exire,
> iam nititur Corde puro,

iamque nimbo vult obscure
JKoculos Mors impediré.
Ut dignetur me exaudire,
Ora sacra, postulate:
pro inimicis supplicate
Eius pissimo Amori…
Sed heu!, Iam illud est mori:
Iam dedit Spiritum.

Frankly, there is nothing unique in Sor Juana's Latinized self. Most serious authors of the Spanish baroque indulged in such linguistic exercises. More interesting are her forays into Nahuatl. She produced two *tocotines*: "La fiesta de la Asunción" and "La fiesta de San Pedro Nolasco." There has been a conversation among scholars about her proficiency in the indigenous language. How much Nahuatl did she know? The consensus is that her grammar is at best shaky and at worse a sign of impostorship. To me the remarkable aspect is that, in spite of her constant exposure to Aztec elements in Nueva España, Sor Juana didn't refer to more aboriginal aspects of her habitat. She had a slave and a *criada* in her cell at the convent of San Gerónimo. In what tongue did she communicate with them? Did these languages contaminate each other?

"La fiesta de la Asunción" (1676)

Tla ya timohuica
totlazo Zuaplli, [sic]
maca ammo, Tonantzin,
titechmoilcahuiliz.

Ma nel in Ilhuicac
huel timomaquitize,
¿amo nozo quenman
timotlalnamictiz?

In moayolque mochtin
huel motilinizque
tlaca amo, tehuatzin
ticmomatlaniliz.

Ca mitztlacamati
motlazo Piltzintl [sic]
mac tel, in tepampa
xicmotlatlauhtili.

Tlaca ammo quinequi,
xicomoilnamiquili
ca monacayotzin
oticmomiquiti.

Mochichihualayo
oquimomitili,
tla motemicitia [sic]
ihuan Tetepitzin.

Ma mopampantzinco
in moayolcatintin,
in itla pohpolin,
tictomacehuizque.

Totlatlacol mochtin
tïololquiztizque;
Ilhuicac tïazque,
timotzittalizque:

In campa cemiac
timonemitiliz,
cemiac mochihuaz
in monahuatiliztin.

Here is a Spanish versión by George Baudot:

Ya que te vas a ir,
amada Reina nuestra,
¡Ojala, Madrecita querida,
no te olvides de nosotros!

Aunque en el Cielo
tanto vas a deleitarte,
¿no habrá algún tiempo
para que recuerdes?

Todos los que por ti viven
grandes esfuerzos hacen;
mas no, ¡O Tu, bien amada!
tú los llevarás de la mano.

Ya que ante ti rendido está
tu amado Hijo, preciadísimo
así, por toda esta gente
presenta tu súplica.

Mas, si Él no quiere,
por favor recuérdale
que tu preciosa carne
un día le diste,

Que leche de tu pecho
El se la bebió,
que con ella se hartó
cuando pequeñito.

Ojalá, gracias a tu mediación,
tus débiles criaturas,
los siempre olvidados,
merezcamos algo.

Nuestros pecados todos
los arrancaremos.
Al Cielo iremos,
allí te veremos.

Allí donde siempre
tú has de vivir,
donde siempre se hará
tu bendita ley.

"La fiesta de San Pedro Nolasco" (1677)

Los Padres bendito
tiene ô Redentor,
amo nic neltoca
quimati no Dios.

Solo Dios Piltzintli
del Cielo bajó
y nuestro tlatlacol
nos lo perdonó.

Pero estos Teopixqui
dice en so sermón
que este San Nolasco
miechtin compró.

Yo al Santo lo tengo
mucha devoción,
y de Sempual Xuchil
un Xuchil le doy.

Tehuatl so persona
dis que se quedó
con los perros Moro
ipam ce ocasión.

Mati Dios, si allí
lo estoviera yo,
cenzontle matara
con un mojicón.

Y nadie lo piense
lo hablo sin razón,
ca ni panadero,
de mocha opinión.

Huel ni machicahuac,
no soy hablador,
no teco qui mati
que soy valentón.

Se no compañero
lo desafió,
y con se poñete
allí se cayó.

También un Topil
del Gobernador,
ca ipampa tributo
prenderme mandó.

Mas yo con un cuahuitl
un palo lo dio
ipam i sonteco
no sé si morió.

Y quiero comprar
un San Redentor,
yuhqui el del altar
con so bendición.

Again, a Spanish versión by George Baudot:

Los Padres bendito
tiene ô Redentor,
no lo creo yo
lo sabe mi Dios.

Solo Dios Hijito preciado
del Cielo bajó
y nuestro pecado
no lo perdonó.

Pero estos sacerdotes
dice en so sermón
que este San Nolasco
a muchos compró.

Yo al Santo lo tengo
mucha devoción,
y de Viente-Flor
un(a) Flor le doy.

Tú, so persona,
dis que se quedó
con los perros Moro
en una ocasión.

Sabe Dios, si allí
lo estoviera yo,
a cuatrocientos matara
con un mojicón.

Y nadie lo piense
lo hablo sin razón,
porque soy panadero,
de mocha opinión.

Muy de mano dura soy yo,
no soy hablador,
mi amo lo sabe
que soy valentón.

Un mi compañero
lo desafió,
y con un poñete
allí se cayó.

También un alguacil
del Gobernador,
por culpa del tributo
prenderme mandó.

Mas yo con un leño
un palo lo dio
en su cabezota,
no sé si morió

Yo quiero comprar
un San Redentor,
como el del altar
con so bendición.

Tocotines were villancicos specially designed to evangelize the aboriginal population. Sor Juana's audience, therefore, was neither the Spaniards nor the Creole dwellers of Mexico City. By writing in Nahutal, was her intention to legitimize their language? Had she learned Nahuatl only orally since she was little? (Her first poem in Spanish was written when she was eight.) Should we not be critical of the agrammatical approach to it of this underappreciated translator?

On Memes as Semiotic Hand-Grenades
(with Mª Carmen África Vidal Claramonte)

ÁFRICA VIDAL: It is well-known that the term "meme" was coined by Richard Dawkins in his 1976 book *The Selfish Gene*. As a concept related to sociobiology, memes show analogies with genes inasmuch as they are small units of cultural transmission that spread and replicate themselves as genes do. But Ilan, don't you think memes are today much more? In an article you published in the *Daily Hampshire Gazette* (8/9/2018) you refer to the origin of the word which draws on the ancient Greek *mimeme*, meaning "something imitated," *mimeisthai*, "to imitate," and *mimos*, "mime." In this vein, Sarah Maitland argued in a lecture entitled "What Can Memes Teach Us about Cultural Translation?" (University of Edinburgh, 16 October 2019), that the construction of a meme "becomes linked inextricably to ideas of playfulness, mimicry, emulation, imitation, verisimilitude, and metonymy. As cultural reproduction, memes make use of processes of copying and imitation." All these processes are essential in social media and digital spaces but are also the essence (or perhaps not) of translation.

I start this conversation on the premise of conceiving memes in translational terms. I think memes are not simply "copying units" but translated cultural units which incorporate many layers and asymmetrical variations, posts of topical comments taken from the "original" author which modify its content and sometimes localize it. They sometimes even create new words. They are semiotic units that reconfigure, rewrite, and translate contemporary issues based on an original (an image, a film, a song, a text) which the target audience recognizes. In fact, internet memes may function as cues of membership or serve as a sort of creative and social glue that bonds members of a community together. I think they exemplify Gentzler's idea when he argues that the question of what constitutes a translation today is under radical review. The task of the translator no longer takes place between two languages but among "many contemporary parts of social life [...] From this perspective, it is possible to view all language use as a process of translation, thus questioning the assumption that translation is a mapping of items from one code to another [...] all communication involves translation." In this sense, memes could be interpreted as multimodal rewritings that refer to lively topics in social media, or, as Maitland describes them, as "twenty-first century palimpsests, memes add new layers of meaning on top of the cultural phenomena they translate." Would you agree?

ILAN STAVANS: Meme are snippets of knowledge that carry, in their DNA, a vast cultural cosmos that viewers must decode first. This mechanism isn't unlike what takes place in parody: for the audience to appreciate the parodic message, it needs to appreciate what is being parodied. Think of *Don Quixote*. Most readers today have never read Amadís de Gaul, Tirant Lo Blac, or other chivalry novelists. Yet entering Cervantes' book, they immediately recognize how *Don Quixote* is an attempt at ridiculing them. Likewise with memes: upon receiving a meme that reconfigures a scene of *The Wizard of Oz*, viewers must first recognize this 1939 classic film. Creators and recipients must share a common culture for the meme to be effective. But memes include another dimension: they are anonymous. In that sense, to me they are closer to folklore than to art: they are uncredited mechanical reproductions that, while created by an individual, are a product of the collective spirit seeking to give meaning, through the debris produced by internet communication, to the epistemological perplexity of a particular moment. In my view, in 2020, especially during the COVID-19 epidemic and as Donald Trump mastered tweets as the preferred method of dialogue with his political base, the meme, in my view, acquired truly global dimensions. As quarantine settled on the world's population, idle time pushed people to generate epistemic transactions across cultures that defied all types of borders, geographic, ideological, and linguistic. The meme was well-established long before; the pandemic simply emphasized its universal quality.

AV: One of the first scholars in our field who used the concept of meme was Andrew Chesterman in his seminal book *Memes of Translation*, where he argues that memes are ways to translate ideas because they spread them but also change them. From a descriptivist perspective, Chesterman reminds us that translators are agents of change, since the meme metaphor gives "less priority to the notions of 'preserving identity' or 'sameness which underlie the more traditional image of 'carrying something across, a something that somehow remains unchanged. I offer the meme metaphor as a helpful way to look at translation." He views memes as concepts and ideas about translation itself, and about the theory of translation. He goes on to describe his five "supermemes of translation," memes that encapsulate concepts and ideas on translation itself. This is, no doubt, an excellent starting point, especially because Chesterman underlies the fact the translation is not about sameness and mere equivalence. I would suggest to go further in line and start from "a dialogic view of translation premised on the notion of stimulus-and-response: translation responds to its source text (the stimulus), 'talks back' to it, by developing and extrapolating the memes built into the latter, and it does so by way of mobilizing the signifying resources of the target language. Response is not mimicry; it is a creative and calculated rejoinder formulated in the target language triggered by a prior stimulus, which is the meme of the source text." From this perspective, memes can be seen as units of translation of a rhizomatic nature. Memes could be seen as rewritings: "different translations may choose to develop different memes from the same source text; or the same memes may be instantiated in divergent ways in different translations with recourse to their particular repertoires and the affordances available in the languages, modes, and media in use." What do you think?

IS: Using literature again, memes are Menardian: just as Pierre Menard rewrites *Don Quixote* by recontextualizing it – the same exact words acquire an altogether different meaning once they are repeated – the meme extracts an epistemic unit of knowledge from its context and inserts it in another but does something more: it adds to its original meaning by inserting a caustic element in it that turns the original on its head. I remember years ago stumbling upon a volume in an Oxford, UK, bookstore of world literary classics (*Hamlet, Adventures of Huckleberry Finn, The Great Gatsby*, etc.) delivered, in abbreviated form, in tweets. Novelty aside, the question anyone interested in language and culture must ask is: can tweets generate the same emotional reaction in readers that full textual narratives might? Is the "aesthetic moment" one experiences when following the existential odyssey of Prince Hamlet capable of being accessed in a sequence of 137-character messages? I ask this question because memes, while infused with satirical value, are still a language in its early stages of formation. Might a complex plot be composed one day through these linguistic bricks, which is another way of calling them?

AV: You also say in your article I previously cited that the etymology of the word "meme" is useful in that it points to artifacts as cultural capsules passing from one individual to another. I think this is a very important point because it makes us think of the idea that we live in *The Age of Sharing* (2016), to use the title of Nicholas John's well-known book: sharing was once equivalent to caring, but in the digital age it is more related to what we do online, to a model of economic behaviour, or to a type of therapeutic talk. In fact, during the pandemic, imagination helped us to endure the lockdown. As you say in the introduction to *And We Came Outside and Saw the Stars Again*, imagination helped us to "escape mental imprisonment; some share memes, GIFs, or tweets, while others recite poems, dress up, sing, talk on the phone or skype, dream, listen to the dreams of others. Thousands of artists have given away their plays, films, books, and concerts online. The species persists through forms of representation of reality (eliminated from public budgets as the most expendable part of reality).". But sharing may not embody positive values and may be used to disguise racism, sexism, and commercial or even exploitive relations.

IS: Social media is said to be a blessing and also a curse. In my case, it is more an affliction than anything else. Donald Trump: need I say anything else? When Facebook and Twitter took away his accounts, there was, expectedly, an outcry connected with First Amendment rights. But free speech, in the age of the internet, which creates silos of information, is no longer what it was in the 18th century, when the French Encyclopedists reflected on the idea: it has turned individual rights into bastions of social disengagements. Social media in reality should be called *asocial* media: the age of sharing is also the age of minimizing others into misinformed soundbites. If we don't somehow curtail free-speech rights, narrowing the limits without restricting its qualities – I believe this should be done – I will not be surprised if governments in this decade and beyond fall like raindrops. Stabilization is at stake; so is cosmopolitanism. I'm fully aware, obviously, of the implications of my assessment. But the opposite, e.g., inaction, is too dangerous. As a result of social media, mass culture is increasingly ungovernable.

AV: On the other hand, sharing is closely connected with translating. In an interesting article, Varis and Bloomaert argue that "sharing" an update on Facebook is a classic case of "re-entextualization," which they describe as "the process by means of which a piece of 'text' (a broadly defined semiotic object here) is extracted from its original context-of-use and re-inserted into an entirely different one, involving different participation frameworks, a different kind of textuality – an entire text can be condensed into a quote, for instance – and ultimately also very different meaning outcomes. What is marginal in the source text can become important in the re-entextualized version, for instance." Sharing is also a type of "re-semiotization." Re-semiotization, in line with the foregoing, "refers to the process by means of which every 'repetition' of a sign involves an entirely new set of contextualization conditions and thus results in an entirely 'new' semiotic process, allowing new semiotic modes and resources to be involved in the repetition process." They give as an example the meme "Keep Calm and ..." which has been endlessly rewritten, retranslated, combined with other memes, and gone viral since the year 2000. It has even been translated into "lolspeak" in an online translation of the entire Bible. Sharing is a characteristic common to translation and social media. To exist, you say in your article, Ilan, a meme must travel, must be shared. The same can be said of translation. Memes transform us all in subtle ways, you assert. Again, the same goes for translation. Don't you think?

IS: An unused meme (or else, the idea of a meme) is like a manuscript stored in a drawer, or like a tree that falls in the middle of the forest. To exist, a meme must be a bridge between at least two individuals. Needless to say, memes, within themselves, aspire to much more: dozens of recipients, hundreds, thousands, millions. The issue of connectivity starts with the act of deciphering a meme: the recipient must understand, even partially, what the sender's intended meaning is. But more is required. The ecosystem into which the meme is born is defined by irony, parody, sarcasm, mockery, ridicule, and other similar cognitive tools of understanding. Unless there is a channel of shared experience between the sender and the recipient, the meme is ineffective. This frequently happens when it reaches an unintended audience, at which point it is deleted or ignored. It is important to talk about these two responses. Deliberately or otherwise, to ignore a meme is to pre-empt its message. And to delete it – which is possible only in a few platforms – is to outright cancel it. Either way, the life cycle of the meme is suddenly interrupted. When this is done, one time in a million, it matters little. Yet rejecting a meme is a form of self-restraint in the receiver. "I don't like this," the recipient might be stating; or else, I disagree; or even more politically, I'm not ready to perpetuate this message and, therefore, I exclude myself from this community. Clearly, receiving a meme, although seen as a passive form of behaviour, actually requires compliance and even consent.

AV: Such concepts as "text" or "image" have changed in our digital age. Adding more semiotic modes to our contemporary making of meaning also implies to assemble different resources which help us to grasp today's expansion of the idea of what a text is in the era of multimodality. Indeed, language, in the case of memes, is now seen as ancillary to other semiotic modes. The different modes of intermediality appear in Web-based homepages, digital fiction, born digital hypertexts narratives, gaming, MUDS and MOOS, hyperlinked words, electronic literature, the photo-sharing application Flickr, YouTube, sites like Myspace where individuals narrate their stories on blogs, journals, and discussion boards, or Facebook, with its collaborative storytelling ventures, wall posts, comments, microblogging. These modes and genres are used today as new ways to tell stories when words are no longer so prominent. Graphics and animation turn the visual richness of these texts into a challenge for translators because they have altered the traditional conceptions of plot, structure, temporality, originality, or agency, and at the same time have demonstrated that words are only one of many semiotic systems which may be used to communicate.

IS: To me the meme shares qualities with the first linguistic signs recorded in caves in Cantabria in Paleolithic times. Images are stamped on a wall to tell a story. They are anonymous. And while they are in Altamira, for instance, they bridge the local and become universal. Memes are also similar to hieroglyphics in a language that employs characters instead of letters. It goes without saying that countless memes depend on images and letters. But the base is graphic, not literal. And, as in the ancient narratives I'm invoking, they aren't static; instead, they tell stories, with a plot, no matter how incipient, how undeveloped it might be. While our technology makes us feel advanced, it draws from the same tropes humankind has depended on since the beginning of time.

AV: The pandemic has also infected the internet, which has played a role calming nerves during the lockdown. Memes were frequently concerned with the coronavirus. In many cases they reassured people that they were not alone. Humor, subversion, irony are mixed in all memes, and they allow users to address such a sensitive topic and express criticism of how politicians have dealt with the crisis. Some of these memes, highly topical, are difficult to understand to some elders who do not get the context; they do not have the cultural references to translate the different layers and get the cultural references. If they are clever, sometimes in some countries memes are used against state censorship. So, they have been used by the #BLM movement, feminism, queer rights, climate justice, and many other. However, memes can also be a weapon of harm and inflict mental and emotional damage. The coronavirus pandemic has also been an excuse to promote racism, for instance after Trump's use of the phrase "Chinese virus" in a tweet on March 17, 2020. An anti-Asian sentiment was translated into images and language. This had happened in the past with other events and keeps on happening with racism in general. Sometimes these same memes are retranslated to mean the opposite. Memes spread in internet spaces and undergo multiple changes by internet users. In the case of memes related to pandemics, they have included humor, sarcasm, but also racism, (symbolic) violence, and hate. They have used negative stereotypes to expand biased attitudes against China, where it first originated. António Guterres, UN Secretary-General, said that migrants and refugees have been demonized as sources of the virus and denied medical treatment. He called for an "all-out effort to end hate speech globally" amid what he called a "tsunami of hate and xenophobia, scapegoating and scare-mongering" unleashed during the coronavirus pandemic," and added that "anti-foreigner sentiment has surged online and in the streets, anti-Semitic conspiracy theories have spread, and COVID-19-related anti-Muslim attacks have occurred." The so-called Coronavirus Karen could also be an example here. Memes, like translations, are potentially dangerous because they, both memes and translations, are never neutral phenomena but interpretations of public dialogues.

IS: Nothing in language is ever neutral. To engage in communication is to interpret. But memes, I agree, are semiotic hand-grenades. They are deprived of innocence; their intent is to unsettle, or, at least, to interrupt our train of thought, to disrupt it.

AV: As multimodal translations, memes subvert online official (mis)information and distort old "normal" concepts like time, which has been the subject of endless translations which play with tense ("Next week has been exhausting!") in the disruption of temporality; calendars in which celebrity portraits that age decades in months; or which, conversely, are presented by an identical static pose month after month after month. They also take the form of hand-washing guides with joke-lyrics, images of empty grocery shelves, panic-buying of toilet paper, people wearing masks, putting on weight, that parodying government slogans. But memes are more than jokes. Like translations, they help answer the question of how do we all individually understand a joint experience. They are social semiotic artifacts, powerful tools for political commentary and participation, cultural translations of global issues and intersubjective experiences. As such, they serve functions of communication and political participation. Again, like translations, they reflect the heteroglossia of perspectives.

IS: Heteroglossia and heteronomia. Since the pandemic began, social media, obviously, has come to play an enlarged role. Tweets, Facebook, Instagram, and other platforms are the channels through which people establish the parameters of their orbit. Since they are 24-hour endeavors, time as we know it vanishes. A student of mine told me the other day that this past year has been "a year without weekends." What she meant is that she no longer perceives a difference between a working day and a day of rest. She is constantly indoors, unaware of the difference between night and day. She said that in the middle of the night, when suffering from insomnia, she looks at Tik Tok "in order not to be alone." This erasure of time, in connection to translated memes, might be approached from a different angle. After the presidential inauguration of Joe Biden on Wednesday, January 20, 2020, a meme of Senator Bernie Sanders was widely circulated online. Sanders had been photographed sitting on the inaugural platform, wearing his usual informal clothes, with mittens and a mask. It was an inspiring sight: the veteran socialist maverick celebrating the transition of power without the regalia that goes with occasions such as this one. The photograph became an instant success among meme artists. In one meme, Sanders is sitting in Leonardo da Vinci's "The Last Supper." In another, he is at the Yalta Conference with Churchill, Roosevelt, and Stalin. And in a third he is having lunch with workers on the steel beam atop the New York City skyscraper under construction on 30 Rockefeller Plaza, an image immortalized in the iconic John Ebbets photograph. The magic of these images includes the fact that Sanders – anachronistically – is painted by da Vinci around 1495, as though he is an apostle next to Jesus Christ; he is in Manhattan in 1932, and he is in the Crimea on February 12, 1945. In other words, Sanders travels unimpeded through space and time in a way we, in our limited reality, cannot. That is the freedom that memes allow. They project the illusion of ubiquity. And maybe of omnipresence, which is an attribute of God.

AV: The virality of GIF memes (images captioned with texts) can turn an individual's expression of hate or the sharing of stereotypical jokes into the perpetuation of bias online. As you say in your article, the young traffic in memes at astonishing speed. This may give way to very quick and emotional responses, likes and dislikes, (politically) correct (or not) answers to sensitive topics with important consequences in the so-called cancel culture.

IS: Memes, we might say, are impulsive, unpremeditated reactions, of the kind those engaged in them don't think twice about. In that sense, they are instantaneous, automatic, and, therefore, potentially inopportune. This last adjective is particular important: to travel fast, memes need to surprise, to unsettle, to indulge in unpredictable messages. Thus, they have a somewhat disruptive quality in their nature: they amaze, even startle. But, as I mentioned before, their life cycle is that of a firefly. The fact that they have a text delivered in particular languages creates a sense that we're again at the bottom of the Tower of Babel – after the divine wrath. Tongues come and go at astonishing speed from one end of the globe to another without much regard to nuance: it matters less what these GIF memes say than the fact that they exist. That is the phantasmagoric effect of social media: to torpedo everyone with content regardless of meaning; the objective is to stay connected, even while the reasons behind that connectivity might be unclear.

AV: You also argue that young people see memes as democratic items. "Through these memes, they proclaim their ideological loyalties, even when it feels as if those ideologies are hyper-sarcastic. They proclaim pop culture to be everyone's property: There is no private property, especially online; every theft is a type of appropriation. This is unusual because, in our age, the concept of appropriation is highly contested. It is ironic that the young often protest when the narrative of a disenfranchised group is stolen. Yet to create memes, they steal left and right without an ounce of shame." I feel this has to do with what Marjorie Perloff calls in another context "unoriginal genius." But it also made me think of your own theory of translation and self-translation, especially when you say: "I lived in translation without an original. In the past decade and a half, I have come to refine that view: I exist in an echo chamber of self-translated voices, all of them my own". Or when you argue that "ours is a universe infused with translations." In my opinion, this is very Borgean: translation completes the original, broadens its meanings; opens up new interpretations; asks questions, and those questions generate other questions; reads the original text and discovers a journey to a rugged landscape with misty views, which is, however, worth exploring. Would you agree? Memes are translations that by sharing, by travelling, complete the original and broaden its meaning?

IS: In memes, the concept of authenticity is revamped. Authenticity is based on copying. To be original is to exercise the dexterous talent of repurposing. Likewise, in memes the very idea of originals is pushed aside; everything is a copy, and a copy of the copy. One might argue, of course, that the original is the image on which the meme maker reformulates meaning; yet calling that an original is foolish since that image, by definition, is stolen. Indeed, memes make us appreciate culture as an endless sequence of thefts: to steal is to engage in conversation; to steal is to appropriate through anonymity. Perloff is not only right when she talks of "unoriginal genius"; she actually invites us to reconsider our understanding of genius. The best memes are both genial and expressions of genius; but they aren't original. Think of Mozart, Shakespeare, Goethe, and Rimbaud. We refer to them as geniuses because of the way they projected their individuality in their oeuvre. Any aspect of their work *is them*. But in memes genius is the absence of individuality; brilliance isn't confined to individuals; instead, it is the result of group efforts. Memes aren't expressions of personal quality, nor are they representations of intellectual property. Memes are masks behind which pluralities hide.

AV: A seminal characteristic of memes is their multimodality. In this sense, I think they are a very good example of the new concept of text in our visual culture. Communication today implies an inevitable combination of different media. Scholars are moving from a language-centred model of a decade ago to another one which underlines the interconnection among media. Words, images, colours, sounds, bodies, gestures, tastes, spaces, movements, cities, architecture communicate and make clear that no single disciplinary framework can be an adequate approach to our multimodal world. If we want to understand how meaning is produced, expanding the idea of language seems inevitable. The stories told through memes show that non-traditional texts need to be translated in new ways. Given this state of affairs, expanding the field of translation studies seems to be an urgent goal. Within this new semiotic landscape, translation needs to broaden its scope. Developments in multimodal studies in the field of translation have already begun to change our idea of what translation is. In fact, many scholars claim that in our global and visual culture the question of what constitutes a translation is under radical review. In 2011, an article by Siri Nergaard and Stefano Arduini, "Translation: A New Paradigm," published in *Translation. A Transdisciplinary Journal*, urged for a different way of facing the great epistemological questions of what we know and how we know. Edwin Gentzler, in a 2015 article, underlined the need to translate without borders, to understand translation as an ongoing process of movement: manoeuvring, traversing boundaries, changing and adapting. He argued that rather than thinking about translation as a somewhat secondary process of ferrying ideas across borders, we think beyond borders to culture as a whole, reconceiving translation as an always primary, primordial, and proactive process that continually introduces new ideas, forms of expression, and pathways for change into cultures. They are translated communications, one of the best examples of the new concept of "text" in our multimodal culture and, furthermore, an excellent exemplification of the "outward turn" in translation studies. The multimodal nature of memes makes us aware of how urgent it is for translation studies to turn *outwards*, to use Susan Bassnett's concept, meaning that translation studies needs to engage more with other disciplines rather than, as we fear has been happening, with translation studies becoming introspective and with scholars only talking to one another. In an article in dialogue with Anthony Pym, she describes translation in a way that could be applied to memes: "promoting translation as a creative act, one which always involves language and is also political, but which above all is a process of discovery." We learn through translating – we learn about our own language as well as about the language from which we are translating. We learn what cannot be said, what is unsayable, and we also learn about compromise, manipulation, negotiation. I go so far as to believe that it ought to be possible – indeed essential – to teach translation to people who have no foreign language, because in a way everyone engages in intralingual and intersemiotic translation, to go back to good old Jakobson, even if they don't have a foreign language.

IS: The old definitions of translation have become obsolete. By this I mean that translation, as I've said before, is much more than simply conveying a text in a language other than the one that originally housed it. For me translation is a way of life. I'm an immigrant. Switching languages is a daily affair. I negotiate who I am all the time by using different codes depending on the social environment I find myself. Translation, in my eyes, isn't static; it is like jazz – amorphous, nervous, improvisational. To be frank, I have little interest in translation studies as a discipline because it confines what is existential to me to a narrow academic field. Translation is a strategy of survival; it is the tools through which I became different people depending on the circumstance.

AV: Memes are internet translations. They are examples of multimodal, multi-authorial, and multi-layered new texts that do not have a single interpretation and, as Maitland asserts, they are hermeneutic reflections that arise from the co-presence of a literal signification suggestive of a secondary meaning that can only be understood by a detour through the meaning of the first. They are palimpsests, text upon image, image upon image, sound upon sound, all full of parody, humour, hate, ostracism. And always, interpretation upon interpretation. Maitland argues in her lecture: "The cultural stimulus that is copied in the meme functions as the 'source text' of translation. This source text is interpreted, imitated, parodied, transformed, reshaped, and 'translated' by Internet users, turning it into something new, a 'third object,' alike and akin to the original cultural stimulus, yet undeniably different. Just like a translation, this new form is intended to find a new audience in a new time and new place." In some books, you describe yourself not as an original but as a second original who feels attracted by masks. You have also said that you like anthologies because they give the reader multiple points of view and in your book on "cellfies" you argue that "our self isn't a unity but a multiplicity." What similarities do you find between selfies and memes?

IS: Selfies are palimpsests, too; they are curated, instant, ephemeral versions of the self. Like memes, they exist by creating a community of those who are included – the sender of the selfie chooses its recipients – and also those who are excluded. The difference between "selfie" and "cellfie," and even between these two spellings and a third one, "sellfie," is essential: one highlights the self, another the cell phone, and the third the monetary transaction engaged by the photograph that is being shared. To me selfies are marketable versions of who we are; they reduce us to a convenient profile, the equivalent of a meme. In fact, selfies (notice my choice of spelling) are often intervened by the sender or someone else, de facto becoming memes. That intervention might be a way of beautifying the picture; or it might be an aggression, a way of demeaning it. In any case, they are similar to translation in that they refashion a real object in subjective ways, thus modifying its meaning.

AV: COVID-19 has endorsed new meanings to such words as touching, distance, fear, isolation, strangeness, disorientation. In sum, this small virus has had the enormous capacity to rewrite life and death. The virus is today our most powerful rewriter, a translator who is obliging us to reread concepts, even ways of life. It took us by surprise, although this is not new. Similar disasters, taking the form of earthquakes, deluges, famines, plagues of insects, are recurrent visitors in the theater of human affairs. The title of your anthology, *And We Came Outside and Saw the Stars Again*, was inspired by the last line of Dante's *Inferno*, in which the poet and Virgil emerge from their journey through hell to once again view the beauty of the heavens. But this time we have new ways of representing fear, isolation, and loss; we have new forms of translating the virus' translations back. In the story written for *And We Came Outside and Saw the Stars Again*, Juan Villoro argues that memes, GIFs, poems, songs, art, concerts, dreams, or listening to the dreams of others represent forms of imagination which are helping us in this crisis. While governments are cutting funds in the cultural sector, the irony is that we are surviving thanks to the arts. Villoro mentions Churchill's claim that Britain won the war because they decided not to close theaters. "The species persists through forms of representation of reality." Memes are one of these forms of representing and translating reality. By rewriting and translating what is happening, memes and other digital platforms have revealed many things of our own selves, have been a selfie/cellfie of contemporary society. As Carlos Fonseca argues in his story in your anthology, "The paradox behind this pandemic is that it has made evident the world in which we were already living: a world of isolation, of frontiers and walls, a world where the elderly are secluded and forgotten, a xenophobic world, where death is something invisible that happens always behind closed doors and against which we prove incapable of mourning. A world that mixes the possibilities of technological globalization – Zoom, Skype, FaceTime – with the tightening of borders and the rise of contemporary nationalisms [...] Sometimes I feel that the logic of the virus, which is that of repetition and difference, is precisely the logic of rumor and of the media. Tweet and retweet. The logic of post-truth. Perhaps the uncanny sense of unreality that pervades this crisis comes from the fact that now, more than ever, we are living through a catastrophe that is experienced online." But perhaps memes can also offer, to paraphrase John Berger, new ways of translating what will never be normal again.

IS: Memes are astonishingly creative forms of communication. Insofar as social media remain uninterrupted, they are the go-to form of informal encounter, taking people out of their Robinson Crusoe island into a marketplace of meaning. Like guns, they aren't dangerous unto themselves; it is who uses them that gives them an edge. The pandemic is the most sobering event of our lifetime. It is a calamity of the magnitude of the bubonic plague in the Middle Ages, the Napoleonic Wars, the First and Second World Wars, and similar transformative moments in human history. The fact that we have moved into Zoom in order to continue our life, that memes have become transactional capsules, is evidence of human adaptability. As Plato suggests in *The Republic*, "our need will be the real creator." One might take this to mean, in the popular imagination, that "necessity is the mother of creation." I find memes extraordinary in their resourcefulness. Can we one day create with them a narrative that is the equivalent of a novel, one capable of moving us inside? Maybe. The language of memes is infinite.

*– Translation and Social Media Communication
in the Age of the Pandemic* (2022)

Reading Emilio Salgari

I am told that my youthful passion for the adventure novels of Emilio Salgari (1862–1911) puts me in the company of Jorge Luis Borges, Pablo Neruda, Gabriel García Márquez, Carlos Fuentes, and Isabel Allende, who also read him voraciously in their formative years. (And I should add Álvaro Mutis, author of *Adventures of Maqroll*. He explicitly told me he discovered the sea in his native Bogotá thanks to Salgari.)

I'm happy to be part of this illustrious group, but the truth is that it changes nothing. I read Salgari before I read these Latin American precursors. I wasn't an assiduous reader in my early days; but when I did find myself with a book in hand, it was usually one of the twenty-five volumes by Salgari published by Editorial Porrúa. What I liked about him was the sheer, unadulterated adrenaline he offered in his tales of swashbucklers. These days you get that adrenaline at the movies.

Fast-forward twenty years later. *The Washington Post* asked me, then a recent immigrant in New York and writing in the English language, for an autobiographical essay about growing up as a reader in Mexico. One afternoon, as the piece was being readied for publication, I received a call from the copyediting department. In her dutiful fact-checking, the editor had come across my mention of Emilio Salgari.

The internet was still in its infancy at the time. She couldn't find a reference to him anywhere. She asked point blank if I had concocted the name. I said I wished I had.

When I too went out on a fact-checking expedition, I realized that, unlike many of us privileged Latin Americans, our counterparts in the United States had never grown up with Sandokan, the Queen of the Caribbean, and Captain Tempesta.

I felt pity. In my next phone call with the fact-checker, I tried to describe the thrills I still had from these books. She allowed the reference to stay.

One of the aspects I most remember of Salgari was what a liar he was. For instance, he pretended to have traveled to the American Wild West, where he said he met Buffalo Bill. Or he said his books were based on his travels across the "Seven Seas." Truth is, Salgari never went anywhere beyond the Adriatic Sea.

This isn't a criticism. Fine fiction, regardless of the form it comes in, is always a lie – a durable, persuasive lie.

Shakespeare never set foot in Italy, yet he left us with more than a dozen plays that take place in it, from *Romeo and Juliet* to *The Merchant of Venice* and *All's Well That Ends Well*. Likewise, Kafka didn't cross the Atlantic Ocean even once, although his novel *Amerika* unfolds, in part, in New York.

Or think of Karl May, who wrote novels in German set in China and Latin America. He is best known for the ones in the American Old West, with legendary indigenous characters like Winnetou. May didn't know the place either.

This begs the question: Do you need to have been in a place to write "authentically" about it? For what I know, Dante never actually visited Purgatory either.

(By the way, Salgari did meet Buffalo Bill; it was during a tour he did of Italy in a "Wild West" show.)

How many pirates Salgari knew is also subject to debate. But it doesn't matter either, especially now that pirates are Russian technology hackers or bootlegger Africans targeting Western cargo or tourist ships with machine guns.

I mentioned Sandokan before. He is known in Salgari's novels as the Tiger of Malaysia. Sandokan is a kind of 19th-century barbarian: handsome, courageous, gallant, at once an indomitable force and a brave anti-colonial, or maybe anti-capitalist, leader.

At least, that is how I remember him.

He is, I could swear, the inspiration behind the comic-strip Mexican superhero of the 1960s called Kalimán, who wears a turban with a big "K" and is supposedly a descendant of pharaohs. Kalimán is endowed with both muscles and mentalist powers.

As an adolescent, I loved him as much as I loved Sandokan. In fact, I sometimes imagined a combined series where they intrepidly join forces.

Curiously, it never crossed my mind while reading Salgari that he had written in a foreign language. I don't recall noticing any mention of a translator on the covers of his novels. Besides, to me "Emilio Salgari" sounded Mexican.

What a thrill it is now to acknowledge the role translation had on me then.

After Salgari, I graduated to another Italian: Umberto Eco. I remember with astonishing precision the day I bought my copy of *The Name of the Rose* in a Spanish translation. I devoured it in twenty-four hours. It was about Benedictine monks in a 14th-century abbey, a lost treatise on laughter written by Aristotle, and an exercise in deductive thinking rooted in William of Occam's philosophy.

It isn't a figure of speech to say that Eco's novel had much to do with the most crucial decisions I made in that period of my life.

Anyway, while reading it I remember thinking of Salgari. Only later did I discover that Eco too was a Salgari fan.

The classics are books that always feel new. On the other hand, there is wisdom in not going back to one's juvenile infatuations. Not long ago, I tried *The Name of the Rose* again. It didn't fare well: it is verbose, contrived, and predictable.

I still own the Salgari novels I acquired in Mexico. I haven't tried returning to them. They are a reminder of the reader I was at the time.

– *Prahos*, September 2023

On Translating *The Disappearance* into Yiddish (with Beruriah Wiegand)

כ׳האָב אַלערלײַ טויטן פֿאַרזוכט ביז אַהער
און ס׳קען מיך שוין קיינער ניט וווּנדערן מער.

"פֿאַרפֿרוירענע ייִדן" – אַבֿרהם סוצקעווער" (1944)

So far, I have tasted all kinds of death,
None will surprise me, will catch my breath.
– Avrom Sutzkever, "Frozen Jews" (1944),
translated by Barbara and Benjamin Harshav

ILAN STAVANS: The appearance of your Yiddish rendition of *The Disappearance* reminds me of the visit Saul Bellow paid to Shmuel Yosef Agnon in Jerusalem. Two significant moments of this encounter live in my mind. In the first, Agnon asks Bellow: "Young man, do you use Jewish themes in your books?" To which Bellow replies: "Yes, I think I generally do." Agnon then states: "If so, you will have a great future!" And the second moment is when they discuss translation. Agnon tells Bellow that Jewish books need to be in Hebrew. Bellow brings up Heinrich Heine in English translation. "Ah," Agnon says, "we have him beautifully translated into Hebrew. He is safe." My book has appeared in other languages but to me it feels safe in *mame-loshn*.

BERURIAH WIEGAND: I am very happy to read these words. In our recent online conversation in Mexico, one of the presenters said hearing me read from my Yiddish translation of your book gave her the feeling that these stories were originally written in Yiddish. Of course, this was wonderful to hear! But it is true that I translated your stories in a way in which they would sound authentic in Yiddish. The subject matter in all three of your stories is very Jewish, and for that reason, they translate well into Yiddish. I have also been striving to recreate your unique style of writing in my Yiddish translation, and I hope I have succeeded in this.

What is your own connection with Yiddish? I've got the impression that you know it well enough to read and appreciate my Yiddish translation of your stories, but not well enough to translate your work into Yiddish yourself.

IS: I grew up in Yiddish. In school it was one of the languages of instruction at the *Alte Yidishe Shule* in Mexico. I communicated in Yiddish with my grandmothers and at times with my parents. But as a young man, I wasn't a happy Yiddish speaker. I resented it because I didn't see any practical side to knowing it: it was a link to what has been called "a world that was no more." Why not learn English, French, or German instead? I read Peretz's Hasidism-infused stories, Sholem Aleichem's *Tevye der milkhiker*, Israel Joshua Singer's *The Family Carnovsky*, the poetry of Avrom Sutzkever (I remember distinctly being exposed, for the first time, to "Frozen Jews") – yet these efforts were done mechanically. It was only when I moved to New York City, in my mid-twenties, having rejected Yiddish as what I called "a camel for the streets," that I rediscovered it again – and since then I have been possessed by its splendor.

BW: Where were you?

IS: It happened on a Manhattan subway train. Yiddish wasn't altogether a thing of the past for me, but I had grown distant from it. As I saw it, it had lost currency, yet, in Williamsburg, Brooklyn, and elsewhere in the city, it was the tongue of Hasidim. As I understood it, the structure of Yiddish was Babel-like: a mishmash of provenances that made communication an addition rather than a subtraction. After a year or so in New York, where I had arrived as an immigrant, I had begun to fall in love with Spanglish, the mix of Spanish and English, spoken by millions of Latinos of numerous provenances (Mexico, Cuba, Puerto Rico, Dominican Republic, Colombia, etc.), when it suddenly dawned on me that Spanglish was, indeed, *the new Yiddish*, a hybrid, bastard tongue born out of necessity, spontaneously developed by a growing minority uniquely positioned in the intersection between two cultures. I decided then to become a sort of *bal-tshuve*: to re-embrace my Yiddish.

BW: I am intrigued by the comparison with Spanglish. Do you think in it when you are among Spanglish speakers?

IS: I surely do. That mode – not only using the words, but inhabiting them – is what makes a language more than a verbal code. Anyway, nowadays Yiddish colors *everything* I do, even when I'm not conscious of it. When I lecture on Plato's *The Symposium* or Shakespeare's *The Merchant of Venice*, discuss the rise of populism on the global stage and the future of democracy, or meditate 19th-century American poetry, it is Yiddish that forms the substratum of my thoughts. I speak it and read it with joy, but I don't feel comfortable writing a story or poem in it, although years ago I did.

My second son, Isaiah, an actor and playwright, recently played Sholem Asch in Paula Vogel's *Indecent*, at the Chautauqua Theater Festival. He knew the basic grammar but needed to learn how to perform in it.

With the entrance of American Jews into mainstream culture in the United States, a sense of nostalgia colors Yiddish. Assimilated Jews know a few words but, with increasing frequency, they wish they had been taught the language by their forebears. Curiously, those forebears engaged with Yiddish in ways that were noticeably "unlinguistic," that is, they employed it for the children *not* to understand. The strategy is mind-blowing, since language is, by definition, a communicating code. In this case – and it happens often with immigrants of all types – the mother tongue is devised for the next generation not to understand. Fortunately, this nostalgia appears to be prompting young people to return to Yiddish. During the pandemic, the amount of Zoom courses, events, and other online activities in and around Yiddish multiplied to the nth degree.

BW: Yes, I have been taking part in numerous online events in and around Yiddish all over the world, and I've been teaching all my Yiddish courses via Zoom for the past two years. Last year, Professor Judith Olszowy Schlanger, the president of our Oxford Centre for Hebrew and Jewish Studies, set up the Oxford School of Rare Jewish Languages, offering weekly online classes in Yiddish, Ladino, Judeo-Arabic, Judeo-Persian, Judeo-Tat, Judeo-French, Judeo-Italian, etc. I was teaching four Yiddish courses for the OSRJL last year, and I was overwhelmed by the number of applicants for all my courses … We were accepting thirty students per class, but there were hundreds of applications. My students came from all over the world: the UK, the Netherlands, Germany, Italy, Poland, Russia, Ukraine, the United States, Canada, Israel, etc. I had both Jewish and non-Jewish students. There were certainly students wanting to return to the language of their parents or more often grandparents, but also Yiddish singers, students of history who need to read original Yiddish documents, students of modern languages or linguistics, curious to learn another fascinating language, students wanting to read Yiddish literature in the original, and even some students in my advanced class who wish to translate Yiddish literature into their languages, including German and Georgian, which makes me very happy, especially since one of these students is hoping to translate some of my own Yiddish poetry. But it's one thing to translate from Yiddish into another language and quite a different matter to translate literature into Yiddish, which I have done with your stories.

IS: How did you make my stories sound "authentic" in Yiddish? Authenticity is elusive, contested in translation.

BW: The subject matter of your book made it very natural for these stories to be translated into, and recreated in, Yiddish. But all along, I was conscious of the fact that I was translating from one linguistic system to another, very different one, and my translation was often an act of problem solving. For instance, Yiddish syntax is very different from that of English. In Yiddish, the main conjugated verb is always the second sentence unit, which makes it especially tricky when there are long sentences with many subclauses and some insertions in between different parts of a verbal construction, as you tend to have in your stories. English makes extensive use of the passive voice. Yiddish doesn't. Although there is a passive voice, which is sometimes used in the literature and especially in Bible translations, it's much more natural to use the construction with מע / מען, which I have often employed in Yiddish where you had the passive voice in English. English uses a large number of abstract nouns, where Yiddish would often have a verbal construction, which is the way in which I have translated many of your abstract nouns.

Then there was the problem with wordplay and invented words. For example, among the films that the actor Maarten Soëtendrop has made, and is yet to make in the title story "The Disappearance," there is one entitled "Amsterdamned." After much reflection, I came up with the translation "פֿאַראַמסטערדאַמט". Likewise, I was wrestling with the title of your third story, "Xerox Man." How do you translate this into Yiddish דער קסער פאטאקאפיר-מאן ? דער פאטאקאפירן ? אָקס-מאַן ? – Surely not! I went for "דער פֿאָטאָקאָפֿירניק".

IS: I love your restless approach: language is malleable. A translator is also a creator.

BW: My translation was a dialogue with your source text and a quest for meaning in my target language: Yiddish. Translating literature implies creativity. It's not just translation, but "transcreation." Translating into Yiddish is an art form! I wonder if you can relate to this, not just as a translated author, but also as a translator of literature into English and Spanish.

IS: I like the term "transcreation" because it acknowledges the translator as another essential creator.

BW: Yes, indeed. I very much enjoyed "transcreating" the first and the third of your three stories in the book, which I was commissioned to translate by Daniel Galay, the publisher of my two poetry collections at the H.Leyvik-farlag in Tel Aviv. Originally, I was only supposed to translate those two stories and proofread and copyedit the translation of the second story, "Morirse está en hebreo," which had been done by a different translator, Shlomo Lerman. But I soon realized that there was much more work to do on this story than just correcting a few grammatical and orthographic mistakes. There were huge problems with syntax that had to be remedied, and large numbers of old-fashioned, *daytshmerish* words in Yiddish that had to be exchanged for something more modern. There were mistranslations, words and sentences omitted, etc. But above all, there was the question of style. If I wanted to have all the three stories in the book in a consistent modern Yiddish style that would reflect the style of your English original, I knew I had to rewrite the translation of your second story in my own creative way, which I did. And with my Yiddish translation of your book, I have now added to the vast canon of world literature translated into Yiddish, which includes writers like Ibsen, Knut Hamsun, Thomas Mann, Guy de Maupassant, Jules Verne, Sh.Y. Agnon, and more recently books like Antoine de Saint-Exupéry's *Le Petit Prince* and J.K. Rowling's *Harry Potter*.

IS: What makes the history of Yiddish plentiful is the abundance of translations in it. From the start, speakers were bringing into their midst other languages while sending Yiddish back to them. Think of all the other Jewish languages we have created: Ladino, Judeo-Persian, Judeo-Portuguese, Judeo-Italian, etc. None was ever – even remotely – the type of "translation machine" Yiddish became. Spinoza is in Yiddish, Cervantes, Dostoyevsky, Erich Maria Remarque … Except that, in numerous cases, translators engaged in all kinds of cheap tricks: they abbreviated texts, rendering them not from the original but from a second language like German or English; they modified and even deleted characters; and so on. Personally, I've been prone to Shakespeare in Yiddish. In cadence and metrics, the sonnets have been respectfully, though not loyally, approached. Can a translation be both loyal and beautiful? But the plays: oy, oy, oy. They aren't "transcreations"; nor are they "transadaptations."

BW: Yes, even Bashevis engaged in this kind of translation work, long before he became the famous Nobel Prize–winning writer I.B. Singer. In Warsaw in the 1920s and early 30s, he translated works like Thomas Mann's *Der Zauberberg* and Erich Maria Remarque's *Im Westen nichts Neues* into Yiddish from the German original, but he also translated Knut Hamsun's *Pan* from its German translation, not from the original Norwegian, a language which he, of course, didn't know.

But what about Shakespeare? There are many translations of Shakespeare's works into Yiddish. There are also some completely new versions, like דער ייִדישער קעניג ליר or Yankev Gordin's play מירעלע אפרת, which is like a Yiddish/Jewish "Queen Lear" …

IS: In *King Lear* and *Hamlet*, to list two famous examples (though these plays, I should say, were translated into Yiddish more than once), they are entirely new pieces, set in a Jewish milieu, with religious, political, cultural concerns that are absolutely remote from Shakespeare's Elizabethan England. My point is that translators are never innocent. Needless to say, Shakespeare himself was a plagiarist. Many of his plays are rewritings of previous versions of say *Macbeth*, *Richard III*, and *Henry V*. He also inserted segments of Ovid's *Metamorphosis*, maybe his favorite book, which show up in *Cymbeline*, *Titus Andronicus*, and *A Midsummer Night's Dream*. And Montaigne's personal essays (in John Florio's translations) appear in *The Tempest*. Conclusion: there's nothing original in originality, least in the sphere of translation. Anyway, I'm particularly struck by your choice for the title story of *The Disappearance*, "Der Opgang."

BW: I was deliberating for a long time on how to translate the title of the first story and thus the title of the whole book. There was no obvious choice for *The Disappearance* in Yiddish. I checked in the *Comprehensive English-Yiddish Dictionary*, edited by Gitl Schaechter Viswanath and Paul Glasser (Hershl Glezer), originally published by Indiana University Press in 2016, with a second enlarged edition in 2021. They listed both the abstract noun די פֿאַרשווינדונג, which isn't much in use, and the verbal construction דאָס פֿאַרפֿאַלן / נעלם / פֿאַרשוווּנדן ווערן, which is in use, but would sound really clumsy as the title of a book. Then I remembered Dovid Bergelson's novella אָפּגאַנג, first published in the periodical אייגנס in 1920 and later on in book form by the Kultur-lige in Kyiv in 1921.

There is a beautiful bilingual edition of this work in two volumes, edited and translated by Joseph Sherman and published by the Modern Language Association in New York in 1999. Joseph Sherman chose to translate the title of the novella as *Descent*, but the Yiddish אָפּגאַנג has many more possible meanings, including disappearance. I then had a look at the גרויסער ווערטערבוך פֿון דער יידישער שפּראַך, edited by Yudel Mark and published by the Yiddish Dictionary Committee in New York and Jerusalem in 1980, which to this day encompasses four volumes with the letter *alef*... Volume IV lists 10 different meanings for the noun אָפּגאַנג and 25 different meanings for the verb אָפּגײן, from which the noun is derived. Some of the meanings of the noun אָפּגאַנג are: אַ אַקט אָדער רעזולטאַט פֿון אָפּגײן, i.e., departure; אָפּגאַנג פֿון אַקטיאָר פֿון דער בינע, i.e., exit; דאָס פֿאַרשווינדן, i.e., disappearance; פֿאַרלוסט, אָנווער, i.e., loss. Some of the meanings of the verb אָפּגײן are: פֿאַרבײַגײן, passing (e.g., of time); צעגײן, i.e., decay; פֿאַרגײן, זינק אין פּראָצעס פֿון ניט-ווערן, i.e., passing away, disappearing; שטאַרבן, i.e., dying, death.

IS: One singular aspect of what you're conveying is the intimate relationship between the translator and the dictionary. I can't think of a more constant, loyal, and devoted friend. Yet dictionaries – I have a large collection of them – are also treacherous books: they reflect the fancifulness of their creators. One often thinks of the *Oxford English Dictionary*, for instance, as infallible. It isn't, really. The definitions we encounter on its pages have been distilled over three hundred years.

BW: In the process of translation, my dictionaries are most definitely my best friends. But one also needs to know how to use them, and quite often one has to make one's own creative choices. In any case, all these different meanings of the noun אָפּגאַנג and the verb אָפּגײן, listed in the גרױסער װערטערבוך פֿון דער ייִדישער שפּראַך, seem to be very suitable for the first story of your book, as well as for the book as a whole. Thus, my chosen title, דער אָפּגאַנג, not only reflects your original English title, *The Disappearance*, but also has all those other connotations, which are so fitting for all the three stories in your book!

Can you tell me more about what inspired your three stories? I also know that one of the stories was turned into a feature film and another one was adapted for the theater.

IS: Each of the stories had an auspicious birth and has grown to find its own place in the world. "Morirse está en hebreo" was the basis for the script of the Mexican film *My Mexican Shivah*, directed by Alejandro Springall and produced by John Sayles. Seeing it "translated" to the screen was joyful. The adaptation tones down some of the political content. For instance, the death of the Jewish patriarch coincides with the crumbling of the dictatorship of PRI, Mexico's ruling party. That aspect doesn't show up in the movie. But the movie has a dimension the story doesn't have: it has the feel of a telenovela, which goes well with the emotional excesses I sought to convey in the plot. "The Disappearance" has been adapted by Double Edge Theater into a traveling play. And "Xerox Man" was commissioned by the BBC in London, where it aired for the first time in my own reading.

BW: How was it for you to see your work transposed to the stage and to the cinema?

IS: Throughout my life, I have enjoyed collaborating with actors, directors, playwrights, filmmakers, and illustrators. As I see it, it is a natural dialogue across the arts, since culture is, in its essence, promiscuous. The experience has led me to at times to imagine a piece in one format only as "a first draft" and the subsequent adaptations as revisions or recreations. I feel close to Whitman's views on closure in literature. As you know, time and again he kept revising *Leaves of Grass*. In my case, the return to a piece of work I've done often comes in the form of a collaboration. It has happened in my graphic novels, like *Angelitos*, or in plays such as *The Oven*. Plus, when I translate my own stories I give myself permission to rewrite them in the new language, though this happens only occasionally. (I don't like to translate myself.) At any rate, I don't believe a work of art should be trapped in a particular genre or language.

BW: What you say about revisions and recreations of your own work is fascinating. This is something that also happened a lot in Yiddish literature.

The first of the three classic authors of modern Yiddish literature was Sh.Y. Abramovitsh, who published his books in Yiddish under the name of his narrator (at times editor, at times translator, and at times an important protagonist in his novels). Mendele Moykher-Sforim was famous for rewriting and polishing his works many times. He was a bilingual writer, who wrote in both Yiddish and Hebrew and constantly translated his own works from one language to the other. Five of his novels were written in both Yiddish and Hebrew, with his Hebrew recreations following the publication of his works in the original Yiddish. But he also kept enlarging, rewriting, and polishing his novels in Yiddish, like דאָס ווינטשפֿ‏ יִנגערל and פֿישקע דער קרומער. And he wrote some of his stories originally in Hebrew, which he later translated into Yiddish.

IS: Translation implies movement: a text moves to another linguistic ecosystem, a writer is accessible to a reader and vice versa, and also a text is repositioned through the recalibration of its messages. Friedrich Schleiermacher, in his essay "On the Different Methods of Translating," states that "either the translator leaves the writer in peace as much as possible and moves the reader toward him; or he leaves the reader in peace as much as possible and moves the writer toward him." The same happens, I should add, when we translate not a contemporary text but a historical one, meaning one that was written a long time ago: either you bring the reader to the past by means of recreating the original language in the target one, or you move in the opposite direction, allowing the text to travel to the present. When it comes to self-translation, things, obviously, become less complicated, since your original and target language are synchronous.

BW: It is interesting to me, and somewhat surprising, that you don't like to translate yourself. You probably know that apart from being a Yiddish lecturer, teacher, and translator, I'm also a Yiddish poet, with two bilingual collections of my poetry, published by the H.Leyvik-farlag in Tel Aviv, the publisher of my Yiddish translation of your book *The Disappearance*. For the past 22 years at least, I've been writing all my poetry in Yiddish, but also translating much of it into English. All the English translations of my Yiddish poems in my two books, צי האָט איר געזען מײַן ציג? (*Have You Seen My Goat?*, 2012) and כּלת-בראשית (*Bride of Genesis and Other Poems*, 2018), are my own, kindly checked by my friend Vincent Homolka, who made several very useful suggestions on how to improve my poems in English.

IS: Your friend Homolka is crucial in the endeavor, if I can say it, allowing you a certain distance from the text you would otherwise not have, unless you work with an editor capable of doing the same.

BW: Yes, my friend has played an important role in improving my own English translations of my Yiddish poetry. I've always found it easiest to translate myself, as I know exactly what I want to say in my own poetry, and I also feel much freer in translating and recreating my own poems in another language than I would feel when translating another poet or prose writer. I've found it much more difficult to translate A.N. Stencl's poetry into English, for example. I published a bilingual collection of some of Stencl's early work from his time in Berlin together with my fellow poet and co-translator Stephen Watts' *All My Young Years: Yiddish Poetry from Weimar Germany* (Five Leaves, 2007). I was sometimes struggling with Stencl's language when we were translating him. He uses quite a few dialectal words in his own unique dialect from western Poland, which are not in the dictionaries, and the meaning of some of his images and expressions or the connections between two lines of a stanza are not always clear. And I want to be faithful to this charming poet, who lived in the East End of London for decades, who died in 1983, and is no longer around to ask what he meant when there is something slightly unclear in his poetry.

Why don't you like translating yourself?

IS: There are a couple of reasons why I dislike translating myself. First, the lack of objectivity. Whereas when I translate *Don Quixote* into English, *Hamlet* into Spanish, or Bashevis Singer from the Yiddish, I approach the original as a sacred text. Rendering my own work often pushes me to revise the original, which means I'm not only translating but rewriting. If every translation is an interpretation, why not leave it to someone else to interpret the work? The author is often the worst interpreter of their own oeuvre. And secondly, I think to myself: instead of translating yourself, why don't you write something new? The day generally doesn't have enough hours for me to accomplish what I want. Why steal time from new work?

Thus, as a matter of choice, I prefer to translate a dead author: Sor Juana Inés de la Cruz, Jorge Luis Borges, Emily Dickinson, Elizabeth Bishop … That's because I'm interested in the layers of interpretation a book accumulates over the centuries – and I insert myself in between those layers. I'm attuned to how words change meanings and how writers push dictionaries to refresh definitions. But I often translate new authors, too. Translation brings about renewal. It is also about death: the metaphorical death of a text as it metamorphoses across languages. When Sutzkever talks about "tasting all kinds of death," the image brings to mind the taste of original texts and their repositioned translations.

BW: For me personally, it's not so much death, but a change of form and dimension. But maybe this is what death is – a change of form and dimension? In any case, it's a unique situation when you are translating a living author. When I started translating your stories into Yiddish, there were a few things I was wondering about: a couple of English words I didn't know and had to look up, different geographic locations in Belgium and in Mexico that I had to look up, the anti-Semitic play by Rainer Werner Fassbinder, mentioned in your first story, that I had to read up on, and one or two matters that weren't immediately clear to me, but became clearer the more I was working with the text. Then there was the question of what to do with the many words and entire lines in Spanish, French, and Dutch in your English original. At the beginning of my process of translation, I was considering writing to you and asking you some questions, but I wanted to wait until completing at least a first draft of my Yiddish translation. In the end, I decided to go it alone, to look up everything I needed to know and to make my own decisions, and I just hoped you would like my Yiddish translation/transcreation and appreciate my choices!

What prompted you to include so many words in Dutch, lines in French, and words, expressions, and poems in Spanish, as well as the Kaddish prayer in Hebrew (in Hebrew characters). It is highly unusual nowadays for a work of literature written in English to be so multilingual.

IS: I'm thrilled you've asked the question because it is at the heart of how I see things. Languages don't exist in a vacuum, isolated from the others. Quite the contrary: the world is messy, convoluted. Tongues don't only borrow from each other; they also steal shamelessly, creating a symphonic – perhaps the word is "cacophonic" – chaos.

My autobiography *On Borrowed Words: A Memoir of Language*, published in 2001, is made of discreet chapters about disparate periods of my life, each experienced separately through the prism of another major tongue: Yiddish, Spanish, Hebrew, and English, in that order. My original intention was to compose each of the sections about them in that language: the section on Yiddish in Yiddish, on Spanish in Spanish, and so on. Needless to say, my editor said it is all a quixotic dream. I therefore resorted to write the whole book as if it was a translation of each of these languages but without an original. What I learned in the process is that languages step on each other and they push others around. Hebrew penetrates Yiddish, which in turn subverts English from within, only to allow Spanish to reconfigure it. All this, dear Beruriah, is a way to rationalize that multilingualism never exists in a state of purity.

I return again to Schleiermacher's utopian view that translators into a language – in his case, German – enrich it by pushing it beyond its confines. Every time another translator renders Sutzkever's "Frozen

Jews" into English, Shakespeare's tongue is expanded even more. Just as, in translating *The Disappearance* into Yiddish, you've pushed Sutzkever's language further. But tell me about your decisions on what to do with my multilingual insertions in my English texts. Of course, the segments of the Kaddish in Hebrew in *Morirse está en hebreo* appear as such, obviously without the need of a Yiddish translation. There's the song "Desapariciones" by the Panamanian *salsero* Rubén Blades, which you incorporate in Spanish, followed by the Yiddish translation. The epigraphs by Bishop ("One Art") and Shakespeare (*Henry IV*, Part II, Act V) also appear in English, followed by your renditions. These are just examples.

BW: Reading and translating your stories, it was important to me to leave all your Dutch, French, Spanish, and Hebrew words, quotations, poems, and prayers in their original language, some with and some without a translation into Yiddish. And I wanted to have your epigraphs to all the stories both in the English original and translated into Yiddish. There was obviously no need to translate the segments of the Kaddish. I also left the one French quotation and the one note in intentionally messed-up Spanish in your story "The Disappearance" in the original in Latin characters and without a translation. These two instances were a bit separate from the main text. So I could leave it in Latin characters. I decided to leave the Dutch words and titles of publications without a translation, but to transliterate them into Yiddish. To that end, I had to know exactly how they are pronounced in Dutch. The same also applied to all the Dutch proper names and place names. I checked with a young Yiddishist from Amsterdam, David Omar Cohen, who used to be in one of my advanced Yiddish literature classes at Oxford (online), and he told me how everything is pronounced, so I could transliterate it properly in Yiddish. I thought these Dutch words and titles could be easily understood by a Yiddish speaker and didn't require any translation. On the other hand, most Yiddish readers, unless they grew up in Latin America, wouldn't necessarily know Spanish. For your second story, "Morirse está en hebreo," I decided to leave the Spanish, mostly transliterated into Yiddish, but to provide a translation into Yiddish wherever necessary. I thought it would have disturbed the reading experience of the Yiddish reader to have a great deal of Spanish in Latin characters in the Yiddish text in Hebrew characters. Plus employing two different alphabets, one written from right to left and one from left to right, in the same paragraph, always creates great difficulties in the process of typesetting! I only left the Spanish in Latin characters in a few key places in the story, as in the explanation of the phrase "Morirse está en hebreo," and the song "Desapariciones," which was, at any rate, separate from the main text and wouldn't cause any problems with the typesetting. And for this song, I decided to provide a rhymed translation into Yiddish … So I had to make a lot of creative choices here. But I always had my potential Yiddish readers in mind when I made these choices.

IS: Let me return, by way of conclusion, to the idea of translation as a recalibration. Every text has its implied readers. Those readers might have been the author's intended audience. But no author is ever in full control of a text. Once the text is out and about in the world, it finds its public. (To me, this is like parenthood and even like teaching: as a parent, you prepare your children, giving them, as best as you're able to, the tools they need, and as a teacher you do the same with your students; but those preparations have little to do with control, for once they are active in life as adults or as professionals, they find their own ways, either applying or discarding the tools they are equipped with.) But translation reinvents a text's readership; it reorients it by bringing it to the attention of new audiences. This, in and of itself, represents a repositioning of the text. Still, for as much as the translator might have a specific public in mind, the text, once again, will create its own paths. Who did you intend your translation of דער אָפּגאַנג for?

BW: Of course, I intended my Yiddish translation of דער אָפּגאַנג for any Yiddish reader who will want to read it! First and foremost, I wanted YOU to read and appreciate it! I would like all my Yiddishist friends and colleagues around the world to read it, Yiddish scholars, lecturers, poets and writers, as well as a general audience of Yiddish readers and advanced Yiddish students. I very much hope that my Yiddish translation of your book will find its readership, probably much of it in Israel, where the book was published, but also internationally!

I really think that my Yiddish translation of your stories enriches the Yiddish language and pushes it beyond its boundaries, and it adds to the vast canon of literature in Yiddish!

For you as an author of short stories and novellas and for me as a Yiddish poet, there is always the question of when a work of literature is finished. The same applies to a translation of a work of literature into a different language and different cultural and linguistic system. In the Talmud, in *Tractate Kiddushin* 59a–59b, there is a discussion about what causes a vessel, crafted by an artisan, to be finished and thus susceptible to ritual impurity. Is it one last action that makes it a finished vessel? No, it's a thought! The artisan just needs to decide it's a finished work of art or craft, and that's it. On the other hand, if the artisan changes his mind and wants to work on it some more, this will require an action. It's the same for a work of literature or a translation of a literary work. After a long process of writing or translating and of being in dialogue with a text and wrestling with a text, the writer or translator needs to decide at some point that this is enough. This is it. It is now a finished work of art that can go out into the world! And thus, I eventually completed my translation of your book, and now it's out there in the world, waiting for its Yiddish readers!

– In geveb (2022)

Is I *Me*, or Who *Is* I?: Conversation with Jim[1]

JIM: Who dah?
IS: Nobody. I wanna hear about witches, the ones that put you in trance and rode you all over.
JIM: You ain't speak da same way we does.
IS: No.
JIM: You French?
IS: No.
JIM: Huck says, "S'pose a man was to come to you and say *Polly-voo-franzy*. What would you think?" Say, I wouldn' think nuff'n, I says. I'd take en bust him over de head – dat is, if he warn't white.
IS: You would?
JIM: I wouldn't 'low no one to call me dat. But Huck says, "shucks, it ain't calling you anything. It's only saying, do you know how to talk French?" Well, den, why couldn't he *say* it? Huck says again, "why, he *is* a-saying it. That's a Frenchman's *way* of saying it."
IS: You're right.
JIM: Huck says, "Looky here, Jim; does a cat talk like we do?" No, a cat don't, I says. "Well, does a cow?" No, a cow don't, nuther. "Does a cat talk like a cow, or a cow talk like a cat?" No, dey don't. "It's natural and right for 'em to talk different from each other, ain't it?" Course. "And ain't it natural and right for a cat and a cow to talk different from *us*?" Why, mos' sholy it is. "Well, then, why ain't it natural and right for a *Frenchman* to talk different from us? You answer me that." So I says to Huck, "Is a cat a man, Huck?" No. Well, den, dey ain't no sense in a cat talkin' like a man. Is a cow a man? – er is a cow a cat? "No, she ain't

---

1 The following is part of a series of conversations with literary characters, such as Alonso Quijano, Emma Bovary, and Rodion Raskolnikov. This one is with Jim, whose journey to freedom is recounted in *Adventures of Huckleberry Finn* (1884).

either of them." Well, den, she ain't got no business to talk like either one er the yuther of 'em. Is a Frenchman a man? "Yes." *Well*, den! Dad blame it, why doan' he *talk* like a man? You answer me *dat*!

IS: I speak Spanish, Jim.

JIM: Hm! What you know 'bout witches?

IS: Not much. That five-center piece round your neck with a string, is it a charm the devil give to you with his own hands, and said you could cure anybody with it and fetch witches whenever you wanted to just by saying something to it?

JIM: Say, who is you? Dog my cats ef you didn' want sumf'n.

IS: Just catching up.

JIM: Nah. Well, you see, it 'uz dis way. Ole missus – dat's Miss Watson – she pecks on me all de time, en treats me pooty rough, but she awluz said she wouldn' sell me down to Orleans. But I noticed dey wuz a nigger trader roun' de place considable lately, en I begin to git oneasy.

IS: So?

JIM: Well, one night I creeps to de do' pooty late, en de do' warn't quite shet, en I hear old missus tell de widder she gwyne to sell me down to Orleans, but she didn' want to, but she could git eight hund'd dollars for me, en it 'uz sich a big stack o' money. So de widder she try to git her to say she wouldn' do it, but I never waited to hear de res'. I lit out mighty quick, I tell you.

IS: And?

JIM: Well, I had a dream, en de dream tole me to give it to a man name' Balum – Balum's Ass dey call him for short; he's one er dem chuckleheads, you know. But he's lucky, dey say, en I see I warn't lucky. De dream say let Balum inves' de ten cents en he'd make a raise for me. Well, Balum he tuck de money, en when he wuz in church he hear de preacher say dat whoever give to de po' len' to de Lord, en boun' to git his money back a hund'd times. So Balum he tuck en give de ten cents to de po', en laid low to see what wuz gwyne to come of it.

IS: You and Huck always raftin' down, never stoppin'...

JIM: With our ole raf'. She was tore up a good deal; but dey warn't no great harm done. Ef we hadn' dive' so deep en swum so fur under water, en de night hadn' ben so dark, en we warn't so sk'yerd, en ben sich punkinheads, as de sayin' is, we'd a seed de raf'. But it's jis' as well we didn't, 'kase now she's all fixed up agin mos'.

IS: As good as new.

JIM: En we's got a new lot o' stuff, in de place o' what 'uz los'.

IS: You got hold of the raft again.

JIM: Yeah, how I gwyne to ketch her. Some er foun' her ketched on a snag along heah in de ben', en dey hid her in a crick 'mongst de willows, en dey wuz so much jawin' 'bout which un 'um she b'long to de mos' dat I come to heah 'bout it pooty soon, so I ups en settles de trouble by tellin' 'um she don't b'long to none uv um, but to you en me; en I ast 'm if dey gwyne to grab a young white genlman's propaty, en git a hid'n for it?

IS: Did Mark Twain steal from you?

JIM: No, sah.

IS: A good man?

JIM: En pooty smart. But I hain't said a word. I hain't got nuffn but dish yer ole shirt. Enuf.

IS: You seem angry.

JIM: Nah. Oh, it's de ol-blame' witches, sah, en I wisht I was dead, I do.

IS: Twain says his book about you and Huck uses dialects to wit.

JIM: Da witches, dey's awluz at it, sah, en dey do mos' kill me, dey sk'yers me so.

IS: I know.

JIM: Please to don't tell nobody 'bout it sah.

IS: You know about the Missouri dialect'?

JIM: I hain't said nothing, sah. Not as I knows on. How does I talk wild?

IS: *How*?

JIM: Well, looky here, boss, dey's sumf'n wrong, dey is. Is I *me*, or who *is* I? Is I heah, or whah *is* I? Now dat's what I wants to know. I is, is I? Well, you answer me dis.

IS: What?

JIM: Didn't you tote out de line in de canoe fer to make fas' to de tow-head?

IS: What tow-head?

JIM: You hain't see no tow-head? Looky here, didn't de line pull loose en de raf' go a-hummin' down de river, en leave you en de canoe behine in de fog?

IS: What fog?

JIM: Why, de fog! – de fog dat's been aroun'. Nah. Well, it's a blame ridicklous way, en I doan' want to hear no mo' 'bout it. Dey ain' no sense in it.

– *Massachusetts Review*, Spring 2023

Petrarch's Sonnet #132

After reading Chaucer's loose rendition of Petrarch's Sonnet #132, I made the following translation for my students in the course "Love." Obviously, Chaucer believed his rendition to be an emulation. In other words, he felt no loyalty to the original. This triptych starts with the Italian original.

S'amor non è, che dunque è quel ch'io sento?
Ma s'egli è amor, perdio, che cosa et quale?
Se bona, onde l'effecto aspro mortale?
Se ria, onde sí dolce ogni tormento?

S'a mia voglia ardo, onde 'l pianto e lamento?
S'a mal mio grado, il lamentar che vale?
O viva morte, o dilectoso male,
come puoi tanto in me, s'io no 'l consento?

Et s'io 'l consento, a gran torto mi doglio.
Fra sí contrari vènti in frale barca
mi trovo in alto mar senza governo,

sí lieve di saver, d'error sí carca
ch'i' medesmo non so quel ch'io mi voglio,
et tremo a mezza state, ardendo il verno.

— Francesco Petrarca

If no love is, O God, what fele I so?
And if love is, what thing and which is he?
If love be good, from whennes cometh my woo?
If it be wikke, a wonder thynketh me,
When every torment and adversite
That cometh of hym, may to me savory thinke,
For ay thurst I, the more that ich it drynke.

And if that at myn owen lust I brenne,
From whennes cometh my waillynge and my pleynte?
If harm agree me, whereto pleyne I thenne?
I noot, ne whi unwery that I feynte.
O quike deth, O swete harm so queynte,
How may of the in me swich quantite,
But if that I consente that it be?
And if that I consente, I wrongfully
Compleyne, iwis. Thus possed to and fro,
Al sterelees withinne a boot am I
Amydde the see, betwixen wyndes two,
That in contrarie stonden evere mo.
Allas! what is this wondre maladie?
For hete of cold, for cold of hete, I dye.

– Translated by Geoffrey Chaucer

If this is love, what is it that I feel?
And if love it is, God, what is this thing to me?
If good, why its effect is rough, mortal?
If bad, why the sweetness of every torment?

If I burn, why the sobbing and lament?
If my state is bad, is it worth lamenting?
O living death, o delicious evil,
how are you in me, if I do not consent?

And if I consent, a great injustice pains me.
Between contrarian winds a fragile boat
I am, at high sea, without control,

light in wisdom, loaded with error,
not knowing what is it I want:
if to tremble in cold heat, or heated cold.

– Translated by Ilan Stavans,
The Common, Fall 2022

A Lover Alone in Prison
(with Sara Khalili)

ILAN STAVANS: I came serendipitously to translation. It was frustration with the coming-and-going of my own languages, the sense that something was always lost, that kept me imagining an entire poem, a whole novel in the other language. Then came love and after that marriage: the love for the craft and the marriage that comes to an endeavor out of which comes enormous joy. Yet the frustration remains. Robert Frost was both right and wrong in suggesting that "poetry is what gets lost in translation." It is also what gets found – poetry and much more. Did you become a translator out of love?

SARA KHALILI: I was coaxed into becoming a translator, but it didn't take long for me to find myself wanting to do nothing else. I am, or I should say, I was, a financial journalist and worked in my field for many years. I only thought about translation when the late Karim Emami would tell me, yet again, that I was wasting my time, that I should instead dedicate myself to translating Persian literature. He believed I had a talent for it.

IS: Emami translated from Persian to English and back again. He rendered Scott Fitzgerald's *The Great Gatsby* (1965) for Iranian readers, as well as four volumes of *The Adventures of Sherlock Holmes* (1993–1998). And he also translated into English seventy-two quatrains of poetry by Omar Khayyam in the *The Wine of Nishapur* (1997).

SK: Karim was one of Iran's most celebrated literary translators, as well as a renowned editor and literary critic. To me, he was also a dear friend and close relative.

IS: I know he was a lexicographer, too. I wished I had met him.

SK: Karim's arguments for, and my arguments against, what he was urging me to do went on for several years, until in 2004, when he suggested I work with him on the translation of a short story for an anthology of Iranian literature that PEN was publishing. I agreed, thinking it would be an interesting exercise. As we worked together, Karim in Tehran and me in New York, he patiently educated me on the art of translation. I was captivated. Needless to say, I finally did what he had hoped I would do.

IS: Karim Emami's effort was visionary, not only because of the beauty of your translations but, needless to say, because of the unforgivably limited diet of Iranian literature English-language readers have access to. Two titanic cultures, with astonishingly rich literary traditions, at odds with one another. Why is it that, in spite of a number of astonishing books, Iranian literature is almost totally unknown in the United States?

SK: The greatest challenge is the scarcity of skilled literary translators. Unlike countries where governments and cultural organizations fund and support the translation of their writers' works into other languages and actively promote them overseas, no such mechanisms and resources exist in Iran.

IS: A culture without translation is like a lover alone in prison.

SK: Languishing and forlorn. The absence of any meaningful backing has meant that translating Iranian literature has remained mostly as an avocation or an academic exercise, instead of being a profession in literary arts undertaken by talented translators who can dedicate themselves to cultivating and refining their skill and introducing the works of Iranian writers to an English-reading audience.

IS: It isn't only Tehran's nearsightedness. The American market shows little interest too.

SK: Yes, the problem is compounded by the difficulty of finding interested publishers in the United States. As you well know, in general a very small percentage of books published in English are works of literature in translation. And a majority of these are works by established European and Latin American writers. This leaves very little room for as-yet-unknown writers from countries such as Iran.

IS: In spite of the geographical closeness, and of the comparative abundance, at times misguided (even forgettable exercises Roberto Bolaño rightfully never dreamed of publishing are now available in English), we in Latin America complain of a lack of interest as well. Well-balanced, representative interest, I mean.

SK: The situation would have been far worse were it not for small, independent publishers, such as Restless Books, that dedicate themselves to literature in translation. As someone who is a prolific writer, translator, and publisher, you have a multifaceted view of the market. How would you explain this lack of interest?

IS: Americans have little appetite for foreign cultures. Their interests are parochial: the most powerful nation in the world, shallow at its core. Other empires have displayed voracious interest, even, in their neighbors. The United States, in contrast, is marked by a complacency that is linked to its professed individualism. They can do it all alone, without anyone's help. Ah, such spiritual poverty!

SK: In some cases, the problem is more complex. In much of the world, foreign literature is a window into distant lands, a different manner of traveling, seeing, and experiencing other cultures. Literature from some of those distant cultures not only seems to inspire little curiosity here, but it also falls prey to geopolitics. The little interest there is for Persian literature peaks when heated politics land Iran on the front pages of newspapers. And then, the interest is not entirely in the literature itself, but in amplifying the voice of the dissident, the exiled whose work in one way or another spotlights the ills of that country's government and its politics.

IS: An old adage: literature as ideological artifact.

SK: In the years I have worked as a translator, only once has an editor approached me specifically interested in what is actually being written and published today inside Iran. In 2013, Susan Harris, editor of *Words Without Borders*, decided to dedicate an issue of that magazine to short stories by the post-revolution generation of Iranian writers living and working in that country. Shahriar and I curated the stories and I translated them. Other than that collection, the majority of my published translations are works by writers in exile or books that have been banned in Iran. We hardly ever see the vibrant and exciting works of talented writers in Iran who are changing the face and fiber of Persian literature.

IS: It is how capital moves around in the literary marketplace. At Restless Books, I recently received as a submission a novel by a Chinese dissident, for which Ai Waiwai had done some cover art. The work itself wasn't particularly enthralling yet the package did nothing but emphasize dissidence as a marketing tool. Quality was secondary.

SK: In 1990, Edward Said published in *The Nation* an article titled "Embargoed Literature." His argument was that Arab literature is "embargoed" in the West despite the fact that in 1988 the Egyptian writer Naguib Mahfouz was awarded the Nobel Prize for Literature. He wrote, "Of all the major world literatures, Arabic remains relatively unknown and unread in the West for reasons that are unique, and I think remarkable at a time when tastes here for the non-Western are more developed than before and, even more compelling, contemporary Arabic literature is at a particularly interesting juncture." The same holds true for Persian literature.

IS: How do you choose what you translate? Is your personal taste the defining factor? With so few translators from Persian into English active in the marketplace, is what you like the type of literature readers end up associating with Iran today?

SK: Translation is an intimate relationship between a translator and a work of literature that could last for months or years. Better that it be a happy union than a hesitant one. Beyond personally liking a work, I look for a literary value and quality in it that deserves a wider readership and the time I would need to dedicate to it. Then I ask myself, is it a book I might find a publisher for? And in the end, I hope readers consider my choices only as a small sampling of the wealth and variety of Iran's literary arts.

IS: You have translated the poetry of Siavash Kasrai, Fereydoun Moshiri, and Simin Behbahani. How did you come to them?

SK: One of the largest publishing houses in Iran, Sokhan Publishers, set out on a wonderful mission to produce a series of bilingual editions of works by contemporary Iranian poets. They commissioned me to curate and translate a collection by Simin Behbahani. It was the first time I was translating poetry, and I was enormously lucky that Michael Beard, a specialist in Middle Eastern literature and a translator from Persian and Arabic, agreed to work with me as editor. I was then asked to work on three other volumes.

The ones you mentioned survived the scrutiny of the Ministry of Culture and Islamic Guidance, which must approve and issue publishing permits for all books printed in Iran. The manuscript of the fourth volume, the selected works of Forough Farrokhzad, was submitted to the Ministry almost a decade ago. We never even received the usual notice advising us of edits to the text that would be required for it to receive a permit. I imagine it is in some overpopulated manuscript morgue, and in good company.

IS: The bureaucratic ordeal, not only of the Farrokhzad volume but of the set you translated, makes me think of the administrative procedures Cervantes had to go through to get the two volumes of the manuscript of *Don Quixote of La Mancha* through the Holy Inquisition censors. Some of the sections in the novel are quite daring. Did the censors truly read them? If so, they must have been amused by Volume One, Chapter VI, in which the barber, the priest, and Alonso Quijana's niece go through Quijana's personal library while Don Quixote is ill. It's a hilarious scene that results in many volumes ending up in a bonfire. What was accepted and what was rejected by the actual censors, not by Cervantes' characters, is less humorous but just as capricious.

By the way, I am of the view – and I have stated it in *Knowledge and Censorship* (2008) – that censorship is useful in literature. Likewise, I believe in its cleansing power in terms of translation.

SK: What do you mean by cleansing?

IS: Purifying. We cannot live without censorship. Dictatorships regulate the flow of information. But so does an open-market economy, though under a different pretense. A self-translation, which is the most ubiquitous, defines everything we do, even this exchange.

SK: Translators consciously sift, rewrite, reword, compromise, and to some extent filter while rendering a book into another language. We all do the same in our daily lives, but we do it far less consciously and less deliberately.

Translation, by its very nature, shares these functions with censorship. Where the two differ is in their intentions. The translator strives to convey, whereas the censor aims to purge.

IS: Going back to *Don Quixote*, the reader is told numerous times that the original narrative about the deranged knight was written by an Arab historian, Cide Hamete Benengueli, and that what we are reading is a poor, impromptu translation delivered by "un morisco aljamiado," which, loosely translated, is a Spanish-born Arab speaker with a lousy knowledge of his ancestral tongue.

SK: "Traduttore, traditore!"

IS: How does one transpose the gorgeous rhythms of Persian into modern English?

SK: It is near impossible to perfectly carry over from Persian into another language the unique qualities of a poem – what its composer felt and thought, their particular voice and tone, the weight given to each carefully chosen word, the meter and structure of their composition. Added to this are the linguistic and cultural elements that cannot be mirrored. This is especially true of classical Persian poetry. Dick Davis even wrote a famous essay titled "On Not Translating Hafez" – though he did eventually take on the challenge.

IS: I remember reading Davis' essay, published in the *New England Review* (vol. 25, nos. 1–2, 2004), and dreaming for days about what is and isn't untranslatable. One of his paragraphs was emblematic of the entire argument:

Certain poets are held to be untranslatable, or virtually so, and often they are thought of as those that most intimately express the poetic soul of their people: in Russian there is Pushkin; in German, Goethe; in Persian, Hafez. It is often precisely the poets who seem to sum up a poetry's idiosyncratic potential and identity whose works are most resistant to translation; this can give rise to a kind of romantic, quasi-racial canonization of them, the implication being that they cannot be translated because what they express draws so deeply on the culture's specific ethnic soul that it is not communicable in any other terms. This is a variant of the sentimental "To understand, my friend, you have to be Persian/Jewish/Russian …" ploy. (Against this ethnic self-indulgence there is a lovely story of Franco Corelli asking Richard Tucker for tips on how to sing Puccini: "Well," began Tucker, "You have to be Jewish …").

No, you don't have to be Jewish to understand, say, Henry Roth's *Call It Sleep* (1934). That's what literature is about: the opportunity to have out-of-body experiences.

Nabokov translated Pushkin – poorly, I might add. (Edmund Wilson famously shared this opinion.) And Goethe, who championed *Weltliteratur* as a continental project, doesn't sound in English the way he does in German. But should we care? Of the 14th-century Hafez (Borges would have loved his full name, Khwāja Shams-ud-Dīn Muḥammad Ḥāfeẓ-e Shīrāzī), I only know Davis' Penguin Classics edition (2012), which, of course, he ended up doing. Yes, these, and other, poets resist translation. Yet it is crucial that we try anyhow; otherwise we are doomed. For without translation there is no dialogue across civilizations.

SK: Among the greatest works of world literature is the *Shahnameh* (*The Book of Kings*), written by Ferdowsi in the 10th century. It is the longest epic poem ever composed by a single poet, narrating the history of the ancient kings of Persia from mythical beginnings to the Arab conquest in the 7th century. Written in 60,000 rhyming couplets, the book defies translation. But how much poorer we would have been were it not for the efforts of those who have tried. There are several partial and abridged English translations of the epic, but the only complete version went out of print more than 80 years ago. It took Ferdowsi 30 years to write the *Shahnameh* and it took the brothers Arthur and Edmond Warner 20 years to translate it in nine volumes of verse, the first of which was published in London in 1905. More recently, Davis' 2006 translation, which excludes some segments, is a blend of poetry and prose. Having done away with a lot of the antiquated flourishes with occasional explanations interspersed in the text, it is one of the most accessible English renditions of the *Shahnameh*.

IS: The classics inspire awe whereas contemporary works appear less obtuse. I'm not sure this is true. Still, as in life, appearance is everything in literature.

SK: Unlike classical Persian poetry, contemporary works lend themselves often surprisingly well to translation. The poets' use of looser forms of quatrains, free verse, the personal lyric, and metaphoric imagery has made it more possible to retain the aesthetic value of their work in English. Of the poets I have translated, the one leaning most toward classical structures was Simin Behbahani. She composed often in ghazals, which could lose a lot of their musicality and expression in translation. But, even in her case, she took the classical form of the ghazal and infused it with the modern and colloquial, which better survive the journey into English.

IS: Personally, I find translating poetry far more challenging, but also more rewarding, than translating prose. What one is after isn't only meaning but rhythm. Needless to say, translating rhythm is a maddening task because music isn't translatable.

SK: Perhaps almost as challenging are the very elusive and convoluted metaphors, which Persian poetry is riddled with.

IS: I want to hear about the process of translating *Moon Brow*, by Shahriar Mandanipour.

SK: Shahriar and I worked in tandem on *Moon Brow*. As he wrote, I translated. It was not the conventional way of going about it, but seeing a novel take shape in two languages at the same time was quite a unique experience.

Shahriar's intricate prose is always a challenge, but *Moon Brow* proved to be even more so than his other works that I had translated. The inner reflections of the main character (Amir) were particularly difficult. Shahriar has written of the chaotic thoughts and fragmented recollections storming through the mind of a shellshock victim often as poetry in prose or complicated plays on language. To capture their essence while staying true to the structure and meter of his compositions, I needed to first unravel the Persian text, translate it, and then weave the English back into the same construct as the original.

Also, the novel has two narrators – the scribes on Amir's right and left shoulders, who have very different personalities. One is gentle and refined, the other is crude and brash. It is their tone and language that sets them apart, and this had to come across clearly in the translation. The narrative also shifts constantly in time and place. The rapid transitions had to be as smooth and as seamless as possible for the reader to drift through them effortlessly.

IS: Seamlessness in translation is a challenging objective. It reminds me of Flaubert's obsession "to disappear" as an author in order for the narrative to flourish. Also, collaborating with an author might be a double-edge sword. Yet it seems that in this case it was a joyful opportunity.

SK: What I enjoyed most about the actual process was the sense of collaboration between us. The exchanges of ideas, the back-and-forth about what works and what doesn't work in English, the discussions of what to do with a metaphor or a colloquialism that wouldn't survive translation ... The most difficult aspect of it was simply trying to keep track of each other's work. As writers always do, Shahriar would revisit earlier segments to revise, rewrite, add, or delete. For me to know what he had done, Shahriar came up with a color-coding system. Deletions highlighted in red, additions in yellow, rewrites in blue, etc. And invariably, one of us would confuse the colors or lose track of the various versions of the original or the translation. It wasn't uncommon for us to spend a few frustrating hours trying to figure it all out, only to have the same confusion a few weeks later.

IS: In what way was the work you did on *Moon Brow* different from translating Mandanipour's *Censoring an Iranian Story*?

SK: The actual process of Shahriar writing *Censoring* as I translated it was similar to that of *Moon Brow*, albeit even less organized. The difference was rooted elsewhere. *Censoring* was a first for both Shahriar and me. It was his first novel being translated and published in English. It was my first time translating a full-length novel, and a very difficult one at that. I was not as confident in my understanding and interpretation of his style, his language, and his complicated prose. And he wasn't as confident in me being able to recreate his work in English. The trust that exists between us today had not yet been earned. But trust was imperative.

We barely had the first hundred pages of *Censoring* in English when the rights for the novel to be published in several other languages were bought. Given that the book was not going to be published in its original language, all other translations were to be based on the English edition. This made the stakes much higher for Shahriar as the writer, and the weight of the responsibility much greater and far more daunting for me as the translator.

By the time we started working on *Moon Brow*, Shahriar wrote more freely, trusting that I could – and would – be faithful to his prose. And as I translated I became less anxious and more confident that I could – and would – do justice to his art.

IS: As an editor, I love the result. At the same, just as with seamlessness, I'm skeptical of those who say they are faithful in translation. You might imagine why: as in love, a faithful lover is not always truthful and vice versa.

SK: The question is faithful to whom, and when and why. There are times when my loyalty shifts from the writer to the translation itself. In instances where being faithful to a writer's original work would be to the detriment of its English rendition, I will be unfaithful. But always with the writer's knowledge, and hopefully his blessing. In other words, I always confess before I stray.

IS: Do you trust a translation might be better than the original? I think of this question often, not only when I read a text in translation but when I translate myself. I'm in no way tempted to supersede the author, since better isn't really, at least not for me, about quality, but about connection. Can the translation connect with its audience better than the original did?

SK: It is not outside the realm of possibility that a translation supersedes the original, or that its readers better relate to it. However, there are more instances not of translations that are better than their original versions but of translations that are noteworthy works of literature in their own right. To me, most successful translations are in fact a *recreation* of the original work in a different language, with the translator making every effort to remain true to the original without sacrificing literariness.

IS: There are indeed a few cases in which a translation becomes better known – as I mentioned, "more fine-tunely connected" with its readership – than the original. Or at least it acquires a certain autonomy. The King James Version of the Bible, published in 1611, is an example. Another is Edward William Lane's rendition of the *Arabian Nights* (1838–40).

SK: The best example of this in Persian literature is Edward Fitzgerald's translation of *The Rubaiyat of Omar Khayyam*, which stands on its own as a highly celebrated classic and one of the most frequently quoted. But it is important to note that Khayyam's more than 750 quatrains did not comprise one very long poem. Fitzgerald's version is an intuitive, interpretive translation of the original, with much omitted and invented, many of quatrains paraphrased, and some pulped together.

IS: How do you define *recreation*?

SK: To me, it is taking a work of literature and almost rewriting it in another language while trying to strike a delicate balance between the aesthetics and sensibilities of the work, the voice and intent of the writer, and the vagaries of language and culture. If a bilingual reader were to compare the original version of *Moon Brow* with my English translation of it, they will find many instances where the two diverge. These are often occasions where Shahriar and I have realized that staying true to the original and his particular plays on form and language simply would not work in English. As the translator, I have come up with alternatives, with different constructs of Shahriar's words. The effort there has been to remain true to his voice and intent, but not necessarily to his precise words and composition.

IS: A sharp distinction.

SK: I would hazard the guess that the majority of translations that have succeeded have undergone the same. In the end, the two versions of these books are in fact two works that I believe should be considered and judged based on their own merits.

IS: Have you ever been tempted to add material – more than a subtle sentence, maybe a paragraph – in a translation? Such idea, needless to say, is anathema today, such is the commitment, blind in my eyes, we have to the topic we've already discussed, faithfulness. Yet let's not forget that characters like Ali-Baba, Aladdin, and Sinbad were inserted by European translators like Antoine Galland. In the case of *Don Quixote*, one of the French versions of the novel had an entirely new final chapter, after which another volume, all concocted by a translator, was attached. Love blinds ... Translators aren't innocent creatures.

SK: Of course, I have been tempted. But I always remember the indignation and sense of violation I felt when I realized a writer had taken the liberty of meddling with a segment of my translation without my knowledge. The fact that the writer's knowledge of English was at best rudimentary was almost irrelevant. If I believe I can write a finer story than the one I am translating, then I should go ahead and write my own story. As a publisher, what qualities do you look for in a translation? How do you evaluate a translation from a language you do not know?

IS: The matching of the writer and the translator must result in a waltz of compatible sensibilities. Otherwise the overall effort ends in shame. I believe a good book – and in this case I think of classics – needs not only to survive but to thrive in translation.

SK: In pondering the difficulties of the US market, what are the obstacles, or say challenges, you as a publisher of literature in translation face? How you overcome them? And how do you manage to continue in spite of them?

IS: The fallacy in the industry is that independent publishers publish books and readers find them. In truth, you have to find the readers before you agree to acquire the book. To be successful, books need to find their audience and vice versa, audiences need to find the books they are looking for. If you aren't sure you can find that audience, you're doing the book and its author a disservice. In other words, throwing a wide net isn't the right approach, at least not for independent publishers.

Actually, that's the approach of corporate publishers: bring out as many titles as possible, as quickly as possible, and hope that something sticks. They are behemoths, meaning they are clumsy, abrasive, and heavy-handed. It's the wholesale strategy: the more the merrier. Small publishers, instead, with their limited resources, need to be intentional. Since it's always a matter of life and death, each book is a gem. Each needs to find a home.

From the market perspective, a book in translation is born with a handicap. It is an ugly duckling. Why read it if others are directly in English and therefore not prone to misunderstanding? It takes a minimum of two years from the moment a foreign book is acquired for it to reach its audience. A major stage of the process is making sure the translation is right: every word, every comma, every intention.

Independent publishers never overcome these hurdles; we just learn to make the most of them. We learn to persevere. There are a lot of people rooting for us, of course. That support is crucial. We'll never be millionaires; at best, we'll be afloat financially, maybe even thriving as a major minor player. What we want is to make a difference, to humanize those who aren't next to us, who live in far-away lands, who speak and think and dream differently.

SK: Your own books have been translated into many languages. How would you characterize those translations?

IS: Mercifully, a handful – say into Turkish or Tamil – I can't judge, since my knowledge of those languages is nil. And those I can assess, I rather not, for I would be undermining the translator's effort. I don't like to be a barricade. I prefer to help but only if and when help is sought.

SK: What is it like to work with a translator who is rendering your work into a language you are fluent in? How much, if any, influence (or interference) do you allow yourself?

IS: I work closely with translators when they ask for advice, given that they've made the effort to reach out. But I do it with the explicit agreement that I don't want to read the final version. I trust what they do, even when I don't.

SK: You speak half a dozen languages. Have you ever translated your own work?

IS: I have and the result isn't satisfying to me. I wrote about it in *On Self-Translation: Meditations on Language* (2018). I am invaded by the temptation to rewrite the piece altogether. And on some occasions, I have done it: a handful of my stories have different endings in Spanish and English, and sometimes the characters also do things differently. What I like about translation and dislike about self-translation is that the text is subjected to a fresh, objective set of eyes.

I wonder if you ever imagined yourself translating an old religious text, Sara. I once translated "Ave María" into Spanglish. And maybe one day I'll translate a couple of chapters of the Hebrew Bible.

SK: No, and I would never even entertain the possibility. Translating a religious text, especially an old script, would require a depth of theological knowledge and understanding of that religion. These, I don't have.

– Michigan Quarterly Review, Spring 2019

Jevel Katz in Yingleñol

Affectionately called Jévele and Kétzele, Jevel Katz (1902–1940) was an immensely popular "cantautor," a Jewish troubadour in Argentina famous for combining Yiddish and Spanish in humorous songs: tangos, vitalitas, rumbas, rancheras, and fox-trots. Born in Vilnius, he immigrated to Buenos Aires in 1930, where he became a star on stage, radio, and in concert halls. Katz toured Argentina's Jewish agricultural colonies, like Moisés Ville, as well as those of Uruguay and Chile. His funeral is said to have been attended by some forty thousand people. In this translation, I have deliberately rendered Katz's Casteidish – the equivalent of Yinglish in the Southern Cone – through a concoction of Yiddish, Spanish, and English. Call it Yingleñol.

"Moisés Ville"
Jews, be happy at this miraculous hour,
in a corner of Argentina, the *meshiach* has arrived!
Here there are no Christians,
nor small- or big-shot Jews,
the *apteiker*, the *bañero*, the *comisar*, and the judge –
in Moisés Ville,
my little *shteitele*,
Moisés Ville.
My beautiful *heimele*,
you're a *yiddishe medine*,
you're the pride of *Argentine*,
Moisés Ville.

In *mitn pueblito*, there's a plaza full of trees,
youth wanders *oif der najt*,
people say *Buenas Noches* and the beasts get out,

and *take*, not once, a *shidaj* comes out from it all –
in Moisés Ville,
my little *shteitele*,
Moisés Ville.
My beautiful *heimele*,
you're a *yiddishe medine*,
you're the pride of *Argentine*,
Moisés Ville.

A radio *shpiels* tangos, and the public takes a stroll,
wives tell *mayses* about what in shtetls *occur*,
who's having a *tnoim*, where there'll be a *bris*,
and who on *fraytik* is burning a knish –
in Moisés Ville,
my little *shteitele*,
Moisés Ville.
My beautiful *heimele*,
you're a *yiddishe medine*,
you're the pride of *Argentine*,
Moisés Ville.
In the plaza stands a *mentch*, a *pundik* no doubt,
with wide *bombaches*, with *alpargatas* in his feet,
through the *bigotes* he whistles a Spanish *lid*,
you can be sure the criollo is a *yid* –
in Moisés Ville,
my little *shteitele*,
Moisés Ville.
My beautiful *heimele*,
you're a *yiddishe medine*,
you're the pride of *Argentine*,
Moisés Ville.

– *Jewish Review of Books*, Fall 2022

Matching Socks in the Dark; Or, How to Translate from Languages You Don't Know

Fidelity to meaning alone in translation is a kind of betrayal.
— Paul Valéry, translated by Jackson Mathews

You love the trade but what are you accomplishing? Lazy thinkers believe that translators are, well, lazy thinkers, that they hide behind someone else's work. You, instead, are convinced translation is an exquisite mental exercise. How to convey in one tongue the silences of another? For a true translation isn't about what's visible on the page; it is about what is hidden, what might only be insinuated.

Needless to say, translation is the art of the impossible. What can be said well in one tongue might only be reinvented in another. It is thus a deception. Who cares? Every intellectual effort is a theft: we domesticate things, setting them free from their original context.

Still, translation is a bona fide business. It isn't for con artists. A translation might be better than the original if the translator is humble, for humility invariably comes across in every sentence. You're always at the risk of being exposed.

You dislike the automatic nature of the craft, though. At some point, between your eyes studying the original and reformulating them on the page, it's easy to feel anesthetized. Translation is mechanical: back and forth, back and forth. Your challenge, when in the middle of it, is to always be alert: awake, though not woke.

That state is essential; the success or failure of the enterprise depends on it. For an interesting translation depends on the nuanced relationship forged between author and translator (even if and when the author is dead).

You've reached these conclusions over time. Now that COVID-19 has injected the bizarre into the mundane, you are in for a surprise: you are interested not in what you know but in what you don't.

The most suitable comparison you are able to think of is matching socks in the dark. On the surface, it is – according to common knowledge – hopeless. With no light, all matches are decided at random. Darkness is seldom full darkness, meaning a state in which you don't see anything. Your eyes just need to be acclimated. After a while, you start figuring out patterns, colors, and silhouettes. While there is still a lot of guesswork, the blind do see. Do you remember one of those seven lectures Borges delivered in Buenos Aires' Teatro Coliseo in 1977 about blindness? In it he describes how the blind, like him, rather than being surrounded by blackness, actually see certain colors? Those colors, he declares, are "loyal" to him. In his sonnet "On His Blindness" Borges writes:

> Others have the world, for better or worse;
> I have this half-dark, and the toil of verse.

In Spanish, he praises that darkness, calling them shadows.

You're fascinated by the challenges posed in translating from languages you don't know. It is like turning darkness into color. How often have you done it? Not infrequently. Predominantly you've translated poetry this way; you've done an occasional story or two as well. For instance, not long ago you rendered a short story – it could be called a soliloquy or perhaps a diatribe – by Anton Chekhov. You might recognize a few dozen words in Cyrillic.

Your volume *Selected Translations: Poems, 2000–2020* contains a number of pieces from unknown tongues: one in German by Paul Celan, one in Russian by Anna Akhmatova, one in Georgian by Besik Kharanauli, and a couple in Portuguese by Ferreira Gullar. Portuguese you know much better, capable as you are of reading Machado de Assis and Graciliano Ramos in the original. Arabic you're still pondering.

Are these worth the effort? It is up to the reader, just as everything else is in literature. I am far from the first to indulge in such an endeavor. Samuel Beckett put together an anthology of Mexican poetry (Octavio Paz introduced it) yet his Spanish was minimal. The authors he chose aren't easy: Sor Juana Inés de la Cruz, Bernardo de Balbuena, Juan Ruíz de Alarcón, *modernistas* like Amado Nervo, Enrique González Martínez, and others. The result is astounding.

You called the preface to the volume "Translation and Hallucination." In it you describe translation as liberation:

> Words caught in a single language jump out, becoming worlds in another. This is all the more noticeable in poetry, where each sound, each cadence is strategically placed.

I approach translation as hallucination. I let myself go as much as possible, attuned to every type of stimulation, happy to wonder as I wander, eventually coming to the realization that the universe I am in actually depends on *me* to perpetuate itself. Throughout the process, my mind isn't fully mine. The fact that I emerge in one piece at the end is nothing short of miraculous.

I'm an immigrant. This is my condition. Immigration is untenable without translation. Translation fosters a kind of immigration. To translate is to survive on a day-to-day basis.

I started my life in Yiddish and Spanish interchangeably, then changed to Hebrew, hoping for redemption, and eventually settled in English, with other companions like Ladino saving me along the way. I am ambivalent about the term "mother tongue" to describe my first language, for where are all subsequent ones left? Are they stepmothers? Mistresses? I also don't like describing them as "firsts" because it gives them an unsustainable location. Whatever tongue one is using at the moment is first. For those reasons, I prefer a leveling of fields: all languages – all *my* languages, for that matter – are equal; I love them just the same. All are engaged in giving birth to reality.

For me it is harder to think that I was born in Mexico than to say that I was born into Yiddish and Spanish. Languages are more than a lexicon; they contain the DNA of entire civilizations. The words we use aren't really ours; we borrow them, using them to communicate not only with our contemporaries but with those who preceded us and those who will follow us. It is our responsibility to safeguard them while we also push them to new heights. And, obviously, while creating new words, for no living language is static.

As for poetry, I disliked it when I was young; I found it remote, pedantic. Age humbles us; it was I, of course, who was being snobbish. Poetry is tradition. In the short time we have on earth, it is up to us to unpack and extend it, to become full-fledged members of that tradition.

In short, I live in translation *without an original*. Yet originals are sacred to me, starting with the Bible. My duty as translator is to inject them with energy, to make them urgent.

You go on to suggest in the preface that your heroes are John Florio, who made Montaigne feel comfortable in English and, on the way, inspired Shakespeare; Richard Burton, whose *One Thousand and One Nights* is exquisite; and Adrienne Rich, who appreciated, perhaps disingenuously, that if language is power, silence is violence.

In translating from languages you don't know, you aren't talking about retellings, e.g., recreations, the famous "after such and such." That's altogether different. In your case, it is more than clear that these are full-fledged renditions.

At this point, you should make a reference to the "informer." You do not always use one – not knowing pushes you to resort to all sorts of strategies – because the technique varies from case to case. In select cases you do. At times your informer is actually a co-translator, as when you translated Gullar with Tal Goldfajn or Kharanauli with Gvantsa Jobava.

This is how you explain it. In a number of instances, after you've made your choice about a poem you've fallen in love with, after you've studied it from top to bottom, you've found a "stoolpigeon," as you once called it. This is a person you trust, often a close friend, who is an insider in the language of the poem. You spend a generous amount of time – a day, a weekend, sometimes up to a month – discussing every detail, every twist and turn of the text, until you feel you know it as if it was in your own language.

It isn't an easy task. You might become intimate with the poem but the language is still "en chino," as Mexicans say. Nevertheless, your foreignness with the original language, you acknowledge, will never cease. It is then a matter of turning your anxiety into art.

The informer is your spy. You want to know everything. You want to make the relationship between the two of you absolutely clear. Unless you've defined it that way (and you have on a few occasions), the translation you've embarked on isn't a joint venture. It is yours alone. You will take full credit, for the good as well as the bad.

That's why the image of matching socks feels right. If you end up with an unmatched pair and put them on, it is you who is subjected to ridicule, no one else.

So what, you ask? Does anyone still care anymore about non-matching socks? The Age of Aquarius has come and gone. To be freaky means being normal.

Is that why you don't care if the translation misses the mark? Actually, you do care. To invoke Elizabeth Bishop's riposte, it isn't a disaster.

Anyway, after the informer informs, does the snitch look at your work? Come on, it's wrong to call it snitching. The insider isn't a censor; that is, very rarely will you show your versions for approval. You share them all the time with friends, not to mention editors. Nevertheless, this is done to help you see what you can't see. In fact, that spy – that's closer to it! – might not even know you ever finished the task. You're unapologetically thankful. And then you take leave.

You said before that translation is the art of the impossible. It is also, as you've stated elsewhere, the art of the inevitable. Without translation, we are trapped in our own solipsism. Translation brings us out; it builds bridges between the self and the world.

It also cures us of our unbearable individualism. In writing, writers foster national literatures; in translating, translators make those writers global.

You hate the Russian proverb that states that translation is like a woman: if she is faithful, she is not beautiful; if she is beautiful, she is not faithful. Gregory Rabassa, the translator of *One Hundred Years of Solitude*, taught it to you. Forget about it being egregiously misogynistic. Its problem is that it builds a vision of the world as an either/or. The world is seldom that way: someone might be good and bad.

The same goes for translation.

– Epilogue, *This Is a Classic: Translators on Making Writers Global* (2023)

Self-translation como survival mecanismo

Publiqué hace un par de años un libro titulado *On Self-Translation* (2018). Quiero aquí regresar al tema, pursuing algunos ecos – acaso con más libertad – que continue to preoccupy me.

La auto-traducción es un exercise de capital importance en la literatura universal. Its pratictioners van de Flavio Josefo y Baruch Spinoza a Josef Conrad, Vladimir Nabokov e Isaac Bashevis Singer, all of them políglotas que, en momentos claves, for reasons de supervivencia (económica, política, cultural), cambiaron de lengua: del arameo al griego, from Dutch to Latin, y del polaco, el francés y el idish to English. En la tradición literaria latinoamericana, la auto-traducción es también típica: Jorge Luis Borges, María Luisa Bombal, Guillermo Cabrera Infante y Manuel Puig son algunos de sus practicantes distinguidos.

Tal como demostré en *The Norton Anthology of Latino Literature* (2011), entre los hispanos in the United States esta actividad es típica, no solo a nivel diario among people of all backgrounds, sino en las esferas artísticas y, obviously, literarias. La minoría exists en un estado en el cual two languages, el español y el inglés, se mantienen en contacto irrevocable. There are countless ejemplos de escritores que escribieron su obra primero in pone idioma and then, en su propia voz, in another. Entre ellos están Tomás Rivera, Julia de Burgos, Roberto G. Fernández y Ariel Dorfman.

I myself have switched de un idioma to the other a number de veces: del idish to español and then al hebreo y el inglés, with brief stays también en French. Escribí mi autobiografía *On Borrowed Words: A Memoir of Language* (2001) en inglés aunque cada capítulo está imaginado in another language: el Yiddish de mi abuela paterna, the Spanish of my childhood, el hebreo de mi aliyah a Israel, and the English I adopted when settling in New York en los ochentas. When Fondo de Cultura Económica publicó el libro en español en el 2013, I decided no traducirlo yo mismo but giving it to a profesional traductor para que hiciera una versión ajena a mí. El material was too raw for me to regresar a él e imaginarlo en otro idioma.

Pero he escrito cuentos en español que yo mismo hace translated al inglés y que, when doing it, come out de forma distinta, con personajes diferentes y hasta endings that don't appear in the original. Confieso que a estas alturas I alone no sé cuál de las dos versiones es el original. In fact, prefiero un término utilizado originalmente por Singer: "second original." El autor que se auto-traduce se desdobla de tal manera que termina with two selves.

Aquí va una sección de mi cuento "Xerox Man" en dos registros distintos:

"And what did you do with those missing pages?"

"Ah, therein the secret … My dream was to serve as a conduit in the production of a masterpiece that shall truly reflect the inextricable ways of God's mind: a random book, arbitrarily made of pages of other books. But this is a doomed, unattainable task, of course, and thus I left these extricated pages in the trash bins of the photocopy shops I frequented." (Ilan Stavans, *The Essential Ilan Stavans*, 307)

And,

-¿Y qué hizo con esas páginas faltantes? –Ah, he ahí el secreto … Mi sueño era servir como intermediario en la producción de una obra maestra que reflejara verazmente los caminos inescrutables de la mente de Dios: un libro hecho al azar, arbitrariamente, con páginas de otros libros. Pero ésta es una tarea condenada al fracaso, irrealizable, por supuesto, y por esto dejé esas páginas desprendidas en los cestos de basura de los centros de copiado que frecuentaba. (Ilan Stavans, *Lengua Fresca,* 137)

Escribí the first primero y and the second después. Al releerlas, me complacen en ese orden descendente, quizás porque el inglés hoy es mi hogar permanente y el español my alternative home.

¿En qué radica entonces el survival mecanismo? La respuesta es fácil: en una total reinvención. Almost sixty years of age, podría yo decir, without a hint of hestitation, que tengo varias vidas, una en cada idioma, y que sobrevivo en cada una de estas dimensiones lingüísticas desdoblándome in new originals.

Hasta acá – roughly y resumidamente – lo que dije en *On Self-Translation*. Hay mucho más, though. Para empezar, el tema de la ansiedad. El escritor que se auto-traduce exists en un permanent state of anxiety.

En mi caso, I don't fully belong a la literatura mexicana o a la latinoamericana; en in the United States, I am seen también como una rara avis. Es decir, ni soy de aquí or from the other side. Este sentimiento, obviamente, isn't new; de hecho, en un siglo en el cual migration is the dividing line, esta ansiedad is rather ubiquituous, o al menos es una constante acendente. To be dislocated, not to belong en ninguna parte, es ahora el *sine qua non*.

Yo soy un proud Spanglish-parlante, que para mí has a lot to do with being hispano en EEUU and also Jewish. Este idioma bastardo es absolutamente democrático: by la gente, for la gente y para la gente. As time goes by, está ordenándose in such a way que se vislumbra ya una standardized sintáxis.

La tradición literaria latina incluye figuras deslumbrantes who used Spanglish in admirable ways. El chicano Tato Laviera, las puertorriqueñas Ana Lydia Vega y Giannina Bracci y la argentina Susana Chávez-Silverman. Su obra es tanto liberadora como libertadora.

¿Es el Spanglish una afronta al español? If so, qué bien. Does it represent its demise? De ninguna manera. ¿Debe el inglés preocuparse del amplio número de hablantes, unos 40 millones a nivel mundial? A little.

Estas preguntas are made de forma recurrente. A mí, francamente, no me importa su respuesta. Language purity is only of concern to those que creen que hay que mantener ciertas reglas sintácticas. Truth is, la lengua existe in constant change. Y el mestizaje is an essential linguistic feature.

En el mundo hispánico, I'm convinced Spanglish is the major force que definirá nuestro metabolismo.

Aquí un párrafo de mi op-ed "Fort the Love of English"/"Jangueando," en el *New York Times*, July 20, 2017:

> Within those nationally defined groups, young people use Spanglish differently from their elders, just as immigrants use a type of Spanglish that is unlike the Spanglish spoken by second-generation Latinos. There is even a palpable difference between Puerto Rican Spanglish and Nuyorican, the Spanglish spoken by Puerto Ricans on the mainland. Each of these varieties is infused with a unique lexicon, accent and even style – "su propio revolú," its own ruckus.

Y,

> Dentro de esos grupos definidos por su nacionalidad, los jóvenes usan el spanglish de manera desemejante que sus mayores, así como los inmigrantes utilizan una modalidad que no es igual al que hablan los latinos de

primera o segunda generación. Incluso hay una diferencia palpable entre el spanglish de Puerto Rico y el "neoyorriqueño", es decir, el que hablan los puertorriqueños en el territorio continental de Estados Unidos. Cada una de esas variedades está permeada de un léxico diverso, un acento e incluso cierto estilo; "su propio revolú", su propia algarabía.

En relación al concepto de "second original", esta opción, el Spanglish, actually prompts a third path: neither inglés nor español, crea una alternativa that we may want to call "tercer original". En mi propio caso, when I write a piece in casteñol – como lo hago ahora – it inhabits su propia estética and, para ser entendida en español o en inglés, it requires translation.

And what type de traducción es esa? No refiero a invertir el esquema de forma endogámica. Take this example:

Esta frase is filled with double enredos.

Translation into Spanglish:

This sentence está llena de tricks dobles.

This exercise leads a ninguna parte; al contrario, it says exactly the same as if through un negative fotográfico. To achieve its true goal, la frase debe traducirse completamente al inglés ("This sentence is filled with double tricks") or al español ("Esta frase está llena de enredos dobles").

There you have it: three originals. Is one truer than el resto? Depende del reader, no del autor. One might find the English easier to access, or el español, o el Spanglish.

I'm writing this as the spread del COVID-19 ha forzado casi al mundo entero to isolate. Todos estamos bunkered in, encerrados en nuestras propias casas. Salvo, claro, los inmigrants, who are in refugee camps, o encimados en apartments, looking for ways para sobrevivir. Ellos don't have redes de apoyo. The future is even more incierto que para el resto de la gente. Viven en dos o más culturas y se comunican en tres o cuatro o cinco lenguages. Son forzado to negotiate su existencia on a daily basis.

However, en mi caso, como en el de muchos de esos refugiados, the option to auto-traducirse no siempre es un either/or. La sobrevivencia isn't about comunicarse en árabe, en francés o en alemán sino in Arabic, French, and German. Es decir, el ir y venir de idiomas often results en un menjurje, un mestizaje.

Aunque soy descendent de inmigrantes europeos to the New World, I feel very close al concepto de mestizaje. La mezcla es la clave y para mí esa mezcla es el Spanglish, que otros llaman inglañol o casteinglés. Although less and less, cada vez es visto con más aceptación. Cuando yo empecé a hablar de él públicamente in the nineties, it was a constant blanco de ridicule. But major universities, gobiernos y editoriales hoy dedican their attention to its development. That's because el Spanglish es un fenómeno inaplazable que precisamente surge del survival mechanism.

– *Ínsula*, September 2020

Simply Gimpl

"Gimpl Tam," as it is known in its Yiddish original, is one of the best short stories of the 20th century. It might be said to have defined the way Americans – in particular, American Jews – ultimately looked at the world destroyed by the Holocaust. First published in Yiddish at the end of the Second World War, it auspiciously arrived in English in 1953, in Saul Bellow's translation, published in *Partisan Review*.

The birth of that translation is surrounded in controversy. Literary critics Irving Howe and Eliezer Greenberg were under contract to edit the anthology *A Treasury of Yiddish Stories* (1954). Greenberg gave "Gimpl Tam" to Howe. Howe, in turn, asked Saul Bellow, who was born in Canada and had been raised in a Yiddish household, to bring it into English. By most accounts, Bellow translated the story in a single sitting, said to have lasted around three hours. He titled it "Gimpel the Fool." Bellow might not have written it down himself, since, according to one account, he dictated it to Greenberg. There are also suggestions that his Yiddish wasn't fully fluent, which explains, in part, the liberties he took, starting with the title: the Yiddish word "tam," coming from Hebrew, doesn't mean fool; yet the alliteration "Gimpel the Simple" was, well, foolish. At any rate, translation *is* about freedom. Bellow's style is everywhere in "Gimpl Tam." That might help explain the story's immediate and far-reaching acclaim. He was the up-and-coming author of *Dangling Man* and *The Victim*, and about to publish *The Adventures of Augie March*, which received the National Book Award.

Even though the story tied these two geniuses at the hip, the truth is that throughout their careers Singer and Bellow developed a courteous if tortured relationship, keeping each other at arm's length, especially Singer, who, as he made it clear in letters and interviews, was jealous of Bellow. More than a decade older than him (he was born in 1903, Bellow in 1915), Singer was a Polish-Jewish immigrant to New York, isolated in a parochial enclave of Yiddish speaking-refugees from Europe, whereas Bellow was widely recognized as a luminous Jewish intellectual, at home in the English language, and part of a cadre that was redefining American letters. Although a novel by Singer, *The Family Moskat*, had been translated into English before, it had gone nowhere. Hence, the fact that Singer ultimately found his footing in America thanks to Bellow's translation of "Gimpl Tam" made him uncomfortable for years. Add to it that he received the Nobel Prize in 1978, two years after Bellow, and you have the reasons for his simmering discomfort.

The register of "Gimpl Tam" is somewhere between a fable and a folk tale. Singer portrays the shtetl as a conniving place. Having a simpleton as the first-person narrator is a winning strategy: tempted by evil and incapable of decoding his surroundings, he chooses the higher ground. In the mid-fifties, readers responded to Gimpl with a mix of awe – in his nearsightedness, he was a sage – and nostalgia for what Singer's older brother Israel Joshua called "a world that is no more." Since then, all sorts of interpretations have accrued: about the nature of truth, about the endurance of Jewish diaspora life, and about what justifies revenge.

In Singer's old age (he was fifty when Bellow's "Gimpel the Fool" appeared), he himself took a stab at rendering the story into English, producing a draft for a dramatization. The present volume features that rendition, called "Simple Gimpl," completed by scholar David Stromberg, along with a brief essay by Stromberg explaining his discovery of the journal that featured it, his view on the collaboration, and his take on crucial aspects of the piece. The "new" version is followed by Bellow's translation and then Singer's Yiddish. They are accompanied by Liana Fink's gorgeous illustrations, in themselves another interpretation of "Gimpl Tam." This structure not only puts Singer and Bellow in dialogue – even if reluctantly – but looks at how the story has been appreciated across generations; it also celebrates translation as an integral component of world literature, for without it, entire civilizations would disappear irrevocably. And then there's the question of self-translation. When an author opts to render their own work in another language, what is it that is gained or lost?

– Preface, *Simple Gimpl* (2023)

Homestead: "La casa pairal," from *The Manuscript of Reus* (with Regina Galasso)

This is a translation, from the Catalan, of Antoni Gaudí's seminal notes on his concept of *casa*.

***

La casa is a family's small nation.

A family, like a nation, has a history, foreign affairs, changes in government, etc.

An independent family has its own *casa*; one that's not, rents a house.

One's own *casa* is the country of birth; a rented one is the country of emigration; that's why *una casa pròpia* is everyone's ideal.

A *casa* without a family is hard to imagine; it's easier with a rented one.

The *casa de familia* is called the *casa pairal*, the homestead, the ancestral home. Given the name, can't everyone think of a fine example of one in the countryside or the city? The desire for money and lifestyle changes have done away with most of the *cases pairals*; the ones that are left are run-down and will ultimately fall into ruin.

It's not just a single epoch or specific families that need a *casa pairal*; it has always been a necessity for everyone. A detached dwelling, a fine orientation, and an abundance of air and light, all generally absent in urban housing, are sought in this infinite number of manors outside the city. It then becomes peculiar that, in this situation, most families have two dwellings for their everyday living. What is even stranger is that the one that is best equipped is the one that is used the least.

To find these qualities, it's not uncommon for inhabitants of foreign cities to leave the city center, if suitable transportation options are available; fortunately, we are also starting to have easier access to these.

Given these circumstances, let's think about the true family dwelling. Combining the urban dwelling and the manor, the *casa pairal* is born. Let's imagine one, neither large nor small, that we could call ordinary. Enriching and enlarging it, it becomes a *palacio*. Making it smaller and using affordable materials and décor, it will be a modest *casa* for a well-off family.

Let's take, for instance, a lot in l'Eixample – its size depends on what the owner can afford – in an aristocratic neighborhood or not, depending on the owner's wealth and position. It's surrounded by a wall, crowned with an ornamental parapet around the gardens, high enough so what's inside can't be seen from the street. A small loggia by the gate breaks up this area. Inside, on one end of the lot, there's a long ramp, a path for carriages, that's across from a staircase. At the top of the stairs, one can make out a garden and, through the foliage of trees and plants, the *casa*. The rooms, arranged according to which way they face, create a picturesque ensemble. The bedroom's large windows face east; the office and the living room, south; the winter dining room and parlor, west; and to the north, the study, the summer dining room, and other rooms. Separate from this area, facing the same direction, there's the kitchen and pantries. Between the bedroom and the study, shaded by acacia and laurel trees, there's a porch decorated with terracotta pieces, where the local sparrows nest. Across from that, an iron and glass greenhouse, the winter garden, that connects to the room for entertaining, which can be used for large family parties. In this *casa*, systematic simplicity is everywhere; good taste is the guide; meeting one's needs and comfort is a must. Everything has its place. Family memories, historical events, local legends, our poets' subtle creations, mother nature's spectacles and scenes, everything with meaning and value, are part of the *casa*.

In short, the *casa* we are imagining has two objectives. The first is to provide a healthy environment so that those who grow up there become strong and robust. The second is to offer an artistic environment to build, to the degree possible, integrity of character. In sum, its purpose is to make the children who are born there true children of the *casa pairal*.

Translation as Home
(with Regina Galasso)

REGINA GALASSO: Congratulations on the publication of *Selected Translations: Poems 2000–2020* with the Pitt Poetry Series of the University of Pittsburgh Press! Before we open this beautiful book, I'd like to talk about the cover. There's a lot going on here. First, "Ilan Stavans." "Ilan Stavans" is larger in size than "selected translations." There's nothing on the front cover that says "translated by" or that points to you as the translator. But, of course, with the font size of your name, you dominate as the major player in this book without a doubt. I'm assuming that the decision to not explicitly point to you in the role of the translator was a deliberate one. I like it because it makes us wonder, what is your relationship to the "selected translations" of this book? What are the roles one must take on to produce a book of selected translations?

ILAN STAVANS: The cover design was in the publisher's hands. I like the image by painter José Gurvich, who was a central figure in the Constructivism art movement in Latin America. His work also illustrated the cover of my book *The Seventh Heaven: Travels through Jewish Latin America* (2019). The font size wasn't my decision. While I see your point on the absence of references to me as a translator, in my eyes it is the other way around: the translator of this book is also the author and vice versa. These are all my translations into English from about a dozen different languages (Spanish, English, Yiddish, Hebrew, and Spanglish the most prominent ones) done in diverse moments of my career, sometimes for specific purposes.

To me, *Selected Translations* is a *carte d'identité*. This is one of my selves, perhaps the most important: I'm a translator. I live through translation and I translate in order to live. I'm an immigrant as well as a descendant of immigrants. Translation and immigration come hand in hand. To me the word "translation" is a synonym of home, or maybe homelessness. When I translate, I'm at home – mind you, a temporary home, never a fixed one. I know some of my homes better than others. What I like about them is that I'm a renter, not an owner. In other words, I'm always in transit. Another way of understanding translation is being alert to foreignness. I don't like the idea of translation as domestication. For me a text is like a stranger knocking at the door. I make the stranger comfortable; I create a suitable atmosphere for the stranger to feel acclimated. But the stranger remains a stranger and I extend the welcoming hand.

RG: That's a great reminder that published books are a collaborative effort. Of course, not all collaborators contribute equally to the final product, but there are several players involved and behind what we are eventually able to hold in our hands. I like the ambiguity and centrality of your role as projected on the cover of *Selected Translations*. Although there is a growing awareness in the United States about the complexities of translation and the work/art of translators, we're in an environment in which many cultured and educated people are still on their way to understanding all that goes into translation and the possibilities of translation. The cover of this book shows that *Selected Translations* does not *just* belong to a translator, but to someone, Ilan Stavans, who as the translator is also the author, the editor, and the life behind the selections. A life probably does need a home. I like that idea of "translation" as a synonym of home or homelessness. "Selected Homes" could be a nice title for a future book that deals with languages and lives.

Speaking of languages and lives, one of the parts I like most from *On Borrowed Words: A Memoir of Language* (2001) is when you talk about your first days in New York City. José Gurvich also moved to New York City with his wife and son in 1970 after having lived in several places; sadly he died there at the young age of 47. New York experiences are so pivotal to the trajectory of the careers of artists and writers from Latin America and the Iberian Peninsula, regardless of the amount of time they spend in the city. I think a lot of this comes from the fact that New York is and always has been a place where so many languages gather. The city asks you to think about your relationship to those languages and your relationship to your own language. Was the New York connection a consideration in choosing Gurvich's artwork for the cover of two of your books? Is there something you see in his work, in the artwork choice for the cover of *Selected Translations* in particular, that sparks thoughts about language and translation?

IS: To me New York, to borrow a descriptor from Uruguayan literary critic Ángel Rama, is "the lettered city," not only because it is the global capital of literary culture, but because the landscape is, literally, a lettered narrative – actually, a multilingual one. Immigrants, through their native languages (Dutch, Italian, Yiddish, Spanish, and so on) have built their collective memory in their native tongue. You, Regina, have done groundbreaking scholarly work on this front, looking at Spanish – and Catalan – in New York through a literary lens: Federico García Lorca, Felipe Alfau, Josep Pla, and others. When I was a student at Columbia, knowing that Federico García Lorca had been in the same building, and that his experience had produced *Poet in New York* (1940), was enormously stimulating. I felt just the same about José Martí and Piri Thomas, whom I met.

Since Yiddish was one of my mother tongues in Mexico, it was equally crucial for me, when I arrived to New York City in the mid-1980s, to know that Isaac Bashevis Singer lived on the corner of 86th Street and Broadway and that Henry Roth, Abraham Cahan, Anzia Yezierska, and Irving Howe accessed the city *through* Yiddish. In my eyes, these forking paths converge in Gurvich, who is one of the most accomplished Jewish artists from Latin America. Born in Lithuania (his full name: Zusmanas Gurvicius) in 1927, when he was four, his father immigrated to Montevideo, Uruguay, and a year later sent for his family. Gurvich was closely associated with the workshop of Joaquín Torres García. As an artist, he traveled Europe, lived in Israel, and settled in New York City in 1970, four years before his death. There is a museum dedicated to Gurvich in Montevideo in which his New York years are emphasized.

Although I was already an incipient Spanish-language writer when I came to New York, it is there where I found my voice – especially in the English language. It was an arduous yet rewarding process. I will be eternally grateful to New York for invading me with its cacophony of sounds. It is still the place I feel most comfortable. When I finally moved out of the city in 1993, the impression I had at first was that I would never be whole again. Truth is, once you've made New York your home, it never leaves you; it travels with you in your tongue. My English, the one I carved in that period of initiation, is rowdy, elastic, and polysemic, that is, New Yorkish.

RG: I had the same impression when I left New York and it still remains. In New York, there's something so big about sharing a network of paths of previous, present, and future lives that transform in profound ways because they are touched by the sounds of multiple languages. García Lorca's path remains visible. I'm glad you included a poem from *Poet in New York*, "Ode to Walt Whitman," in *Selected Translations*. In the preface of the volume, you mention that these translations were done at the request of a friend or an editor. What is the path that led you to this poem? What paths were revealed to you as you translated the poem?

IS: I talked about Whitman with Boris Dralyuk of the *Los Angeles Review of Books*, an astonishing translator from the Russian, whose renditions include Isaac Babel's *Red Cavalry*. Whitman to me is a gravitational force. I love the way he does indeed contain multitudes: Borges admired the elasticity of his language, whereas Neruda favored his generosity of spirit. *Leaves of Grass* is a poetic contract with America – the word America understood both as a nation and as a continent. García Lorca's "Ode to Walt Whitman" inspired, and was in dialogue with, Neruda's "Ode to Walt Whitman." Through my translations, I wanted to give life to this dialogue again. I feel enormous empathy toward García Lorca's foreignness in New York: he is a distant yet compromised observer of the city, appropriating it, turning its agony into an entrance door through which others – strangers, tourists, all kinds of dislocated souls – might access it. I love the rhythm of the ode; I love these two consecutive lines: "Nueva York de alambres y de muerte. / ¿Qué ángel llevas oculto en la mejilla?" They invoke in me the image of Walter Benjamin's Angelus Novus, the angel of history (based on Paul Klee's drawing).

RG: Your translation reads: "New York of wire and death. / What angel do you hide in your cheek?"

IS: It is how the image travels for me from Spanish to English.

RG: Do you love your version?

IS: Love isn't an emotion my own work awakens in me.

RG: More on places and paths … Here we are in Amherst, Massachusetts, working, researching, writing, teaching, translating, and living in Emily Dickinson's town. The appendix of the volume includes your translations into Spanish of six of Emily Dickinson's poems. The book is dedicated to Jules Chametzky, a Brooklyn-born professor emeritus of English at the University of Massachusetts-Amherst and founder of the *Massachusetts Review*. Amherst is here. How has Amherst shaped your literary tastes?

IS: I was familiar with Dickinson and Robert Frost only marginally when I arrived in Amherst. Becoming part of the town to me has meant making them not only my neighbors but my friends. For our life isn't only spent with our contemporaries, but with our ancestors and successors. Our contemporaries are accidental; whom we choose from the past and who chooses us in the future are a matter of decision. Dickinson's imagery, her fractured vision, her radical punctuation – she is the best American poet of the nineteenth century and maybe the best overall. And Frost is almost as stunning. "Mending Wall," which I also include in *Selected Translations*, is, unavoidably in my view, about the US-Mexico border, even though Frost doesn't seem to have thought much about it. Of course, it is about countless other borders, too: the one that separates Israel and Gaza; the Berlin Wall, China's Great Wall, etc.

Over the twenty-five years I've lived in Amherst, the town has shaped me in countless ways. New England was the cradle of transcendentalism. I feel very close to Hawthorne, Melville, and Emerson. I live in an old house with beautiful trees from all over the world; that landscape alone inspires me at all times. I have also been in communication with an assortment of terrific writers from around the world who have lived in the area, including Richard Wilbur, David Foster Wallace, Norton Juster, Agha Shahid Ali, and Martín Espada.

RG: Translation is a way to get to know and be with our ancestors, cities, towns, and homes. Homes … and being at home when you translate. If translation is a synonym for home, then what about the original? Where is the original, Ilan? What is the original? In other places, we've both talked about translations without originals, and the original as the translation, in the context of specific writers. Felipe Alfau's *Chromos* (1990) has so much to say about translations and originals, especially when writers produce literature in second or third languages, and outside their birthplace. I've heard you talk about this in the classroom with students and you've shared in other publications that translation might supersede the original. And when we look at the pages of *Selected Translations*, readers don't see the originals with the translations. This once again might have been an editorial decision.

IS: It certainly was. Some of the versions appeared in *The FSG Book of Twentieth-Century Latin American Poetry* (2011), where every original is paired with its translation. Others were featured in newspapers, magazines, and other periodicals, or were read in festivals, on radio and TV. This volume focuses on the translations alone.

I met Alfau in a retirement home in Queens. I translated his poetry and introduced his novels, especially *Locos: A Comedy of Gestures* (1936) to Spanish-language readers. His multilingualism is enthralling in that he never became fully comfortable in English – which he mostly used as a writing strategy – while his Spanish and Catalan became stilted. He is an example of translingual authors: linguistic travelers. Alfau was like a vampire: sucking blood at night from maidens, while sleeping in a sarcophagus.

I'm of the opinion that translation isn't a kitchen sink endeavor, a mere transaction in order to offer in one language what is available in another. Translation is art. It has its own aesthetic aspirations. It isn't difficult to think of translations that improve on the original, maybe even supplanting it. Is the King James Version of the Bible better than the Hebrew and Aramaic original? I'm conscious that such a suggestion is blasphemous. After all, the original is sacred because God conceded to deliver the narrative in those languages; nothing in that narrative – not one iota – might be supplanted. Yet the forty-seven translators had at their disposal an ampler lexicon than the authors of the Bible; they also paid more attention to style, coherence, music, and so on. One might engage in similar explorations when talking about other classics, though far from all. There is also a hint in Borges' "Pierre Menard, Author of the Quixote" that the nineteenth-century French symbolist is a superior writer to Cervantes' "genio lego."

RG: I am glad you brought up the classics. Are these poems in *Selected Translations* your classics? I would love to see volumes of selected translations from individual writers that reveal the writer's development and literary tastes. Might we anticipate seeing another volume like that?

IS: In 2004, to celebrate his centennial, I did a volume of translations called *The Poetry of Pablo Neruda*. It showcases the work of various translators; in fact, some poems appear in multiple versions. For Penguin Classics, I have also edited – though not translated – the poetry of Sor Juana Inés de la Cruz, Rubén Darío, and César Vallejo. Depending on how much time I have left, I certainly would return to a number of authors, granting more space than *Selected Translations* does. Others I would leave alone. Borges, for instance, never ceases to amaze me but mostly as an essayist and in his *ficciones*; I'm less engaged with his poetry. In any case, because it uses standard metrics – sonnets, especially – it is impossible to do justice to it in translation; something similar happens to Quevedo, who will forever be imprisoned in the original. In perusing Alexander Coleman's edition of Borges' *Selected Poems* (2000), I found very little that was satisfying.

Roughly, the year 2000 is when I finally felt confident enough to translate poetry into English. It is also the start of my interest, in terms of commitment, in Spanglish and other hybrid languages. *Selected Translations* includes versions into Spanglish of Shakespeare's soliloquy "To Be or Not to Be," among other texts. The hundred-or-so poems in the volume are a record of my affinities. To me, a translator must engage in myopic reading; the translator is the closest reader a text ever gets, to the point that, from my perspective, translators end up knowing more about the author than the author himself. I'm not being facetious.

Yes, these are *my* classics, i.e., authors without whose oeuvre I cannot conceive of the world. There is a distinction between a sacred book and a literary classic: the former is supposedly written by a supernatural entity and, therefore, is perfect; the latter, instead, are books that survive their authors to become staples of their time. At the age of fifty-nine, I devote most of my time to rereading classic works. I find *re*reading far more rewarding than reading.

RG: Finally, tell us more about rereading the classics in the context of language and translation. You touch on this a bit in your conversation with

Jenna Tang. Many readers of classics forget that they're often reading a translation. What is more, when they choose to read a classic – *Madame Bovary* (1856), for example – they don't think about which translation to read, if they can't read the French. They don't realize they could pick up a 19th-century translation or a 20th-century translation. How do language choices and available translations figure into your decision to reread a classic?

IS: There are multiple definitions of a classic. One I personally like is "a book capable of surviving translation." In order to find a readership beyond their habitat, books need translation. But translations aren't always good; plus, more so than the original, they are bound to an age. Let me expound on this. A classic is a book frozen in time. Shakespeare's English is challenging, yet the idea of retouching is anathema. That isn't the case of translations of Shakespeare's work. No sooner do they feel dated, fresh new ones emerge. Thus, reading a classic in translation means that there inevitably is a choice, at least in most "majority" languages, e.g., languages with a commanding demographic stake: what translation should I choose? Because by reading Lydia Davis' translation of *Madame Bovary* (2010), I'm automatically not selecting any of the other seventeen ones.

The first one ever to appear was by Eleanor Marx-Aveling (1886). It was published thirty years after Flaubert's novel came out in French and has been revised at least once. Others I like are by Francis Steegmuller (1957), Lowell Bair (1959), Mildred Marmur (1964), Geoffrey Wall (1992), Margaret Mouldon (2004), Raymond N. MacKensie (2009), Christopher Moncrieff (also 2009), and Adam Thorpe (2011). Given that translation is a subjective endeavor, each of these translations, consciously and otherwise, emphasizes another dimension of the narrative. In general, there are two types of translations of a classic: one brings the text to the present, meaning it modernizes the language; the other brings the reader to the past, recreating the "archaic" worldview by using old elements in the target language. Their overall intentions are hence very different. In response to your question, when I reread a classic with a group of readers, I always keep in mind the objective of the group. Is our reading shaped by scholarship? Are the readers part of a general audience interested in "enjoying" the narrative? If, for instance, I'm leading a group of high-schoolers or senior readers, I selected a version that modernizes the original. If, on the contrary, I'm studying the text with graduate students, I opt for a more scholarly translation. These forking paths are a luxury one doesn't have with a contemporary book. With a classic, it isn't only what book you're reading but how. In other words, it isn't solely what the classic says but what the classic means.

– *Latin American Literature Today*, May/June 2021

Immigrants in Quarantine (with Jhumpa Lahiri and Eduardo Halfon)

ILAN STAVANS: My dreams lately have been more vivid that usual. The texture in which they unfold is intense. I seldom remember my dreams but now I wake up disturbed in the middle of the night, not because of the images I witnessed in my dreams but because I feel that the emotions they're conveying are raw, urgent. Years ago, an Indian friend told me that we don't dream of a tiger and then feel scared. It is the other way around: we are scared and then we dream of a tiger. Have your dreams been different since the pandemic began?

JHUMPA LAHIRI: Yesterday night I had a classic COVID nightmare. My brother-in-law was coming to visit. He had a fever. Then my son Octavio also had a fever. I was frantically trying to understand what to do. I also had an interesting dream early on in the pandemic, while I was still at Princeton. I was flying in a very small airplane with a couple of friends. I was exhilarated to be in the air. I looked down at some point and saw the ocean, which, as you know, Ilan, I have a great passion for. I hadn't seen it in a long time. At first I was thrilled. But then I saw hundreds and hundreds of people on the beach. My friends on the plane and I decided we needed to go somewhere else and I was relieved to leave the crowds behind. Clearly, these dreams are expressions of basic fears, about searching for safety.

IS: Did you wake up anxious after either of these dreams?

JL: I don't know if I can draw that type of connection. Dreams are inherently mysterious. Some remain with us, others are just fragments. But yes, my dreams, in general, have been more intense in recent months. There is also the awareness of waking up and every day having to confront the truth again.

One of the reasons I'm grateful to be in Rome is that it is a place I love very deeply. When I wake up, I'm concerned. But I'm also happy to be here. I would feel similarly if I were in Wellfleet, another place I very much love and feel at peace in.

When COVID broke and we realized what we were headed for, I remember thinking I wanted to be in a coma for the next year. Wake me up when it's over. I don't want to deal with it. Then I stopped saying it, because sometimes you get what you wish for. It is all so grim, and we are getting so tired of it. It has been disheartening for those of us in the United States who followed the rules. In Italy, my friends say, "we made an intense sacrifice, the whole country, every single person took part, otherwise we would have faced the consequences, including fines." And now that they've emerged from it, after truly flattening the curve, there's a sense of relief, even of cautious exhilaration. Of course, people are on standby, wondering if there will be a second wave.

On the whole, in Italy, the entire country can now say, that was then and this is now. We can't say that in the United States. There has been one tsunami followed by another. It's all a big mess. It's hard to sustain mentally and emotionally.

Going back to dreams, I'm sure we're hungrier than ever to explore our unconscious. Especially those of us who haven't been able to travel. My family and I are fortunate in that we managed to come to Italy. Most people I know have been stranded.

EDUARDO HALFON: From the beginning, more than my dreams it was my sleep that was affected. The pandemic hit us in Paris. It was painful to see a deserted Paris. And the uncertainty of what was happening outside affected my sleep. We were away from home. We were guests in Paris – I had a fellowship from Columbia to spend a year there, writing. And not being in my own environment, not having a personal doctor, not knowing how the health-care system worked – these variables disturbed me. I was thrown into a constant state of anxiety.

I also started dreaming about family members getting sick. Not with COVID, necessarily, more of a general sickness. I think it stemmed from the fact that if someone did get sick – my father, my mother, my brother, my sister – I would not be able to be with them. That made me feel even closer to my wife and my son, who were there with me.

But I kept thinking how the pandemic would have affected me if I weren't a father or a husband, if it was just me. Would it have been easier? Would I have been able to work more? I wouldn't have had to take care of anyone, or to worry about either of them getting sick – my biggest concern. Although, at the same time, I couldn't imagine spending two months of lockdown without them. Yes, writing was difficult if not impossible with a toddler at home, but I was also too busy keeping him busy, playing and inventing with him new games, sheltering him from what was going on outside, in the streets. We were bunkered down together.

IS: In spite of the anxiety, I confess to also have enjoyed quarantine. I'm sure I'm not the only one. It has come as a respite. Not to travel, not to be constantly on the move. In my case, I confess to have discovered the tranquility my home has always given me. I had taken it for granted. Now I cook more. Alison and I take long walks. Mixed with the anxiety, and frankly the fury at the ineptitude of our government, is a sense of gratitude. My writing feels different, too. I relax better while I'm writing. I've always enjoyed it. But now I do more. Perhaps it is because I have thought much more seriously about finitude. I only have a limited time. Things will suddenly end. I will not be myself at some point.

Somehow, I have noticed the birds more than before. Cardinals, finches, hummingbirds, blue jays. Alison put up some feeders. The birds come regularly. Their movements are nervous. They have always been. But I see that nervousness now more emphatically. In Wellfleet, we have also been visited by wild turkeys. One large family: the parents and about eight chicks. They go about their way without worry. I envy them, honestly.

Jhumpa, I notice in your words anger toward the United States, a feeling to want to keep the country at arm's length, far away from you. We've talked about it at dinners. Is it more pronounced? Isn't what is happening to this country predictable? The excess of individualism, the libertarian response to government rules, the conviction that everyone is exceptional. It all has been in the collective DNA. The pandemic and Donald Trump's ineptitude have simply made the fault lines more visible.

JL: It certainly helps me, when I live in the United States, to have another point of reference, another home – socially, culturally, linguistically. Octavio was going to school in Italy this year while the rest of us were living in Princeton. Having my son in Rome meant that I was always, mentally and emotionally, in two places, and this caused me to have even more perspective.

For the past eight years, I have been cultivating an intense relationship with Italy, and especially with Rome, where I now live part of the time. Of course this is a big investment: of time, of energy, of finances. But as a result I always thought to myself: if things get bad in the United States, we can leave. I especially felt it after Trump was elected. It was enormously reassuring. Like so many, I was in a deep state of shock, mourning, and terror. But I had the keys to my Roman apartment in a coffee can in my study in Princeton. All we had to do was book tickets.

Ironically, when COVID hit, I couldn't leave. I had a job. There were roots, responsibilities. Literally, the solution I had created wasn't possible. That was hard for me to accept. I had to stay put, obey the rules, and hope things would slowly improve. And they have, otherwise I wouldn't be in Italy now. However, the freedom one feels is tentative. It's still a risk to move around. Things are uncertain.

I feel anger, of course. I think one of the best aspects of America is also one of its limitations: freedom to a fault. The insistence on doing it my way without thinking about the collective. False statements of patriotism mean nothing to me, but sacrificing for the greater good means a great deal. There has been a total lack of leadership, by a dangerous man. It's the perfect storm. We needed someone to say, "Listen up everyone! This is very serious. We have to all work together. We have to listen to the scientists." That message never came. It's a buffet-style approach to culture. We needed a seated dinner with a fixed menu.

In Italy, on the whole, there's a greater sense of community, and more day-to-day interaction in living one's basic life. There's less isolation, less alienation. I miss that when I'm in America.

IS: I haven't been able to be with my mother, who lives in Mexico City, for a long time. She is absolutely alone in her apartment. I talk to her every other day but it isn't the same. And I haven't been able to hug my son Josh, who is in Brooklyn. I miss the love that comes from the day-to-day physicality. You come from a diasporic Jewish family, Eduardo. You were raised in Guatemala and studied in the United States. I think of you as an ex-pat, although I don't know what the "ex" refers to, what is the center of gravity for you and your family. Do you also approach the pandemic as an immigrant?

EH: I approach everything as an immigrant. I've always approached everything as an immigrant. I come from an immigrant family. I was raised that way. Always on the move.

In my life, I've experienced two different United States: in the eighties growing up in South Florida, and then the decade I spent recently in the Midwest – in Nebraska and Iowa. Two completely different experiences. In the latter, I arrived in Lincoln just as Obama had been elected. The atmosphere was optimistic. Like both of you, I had always been attached to universities, which are like an oasis. International students, international faculty. It was easy. Then came the nightmare of Trump's victory. As a Latin American, I immediately sensed in him the type of bully we are accustomed to south of the border. A con man. A shyster – a wonderful word, difficult to translate into Spanish. It isn't an accident that what is happening in the United States right now, with the pandemic out of control because of a complete lack of leadership, is also happening in Brazil and other Latin American countries, Guatemala included.

But I see all of this from the outside. Although I've lived in the US almost half of my life, I have always seen the country as an outsider. I never became an insider, never became a citizen (I was always there on some type of visa), never felt like an American, although I could pretend to be one. But when I'm in Guatemala I feel the same. Likewise in Spain. Likewise here in France. I'm never completely at home anywhere. You see those suitcases behind me? They're still full. I haven't taken all of my clothes out. I didn't while I was in Nebraska, either. I always have them ready to go. Mine is an itinerant life.

I like, Ilan, that you used the word "diaspora." My grandparents were Jews from Poland, from Lebanon, from Syrian, from Egypt. Like them, I live on the move, ready for the next place. Always hovering everywhere, never landing anywhere. I was educated that way: to always be at the ready. So when COVID arrived, I was of course ready to move. Suitcases packed, let's get out of Paris. And we did, to a small town in southern France. In due time, however, I'll also get out of southern France.

My son is three and a half. He has already moved six times. He has three passports. Clearly, this itinerant life is continuing. It's a nomadic existence, a Jewish type of life.

IS: In the earlier days of the pandemic, my sons, just like everyone else, kept talking about going back to "normal." In the last few weeks, I have noticed they no longer use the word. They are in their twenties. I have asked them, separately in each case, what they think the future will look like. Neither believes it is the same future they envisioned in December, for instance. The future, as a dimension, has been utterly reconfigured. To them it now feels more tentative, less forgiving. By this I mean the conviction that you might do anything you dreamed of in it. Maybe not anymore. What do you think?

JL: The future is by definition an unknown. We all have hopes, plans, expectations. But life teaches us again and again that nothing apart from the present moment is within our grasp. This has been one of the great lessons of Rome for me personally and, I hope, also for my children: to live each day with appreciation and with awareness, knowing that tomorrow everything could change. History teaches us and the pandemic now reminds us of how precarious life is, how little we still know. It's a sobering reality, especially for young people. But honestly, my children have faced the considerable disruptions caused by the pandemic with extraordinary strength, patience, and clear-headedness. They have never despaired the way they did the night Trump was elected.

EH: I can't help thinking that the opinion on this of someone like me, that is, someone of my socio-economic standing, would be radically different from, say, the opinion of a poor indigenous Guatemalan or a poor rural Nigerian. For them, the future has always been tentative, unforgiving, devoid of any possibility of plans or dreams. Their situation hasn't changed it's still day to day, still hand to mouth. They still struggle every day to put food on the table. They still have no access to health care or adequate schools. Their daily existence is as precarious now as it was before the appearance of any virus. It is only for us, the more privileged, the ones who have lived under the illusion of planning and dreaming up fairytale futures, that things feel as though they've now dramatically changed. The rest of the world just puts on a mask.

– *LitHub*, March 2020

Coda: The Hermeneutics of Translation

Reading the Talmud in Mexico: A Confession

To Rabbi Justin David

You misunderstand everything, even silence.
— Franz Kafka, *The Castle* (1926),
translated from the German by Ilan Stavans

In Mexico in the eighties, a *daf yomi*, for a neophyte like you, was a daunting endeavor. You were just in your early twenties, studying with a Mizrahi mother and daughter. You don't recall much about them other than the fact that they were Lebanese immigrants. What you do remember is the pride in your nascent capacity to interpret.

Even in its premodern stage, your country has always existed peripherally, on the outskirts. This is all the more so with modernity. It is as if Mexico had been left unfinished at the time of creation. You once saw a black-and-white film by Luis Buñuel, *Los olvidados* (1950), called in English *The Young and the Damned*, about homeless children living in slums. There is one singular scene with a blind old man and a boy that takes place in an abandoned construction site. Modernity in Mexico City to you is symbolized by that scene.

When you were growing up there, the country had a one-party dictatorship. Democracy was quelled by means of all sorts of strategies. Dissent was tolerated as long as it didn't undermine the nation's hierarchical structure; otherwise, it was met, first with ostracism, then with torture, followed by prison and death.

How can you stand all of it now? You were oblivious to these political tides, though. That's why the political undertone of the Talmudic story didn't ring a bell. Could anything have been further from your day-to-day reality then? Although you look back at it with remorse, you realize maturity is about playing peek-a-boo.

Are you sure "The Oven of Akhnai" should be called a story? Its narrative flows like an unimpeded river, without beginning, middle, or end. Its plotline meanders. And it isn't populated with recognizable characters whose inner and outer worlds we survey.

It was in Bava Metzia, the first of a three-part Talmudic tractate called Nezikim (the other two are Bava Kamma and Bava Batra), chapter 4, 59a–59b.[1] The general topic of the tractate is properly law. You were reading it in a bilingual Hebrew/Spanish edition from Buenos Aires.

With typos ... You can't quite recall any in particular. Why was it embarrassing to come across them? Because you believe the Talmud should be treated with utmost respect. A single page of it is something to behold. Perhaps they added to your feeling of existing on the periphery. Printed matter circulates in the Spanish-speaking world without much quality control. Still, the sheer fact that the Talmud was available to you was a source of joy.

You don't really like what the story is called, "The Oven of Akhnai." It isn't its real title. Talmudic stories don't have titles. But that isn't the problem. The problem is that the story is neither about an oven nor about a person called Akhnai.

There is no information about Akhnai. Was he a baker? If not, why did he have an oven? You've seen reproductions of this type of oven. They look like the upper half of a beehive, their walls made of concentric horizontal structures and an opening at the top. You have found in the Tosafot that Akhnai was a popular name in the second century, its roots probably in Phoenicia. Could the title be a reference to a "Joe the oven owner"?

You have read that the word *akhnai* is an Aramaic version of the Greek word for "snake." Does Akhnai's oven look like a dormant snake? Inevitably, the snake – in Hebrew, *naḥash* – is a symbol that refers you to Genesis 3:1, where the animal persuades Eve to disobey God's prohibition against the Tree of Life.

You know other Talmudic stories about ovens. One in particular (Kiddushin 81b:2–4) has an important female character. It is about a rabbi, Hiyya bar Ashi, who prays to God to protect him against the *yetzer ha-ra*, "the evil inclination." His wife, Heruta, wonders why, since they have not had sexual relations in a long time. She decides to dress up like a prostitute to seduce him in the garden. He possesses her. Later on, as she is kindling an oven, he confesses to Heruta. She tells him it was she who seduced him. Rabbi Hiyya bar Ashi then responds: "But I, anyhow, intended to do something forbidden."

---

1 You digressed on "The Oven of Akhnai" with a Talmudic lesson you offered in 2014, in which you also talked about Jacob's usurpation of the first son rights in front of Isaac (Gen. 27): "God's Smile," *The Common* 8 (2014): 36–51. And you touched on it in *The Oven: An Anti-lecture* (Amherst: University of Massachusetts Press, 2018).

A page or two before, before "The Oven of Akhnai" even starts, it addresses a theme of deep concern for the rabbis: *ona'at dvarim*, "aggression through words." It states that there is no more serious sin; so serious, God never fails to notice it.

As the plot unfolds, the reader is told a *mishna* from tractate Kelim about utensils susceptible to ritual impurity. An assortment of rabbis react to it. They eventually line up in two opposing sides: Rabbi Eliezer – his full name is Rabbi Eliezer ben Hyrcanus, one of the *tanna'im* and a student of Rabbi Yohanan ben Zakai known for having learned the Torah late yet having amassed knowledge superior to all his peers – argues that if the oven of Akhnai is broken into parts, it isn't susceptible to ritual impurity; the Sages disagree with him.

Who are these rabbis? The story doesn't seem to care. It ignores biographical background, turning the rabbis into mere mouthpieces.

Anyway, Rabbi Eliezer uses logical arguments to prove his point, but in the end fails to convince his opponents. He decides to switch strategies. To prove his point, he makes a number of what you think are outlandish remarks. For instance, he tells the Sages: "If the *halakha* is in accordance with me"[2] (this phrase will become a leitmotif), "the carob tree will immediately uproot itself." Soon the carob tree does, moving one hundred cubits – some say four hundred – from its original place.

The Sages dismiss Rabbi Eliezer's evidence, saying that "proof cannot be obtained from a carob tree."

In Mexico, you recollect being struck by this opening scene, or what amounts to a scene. In that period, you were reading *One Hundred Years of Solitude* (1967), said to be the cornerstone of the movement known as *lo real maravilloso*, "magical realism." Animism permeates such aesthetics: all of a sudden, objects mysteriously move from place to place. For instance, in a crucial episode, *el hilo de sangre*, "a thread of blood," travels from the dying body of José Arcadio Buendía Hijo to his mother, Úrsula Iguarán. And a bag of bones brought to Macondo, the mythical town where the novel is set, by Rebecca keeps showing up, autonomously, at unexpected moments.

Magical realism was described as a by-product of Latin America, a continent where reality remains in formation, mixing dreams with factual information, thus bending our sense of what's conceivable. The episode of the carob tree seems to you to share these traits.

---

2 Quotations come from Adin Steinsaltz's edition of *The Talmud* (New York: Random House, 1990), vol. 3, Tractate Bava Metzia, pt. 3:233–8.

It used to bother you that, in people's eyes, you came from a landscape defined by magic. But it doesn't anymore. Actually, you like it. In Mexico, spirits coexist with people; they guide them in their daily endeavors. Where you live now, reality is too blunt, too scientific. It doesn't bend.

You have asked yourself countless times: Why does *lo real maravilloso* flourish so robustly in that part of the world? Your answer has to do with the arrival of *modernismo*, an aesthetic wave sweeping the region for three decades, starting around 1880, when Nicaraguan poet Rubén Darío published his influential book *Azul* … (Blue …).

Darío and his cohorts (José Martí, Leopoldo Lugones, Delmira Agustini, José Asunción Silva, Amado Nervo, et al.) drank coffee, dressed like French intellectuals, and wrote precious poetry. A few were Orientalists; others sought to give voice to the nativist folktales. It was a period of turmoil: Italian and Jewish immigrants were seeking a new life in Buenos Aires, Montevideo, Bogotá, and Mexico, among other places. Gas lighting, sewer systems, and public transportation were redefining the Latin American city. The Modernistas were convinced their nations would soon catch up with Europe. Was it the wrong aspiration?

Half a century later, another generation of writers – Gabriel García Márquez, Mario Vargas Llosa, Julio Cortázar, and others – will be more skeptical. The wounds of colonialism run deep. They don't all of a sudden disappear. Power corrupts everything. Latin America has its own path. It doesn't have to be like Europe. Pre- and post-modernity coexist in its midst. This generation will embrace other modes of being, like jazz, Buddhism, and a return to the pre-Columbian past.

The Talmud, indeed Jewish sources in general, aren't part of their menu. That's why you felt, next to your Lebanese study mates, like an anachronism. You were finding your own path. The *daf yomi* was your ticket to freedom. It was a bubble almost for yourself alone. Yet it blinded you, too. It was an exercise in solipsism. You thought it connected with your own ancestral roots but nothing else.

Rabbi Eliezer tries again. He states: "If the halakha is in accordance with me, a nearby channel of water will flow backward." And miraculously, it does. But the Sages remain unconvinced: "Proof cannot be brought by the channel of water either."

To which Rabbi Eliezer adds another proof: the walls of the House of Study will lean sideways, almost falling to the ground.

Rabbi Eliezer's chief antagonist, Rabbi Yehoshua (full name: Rabbi Yehoshua ben Hananiah, another *tanna'*), enters the stage, proudly saying: "If Talmudic scholars argue with one another in their discussion about the *halakha*, what affair is it of yours?" In other words, he is categorical that no extemporaneous proof should be used to make a logical point.

At this point, the two sides cannot define their turf in clearer terms: one (Rabbi Eliezer) believes in revelation; the other (Rabbi Yehoshua and the Sages), in human reason. To you, *this* is what "The Oven of Akhnai" is about.

Astoundingly, the story states that out of respect for Rabbi Yehoshua, the walls of the House of Study didn't fall down; and out of respect for Rabbi Eliezer, they didn't go back to their original position either. They remained tilted. (By the way, that's how a *mezuzah* is supposed to hang on the door frame.)

Does this mean God is taking no position? On the contrary, God is on Rabbi Eliezer's side; otherwise, the walls would have returned to their original position.

Unbearably stubborn, Rabbi Eliezer finally states that if the *halakha* is in accordance with him (by now you're tired of this line!), "let it be proved directly from Heaven."

It's the kind of statement that frequently comes from a desperate person: "I am right and God is my witness." Not being a prophetic text like the Torah, the Talmud, you think, should be neutral about this statement. You're therefore flabbergasted when a heavenly voice tells the Sages: "Why are you disputing with Rabbi Eliezer? The *halakha* is in accordance with him in all circumstances!"

These lines leave you speechless since you read them in Mexico with the Mizrahi mother and daughter. You thought God was neutral. Since when does God take sides, interfering in human affairs?

You're furious. You feel betrayed. You smile.

Undeterred, Rabbi Yehoshua rises to his feet and quotes Deuteronomy 30:12: "Lo bashamayim hi'" (it [the Torah] is not in heaven).

You tell yourself he's right: the Torah is not in heaven.

But the Torah is from heaven. God likes to be revealed. Rabbi Yehoshua is putting a stop to it. God must feel upset.

From here on, the story turns ugly, moving from verbal dispute to physical violence. In punishment for his stubbornness, the Sages decide to ostracize Rabbi Eliezer, to excommunicate him. No one will be allowed to talk to him again.

Suddenly, you sympathize with Rabbi Eliezer. But is he an underdog? You're amazed by the partnership he has forged with God. To you it looks impure.

You brace yourself for what is coming. Since the Sages are ready to stand their ground, havoc is likely to ensue. Since no one wants to convey the bad news to Rabbi Eliezer (who by this point is wearing black clothes and sitting *shiva*), Rabbi Akiva, his student and a young rabbinical scholar known for his compassion, volunteers. You realize this is why the story of "The Oven of Akhnai" is about *ona'at dvarim*: because a lesson must be learned – this is the Talmud, after all – in terms of reconciliation.

There is no such thing, though. After Rabbi Akiva conveys his message, Rabbi Eliezer's fury not only persist but increases. "The world was smitten," we are told. "One-third of the olives, one-third of the wheat, and one-third of the barley were destroyed. Indeed, some say that even the dough in women's kitchens swelled and spoiled." The Gemara adds that "there was great divine wrath on the day that Rabbi Eliezer was excommunicated and a great calamity befell the world, for whatever Rabbi Eliezer laid his eyes upon was burnt."

This is atrocious: God is vengeful.

The story states that years later, another religious leader, Rabbi Nathan, in a dream, meets the Prophet Elijah, who in the Talmud is a frequent discussant with the Sages. Rabbi Nathan wants to know if and how God reacted to the debate between Rabbi Eliezer and Rabbi Yehoshua. Elijah says: "God smiles and repeated: 'My sons have defeated me! My sons have defeated me!"

You wonder: why does God smile? Is it a gesture of empathy, a father's expression of pride in his children's development? Or is it a sign referring to loss? And why does God repeat the sentence?

The answer, you tell yourself, might be rather simple: by endorsing Rabbi Yehoshua in the argument, the Sages defeated Rabbi Eliezer. God regrets having lost the argument.

There's a coda to the story, though, or perhaps it's another chapter. The Sages, to make clear what the winning argument was, burned all the food cooked in an Akhnai oven after it was reassembled, to show how things connected to it are ritually impure.

The two sides are in retaliation mode: Rabbi Eliezer has supernatural powers, which the Sages must contain.

At that time, Rabbi Gamliel, a great *tanna'* as well, who was responsible for the decision to excommunicate Rabbi Eliezer, was traveling on a boat. A huge wave suddenly rose over him to drown him. He quickly realized that it was brought on by heaven, so he said to God: "It seems to me that this can only be happening to me because of the anguish caused to Rabbi Eliezer ben Hyrcanus." He rose to his feet and said: "Master of the Universe, You know full well that I did not excommunicate Rabbi Eliezer for my own personal honor, or for the honor of my father's house. Rather, Rabbi Eliezer was excommunicated for Your honor, because it is essential that no individual, great as he might be, should reject a decision reached by the majority, so that controversies will not multiply in Israel."

Majority rules. But is God happy?

Rabbi Gamliel does die. The story states that Rabbi Eliezer's wife, Imma Shalom, who was the sister of Rabbi Gamliel, would not allow her husband to pray. One day, when she wasn't paying attention – the story doesn't make clear whether she made an error in calculating the day of Rosh Hodesh or whether a pauper asking for money at her door distracted her – Rabbi Eliezer did pray. She asked him to rise, saying: "You have killed my brother." He wanted to know how she knew Rabbi Gamliel was dead. She answered that the shofar had just been blown in town to make such an announcement.

Did she feel remorse for being distracted and allowing her husband to pray? The story doesn't say. There are only a few women who appear in the Talmud. Heruta is one; Bruria, the wife of Rabbi Meyer, is another. Imma Shalom is a superb if flawed character. You like her. In cases of *ona'ah*, women like her have a direct line to God. She has the capacity to prevent her husband's apparent revenge – since, it seems to me, Rabbi Eliezer senses that if he prayed, something bad would happen – but makes a mistake and, as a result, her brother dies.

"The Oven of Akhnai," now you know, is about a colossal political fight, one in which the two sides suffer enormous losses. In your view, the character who comes out the worst – petty, vengeful, intolerant – is God. Human affairs are always messy. We don't need God to complicate them even more.

Rabbis aren't saintly; they can be antagonistic and rancorous, like everyone else. In its essence, the story is about authority. To you it reads as an invaluable statement of the transition from prophetic to rabbinical Judaism, when biblical revelation ceased in favor of human consensus. This is an exploration of the tension between a single tyrannical form of government that is validated by heaven and a messy, fragile one we call democracy. Rabbi Eliezer represents the former; the Sages, the latter.

Why did you miss all this when you first read the story in Mexico? You failed to see how the story is also magical realist (a version of it could be part of *One Hundred Years of Solitude*), a vicious power struggle that could have helped you understand the drive for democratic change people were looking for. The Talmud was talking directly to *you*. But you yourself were peripheral. You preferred to enshrine the rabbinical debate you were studying in a mythical past.

As you read the story now, the COVID-19 pandemic – you're hunkered down at home – has forced millions into confinement. You're now in a state of heightened awareness. Worldwide the stakes are high. Obviously this rabbinical dispute is symbolic of the larger forces enwrapping you.

You live in the richest country in the world, yet the one most ravaged by the virus. More than two hundred thousand people have died. Millions are infected. Unemployment is high. Relief organizations aren't capable of helping those who are hungry. All this is happening while the bullying president of the nation you've chosen to live in, to which you immigrated, can't stop himself from engaging in *ona'at dvarim*, demeaning one opponent after another without regret.

Are you any wiser now? Perhaps just a bit but wisdom is like sand trickling through one's fingers. Truth is, we are always condemned to misinterpret the universe.

You've come to the realization that Akhnai's oven is a proxy for the destroyed Jerusalem temple. The *tanna'im* were engaging in this debate as they pondered why their temple had fallen. Was it a form of divine punishment, they wondered? It is the same type of response that developed in religious circles after the Shoah: Did it befall us, rabbis asked, because of our sins? Could it have been averted?

The Torah is not in heaven; but the Torah is from heaven.

The possibility exists, of course, that you're misinterpreting the story yet again. You are left with a sliver of hope as you read the last line of "The Oven of Akhnai": "All the heavenly gates are locked except for the gates through which prayers concerning *ona'ah* pass."

In other words, we cannot be pardoned – by others, by ourselves – unless we recognize that words are weapons. That they can be used not only to build the world but also to demolish it.

– *Dibur*, issue 9, Fall 2020

Contributors

Youssef Boucetta is a doctoral student in the Comparative Literary Studies Program at Northwestern University, with a home department in French and Francophone Studies.

Margaret Boyle is Associate Professor of Romance Languages and Literatures; Director of Latin American, Caribbean, and Latinx Studies Program at Bowdoin College; and author of *Unruly Women: Performance, Penitence, and Punishment in Early Modern Spain* (2014), among other books.

Priyanka Champaneri is a fellow at the Virginia Center for the Creative Arts and author of *The City of Good Death* (2021).

Peter Cole is Senior Lecturer in the Department of Judaic Studies and Comparative Literature at Yale University, translator of *The Dream of the Poem: Hebrew Poetry from Muslim and Christian Spain, 950–1492* (2007), and author of *Sacred Trash: The Lost and Found World of the Cairo Geniza* (2016, with Adina Hoffman), and *Hymns and Qualms: New and Selected Poems and Translations* (2017), among other books.

Robert Croll is the translator of Ricardo Piglia's three-volume *The Diaries of Emilio Renzi* (2017 to 2020) and *The Way Out* (2020), and of Javier Sinay's *The Murders of Moisés Ville* (2022), among other books.

Regina Galasso is Associate Professor in the Spanish and Portuguese Studies Program and Director of the Translation Center at the University of Massachusetts Amherst, author of *Translating New York: The City's Languages in Iberian Literatures* (2018), and editor of *This Is a Classic: Translators on Making Writers Global* (2023), among other books.

Contributors

Eduardo Halfon is the Guatemalan author of *The Polish Boxer* (2012), *Monastery (2014), Mourning (2018),* and *Canción* (2022), among other books.

Sara Khalili is a translator of contemporary Iranian literature, including Shahriar Mandanipour's novels *Censoring an Iranian Love Story* (2009), *Moon Brow* (2018), and *Seasons of Purgatory* (2022).

Steven G. Kellman is Professor of Comparative Literature at the University of Texas at San Antonio and author of *The Translingual Imagination (2000), Redemption: The Life of Henry Roth* (2005), *and The Restless Ilan Stavans: Outsider on the Inside* (2019), among other books.

Jhumpa Lahiri is Millicent C. McIntosh Professor of English and Director of the Creative Writing Program at Barnard College and author of *Interpreter of Maladies* (1999), *The Namesake* (2003), *The Lowland* (2013), and *In Other Word* (2017), among other books.

Josh Lambert is Sophia Moses Robison Associate Professor of Jewish Studies and English and author of *Unclean Lips: Obscenity, Jews, and American Culture* (2014) and *The Literary Mafia: Jews, Publishing, and Postwar American Literature* (2022), among other books.

Jenna Tang is the Taiwanese translator of Lin Yi-Han's novel, *Fang Si-Chi's First Love Paradise* (2024).

Haoran Tong, a poet from Beijing, China, is a graduate of Amherst College.

Max Ubelaker Andrade is Associate Teaching Professor in Latin American Studies at University of Massachusetts Lowell and author of *Borges beyond the Visible* (2019).

MªCarmen África Vidal Claramonte is Professor of Translation at the University of Salamanca and author of *Translating Borrowed Tongues: The Verbal Quest of Ilan Stavans* (2023) and *Translation and Repetition: Translating (Un)Original Literature* (also 2023), among other books.

Beruriah Wiegand is the Woolf Corob Lector in Yiddish at the University of Oxford and author of *Tsi hot ir gezen mayn tsig? – Have You Seen My Goat?* (2012) and *Kales-breyshis – Kalat Bereshit* (2018).

Index

Académie française, 68, 173, 210, 231
Accademia della Crusca, 68, 213
Adams, John, 36, 68–9, 74, 79, 80
adaptation, vs. translation, 151
Adler, Misha, 83, 84, 85, 86
Adler, Noemí, 84, 85, 86
Agnon, S.Y., 191, 271
Akhmatova, Anna, 57–8, 303
Alatorre, Antonio, *Los 1001 años de la lengua española*, 168, 196–7, 196n9
Alfau, Felipe, 14–15, 24, 318
  Chromos, 14, 15, 320
  Locos: A Comedy of Gestures, 14–15, 320
  Sentimental Songs: La poesía cursi, 14
Alfonso El Sabio, 93
Alfonso X "El Sabio," 170–1
Alonso, Amado, 194–5, 196
  Castellano, español, idioma nacional: Historia espiritual de tres nombres, 175
  Gramática castellana, 174
alphabets, 180
  Hebrew alphabet, 142, 281
  Latin alphabet, 281
alter egos, 122–8
Alzheimer's, 58–9, 129
American, definition of, 69–70
American Academy of Motion Picture Arts and Sciences, 44–5
"American century," 72, 74–5, 78

An American Dictionary of the English Language (Webster), 69, 182, 217, 235, 238
American English, 34–9, 64–81, 165–6, 235
American Indians. *See* Native Americans
Americanisms, 85, 211, 212, 236
American literature, 47–8
American studies, fallacy of, 35–49
Americas
  Spanish in, 210–11, 218, 238–9
  wars of independence in, 238
Amherst, Massachusetts, 3, 319, 320
Amherst College, 8–9, 38
Amr Mosque, 135, 136
Andrade, Max Ubelaker, 129–39
Antin, Mary, *The Promised Land*, 73–4
anti-Semitism, 50, 53, 55, 85, 86, 127, 213, 261
The Arabian Nights, 28, 34
Arabic, 24, 163, 170, 180, 201, 202, 211, 239, 292, 303
Arabic culture, 40, 170, 171, 180, 291
Aramaic, 25, 40, 307, 320, 332
Araujo, Blanca, *Educating across Borders: The Case of a Dual Language Program on the U.S.- Mexico Border*, 200–1
Arendt, Hannah, 86, 226

Argentina, 8, 95–6, 97, 147, 173, 174, 175, 188, 189, 239, 334
dictatorships in, 234
Italian immigrants in, 176
Jewish agricultural colonies in, 300–1
Spanish in, 188, 189, 190–1
Yiddish in, 29
Argentine Jewish literature, 29, 300–1
Arguedas, José María, *El zorro de arriba y el zorro de abajo*, 176
Aristotle, 93, 231, 270
Arizona, 67, 174
Asch, Sholem, 144–5
Ashkenazi Jews, 82, 140–7, 327
assimilation, 66, 200
 as conversion, 24
 education and, 76–7
 Yiddish and, 141
authenticity
 memes and, 263
 translation and, 273–4
authority, 337. *See also* linguistic authority
autobiography, 82–8
automatic translation machines, 80, 152
auto-traducción, 307–11. *See also* self-translation
Averroes, 180, 231
awareness
 COVID-19 pandemic and, 337–8
 political power and, 234–5
ayahuasca, 138, 157
Aztec culture, 33–4, 249

Babel, Isaac, 62, 319
"Babel Proclamation," 41
Baena, Juan Alfonso de, *Cancionero de Baena*, 171
Balderston, Daniel, 190, 191–2
Barcelona, 7, 9–10, 18
Barlow, Julie, 195, 195n5
Bartlett, John Russell, *Dictionary of Americanisms*, 236, 237

Bassnett, Susan, 16, 264
Baudot, George, 250–1, 252–4
Beckett, Samuel, 151, 156, 303
Behbahani, Simin, 292, 294–5
Bello, Andrés, 196, 238
 Gramática de la lengua castellana: Destinada al uso de los americanos, 167, 173–4, 210–11, 238–9
Bellow, Saul, 271
 translation of "Gimpel the Fool," 312–13
Benjamin, Walter, 5, 27–8, 86, 124, 319
Beowulf, 34
Berceo, Gonzalo d, 166
Berceo, Gonzalo de, 170–1
Bergelson, Dovid, *Descent*, 276
Berlin, Germany, 47, 86
the Bible, 29, 34, 42, 90, 165, 166, 180, 259, 297, 320–1. *See also specific books*
Biden, Joe, 261–2
Bierce, Ambrose, 62
 celebration of dictionaries by, 182–3
 The Devil's Dictionary, 70, 182
 "An Occurrence at Owl Creek Bridge," 182
bilingualism, 11, 77, 233
 of Barcelona, 9–10
 bilingual editions, 292
 bilingual education, 77
 bilingual writers, 278, 307
 in the US, 11, 307
Bishop, Elizabeth, 279, 305
Black people, 48
 Black diaspora, 73
 Black vernaculars, 236
 emancipated, 73
blindness, 129–39
Bolaño, Roberto, 233, 290
Bolívar, Simón, 238, 239
Bolivia, 29, 188
Bong Joon-ho, 44–5
books, 26–31. *See also* libraries
 book covers, 316

booksellers, 30
  collecting, 27
  as friends, 27
  Jewishness and, 26–7, 161–2
  picture books, 237–8
  rescuing, 30
Borges, Jorge Luis, 5, 29, 62, 123, 176, 190–2, 196, 268, 279, 319, 321
  "El Aleph," 134–7
  El Aleph, 190
  "The Analytical Language of John Wilkins," 184
  "The Argentine Writers and Tradition," 190
  "An Autobiographical Essay," 191
  "Averroes' Search," 93
  blindness of, 129–39, 303
  "Borges and I," 125, 175
  on colors, 130, 303
  "El concepto de la academia y los celtas," 133
  darkness in, 137
  dictionaries and, 184
  as director of Argentina's National Library, 130, 132
  encyclopedias and, 184
  English and, 190–2
  "El enigma de Shakespeare," 132
  "El escritor argentino y la tradición," 132
  "El hacedor," 138
  El hacedor, 137, 175
  "On His Blindness," 303
  El informe de Brodie, 138
  "La inmortalidad," 132
  Jews and, 134, 191
  lectures by, 130, 131, 132–4, 190, 303
  literary estate of, 132
  "Man on Pink Corner," 190–1
  "El milagro secreto," 137
  "El Otro" ("El Libro de Arena"), 97
  "Pierre Menard, autor del *Quijote*," 95–121, 238, 257, 321
  "Poema de los dones," 130–1
  as polyglot, 190
  polyphony and, 97–8
  "In Praise of Darkness," 137
  reading and, 129, 132
  register of, 97
  relativism and, 99
  "Las ruinas circulares," 138
  seeing and, 134–6, 137
  Selected Poems, 321
  self-translation and, 307
  Seven Nights, 132, 133
  Siete noches, 130
  "Spinoza," 190
  "Tlön, Uqbar, *Orbis Tertius*," 184, 190, 233
  as translator, 226
  universalism and, 99
  "Utopía de un hombre que está cansado," 137
  vision and, 134–6, 137
  writing and, 129, 132
  "Yo," 129
Boswell, James, 41, 165
Boucetta, Youssef, 14, 95–121
Bowdoin College, 236, 240
Boyle, Margaret, 3, 14, 17, 228–43
Bradbury, Ray, 80–1
Brazil, 29, 326
Brazilians, 30, 47
British English, 39, 65–6, 71, 74, 76, 165–6, 235
Buenos Aires, Argentina, 29, 97, 300–1, 334
Burton, Robert
  The Anatomy of Melancholy, 138–9
  One Thousand and One Nights, 304

Cabrera Infante, Guillermo, 176, 192, 307
Calderón de la Barca, Pedro, 47, 218
Calvino, Italo, 178, 179
Cancionero del Judino Juan Alfonso de Baena, 171

Cantar del Mío Cid, 171
capitalism, 43–4
Caribbean Spanish, 174, 198, 199
Carolino, Pedro, 42–4, 66
Caro Tobar, Miguel Antonio, 196
Carroll, Lewis, *Alice's Adventures in Wonderland*, 206
casa, concept of, 314–15
Casteidish, 29, 188, 300–1
Castile, Spain, 168, 170, 172
Castilian, 170–1, 175, 196, 212
Catalan, 18, 318, 320
  as language of resistance, 18
  Spanish and, 9, 10, 18
  translation of *Don Quijote* into, 8
Catholic Church, 65, 85, 166, 170, 212, 213
Celan, Paul, 58, 303
censorship, 41, 92, 219, 292
center, vs. Periphery, 44, 47, 134
Cervantes, Miguel de, 181, 212, 218
  Battle of Lepanto and, 130
  as creator of words, 180
  Don Quixote of La Mancha, 3, 7–8, 18, 29, 40, 56–7, 89, 91, 95–9, 130, 138–9, 164, 166, 172, 180, 191–2, 213, 219–20, 232, 240, 256, 279, 292–3, 298, 321
  La Galatea, 219
  Martorell and, 18
  Voyage to Parnassus, 219
Champaneri, Priyanka, 14, 56–63, 92
Chaucer, Geoffrey
  Canterbury Tales, 6, 65
  translation of Petrarch's Sonnet #132, 287–8
Chekhov, Anton, 48, 303
Chen Yang, 32–3, 34
Cherokee, 69
Chesterman, Andrew, 256–7
children
  Indigenous, 76
  picture books and, 237–8
Chile, 29, 82, 87, 175, 234, 239

China, 33, 47
Chinese, 24, 42, 48, 78, 188, 203, 204
  graphic quality of, 33–4, 206
  translation from, 32–4
Chinese astrology, 33
Chinese culture, 33
Chinese literature, 33, 204, 205
Chinese mythology, 33
Chinese poetry, 204, 205, 206
Chinglish, 203
Christian Nationalism, 40, 41–2
Civil War, 71, 72
class, 45, 46
classics, literary, 95, 298, 321
  change over time, 93
  definition of, 89, 322
  future of classics in translation, 93–4
  modernizations of, 322
  rereading, 321–2
  rethinking, 89–94
  retranslation of, 150
  translation and, 89, 93–4, 150, 322
  undiscovered, 4
close reading, 321
code switching, 54
Cole, Peter, 14, 155–8
collaboration, 13–14, 277, 317
  reading and, 132
  translation and, 91, 151, 295–6, 299, 305
  writing and, 132
collectivism, vs. individualism, 24–5
Colombia, 8, 82, 84, 87, 173, 188, 239, 334
colonialism, 65, 69, 171, 196, 207, 334
communications, 72–3, 80
Comprehensive Aramaic Lexicon Project, 40
Comprehensive English-Yiddish Dictionary, 276
conquistadores, 172–3, 176
context, translation and, 5
conversion, 24, 52
conversos, 212, 234
copyright, 92

Corominas, Joan, *Diccionario critico etimológico de la lengua castellana*, 166, 175–6
Cortázar, Julio, 189, 334
 "Axólotl," 234
cosmopolitanism, 48–9, 80, 83, 85, 182
Covarrubias y Orozco, Sebastián de, 212–13, 218
 Tesoro de la lengua castellana o española, 29, 40–1, 166, 172, 180, 213, 239–40
COVID-19 pandemic, 3, 30, 92, 130, 228–43, 256, 266–7, 273, 302, 310, 337–8
 dreams during, 323–4
 immigrants and, 323–7
 impact on language, 17
 internet and, 260–1
crisis, language in, 228–35
Croll, Robert, 14, 148–54
crypto-Judaism/crypto-Jews, 30, 234
Cuba, 29, 72, 174, 198, 200
culture, translation and, 92–3

Da Fonseca, José, 66. *See also* Carolino, Pedro
Dante Alighieri, 33, 90, 132, 269
Darío, Rubén, 62, 174, 196, 321, 334
Davis, Dick, 293, 294
death, 279–80
 idea of "good," 56–63
 memory and, 60–1
 preservation of the dead, 60
 sleep and, 59–60
 translation and, 57–8
decidophobia, 203–8
De la Piedra, María Teresa, 200–1
democracy, 67–8, 73, 331, 337
De Tocqueville, Alexis, 23, 67–8
dialects, 46, 163, 176, 179
diaspora
 Black diaspora, 73
 Jewish, 326, 327
 of Latinos in the US, 42

Diccionario Clave, 176
Diccionario de anglicismos del español estadounidense (Moreno Fernández), 196
Diccionario de autoridades (RAE), 173–4, 181, 209–20
Diccionario de la lengua española (RAE), 167, 173, 190, 192, 209, 220, 241
Diccionario del uso del español (Moliner), 176, 209, 241
Diccionario panhispánico de dudas (*DPD*), 192–3
Dickinson, Emily, 24, 48, 64, 74, 182, 279, 319
dictatorships, 92, 127, 234, 292
dictionaries, 3, 5, 17, 29, 36–41, 48–9, 70, 181, 184, 189, 192, 209–20, 225. *See also specific dictionaries*
 based in cities, 49
 bilingual, 166, 241–2
 Borges and, 184
 celebration of, 182–3
 as communities, 230, 240–1
 conception of, 181
 as confidants, 235–43
 dialects and, 179
 history of, 167
 how they define us, 228–43
 linguistic authority and, 79–80, 230
 as literature, 178–87
 as narrative, 178
 nationalism and, 179, 238–9
 as nation-building machines, 179
 as natural history, 235–43
 paratexts of, 179
 proliferation of in the twentieth century, 175–6
 reading, 179
 slang and, 179
 in *Spanglish: The Making of a New American Language*, 164
 as symbol of amalgamation, 179
 vs. thesauruses, 237

dictionaries (cont.)
  translators and, 276–7
  treachery of, 276
Dictionarium ex hispaniense in latinum sermonem (Nebrija), 212
Dictionary of American Regional English, 49
Dictionary of Modern American Usage (Garner), 70
Dictionary of the American Language (Webster), 37, 38–9
Diderot, Denis, 181, 182
Didion, Joan, 60–1
Dominican Republic, 47, 174, 234
dreams, during COVID-19 pandemic, 323–4
Dutch, 40, 65, 236, 242, 280, 307

Eco, Umberto, 186, 270
  On Beauty, 186
  The Name of the Rose, 186, 270
  Serendipities: Language and Lunacy, 186
  On Ugliness, 186
Editorial Gredos, 210
Editorial Porrúa, 268
education
  assimilation and, 76–7
  bilingual, 77, 200
  immigrants and, 200
  standardization of language and, 65–6
Einstein, Albert, 74–5
Eliot, T.S., 163, 179, 183
Ellis Island, 47, 67
Emami, Karim, 289–90
Emerson, Ralph Waldo, 49, 182, 320
emotions, 231–2
encyclopedias, 181, 184, 186, 233
Encyclopédistes, 181, 213–14
English, 2–4, 29, 316
  Alfau and, 14–15, 320
  American, 34–9, 64–81, 165–6, 235

  Americanization of, 65–6
  ascent of, 201–2
  Borges and, 190–2
  British, 39, 65–6, 71, 74, 76, 165–6, 235
  capitalism and, 43–4
  Caribbean, 49
  dominance of, 24, 46, 142, 197
  French and, 217–18
  Gallicisms in, 217
  globalization of, 66, 78, 197, 201
  historical roots of, 71
  lexicography and, 37–9, 167, 235–8, 242
  as lingua franca, 78
  linguistic authority and, 231
  monopolistic and oppressive control the culture, 48
  as non-native language, 42, 45, 188
  as official language of US, 35, 67, 76–7
  Pessoa and, 126, 127
  precision of, 206
  self-translation and, 279–80
  of Shakespeare, 322
  as social medium, 46
  South African, 49
  Spanglish and, 163–4, 176–7, 188–9, 203, 206, 272, 307–11
  Spanish and, 163–4, 197–200, 202, 307–11
  syntax of, 273
  thesauruses and, 237
  translations into, 83–4, 97, 205, 289–99
  variants of, 49 (*see also specific variants*)
  Yiddish and, 74
English-language studies, 48–9
English-only/English first movements, 41–2, 77
Enlightenment, 37, 167, 181, 209, 220. See also *Haskalah* (Jewish Enlightenment)

Esperanto, 35, 47, 49, 84
Esquinca, Alberto, 200–1
etymologies, 76, 211, 216, 218, 220, 257
Europe, 28–9
   colonialism and, 23, 33–4
   Muslim translators and, 92–3
   pre-Columbian languages and, 33–4
exile, 23. *See also* migrants; refugees

Farrokhzad, Forough, 289–99
fascism, 126, 127
Faulkner, William, 48, 62, 226
Federalist Papers, 64
Felipe V, King, 181, 210
Ferdinand, King, 36, 168
film, 44–5, 75, 277. *See also* adaptation; specific films
Flaubert, Gustave, 180, 190, 295
   Bouvard et Pécuchet, 182
   Le dictionnaire des idees recues, 182
   Madame Bovary, 95, 322
Florida, 77, 200, 219, 326
Florio, John, 276, 304
Fondo de Cultura Económica, 132, 307–8
food, Yiddish and, 145–6
form, change of, 279–80
Forverts, 145
Founding Fathers, 64, 65, 67, 76, 78, 80
France, 180, 210, 213–14, 219, 324, 326, 327
Franglais, 163, 203
Frank, Eve, 53–4
Frank, Jacob, 50, 53–5
Frankists, 50, 52, 53, 54–5
freedom. *See* liberation
French, 2, 29, 36, 45, 49, 71, 142, 216, 280, 307
   Americanisms and, 236
   Borges and, 190
   dictionaries of synonyms and, 237
   English and, 217–18
   Founding Fathers and, 65, 68
   Franglais and, 163, 203
   Frespañol and, 170, 188
   Gallicisms, 217–18
   globalization and, 96
   language academies and, 68, 173, 188, 210, 231
   lexicography and, 239, 242
   Lomnitz and, 83
   Pessoa and, 126, 127
   Spanish and, 202, 217–18
   translation of Borges' "Pierre Menard, autor del *Quijote*" into, 95–8
   translation(s) of, 197
Frespañol, 170, 188
Freud, Sigmund, 84, 125
Frost, Robert, 23, 289, 319
Fuentes, Carlos, 184, 211, 268

Gaelic, 24, 67
Galasso, Regina, 7, 11
   translation as home and, 316–22
   translation of "La casa pairal," 18, 314–15
Gallicisms, 217–18
Gamliel, 336–7
García Lorca, Federico, 175, 318
García Márquez, Gabriel, 29, 62, 166, 189, 192, 239, 241, 268, 334
   Moliner and, 176
   One Hundred Years of Solitude, 172, 176, 184–5, 306, 333, 337
Garner, Bryan A., *A Dictionary of Modern American Usage*, 70
gauchos, 174, 191
Gaudí i Cornet, Antoni, 18
   "La casa pairal," 18, 314–15
   El manuscrit de Reus, 18
Geisel, Theodor Seuss (Dr. Seuss), 75
gender, 45, 92
   gendered language, 45–6, 80, 201
   gender-neutral language, 232–3
   gender pronouns, 45
   in German, 45
   Latin and, 80
   in Romance languages, 45, 232–3

348 Index

Genesis, 42, 90
Genizahs, 26–7, 28–9, 30–1
genocide, languages and, 35
Gentzler, Edwin, 16, 255, 264
German, 4, 29, 48, 49, 54, 65, 83, 97, 142, 190, 218, 303
  capitalism and, 44
  gender in, 45
  literature, 275
  Spanish and, 202
  translation and, 197, 280–1
  in the US, 35–6, 41, 74, 236, 237
Germanic languages, 71, 142
Germany, 47, 85, 219
ghazals, 294–5
Glosas Emlianenses, 170
Glosas Silenses, 170
glossaries, 179, 181
glosses, 170
Goethe, Johann Wolfgang von, 139, 293, 294
Góngora, Luis de, 172, 181, 210, 218
Google Translate, 80, 233
Gramática de la lengua castellana (Nebrija), 171, 177, 239
grammar
  changes to, 80
  teaching of, 76
graphic artists, 146–7
graphic novels, 277
Great Britain, 39, 219. *See also* British English
Greek, 49, 65, 68, 96, 239, 242, 255, 307
Greenberg, Eliezar
  Ashes Out of Hope: Fiction by Soviet-Yiddish Writers, 141
  A Treasury of Yiddish Stories, 140–1, 312
Grimm, Brothers, *Deutsches Worterbuch*, 37
Groussac, Paul, 130
Gua de Malves, Juan Paul de, *Cyclopaedia*, 214
Guatemala, 34, 326

Gullaf, Ferreira, 303, 305
Gurvich, José, 316, 317
Gurvich, José (Zusmanas Gurvicius), 318
Guterres, António, 260–1

Hafez (Khwāja Shams-ud-Dīn Muḥammad Ḥāfeẓ-e Shīrāzī), 293, 294
halakha, 333, 334–6
Halfon, Eduardo, 3, 14, 323–7, 324, 326
Hampshire College, 48. *See also* Yiddish Book Center
Han Shaogong, *A Dictionary of Maqiao*, 186
Harding, William L., 77
  "Babel Proclamation," 41
Harshav, Barbara, 141, 271
Harshav, Benjamin, 141, 271
Harvard University, Longfellow Institute, 48
Hasidism, 50–1, 272
Haskalah (Jewish Enlightenment), 53, 83
hate speech, 260–1
Hawthorne, Nathaniel, 48, 320
Hayakawa, Samuel Ichiye, 76–7
Hebrew, 25, 29, 36, 307, 312, 320
  Agnon and, 271
  biblical, 65, 164
  Borges and, 190
  expressing possessiveness in, 44
  gender in, 45
  Hebrew alphabet, 142, 281
  Hebreya and, 163
  Israel and, 141
  letters of, 136
  lexicography and, 211, 239, 242
  Lomnitz and, 83, 84
  Moykher-Sforim and, 278
  personal experience with, 3, 4, 203, 205, 280
  poetry, 180
  reading right to left in, 54
  translations from, 316
  Zionism and, 164

Heine, Heinrich, 151, 271
Henríquez Ureña, Pedro, 168, 174, 196
Herbert D. Katz Center, University
   of Pennsylvania, acquisition of
   personal library by, 30–1
"heritage speakers," 11
hermeneutics, 165
Hernández, José, 174, 176
heteroglossia, 261, 280
heteronomia, 261
heteronymous works, 122, 123
Hinduism, 60, 62
Hispania, 169–70, 171
Hispanophones. *See* Spanish speakers
H.Leyvik-farag, 274, 278
Holocaust, 142, 338
home
   concept of, 314–15
   immigrants and, 23
Homer, 34, 131, 138, 169
hope, 35–6
Hornby, A.S., *Learner's Dictionary of
   Current English*, 241
Howe, Irving, 318
   *Ashes Out of Hope: Fiction by Soviet-
      Yiddish Writers*, 141
   *The Penguin Book of Modern Yiddish
      Verse*, 141
   A Treasury of Yiddish Stories, 140–1, 312

Iberian Peninsula, 169–70, 172, 211,
   218, 238. *See also* Portugal; Spain
The Idler, 165
illustrations, 89, 313, 316
illustrators, 6, 316
immigrants, 23–5, 35, 39, 41, 66, 67, 73,
   75, 260–1, 310
   Central American, 34
   COVID-19 pandemic and, 323–7
   education and, 200
   English as "a second language"
      and, 45
   German, 237
   home and, 23

Immigrant Writing Workshops, 92
   indicating health of a language, 24
   Italian, 74, 176
   Jewish, 142–5
      from Latin America, 31
   Lebanese, 331, 334, 335
   in Mexico, 331
   "nations of," 47
   in New York City, 317–18, 319
immigrant writers, 24
immigration, 2, 23–5, 225, 316–17
imperialism, 65, 153–4
Incas, 33–4
independent publishers, 90–1, 92, 126,
   127, 299
Indiana University Press, 276
Indigenous children, relocation and
   "Americanization" of, 76
Indigenous languages, 173, 236,
   247–54. *See also specific languages*
Indigenous peoples, 23, 33–4, 83, 85.
   See also specific groups
Indigenous vernaculars, 236
individualism, 24–5, 74, 306
industrial revolution, 72–3
inglañol, 311
injustice, languages and, 46
Inquisition, 172, 212, 217, 219, 234
intermediality, 259–60
interpretation, translation and, 99
interpreters, 13, 152
Iran, 289–99
Iranian literature, 289–99, 294–5
Iroquois, 69
Isabella, Queen, 36, 168, 239
Islam, 52, 92–3
Israel, 28–9, 30, 36, 86, 141, 164, 307
Israel ben Eliezer (Baal Shem Tov),
   50–1
Italian, 24, 45, 67, 68, 74, 142, 170, 216,
   218, 239
   dictionaries of synonyms and, 237
   lexicography and, 242
   translation(s) of, 197

Italian immigrants, 176, 334
Italy, 210
   during COVID-19 pandemic, 323, 324, 325, 326
   immigrants from, 73

Las Jarchas, 170
Jefferson, Thomas, 68, 80
Jewish cuisine, 145–6
Jewish cultures, 2, 82, 90
Jewish emancipation, 53
Jewish history, 86
Jewish immigrants, 327, 334
Jewish languages, 273, 275. *See also specific languages*
Jewish messianism, 50
Jewish mysticism, 50, 132, 136. *See also* Kabbalah
Jewishness, 5, 6, 85, 90, 309
   books and, 161–2
   in the Hispanic world, 29
   language(s) and, 5
   literacy and, 161–2
   translation and, 157
Jewish scholarship, 25
Jewish writers, 318
Jews, 35, 48, 171
   American, 273
   Ashkenazi, 140–7, 327
   Borges and, 134
   Covarrubias and, 40
   expelled from Spain, 29, 141, 171
   Latin American, 30, 31, 82–8, 300–1
   Latino, 29, 309
   Mizrahi, 141–2, 327, 331, 334, 335
   persecution in Spain, 212
   Sephardic, 141, 327
   Yiddish and, 140–7
John, Nicholas, *The Age of Sharing*, 257–8
Johnson, Samuel, 29, 37–8, 41, 69, 165, 167, 186, 239
   appearance in Thackeray's *Vanity Fair*, 181–2
   definitions of language, 235–6
   A Dictionary of the English Language, 38–9, 165, 181, 217, 235, 236
Joyce, James, 131, 162
Juana Inés de la Cruz, Sor, 172, 211, 279, 303, 321
   "Allegoric Neptune," 247
   Carta Atenagórica, 211
   coplas castellanas by, 247–8
   décimas by, 248–9
   Dísticos, 247
   "La fiesta de la Asunción," 249–51
   "La fiesta de San Pedro Nolasco," 249, 251–2
   Nahuatl and, 247–54
   Obras Completas, 248
   Respuesta a Sor Filotea, 211, 247
   tocotines by, 249–54
   translation and, 247–54
Judaica, 85
Judaism, 86–7
   books in, 26–7
   Hasidism, 50–1
   High Holidays, 59
   Passover, 59
   transition from prophetic to rabbinical, 337
Judeo-Arabic, 141–2, 273
Judeo-French, 273
Judeo-Italian, 273, 275
Judeo-Persian, 273, 275
Judeo-Portuguese, 275
Judeo-Spanish. *See* Ladino
Juster, Norton, 184, 320

Kabbalah, 50, 132, 136, 191
Kaddish, 280, 281
Kafka, Franz, 28, 89, 191, 269, 331
Katz, Jevel, 29, 300–1
Kellman, Steven G., 4–5, 14, 35–49
   The Restless Ilan Stavans: Outsider on the Inside, 15
   The Translingual Imagination, 15
Khalili, Sara, 14, 289–99

Kharanauli, 303, 305
kibbutzim, 86
K'iche,' 6, 29, 32, 33–4
Knesset, 86
knowledge, 167, 168, 179, 181
Kodama, María, 132, 138

Ladino, 4, 29, 54, 141, 165, 176, 273, 275
Lahiri, Jhumpa, 3, 14, 24, 323–7
La Jornada, 87
Lane, Edward William, *Arabian Nights*, 297
language academies, 68–9, 189–90. *See also specific academies*
language channels, 75
language(s), 2, 3, 24, 48
 "anchor language," 206
 appropriation and, 207
 change and, 45–6, 80, 98, 149, 165–6, 168–77, 202, 235, 242–3
 as character, 64–81
 class and, 45, 46
 colonialism and, 65
 convergence of, 203–4, 205
 in crisis, 228–35
 cultural approaches to, 237–8
 democracy and, 67–8
 vs. dialects, 163
 dominant, 203, 204, 207
 enriched by translators, 280–1
 gender and, 45–6
 genocide and, 35
 global community, 48
 global maritime, 65
 graphic, 260
 hieroglyphic, 260
 hybrid, 73–4, 163, 176–7, 188, 200, 203–4, 206, 272, 310–11, 321 (*see also specific hybrids*)
 impact of COVID-19 on, 17
 imperialism and, 65
 Indigenous, 65, 69, 173, 247–54 (*see also specific languages*)
 injustice and, 46
 as instrument of oppression, 47
 Jewish, 271–83 (*see also specific languages*)
 Jewishness and, 5
 Johnson's definition of, 235–6
 learning, 149
 legitimizing "misuse" of, 207–8
 linguistic authority, 69, 78, 79–80, 173–4, 189–90, 201, 230, 231
 linguistic centralization, 210
 linguistic chauvinism, 35, 36, 40–1, 43–4, 49
 linguistic confusion, 205
 linguistic differences, 47
 linguistic pollution, 71
 linguistic purity, 309
 linguistic xenophobia, 41–2, 77
 love for, 12
 media and, 189
 minor, 161–77
 minority, 46, 92
 "mongrel" jargons, 46–7
 mysticism and, 136
 nationalism and, 235–6
 nationality and, 45–6
 native vs. non-native, 149–50, 207
 "non-native" vs. "native" labels, 11
 official, 35
 Paleolithic, 260
 peace and, 35, 47
 politics and, 234, 239
 power and, 36, 234, 304
 race and, 45
 resistance and, 207
 second, 149–50
 slavery and, 71–2
 social media and, 46
 standardization of, 65, 161, 239
 status of foreign languages in the US, 41
 study of, 162
 target, 257
 thought and, 203
 tolerance for, 36

352 Index

language(s) (*cont.*)
  translating unfamiliar, 151, 226,
    302–6
  truth and, 205, 234
  of tyrants, 234
  visuality and, 33–4
  words as weapons, 338
Lansky, Aaron, 30, 143–4
Latin, 122, 142, 198, 211, 216, 231,
  239, 307
  Borges and, 190
  Founding Fathers and, 65, 68
  gender and, 80
  Latin alphabet, 281
  lexicography and, 242
  personal experience with, 3
  in Sor Juana, 247–9
  Spanish and, 168, 169, 170, 202
  Vulgar, 170
Latin America, 28–9, 36, 95–6
  history of, 82
  immigrants from, 31
  modernity in, 334
  Nazis in, 29–30
  Spanish speakers in, 166
  Yiddish in, 300–1
Latin American Jews, 30, 31, 82–8,
  300–1
Latin American literature, 29, 174–5, 309
Latin American Literature Today
  (LALT), 18
Latin Americanness, 85
Latin American writers, 134
Latino culture, 97
Latino identity, 163, 309
Latino Jews, 29, 309
Latino literature, 14–15, 309
Latino philology, 161–77
Latinos, 48, 233, 307, 309–10
  assimilation and, 200
  population of, 42
Latino studies, 167
Latino writers, 14–15, 309
Latinx, 45, 80, 233

Lazarillo de Tormes, 219
Lazarus, Emma, 23, 41, 67, 151
Learner's Dictionary of Current English
  (Hornby), 241
Lebanese immigrants, 331, 334, 335
Leguía, Augusto B., 84, 85
lexicographers, 235–43
lexicography, 37–9, 41, 49, 189, 213,
  220, 231, 234, 235–43, 289. *See also*
  dictionaries
  English and, 167
  linguistic chauvinism and, 40–1
  literature and, 178–87
  nationalism and, 40–1, 238–9
  nation-building, 70
  Spanish and, 167, 212
  truth and, 234
Lexicon hoc est Dictionarium ex sermone
  latino in hispaniensem (Nebrija), 212
liberation, translation as, 150, 157,
  303–4, 312
libraries, 26–31
  acquisitions of, 30–1
  personal, 26–31, 166
Libro de Alexandre, 170
Lida de Malkiel, María Rosa, 168, 195
Lingua Franca, 165
literacy, Jewishness and, 161–2
literature
  censorship and, 292
  dying and, 56–63
  lexicography and, 178–87
  literary artifacts, 27
  literary classics (*see* classics)
  in translation, 289–99
  traveling through translation, 32–4
Little, Brown and Company, 236, 237
"lolspeak," 259
Lomnitz, Claudio, 82–8
  Death and the Idea of Mexico, 87
  My Family in the Vertigo of
    Translation, 83
  Nuestra América, 82–8
Lopez, George, 75, 181

Los Angeles Review of Books, 319
Lozano, Rosina, 198–200
Lugones, Leopoldo, 174, 176, 334
Lunfardo, 176, 188

Macfarlane, Robert, *The Lost Words*, 238
machine translation, 80, 152
magical realism, 333–4, 337
Maimonides, 25, 179, 231
Maitland, Sarah, 255, 256, 265
Mandanipour, Shahriar, 291
   Censoring an Iranian Story, 296
   Moon Brow, 295–6, 297
Manifest Destiny, 23, 47
Mariátegui, José Carlos, 83, 84, 85
marranos, 29, 171, 234
Martí, José, 174, 318, 334
   "Dos patrias," 156
   "Nuestra América," 82
Marx, Karl, 44, 86
Massachusetts, 65, 67
Massachusetts Review, 319
Mayas, 33–4, 173
   Mayan culture, 33
   Mayan mythology, 33
   possible Asian roots of, 34
media, 189, 197. *See also* social media
Melville, Herman, 41, 48, 320
meme metaphor, 256–7
memes, 255–67
memoir, 82–8
memory, 60–1
Mencken, H.L., 24, 74, 199, 199n11
Menéndez Pidal, Ramón, 194, 195
Merriam-Webster, 17, 36, 38, 48, 49, 70, 79, 80, 167, 180, 186, 228
messianism, 28, 50–5
mestizaje, 172, 188–9, 201, 310–11
Mexican Americans, 77, 199, 200. *See also* Latinos
Mexican-American War, 174, 199
Mexican literature, 247–54, 309
Mexico, 8, 30, 42, 82, 87, 173, 175, 188, 189, 204, 213, 228, 333, 334

Alte Yidishe Shule in, 272
communion with the dead in, 59
democracy in, 331
growing up in, 268
immigrants in, 331
independence movement in, 220
modernity in, 331
PRI in, 277, 331
reading Talmud in, 3, 331–8
United States and, 174, 199, 201
Yiddish in, 318
Mexico City, 3, 87, 125, 326, 331
Middle Eastern literature, 289–99
migrants, 16–17, 260–1. *See also* immigrants; immigration; refugees
migration, 309
   internal, 69
   Spanish and, 176
   translation(s) and, 157
minority cultures and language(s), 46, 92
Minsheu, John, 241–2
mirhab, 136–7
mistranslation, 42–4, 153, 275, 305
Mizrahi Jews, 141–2, 331, 334, 335
modernism, 123–4, 179
modernismo, 174, 303, 334
modernity, 96, 220, 331, 334
Modern Language Association, 276
Moisés Ville, 300–1
Moliner, María, 166, 192, 239, 241
   Diccionario del uso del español actual, 176, 209, 241
"mongrel" jargons, 46–7
monolingualism, 11, 41–2, 207
Montaigne, Michel de, 180, 276, 304
Montevideo, Uruguay, 318, 334
Moreno Fernández, Francisco, 195–6, 199–200
   Diccionario de anglicismos del español estadounidense, 196
   La maravillosa historia del espanol, 196

multiculturalism, 15, 76–7
multilingualism, 4–5, 11, 45–6, 83–4, 126, 179, 203–8, 280, 320. *See also* bilingualism; translingualism
   of Founding Fathers, 65
   Jewish, 5
   in New York City, 163, 203–4, 317–18
   translation and, 10
   writing and, 14–15
multimodality, 259–60, 261, 263–5
multinational corporations, 44, 45
Murray, James, 39, 182
My Mexican Shivah, 277
mysticism, 50–1
   Jewish, 50, 132, 136 (*see also* Kabbalah)
   language(s) and, 136
mythology, 32–3

Nabokov, Vladimir, 24, 294, 307
Nadeau, Jean-Benoît, 195, 195n5
Nahuatl, 3, 173, 247–54
narrative, 162, 169, 184
   collective, 32
   dictionaries as, 178
   philosophy and, 182
nationalism, 40
   Christian Nationalism, 40, 41–2
   dictionaries and, 179, 238–9
   film and, 44–5
   language(s) and, 235–6
   lexicography and, 40–1, 238–9
   messianism and, 55
   Spanish and, 238–9
nationality, languages and, 45–6
   (*see also* nationalism)
National Public Radio, 4, 90
Native Americans, 23, 41, 47, 48. *See also specific groups*
   forced migration of, 69
   names of, 71
   relocation and "Americanization" of children, 76

Navajo, 48
Nazis, former, 29–30
Nazism, 35, 55, 85, 126
Nebrija, Antonio de, 212–13, 218
   Dictionarium ex hispaniense in latinum sermonem, 212
   Gramática de la lengua castellana, 171, 177, 239
   Lexicon hoc est Dictionarium ex sermone latino in hispaniensem, 212
Nergaard, Siri, 16, 264
Neruda, Pablo, 29, 86, 220, 268, 319
   Canto General, 175
   "Ode to the Dictionary," 158, 185, 221–4
   The Poetry of Pablo Neruda, 321
Nervo, Amado, 303, 334
The New England Primer, 65–6
New England Review, 293
New England settlers, 64–6
New English Dictionary, 178–9
New Mexico, 174, 199
newspapers, 27, 236, 241
New York City, 3, 14, 28, 29, 272, 307
   convergence of languages in, 163, 203–4, 317–18
   demographics of, 73
   García Lorca in, 319
   immigrants in, 317–18, 319
   as "lettered city," 317–18
   Spangish in, 164
   Yiddish and, 318
The New Yorker, 70, 79
New York Times, 78, 79, 238
New York Times en Español, 200–1
Nezikim, 332
Nimoy, Leonard, 44, 75, 146
Nueva España, 249. *See also* Mexico
Nuyoricans, 200, 309–10

Olisipo, 126, 127
Los olvidados, 331
ona'at dvarim, 333, 338
oral tradition, 32, 169

originality, 95, 150
originals, 11–12, 304. *See also* source texts
   exoticization of, 153–4
   modernization of, 322
   reduction of, 153
   "second original," 308, 310
   third original, 310
   translations better than, 320
Ormsby, John, 8, 96, 97
Ortiz, Fernando, 168, 174
Orwell, George, 183–4
Oscars, 44–5
outsiders, 5, 23, 25
"The Oven of Akhnai," 331–2, 333, 334–7, 338
Ovid, 219, 276
Oxford Classics, 91
Oxford English Dictionary (OED), 29, 38, 39, 40, 70, 79, 161, 167, 182, 183, 186, 213, 232, 237, 276
Oxford Junior Dictionary, 238
Oxford School of Rare Jewish Languages, 273

Pakn Treger (*The Book Peddler*), 144
Pale of Settlement, 53, 82, 157
pampas, 29, 174, 191
Parasite, 44–5
Partisan Review, 312
Pavić, Milorad, 185, 186, 233
Paz, Octavio, 125, 175, 211, 303
PEN, 289–90
Penguin Classics, 91, 321
Penny, Ralph, 195, 195n7
Peretz, I.L., 141, 272
periphery, vs. center, 44, 47, 134
Persian, 49, 289, 291–2, 293, 294
Persian literature, 289–99
Peru, 82, 83, 84–5, 87, 213, 219
Peruvian Jewish literature, 29
Pessoa, Fernando, 122–8
   anti-Semitism and, 126, 127
   biography of, 122–8

   The Book of Disquiet, 123, 127
   death of, 128
   fascism and, 126, 127
   heteronyms of, 227
   The Interregnum, 127
   Mensagem, 123, 127–8
   modernism and, 123–4
   "The Mommy," 127
   multilingualism of, 126
   occultism and, 126–7
   pseudonyms of, 123, 126
   translations of, 127–8
Petrarch, Sonnet #132, 287–8
Pharies, David, 195, 195–6n8
Philippines, 174, 198, 199
philology, 195
   Arabic, 180
   on becoming a philologist, 161–7
   English, 165–6
   Latino, 161–77
   politics and, 239
   Spanish, 166
philosophy
   Arabic, 180
   narrative and, 182
picture books, 237–8
pidgin, 74
Pitt Poetry Series, 4
Plato, 267, 272
poetry, 304
   Chinese, 204, 205
   translation of, 155–8, 295
   translingual, 204, 205–7
   untranslatable, 293–4
Pokagon Band of Potawatomis, 69
Poland, 50, 55, 327
Polish, 4, 29, 54, 74, 307
political power, awareness and, 234–5
Popol Vuh, 6
   reading in Chinese, 32–4
   retelling of, 6
popular culture, 32–3
Portugal, 124–5, 126

356 Index

Portuguese, 2, 4, 42–3, 122–8, 206, 303
  dictionaries of synonyms and, 237
  gender in, 45
  history of, 170
  imperialism and, 65
  lexicography and, 242
  Portuñol and, 163, 188
Portuñol, 163, 188
Potawatomi, 69
Pound, Ezra, 183, 184
power, language(s) and, 36, 304
pre-Columbian language(s), 33–4.
  See also Indigenous languages;
  specific languages
PRI, 277, 331
profanity, 75, 79–80
The Professor and the Madman, 167, 237
The Protocols of the Elders of Zion, 127
provinciality, 47–9
pseudonymous works, 122, 123
publishers, 27–8, 90–1, 92, 126, 127,
  298–9
publishing, 90–1, 92, 298–9
Puerto Rican Spanish, 309–10
Puerto Rico, 72, 174, 198, 199, 200
Puritan religious manuals, 23
Pushkin, Alexander, 154, 293, 294

quarantine, 323–7
Quechua, 173
queer rights, 260
Queiroz, Ophelia, 126
Quevedo, Francisco de, 172, 181, 218, 321
Q'uq'umatz (Great Feathered
  Serpent), 33

Rabassa, Gregory, 12, 306
racial slurs, 75, 260
Rafael, Vicente L., 197–8, 197n10
The Rambler, 165
readership, 282, 322
reading
  Borges and, 129, 132
  close reading, 321
  collaboration and, 132
  myopic, 321
  as an outsider, 5
  Popol Vuh in Chinese, 32–4
  translation and, 153
Real Academia Española (RAE), 7, 9,
  68, 166–7, 173, 189–90, 193, 210
  Diccionario de Autoridades, 173–4,
    181, 209–20
  Diccionario de la Lengua Española, 92,
    167, 173, 190, 209, 220, 241
lo real maravilloso, 333–4
La Reconquista, 171
recreations, 277–8, 297
Reed, Joseph W. Jr., 38–9
refugees, 260–1, 310
register, 308, 313
reinvention, 23, 308
Reis, Ricardo, 123, 126
religious texts, translation of, 299
Renaissance, 179, 219, 231
Repertorio Hebreo, 84
rereading, 4, 321–2
re-semiotization, 258–9
Restless Books, 4, 13–14, 90, 91–2, 154,
  290, 291
  The Face series, 92
  Immigrant Writing Workshops, 92
  Prize for Immigrant Writing, 92
  Prize for New Immigrant
    Writing, 4
  Shakespeare and, 94
Restless Classics, 4, 90, 91–2
retranslation, 95–121, 150, 263
Review of Contemporary Fiction, 14
rewriting, 6, 277–8, 279
Reyes, Alfonso, 168, 196
Romance languages, 45, 80, 142, 170,
  201, 232–3
Roman Empire, 169–70, 171, 218
Romanian, 83, 170
Romans, 169, 170
Roosevelt, Theodore, 36, 77
Roth, Henry, 74, 294, 318

Russia, 35. *See also* Soviet Union
  immigrants from, 73
Russian, 4, 29, 35, 48, 54, 83, 98, 179, 303

Said, Edward, "Embargoed Literature, 291
Saint-Exupéry, Antoine, *The Little Prince*, 89–90
Salazar, Antonio Oliveira, 124–5, 126
Salgari, Emilio, 268–70
Sanders, Bernie, 261–2
Schleiermacher, Friedrich, 5, 226, 280–1
  "On the Different Methods of Translating," 278
Second Punic War, 169, 170
seeing, 134–6, 137
Sefer ha-Bahir, 50
Sefer Yetzirah, 136
the self, 24–5
self-definition, 24
self-translation, 3, 151, 277, 278–9, 293, 307–11
  anxiety of, 308–9
  register and, 308
  reinvention and, 308
  Singer and, 313
semiotic modes, 258–60
Semitic languages, 142
Sephardic Jews, 141, 327
Seuss, Dr. *See* Geisel, Theodor Seuss (Dr. Seuss)
Shakespeare, William, 47, 62, 94, 125, 130, 165, 180, 181, 269, 272, 275, 304
  as creator of words, 180
  Cymbeline, 276
  English of, 322
  Hamlet, 275, 279
  Henry V, 276
  King Lear, 275
  Macbeth, 276
  Measure for Measure, 180
  A Midsummer Night's Dream, 276
  Richard III, 276

Titus Andronicus, 276
  translations of, 321
  sharing, 257–60
Shaw, George Bernard, 39, 46, 71, 183, 235
Shoah, 142, 338
Sholem Aleichem, 141, 272
Shorter Oxford Dictionary, 183
shtetlekh, 141
siglo de oro, 171–2, 181, 213, 219, 240
sign language, 71
Simon, Sherry, 9, 16
Simon & Schuster, 231
Singer, Isaac Bashevis, 24, 29, 62, 140, 146, 151, 272, 275, 279, 307, 312–13, 318
  The Family Moskat, 313
  "Gimpl Tam," 312–13
  Nobel Prize for Literature and, 313
  "second original" and, 308, 310
  self-translation and, 313
  "Simple Gimpl," 313
Singer, Israel Joshua, 141, 313
slang, dictionaries and, 179
slave-narrative, 92
slavery, 71–2, 73
Slavic languages, 74, 142
sleep, death and, 59–60
Smyrna, 51, 52
social media, 46, 78–9, 197, 255–67
Sokhan Publishers, 292
Sontag, Susan, 5, 80, 226
source texts, 257, 296–7. *See also* originals
South Africa, 47
South African English, 49
South America, 29–30
South Korea, 44–5
Soviet Union, 35, 47, 142
Spain, 8, 36, 72, 95–6, 168, 175, 188, 213, 326
  dictatorships in, 234
  Enlightenment in, 209

Spain (*cont.*)
  expulsion of Jews from, 29, 141, 171
  Hebrew poets of, 180
  history of, 169–70
  Jewish identity in, 234
  Muslim, 233
  persecution of Jews in, 212
  La Reconquista and, 171
  renewal in, 220
  siglo de oro in, 171–2, 181, 213, 219, 240
  Spanish in, 166, 188, 189, 218, 238
  Spanish speakers in, 166, 188, 189
  unification of, 239
Spanglish, 46, 164, 176–7, 188–9, 203, 206, 233, 272, 321
  emergence out of clash between Spanish and English, 200
  English and, 163–4, 309–10
  essay in, 307–11
  glossary of, 40
  history of, 170–1
  lexicon of, 238, 241
  mestizaje and, 310–11
  as the new Yiddish, 272
  personal experience with, 3–4, 7–8
  Spanglish speakers, 309
  Spanish and, 163–4, 307–11
  translation of *Don Quijote* into, 7–8
  translations from, 316
  in United States, 177
  as "a way of accessing reality," 10
Spanish, 2, 14–15, 29, 36, 42, 45, 48, 65, 95, 126, 320
  American, 168, 174–6, 188–202, 210–11, 218, 238–9
  Americanisms and, 236
  Caribbean, 174, 198, 199
  Catalan and, 9, 10, 18
  change and, 170–7, 202
  colonialism and, 171
  Creolizations of, 176
  dialects of, 176
  dictionaries of synonyms and, 237
  eclipse of, 198
  English and, 163–4, 197–200, 307–11
  foreign influence on, 218
  French and, 217–18
  gendered language and, 201, 232–3
  as global language, 175
  grammar of, 173
  history of, 168–77, 194–7, 218
  Iberian, 189, 196, 211, 218, 239
  (*see also* Castilian)
  immigrant languages and, 176
  imperialism and, 65, 171
  as "kitchen language" in the US, 42
  Latin American, 168, 173, 174–5, 188–202
  Latino philology and, 163–4, 166
  lexicography and, 167, 209–20, 238–9, 242
  Lomnitz and, 83, 84
  loyalties to, 197–8, 201
  migration and, 176
  nationalism and, 238–9
  nonstandard varieties of, 188
  as an official language, 188
  personal experience with, 3–4, 166, 203–5, 279–81, 304, 307–11, 318
  plurality of Spanishes, 218
  Puerto Rican, 309–10
  self-translation and, 279–81, 299
  Spanglish and, 163–4, 166, 176–7, 202, 203, 206, 272, 307–11, 309–10
  standardization of, 171, 173, 189, 239
  syntax of, 173
  translations from, 197, 303, 316, 319
  translingualism and, 203–5, 307–11, 318
  in the US, 42, 188–9, 307
  variants of, 4, 176–7, 188
Spanish-American War, 72, 174, 199
Spanish culture, pre-Columbian languages and, 33–4
Spanish Empire, 72, 171, 172–3, 174, 198, 199, 220, 239
Spanish literature, 218–20
  history of, 170–5
  lexicon and, 181

Spanish speakers
  in Latin America, 166, 188, 189
  in Spain, 166, 188, 189
  in the US, 42, 168–77, 307, 309
  worldwide, 188
spelling, 76
Spinoza, Baruch, 53, 231–2, 307
Star Trek, 75
Star Wars, 44, 75
Stavans, Ilan
  aliyah in Israel, 307
  biographical background of, 3–4
  collaboration and, 13–14
  connection with Yiddish,
    271–2
  conversations and, 13–14
  death threats against, 7, 8–9
  early experience reading
    translations, 269
  emigration from Mexico, 3, 16, 28,
    71, 163, 203, 272
  family of, 3, 58–9, 129, 130,
    273, 326
  growing up in Mexico, 268, 269
  Jewish heritage of, 5, 28, 271–2, 307
  library of, 166
  love for languages and, 12
  Mexican heritage of, 28, 268, 269
  in Mexico City, 87, 125, 318
  personal library of, 26–31, 166
Stavans, Ilan, works of
  "Amsterdamned," 274
  Angelitos, 277
  Borges, the Jew, 134, 191
  *On Borrowed Words: A Memoir of
    Language*, 6, 28, 280, 307–8, 317
  contributions to *The FSG Book of
    Twentieth- Century Latin American
    Poetry*, 320
  contribution to *The Norton Anthology
    of Latino Literature*, 307
  A Critic's Journey, 165
  Dictionary Days: A Defining Passion,
    165, 166, 186

different endings in Spanish and
  English, 299
"The Disappearance," 271–83
The Disappearance, 271–83
film and theatrical adaptations of, 277
graphic novels, 277
*How Yiddish Changed America and How
  America Changed Yiddish*, 165
Introduction to *The People's Tongue:
  Americans and the English
  Language*, 64–81
Knowledge and Censorship, 292
"Letter to a Young Translator," 225–7
"For the Love of
  English"/"Jangueando," 309–10
"Morirse está en hebreo," 274,
  277, 281
New World: Young Latino Writers,
  14–15
op-ed on gendered language in *New
  York Times en Español*, 200–1
The Oven: An Anti-Lecture, 138, 277
*The Oxford Handbook of Latino
  Studies*, 45
Popol Vuh: A Retelling, 6
Resurrecting Hebrew, 164
revisions and recreations of,
  277–8
*The Schocken Book of Modern
  Sephardic Literature*, 165
*Selected Translations: Poems, 2000–
  2020*, 4, 185, 303, 316–17, 318–19,
  320, 321
self-translation and, 277, 278–9,
  307–11
*On Self-Translation: Meditations on
  Language*, 2, 3, 6, 165, 299, 307,
  308–9
*The Seventh Heaven: Travels through
  Jewish Latin America*, 29, 316
The Silence of Professor Tösla, 6
Singer's Typewriter and Mine, 165
Spanglish graphic novel adaptation of
  Don Quixote of La Mancha, 9, 13–14

Spanglish: The Making of a New American Language, 164
"Translation and Hallucination," 303–4
translation of Alfau, 14
translation of Borges' "Pierre Menard, autor del *Quijote*," 95–121
translation of Carroll's *Alice's Adventures in Wonderland*, 206
translation of Frost's "Mending Wall," 319
translation of García Lorca's "Ode to Walt Whitman," 318–19
translation of Jevel Katz, 300–1
translation of Katz's "Moisés Ville," 300–1
translation of "La casa pairal," 18, 314–15
translation of Neruda's "Ode to the Dictionary," 158, 185, 221–4
translation of Petrarch's Sonnet #132, 287–8
translation of *The Disappearance*, 271–83
translations by, 4, 7–8, 13–14, 95–121, 185, 206, 221–4, 271–83, 287–8, 300–1, 314–15, 318–19, 321
translations in *The Poetry of Pablo Neruda*, 321
translations of, 271–83, 299, 307–8
And We Came Outside and Saw the Stars Again, 258, 266
"Xerox Man," 274, 277, 308
Stavans, Isaiah, 273
Stavans, Josh, 326
stereotypes, 260–1
Strunk, William, 78
style manuals, 78
subtitles, 44–5
survival mechanisms, 307–11
Sutzkever, Avrom, 271, 272, 279, 280–1
Swahili, 24, 179
synesthesia, 205
syntax, teaching of, 76

Tagalog, 188, 198
Talmud, 3, 25, 50, 95, 191, 282, 331, 334–7
on death, 59–60
reading, 331–8
Tang, Jenna, 14, 89, 321–2
Tang dynasty poems, 204, 206
tanna'im, 333, 334, 336, 338
target language, 257
Teatro Coliseo, 130, 131, 303
television, 75–6
Tesoro de la lengua castellana o española (Covarrubias), 29, 40–1, 166, 172, 180, 213, 239–40
Texas, 42, 76
Texas Revolution, 41
text, concept of, 259
Thackeray, William, 181–2
thesauruses, 213, 237
"they," 80
The Young and the Damned, 331
third original, 310
thought, language(s) and, 203
The Thousand and One Nights, 132. See also *The Arabian Nights*
Tokarczuk, Olga, *The Books of Jacob*, 50–5
Toledo School, Muslim translators of, 92–3
Tolstoy, Leo, 62, 98
Tong, Haoran, 14, 15, 203–8
Toraja people, 60
Tower of Babel, 42
"Trail of Tears," 69
"transadaptation," 6, 275
"transcreation," 274, 275
"transfronterizxs," 200
"Translating the Classics" course, 11
translation(s), 2–3, 4, 197, 269, 289–99. *See also specific languages*
vs. adaptation, 151
anxiety of, 148–54
as approximation, 152
as an art, 320

as art of the impossible, 302, 305
authenticity and, 273–4
automatic translation machines, 80
better than originals, 296–7, 320
as a business, 302
as a career, 227
censorship and, 292–3
change and, 92–3, 153, 279–80
close reading and, 321
collaboration and, 151, 295–6
completion and, 226, 282–3
context and, 5, 9
at core of American experiment, 76
culture and, 92–3
as cure for individualism, 306
death and, 57–8, 279–80
death threats and, 7
definitions of, 265
dialogic view of, 257
empathy and, 155
erotics of, 155–8
exoticization and, 153–4
experimentation with,
  226–7
future of classics in translation,
  93–4
globalism and, 154
as hallucination, 157, 304
as home, 18–19, 316, 316–22
of ideas, 256
immigration and, 225, 316–17
imperialism and, 153–4
impossibility of, 151, 152
interpretation and, 99
Jewishness and, 157
learning, 225–7
as lens, 10
as liberation, 150, 157, 303–4, 312
linguistic domination and, 153–4
literary classics and, 89
of living writers, 280
love for languages and, 12
machine translation, 80, 152
meme metaphor and, 256–7

memes and, 263, 265
as mental exercise, 302
migrant experience and, 16–17
migration and, 157
mistranslation and, 42–4, 305
modernizations, 322
movement and, 278
multilingualism and, 10
multimodal, 261
mystery and, 154
original and, 226
passion about, 5–6
perpetual, 99
of poetry, 155–8, 295
in postmonolingual era, 16
as a production of their time, 98
propaganda and, 153–4
publishing market and, 298–9
reading and, 153
as recalibration, 282
as recreations, 297
reinvention of readership
  by, 282
in the Renaissance, 219
reviews of, 154
rewriting and, 95, 156, 279
seamlessness in, 295, 296
scholarly, 322
self-translation, 3, 151, 277, 278–9,
  307–11
"source" and, 11–12 (*see also*
  originals)
by Stavans, 95–121, 185, 206, 221–4,
  271–83, 287–8, 300–1, 314–15,
  318–19, 321
as subjective endeavor, 322
sympathy and, 155
"target" and, 11–12
technology and, 80, 152
vs. "transadaptation," 6
transcription and, 32
translingual writing and, 206–7
travels of literature and, 32–4
ubiquity of, 13

translation(s) (*cont.*)
  of unfamiliar languages, 151, 226, 302–6
  as way of thinking, 10
  what constitutes translation today, 255–6
translation studies, 16, 264
translators, 2–6, 13, 82. *See also specific translators*
  as agents of change, 92–3
  becoming a translator, 225–7, 289
  collaboration and, 13–14, 91, 299, 305
  as commentators, 32
  culpability of, 275–6
  dictionaries and, 276–7
  enrichment of language by, 280–1
  as interpreters, 32
  as linguistic refreshers, 76
  mistranslation and, 42–4
  roles of, 6
  scarcity of, 290
  writers and, 298–9, 302, 321
translingualism, 15–16, 82, 203–8
translingual writing, translation and, 206–7
transportation, 72–3
Treaty of Guadalupe Hidalgo, 174, 199
Trujillo, Rafael Leónidas, 47, 234
Trump, Donald, 41–5, 92, 234, 256, 258, 260, 326
  COVID-19 pandemic and, 338
  era of, 41–4, 78
  social media and, 79
truth, language(s) and, 205, 234
Turkish, 54, 299
Twain, Mark, 42
  Adventures of Huckleberry Finn, 72, 284–6
Tyrant Books, 89
tyrants, 234. *See also* dictatorships
Tzvi, Shabtai, 50, 51, 53

United Kingdom, 167. *See also* Great Britain
United States, 28–9
  bilingualism in, 11, 307
  during COVID-19 pandemic, 323–7, 338
  demographic change in, 73
  diaspora of Latinos in, 42
  emergence as empire, 174, 199
  English in, 34–49
  founding of, 64
  Hispanophones in, 42
  as land of immigrants, 39
  Mexico and, 174, 199, 201
  parochial tastes of, 290–2
  Spanglish in, 177
  Spanish speakers in, 307, 309
  status of foreign languages in, 41
  War of Independence and, 220
  Yiddish and, 140–7
universalism, 46, 99, 181
University of Massachusetts, Amherst, 7, 319
University of Pennsylvania, archives at, 132
University of Pittsburgh Press, 4
untranslatability, 151, 152, 293–4, 302, 305
Uruguayans, 30, 318, 334
US Constitution, 41, 67
US Hispanic Literary Heritage project, 48
US-Mexican border, 34, 201, 319
US Southwest, 30, 174
Utah, 174, 199

Valdés, Juan de, *Diálogos de la lengua*, 171–2
Valéry, Paul, 191, 302
Vallejo, César, 58, 321
La Vanguardia, 7, 8, 9
Vargas Llosa, Mario, 211, 334
Venezuela, 8, 189, 234, 239
Vidal Claramonte, María Carmen África, 3, 12, 14, 15–16, 255–67
  Ilan Stavans, traductor, 15, 16
  Translating Borrowed Tongues: The Verbal Quest of Ilan Stavans, 15, 16

Vila-Sanjuán, Sergio, 7, 8, 9
visuality, language and, 33–4
visual storytelling, 78. *See also* graphic novels
vocabularies, expansion of, 76
Vocabulario degli Accademici della Crusca, 213
Vogel, Paula, 146, 273

Wallace, David Foster, 70, 320
Washington Post, 268
"wave-crossing," 205
Webster, Noah, 29, 36, 40, 49, 69–70, 80, 167, 186, 237
  An American Dictionary of the English Language, 69, 182, 217, 235, 238
  death of, 70
  Dictionary of the American Language, 37, 38–9
  as "forgotten" founding father, 69
Webster's Second New International Dictionary of the English Language, Unabridged, 70
Webster's Third New International Dictionary of the English Language, Unabridged, 29, 40, 70
Weinberger, Eliot, 130–1
White, E.B., 78
Whitman, Walt, 48, 128, 226, 318–19
  on American slang, 71
  Leaves of Grass, 277, 319
  "Song of Myself," 24, 128
Wiegand, Beruriah, 271–83
Wilbur, Richard, 151, 320
Winchester, Simon
  The Meaning of Everything: The Story of the Oxford English Dictionary, 186
  The Surgeon of Crowthorne: A Tale of Murder, Madness and the Love of Words, 167, 186, 237
Wisse, Ruth, *The Penguin Book of Modern Yiddish Verse*, 141
Wizard of Oz, 256
Woordenboek der Nederlandische Taal, 40

words, as weapons, 338
World War I, 77
World War II, 74, 142, 199
writers, 2
  as thermometers of a language, 189
  translators and, 298–9, 302, 321
writing, 129, 132

xenolinguaphobia, 41–2, 77
Xiaolu Guo, *A Concise Chinese-English Dictionary for Lovers*, 186
Ximénez, Juan, 240
Xu Yuanchong, 206, 207

Yeats, William Butler, 123
Yehuda ha-Levi, 180
  Sefer ha-Kuzari, 233
Yezierska, Anzia, 318
Yiddish literature, 29
Yiddish, 48, 67, 312
  in the Americas, 140–7
  assimilation and, 141
  Casteidish and, 188
  classes in, 273
  defining, 141–2
  descendants of Yiddish speakers, 146–7
  development of, 165
  dialects of, 142
  English and, 74
  fate of, 142
  food and, 145–6
  as hybrid language, 46, 272
  immigration and, 140–7, 176, 300–1
  in Latin America, 300–1
  Lomnitz and, 83, 84
  in Mexico, 318
  as "mongrel" language, 46
  New York City and, 318
  as official language in Soviet Union, 142
  as official language in Sweden, 142
  personal experience with, 3, 4, 29, 203, 204, 205, 304, 307, 318

Yiddish (cont.)
  publications in, 142, 143–4, 145
  return to, 273
  Spanglish as the new, 272
  status as language, 46, 142
  syntax of, 273
  theater in, 143, 144
  translations from, 316
  translations into, 271–83
  United States and, 140–7
  written in Hebrew
    alphabet, 142
  as *zhargon*, 142
Yiddish Book Center, 2, 3, 29, 30, 48, 54, 143–4
Yiddish Dictionary Committee, 276

Yiddish literature, 141, 146, 271–83
Yiddish material, 29
Yiddish music, 29
Yiddish novels, 29
Yiddish poetry, 29, 273, 278–9
Yiddish theater, 29
Yiddish writers, 140–1
Yingleñol, 300–1
"Yinglish," 145

Zamenhof, Ludwik, 35, 47
zamlers, 144
Zappa, Frank, 80
Zenith, Richard, 122–8, 155
Zionism, 164
Zohar, 50

www.ingramcontent.com/pod-product-compliance
Ingram Content Group UK Ltd.
Pitfield, Milton Keynes, MK11 3LW, UK
UKHW040859140325
456137UK00013B/75/J

9 781487 547929